Information, incentives, and bargaining
in the Japanese economy

Information, incentives, and bargaining in the Japanese economy

MASAHIKO AOKI
Stanford University and University of Kyoto

*The right of the
University of Cambridge
to print and sell
all manner of books
was granted by
Henry VIII in 1534.
The University has printed
and published continuously
since 1584.*

CAMBRIDGE UNIVERSITY PRESS

Cambridge
New York   Port Chester   Melbourne   Sydney

Published by the Press Syndicate of the University of Cambridge
The Pitt Building, Trumpington Street, Cambridge CB2 1RP
40 West 20th Street, New York, NY 10011, USA
10 Stamford Road, Oakleigh, Melbourne 3166, Australia

First published 1988
First paperback edition 1989

Printed in the United States of America

Library of Congress Cataloging-in-Publication Data
Aoki, Masahiko, 1938-
Information, incentives, and bargaining in the Japanese economy / Masahiko
Aoki.
p. cm.
ISBN 0 521 35473 0 hard covers
ISBN 0 521 38681 0 paperback
I. Industrial management — Japan. 2. Industrial organization — Japan. 3.
Industrial relations — Japan. I. Title.
HD70.J3A586 1988
658.4'00952 —dc 19 88-2976

British Library Cataloguing in Publication Data
Aoki, Masahiko, 1938-
Information, incentives, and bargaining in the Japanese economy.
I. Japan. Economic conditions
I. Title
330.952'048

ISBN 0 521 35473 0 hard covers
ISBN 0 521 38681 0 paperback

Contents

Figures

Tables

Preface

This book presents a microanalysis of the Japanese economy from the perspectives of information, incentive, and bargaining-game theories. It is not another parable of Japan's economic success.

Many people think that the Japanese economic system does not altogether fit the textbook model of the market economy. Is it because the Japanese economic system is culturally unique? Or is it that the textbook description is too simplistic for analyzing the rich reality of modern market economies of various types? In this book, I have sought to describe and explain the competitive workings of the Japanese microeconomic system in terms familiar to Western economists, although I have tried not to ignore entirely the possible impact of cultural factors.

In pursuing this goal, however, I have been compelled to examine critically some textbook notions about the microstructure of the market economy (e.g., hierarchy as *the* alternative to the market, the firm as a property of stockholders, market-oriented contracts as *the* incentive scheme, innovation as a direct application of invention, among others) that have strongly shaped and influenced the economists' approach to industrial organization. Although these notions constitute an appropriate foundation for the analysis of the highly market-oriented Western economy, it is necessary to go beyond those "specific" notions in order to arrive at a more complete understanding of the Japanese economy. At one level, therefore, this book may be regarded as a study of comparative industrial organization. To the extent that my approach is convincing, I hope it suggests the need for a somewhat different focus and emphasis in the study of industrial organization.

The analysis and conclusions are the results of my research and teaching on the Japanese economy, comparative industrial organization, and the theory of the firm at both the graduate and undergraduate levels at Stanford University from 1984 to 1987. I have been fortunate to have been affiliated jointly with Stanford University and the University of Kyoto since 1984. At Kyoto, I have been in close touch with the making of some insightful empirical studies on aspects of modern Japan not available anywhere else. At Stanford, I have been exposed to an excellent disciplinary atmosphere that fosters a rigorous scientific approach to microeconomics. Stanford also has many researchers from diverse disciplines (including engineering) who take the comparison between the West and Japan seriously. This book could not have been written without the interactions with students and colleagues at both of these institutions, and I am very grateful to them for their stimulating discussions, amiable encouragement, and critical comments.

In particular, I would like to acknowledge the following individuals for their helpful discussions at various stages of the making of this book: Kenneth Arrow, Banri Asanuma, Samuel Bowles, Ronald Coase, Bo Gustafsson, Ken-ich Imai, Hideshi Itoh, Kent Caldor, Kazuo Koike, Ryutaro Komiya, Stephen Krasner, Sunpei Kumon, Harvey Leibenstein, Kurt Lundgren, Stephen Marglin, Robin Marris, Hajime Miyazaki, Yasusuke Murakami, Michio Muramatsu, Daniel Okimoto, Hugh Patrick, Michael Riordan, Thomas Rohlen, Nathan Rosenberg, Henry Rosovsky, and Oliver Williamson. I have also received excellent editorial assistance from Vicky Macintyre, Jeff Sundberg, and Roxanne Guilhamet.

I am deeply indebted to the following organizations for financial assistance to the research that culminated in this book: the Center for Economic Policy Research, the Center for Research in International Studies, and the North East Asia–U.S. Forum on Public Policy, all at Stanford, and the Twenty-first Century (Kigawada) Foundation in Tokyo.

Kyoto
March 1988

CHAPTER 1

Introduction

By the time the Pacific War ended with the unconditional surrender of Japan in August 1945, about one-quarter of Japan's national assets (excluding weaponry) existing at the beginning of the year had been destroyed.[1] In the ensuing years, soldiers returning from the battlefields and immigrants from former colonial lands, as well as those released from war materials production, joined the ranks of the job seekers. The number of job seekers during the first few years of the postwar period was about one-quarter of the total labor force.[2] The level of production in 1946 dropped to about 40 percent of the prewar level of 1934–6. For most Japanese, the 1940s were nothing but a series of daily struggles for survival. The entire nation was swept up in great social turmoil and drastic institutional changes.

Upon the new ground of the institutions shaped in the turmoil, however, the engine of growth started to run in the 1950s. An unprecedented growth rate of more than 10 percent per annum was realized throughout the 1960s, and the gains from this growth were widely distributed among diverse social groups. Even so, Japan was still considered a "fragile flower" because of its meager natural resources. Then in the 1970s Japan was hit by a series of shocks – environmental pollution, escalating oil prices, the shift to a flexible exchange system, and new waves of technological innovation. But each time it managed to steer itself out of the ordeal and in the process demonstrated that its economy was remarkably robust.

By the mid-1980s Japan's national product had surpassed 10 percent of the Gross World's Product and it had become the world's largest net credit holder abroad in history. Once considered a shrewd technological follower, Japan now seems to be gathering its industrial strength and is on its way to becoming a formidable technological leader in a number of global markets. Today Japanese companies are visible all over the world, although they have been greeted with some ambiva-

---

[1] Economic Planning Agency, *Sengo Keizaishi – Soukan* (The post war economic history – A Survey), 1957.
[2] Mataji Umemura, *Sengo Nihon no Roudouryoku* (Labor force in post war Japan), Iwanami Shoten, 1964, pp. 63–5.

1

lence since they are seen as both unwelcome invaders and as gratifying job creators. Considering the devastation existing immediately after the Pacific war, these are, approved or not, amazing achievements indeed.

What is the key to the developmental capability and adaptability of the Japanese economy? Is there a specific Japanese way of managing the competitive industry? If so, is it culturally unique, or can it be emulated in the Western context when desirable? Or do some Japanese economic institutions act as subtle barriers insulating domestic economic interests from foreign competition while allowing them to freeride on the international liberal economic order? Should Japan therefore try to make its economic structure conform more with the Western norm to make global competition fair? If so, is the Japanese polity capable of doing so? The social scientists' views on these questions are diverse and inconclusive.

The neoclassical economists see nothing mystical about the Japanese economy. In spite of its apparent cultural uniqueness, the Japanese economy is sufficiently competitive for the usual neoclassical paradigm (built on the postulate of maximizing behaviors of economic agents mediated by the market mechanism) to explain and predict Japan's economic performance reasonably well. Behavioral equations of economic agents in the market for Japan and any neoclassical homeland should reflect structural isomorphism. The only difference would be in the values for parameters representing the saving propensity of households, their willingness to supply effort, the government's tax rates, and so on. According to this view, any international imbalances may be corrected by realigning foreign exchange rates and appropriate internationally coordinated public policies affecting the maximizing behavior of economic agents.

Another important school of thought – the culturalist – regards the Japanese economy as a coherent system consistent with the Japanese cultural tradition. Cultural factors such as emphasis on the small group, the gift exchange of employee loyalty and employer paternalism, and the penetration of the workplace into what seem to Western eyes to be the personal and private affairs of the employee are the driving forces of the system. Thus the Japanese system is regarded as distinct from the individual-oriented Western system. If that is the case, the implication may be a dismal one: The current trade conflict may be impossible to resolve unless the Japanese change their culture or protectionist walls are erected to insulate the Western and the Japanese economies from each other.

Yet another view of the Japanese economy emerging in recent years is that, although some aspects of Japanese institutions may have cultural origins, the institutional differences between the West and Japan are not absolute. Proponents of this view would argue that the problems facing researchers are related to economic, political, and technological phenomena integral to advanced levels of capitalism and industrialization rather than to specifically Western or Japanese traits, and therefore that propositions applicable to both the Japanese and Western cases should be sought. But, unlike the neoclassical economists, they would contend that this could only be done by enlarging and enriching the existing theoretical models developed primarily for explaining the Western phenomena. In practice, they leave open the possibility that some aspects of Japanese institutions may prove superior to some aspects of corresponding Western institutions and thus be potentially worthy of emulation in the Western context, and vice versa.

Such studies are taking shape in diverse disciplines, although they are at different stages of development. Industrial engineers, for example, are focusing on factory organization, labor economists and sociologists on industrial relations and incentive schemes, business economists on the management system, financial economists on corporate finance, industrial organizational economists on subcontracting and corporate grouping, technology specialists on the R&D process, and political scientists on the government bureaucracy. This work has already produced a stock of interesting results, but no earnest attempt has yet been made to relate them to each other. This situation is unsatisfactory from the social scientist's point of view, however, for we need a consistent and unified theory that covers the micro-micro structure of the business firm through the performance characteristics of markets to the political and economic role of the government bureaucracy. In this book I venture to present a simple, yet coherent account of the Japanese economy along such lines. In so doing I rely extensively on recent contributions in diverse disciplines, but try to reformulate and reinterpret these earlier results in accepted economic terms as much as possible. The analysis is descriptive and does not deal directly with policy issues, except to consider the functioning of the political process.

I open the discussion in Chapter 2 with a micro-micro analysis of the Japanese firm. I draw on the contributions of industrial engineers and labor specialists to illustrate that work organization and intershop coordination in the Japanese firm form one type of information structure, distinct from the conventional model of the functional hierarchy, and I compare the performance characteristics of the two. The central point here is that the internal information structure of the Japanese firm is more decentralized, as it relies on horizontal communication among functional units and autonomous problem solving at individual work units, made possible through the development of workers' integrative skills as opposed to segmented and specialized skills. Such decentralized structure is shown to be effective in adapting the work process flexibly and swiftly to a continually changing market and technological environment.

Chapter 3 is about the types of incentives used to develop the skills (information-processing capacities) needed to operate the information structure studied in Chapter 2 efficiently. The nature and function of what are thought to be culturally unique organizational practices – such as "lifetime" employment, seniority pay, bonuses and retirement allowances, and enterprise unionism – are reexamined in the light of the growing incentive literature developed within the framework of neoclassical economics. In short, I argue that the essence of Japanese incentive structure is the *ranking hierarchy,* in which employees of the firm compete for faster promotion on the basis of their learning achievements. The centralized administration of the ranking hierarchy by the Japanese firm complements the decentralized approach to handling information and safeguards the integrity of the organization.

Chapter 4 turns to the financial aspect of the Japanese firm, specifically, the roles of different types of investors in corporate finance and the corporate governance structure: individual investors, banks, and other corporate firms. In this chapter I try to demystify Japanese corporate finance and refute the widely held view that the interests of stockholders are ignored in the Japanese firm and that the cost of capital is lower in Japan than in other developed economies.

The first four chapters pave the way for the hypothesis that the Japanese firm should be regarded as a *coalition* of the body of employees and the body of stockholders rather than the sole property of stockholders, as postulated in the neoclassical paradigm. In Chapter 5, I utilize the results of recent contributions to bargaining game theory to examine various aspects of management in the coalitional structure and analyze the behavior of the Japanese firm as an equilibrium outcome of a bargaining game between the constituent bodies. For example, the gift exchange of diligent work by the employee for a job guarantee by the employer, which is conventionally thought to be culturally conditioned, is seen as the efficient and equilibrium resolution of the partly conflicting, partly harmonizing interests of both parties.

Chapter 6 deals with various aspects of industrial organization. Section 6.1 analyzes the transactional mode of the subcontracting group in the manufacturing industry from the viewpoint of the growing economic theory of contracts and relates its prevalence to the informational structural characteristics of the Japanese firm outlined in Chapter 2. Section 6.2 takes up the phenomenon of corporate grouping brought about by mutual stockholding among major firms. Here I argue that one of its major roles, besides takeover insulation, is to share business risk. The need for risk sharing (group insurance), although on the decline at present, arose from the long-term association of employees with the firm under the incentive scheme discussed in Chapter 3, which cannot be met through the financial markets. In Section 6.3 I discuss the R&D process of the Japanese firm and show how the type of information produced is related to and conditioned by the way it is utilized. I also call into question the conventional wisdom that the Japanese are technological followers and not innovators and attempt to explain why intercorporate linkages for multidisciplinary research and development are emerging. In Section 6.4 I discuss the role of social reputational ranking as an incentive for top managers, which may be considered unique to Japan.

Chapter 7 deals with the political-economic process and the role of the government bureaucracy in it. By breaking open the black box of the bureaucracy, as I do for the Japanese firm, and examining its internal information and incentive characteristics, I endeavor to clarify the dual role of the ministry, which is to represent constituent interests and to delineate the national interest. By using the theoretic framework of the n-person bargaining game, I show that the politically stable outcome of the bureaucratic process ought to be a democratic aggregation of constituents' utilities in a specified sense and that the converse is also true. From this perspective, I then describe the evolution of pluralistic politics mediated by the bureaucracy, which I call *bureaupluralism,* and its current dilemma.

Chapter 8 focuses on the mutual lessons to be learned from the experiences of Japan and the West. Most cultural and business anthropologists consider small-group orientation to be an essential element of Japanese organizations, the implication being that Japanese organizational practices, however efficient they may be, cannot be transplanted to individual-oriented firms. Although the recurrence of the decentralized information structure and the centralized incentive-ranking hierarchy at various levels of Japanese social organizations suggests that these characteristics have cultural origins, I contend that emphasis on the small group is neither a necessary nor sufficient condition for the future viability of a Japanese-like system in an environment where individual integrative skills and communication technology are highly developed.

A sincere effort at mutual learning by the West and Japan may well lead to some form of hybrid, but it will not be easy to find a path toward it. This book is not intended to guide readers along that path, but only to foster a theoretical understanding of some fundamental issues that may arise as the two sides move in this direction.

CHAPTER 2

The information structure of the J-firm

In microeconomic textbooks, the firm is treated as a profit-maximizing agent whose technological opportunities are exogenously given in the form of the production function or the cost function. In other words, economists have treated phenomena that determine the costs of the firm as purely technological events occurring inside a "black box" and have relegated the task of inquiring about what occurs inside that box to industrial engineers. Thus, in microeconomics the firm can be identified with a single-minded entrepreneur who operates the black box to maximize profits in response to market signals.

This mechanical view of the firm was challenged some half century ago in a celebrated article by Ronald Coase entitled "The Nature of the Firm," in which he asked why the firm emerged at all in the market mechanism.[1] His answer was that a firm would arise and attempt to extend the range of its control as long as its costs were less than the costs of achieving the same result by market transactions. However, the significance of this article was not fully recognized until transaction cost economics, or the new institutional economics, revived interest in the question.[2] As an alternative to market transactions, transaction cost economics identified the mode of transactions internalized in the firm with hierarchies.

The firm as a hierarchy may be visualized as follows: It is composed of many specialized operating units. The activities of these units are coordinated through layers of administrative offices. We may imagine that the optimal design of the hierarchy specifies the order of administrative offices and assigns to each office therein information-processing tasks that will maximize savings on the market-using cost. We may then suppose that viable hierarchies in any particular industry tend to

---

[1] R. Coase, "The nature of the firm," *Economica*, n.s.4 (1937), pp. 386–405.
[2] K. J. Arrow, "The organization of economic activity: issues pertinent to the choice of market versus nonmarket allocation," in *The Analysis and Evaluation of Public Expenditure: The PPB System*, vol. 1, Joint Economic Committee, 91st U.S. Congress; Oliver E. Williamson, *Markets and Hierarchies, Analysis and Antitrust Implications*, Free Press, 1975.

realize similar cost savings to a degree differentiated only by the abilities of managers to design and run hierarchies.

But there are industries in which wide differences in productivity across countries do not seem to be attributable to a mere difference in managerial abilities. For example, from the numerous accounting and econometric studies that have attempted to measure the productivity differential between Japanese and American automobile producers, it appears indisputable that Japanese auto producers have a systematic productivity advantage over U.S. producers.[3] What accounts for the

---

[3] According to various "accounting" studies that have been reviewed in Robert Cole and Taizo Yakushiji, *The American and Japanese Auto Industries in Transition,* Center for Japanese Studies, University of Michigan, 1984, chap. 7, the ratio of Japanese to U.S. labor productivity in the automobile industry ranged from about 1.2:1 to 2.4:1; that is, the Japanese automobile industry was estimated to produce anywhere from 6 to 12 vehicles in the labor time it takes the U.S. industry to produce 5. But there are many problems associated with simple estimates of differences in per vehicle labor costs as reported in those studies. Product mix and vertical integration are dealt with by simply adjusting figures by a constant. Also, the analysis ignores such issues as capital/labor differences and capacity utilization differences, and sometimes confuses factor price differences vs. productivity.

Michael Cusmano has rightly acknowledged these issues and has provided valuable data for productivity mix differences, capacity utilization differences, and fixed assets per labor differences. He has argued that since the amount of fixed assets required to produce one vehicle is roughly comparable in Japan and the United States, capital productivity in the two nations is equal and hence differences in output per labor between the two are attributable to labor productivity. However, output per labor is a function of capital per labor and hence Japanese labor productivity would be overestimated if it were not adjusted for higher fixed assets per labor in Japan. See M. A. Cusmano, *The Japanese Automobile Industry, Technology and Management at Nissan and Toyota,* Harvard University Press, 1985.

The only productivity study based on the econometric method that I know of is the one by Melvyn Fuss and L. Waverman: "Productivity growth in the automobile industry, 1970–1980; A comparison of Canada, Japan, and the United States," *National Bureau of Economic Research Paper,* no. 1735, Cambridge, 1985; "The extent and sources of cost and efficiency differences between U.S. and Japanese automobile producers," ibid., no. 1849, 1986. Fuss and Waverman have found that Japanese producers had a 34.4 percent unit cost advantage in 1980 over U.S. producers. Even after the yen–dollar exchange ratio is adjusted relative to its purchasing power parity rate and assuming that the U.S. producers had utilized their capacity at the level of Japanese producers, the Japanese efficiency advantage in 1980 was still at 5.2 percent. Also they have found that, although the Japanese automobile producers enjoyed a total factor productivity growth of 4.3 percent per annum during the period 1970–80, the U.S. producers experienced only 1.6 percent growth.

Many interesting empirical and theoretical issues related to the comparison between auto manufacturing productivity in the United States and Japan are discussed and the existing literature on the subject is critically reviewed in a promising term paper submitted to a graduate course on Japanese economic models at Stanford by Joji Tatsugi, "Measurement of labor productivity in the U.S. and Japanese automobile industry: a survey, critique, and proposal," June 1986.

differential in labor, as well as total, productivity?[4] One possible explanation lies in the exceptional diligence of Japanese workers and their loyalty to the employing firm, which in turn promises them the security of lifetime employment. But if this is so, how can we explain the fact that Japanese labor productivities are considerably lower than American productivities in certain industries – such as petrochemical, food processing, and pharmaceutical – despite the lifetime employment of equally diligent workers?[5] Moreover, in the hierarchies of Chinese firms, where the assurance of lifetime employment is even stronger, workers' diligence does not seem to be as high.

Another possible explanation for the productivity differential among firms is that they may be using different methods of organizing and coordinating production. For example, some attribute the higher labor (and total) productivity observed in the Japanese automobile and some other industries to efficient team-oriented work organization on the shopfloor. An econometric study by M. Fuss and L. Waverman also indicates that the level of capacity utilization accounts in large part for the cost and efficiency differences between U.S. and Japanese auto producers. These authors note that, since the automobile industry is characterized by significant quasi-fixed factors such as capital plant, administrative and designing jobs, product-specific manufacturing facilities, shifts in consumers' tastes, or economic downturn can have severe effects on cost and efficiency.[6] How then, is the Japanese auto manufacturer able to respond to such external shocks and reorganize internal work more quickly and efficiently? Some attribute this to speedier and more timely horizontal coordination between shops and the subsequent reduction in costly inventory. But do those characteristics of teamwork, horizontal communication, and so on fit the traditional notion of hierarchies?

In Section 1 of this chapter, I summarize some important contri-

---

[4] In a lecture celebrating the fiftieth anniversary of the publication of "The nature of the firm," Coase maintained: "In that article I emphasized the comparison of the costs of transacting with the costs of organizing and did not investigate the factors that would make the costs of organizing lower for some firms than others. This was quite satisfactory if the main purpose was, as mine was, to explain why there are firms. But if one is to explain the institutional structure of production in the system as a whole it is necessary to uncover the reasons why the costs of organizing particular activities differ among firms." (R. Coase, "Lecture on the nature of the firm, 3: influence," 1987; to be published by Cambridge University Press.)

[5] See Dale W. Jorgenson, Masahiro Kuroda, and Mieko Nishimizu, "Japan–U.S. industry level productivity comparisons, 1960–1979," *Journal of the Japanese and International Economies,* 1 (1987), pp. 1–30.

[6] Fuss and Waverman, "Productivity growth in the automobile industry."

butions by labor economists, sociologists, and industrial engineers and make stylized comparisons of shopfloor work organizations and inter-shop coordination mechanisms in the typical Japanese firm and the traditional "unionized" American firm in the automobile industry. (Some readers may think the comparison inappropriate or uninterest-ing, because it places a newly developing entity alongside something widely recognized as outmoded, even in the West. However, the point of the comparison is to explore the theoretical implications of alter-native modes of organizing production.)

Whereas American industrialization has generated an exceptionally high degree of job differentiation and attached a high value to special-ization, the Japanese work organization seems to rely more on the ver-satility of workers and flexibility in job demarcation. In the Japanese work organization, problem-solving tasks – such as coping with absen-teeism, malfunctioning machines, and defective products – tend to be entrusted to a team of operating workers, whereas in the American organization they are entrusted to specialists. This difference can also be seen in the type of intrafirm coordinating mechanism used. In the American firm, coordination between different jobs as well as different shops has itself become the "specialized" function of supervisors and managers, and has helped to make professional hierarchical control more sophisticated. In contrast, the Japanese firm seems to rely on a less hierarchical structure that facilitates coordination through hori-zontal flows of communication among peers and among shops (the well-publicized decision making based on consensus is but one such phenomenon).

The assertion that the Japanese way of organizing production is less hierarchical may appear to run counter to the conventional notion that Japanese society is more hierarchical, but the stylized facts presented in Section 1 help to clarify this point. In Chapter 3 I show that the Japanese organization is indeed hierarchical, but in a different sense. The Japanese firm utilizes the hierarchy of ranking as an incentive for its employees to develop skills useful for the work organization, which is less hierarchical in the functional sense. In the Japanese firm, rank-ing is not necessarily directly associated with functionally specialized job descriptions.

In Section 2, I present the orthodox efficiency argument put forth in defense of hierarchical work organization and coordination and exam-ine it in the context of emerging market and technological conditions. My purpose is to elucidate the limited capacity of hierarchical control and pave the way for my discussion of the nature of the Japanese practice, which needs to be understood from the perspective of economics rather than dismissed as a unique cultural phenomenon. In Section 3, I compare the informational characteristics of the Japanese model of organizing and coordinating production in the firm with the hierarchical model and try to clarify the conditions under which the less hierarchical Japanese model helps to improve the internal efficiency of the firm in certain industries. I show that the relative efficiency of the emerging Japanese practice vis-à-vis traditional hierarchies depends on various technological and market factors. In the concluding section I summarize the main point of the preceding discussion.

1. Stylized comparison: United States versus Japan

A. *Job control unionism versus integrative learning*

Before analyzing the information structure of the Japanese firm, I describe some of the stylized differences between the Japanese and American method of organizing work at the shopfloor level and of coordinating operations among shops responding to random shocks. The discussion here refers mainly to large *unionized* firms in manufacturing industries such as automobile and steel.

Shopfloor practices as well as the management of intershop coordination at some unionized American firms are currently undergoing substantial modification as a result of a significant change in attitude both on the part of the union and of management, under growing international competitive pressure. Also there is a growing nonunionized segment even in traditional unionized industries. In the steel industry, for example, minimills that specialize in high value-added products and are thought to have a considerable competitive edge now account for 25 percent of industry sales; they are largely nonunionized firms that are developing a significantly different work practice from that of unionized steel plants. Thus the stylized picture of the American firm presented in the following paragraphs is that of a somewhat obsolete stereotype, which may have been more common up to the mid-1970s. Nonetheless, it can serve as a backdrop for highlighting essential elements of Japanese practice. For ease of reference and to indicate that the characterization of the typical American and Japanese firms below is highly stylized, hereafter I refer to them symbolically as the *A-firm* and the *J-firm*.

The purpose of the following description is to indicate how different practices at the shopfloor level affect the formation, utilization, and transmission of workers' skills. Certain types of skills can be acquired through formal training – such as apprenticeship, technical training, and professional schooling prior to production experiences – and can be maintained throughout the worker's life. Various craft skills, technical skills in programming, typing, and the like are obvious examples. The allocation of these skills is more likely to be regulated by the craft union (in the case of craft skills) or the competitive market mechanism.

But most skills relevant to modern factories are acquired and developed through production experience. Therefore, the way work is organized at the shopfloor level of a modern factory is such that the skills of workers are developed step by step through learning by doing on the shopfloor. The work process is subdivided into various jobs, and inexperienced workers who have just entered the factory are normally assigned to relatively easier jobs, which labor economists customarily refer to as the "port of entry."[7] Once workers acquire skills relevant to those elementary jobs, they progress to more advanced, yet technically related jobs where they can develop further skills, which in turn prepare them for further advancements. Job ladders have become more or less universal phenomena of the modern factory, West and East. Even so, there are some interesting differences in the way that the A-firm and J-firm organize these job ladders, which have important efficiency implications.

Historically, the United States emphasized worker specialization and job differentiation throughout its industrial development. This approach stemmed from the belief that, through the application of the principle of "a right man in the right place," each worker and the firm would be able to make the best use of any particular talents or different skills. Consequently a much finer job differentiation has developed at American factories. The 1977 edition of the *Dictionary of Occupational Titles* lists some 20,000 job titles. At the micro-micro level, there may be more than one hundred job titles in a typical American automobile assembly factory. As a result of the detailed specification of job duties, each worker tends to follow a rather narrow job path throughout his or her career. Thus a particular skill may be highly perfected, yet rather limited in its range.

[7] This term originates in Clark Kerr, "The Balkanization of the labor markets," in E. W. Bakke (ed.), *Labor Mobility and Economic Opportunity,* MIT Press, 1954, pp. 92–110. Also see Peter Doeringer and Michael Piore, *Internal Labor Markets and Manpower Analysis,* D. C. Heath, 1971, for a detailed description of the organization of job ladders at American factories as described below.

One important outcome of such specialization is that operating tasks become separated from emergency tasks. Each operating worker is required to perform a specific task assigned by a supervisor, according to formal or customary rules, operating manuals, or a supervisor's directives. When something unexpected occurs – for example, workers are absent, machinery breaks down, or there is an abnormally high rate of defective products – remedies are usually sought, under the direction of the supervisor, by the appropriate specialists, such as reliefmen, repairmen, craft workers, and inspectors. Operating workers are normally not responsible for coping with unexpected emergencies, as is evident from a long-standing custom at the American factory that prohibits the worker from stopping the production line on his or her own initiative, even when an event takes place that makes it desirable.

In contrast, in the J-firm, job classification tends to be much simpler and broader. Job demarcation is fluid and ambiguous and job assignments are more flexible. The lower degree of specialization in the J-firm in comparison with the A-firm has been reported in various case studies, for example, by Kazuo Koike and by Robert Cole, among others.[8] Results of recent statistical studies, such as the one by James Lincoln, Mitsuyo Hanada, and Kerry McBird, are also consistent with those case study findings.[9]

How is the degree of specialization reduced in the J-firm? To begin with, the J-firm does not have a specialized reliefman to cope with absenteeism. Instead, it relies on mass relief or the ad hoc reassignment of jobs at the discretion of the foreman. Inspection positions are

---

[8] Kazuo Koike, *Shokuba no Rodo Kumiai to Sanka* (Labor union and participation at the shopfloor), Toyo-Keizai Shinpo Sha, 1975. A succinct summary of this book is found in K. Koike, "Skill formation system in the U.S. and Japan," in M. Aoki (ed.), *The Economic Analysis of the Japanese Firm,* North-Holland, 1984, pp. 44–75; and Robert Cole, *Work, Mobility and Participation: A Comparative Study of American and Japanese Industry,* University of California Press, 1979.

[9] See their "Organizational Structures in Japanese and U.S. Manufacturing," *Administrative Science Quarterly,* 31 (1986), pp. 334–64. They have used carefully designed data on 55 manufacturing plants in central Indiana and 51 plants in the Atsugi region in Japan, selected so that there would be roughly equal numbers of organizations in each country in each cell of a size-by-industry classification. They constructed the functional specialization scale for those plants by asking what proportion of 20 selected functions were assigned to individuals as full-time responsibilities. After controlling for variations in technology (the extent of custom and small batch, large batch and mass production, or continuous process technologies), size, and unionization, they found that the difference in the scale between the two countries is as great as 0.455; that is, about nine more functions are assigned to specialists in the U.S. plant, which is otherwise identical to the Japanese plant. See also Koya Azumi and Charles McMillan, "Management strategy and organization structure: a Japanese comparative study," in David Hickson and Charles McMillan (eds.), *Organization and Nation,* the Ashton Programme IV, Gower, 1981.

also often rotated among operating workers on the shopfloor. When a high number of defective products are found, the cause of and the solution to the problem are sought on the spot before calling in help from outside. As a result of the broader job classification and more flexible job assignments, workers tend to undertake a wider range of jobs and are given an opportunity to develop different skills. This makes it possible, for instance, to lay out different machines in a continuous pattern (such as a U-shape pattern) that will enable individual workers to operate several types of machines, say, a lathe and drilling and milling machines, and thus save time in walking between machines, setting up machines, and transporting and loading in-process products, while reducing in-shop inventories.

Some advanced factories have taken the fluid and flexible approach a step further by introducing regular job rotation. In these factories, workers are usually organized into teams, which are assigned clusters of jobs, and workers within teams are rotated among various jobs quite regularly. Koike describes how this works in a blast furnace workshop in a large steel plant: "This workshop consists of ten workers operating five positions under a subforeman. The way to allocate ten workers to five positions is clear in practice; every half a day, they rotate all positions egalitarianly. The subforeman (after finishing administrative work) works sometimes in place of an absentee."[10] Yasuo Monden illustrates the principle of job rotation at the Toyota factory as follows:

Obviously, cultivating or training the individual worker to become multifunctioned is an important part of achieving *shojinka* [a reduction in the number of workers required]. Toyota cultivates their workers using a system called *job rotation,* where each worker rotates through and performs every job in his workshop. After a period, the individual worker develops proficiency in each job and thereby becomes a multifunctioned worker. The job rotation system consists of three major parts. First, each manager and supervisor must rotate through every job and prove their own abilities to the general workers in the shop. Second, each worker within the shops is rotated through and trained to perform each job in rotation. The final step is scheduling the workers through job rotation at a frequency of several times each day.[11]

Interestingly, the Japanese job rotation scheme is not the product of a prescribed managerial policy or of a formal collective agreement. Rather, through the initiative of foremen and subforemen at some advanced factories in the steel industry, the idea developed autonomously from the level of shopfloor around the late 1950s, and it has

---

[10] K. Koike, "Skill formation system in the U.S. and Japan," p. 61

[11] Y. Monden, *Toyota Production System,* Industrial Engineering and Management Press, Atlanta, 1983, pp. 105–6.

2 The information structure of the J-firm

gradually spread to other industries. This pattern of development suggests that even where jobs are specialized, job demarcation is less rigid in Japanese factories than in American ones.

In most instances where the job rotation scheme is used, even inexperienced workers may be assigned to a very difficult job, in which case the most experienced workers may assist in a side-by-side position. Job rotation allows every worker to become familiar with the whole work process at the shop, which is not possible when work is organized around rigid job classification and sharp job demarcation. Thus the job rotation system facilitates *knowledge sharing* among workers in the following sense: The knowledge possessed by a single worker extends beyond a particular job jurisdiction, so that there is considerable overlap in the knowledge of individual workers of different status on the shopfloor. In contrast, in the specialized scheme the knowledge of individual workers is in principle narrow and confined to one category of job.

Obviously the wider range of job experience in general and the regular rotation system in particular sacrifice some economies of specialization. The loss in static efficiency may be compensated for by other benefits, however. In the rotation system, the diffusion of skills from senior workers to junior workers may be continuously facilitated on an informal basis through the assistance and advice of senior workers and imitation by junior workers. A more subtle, yet probably even more significant aspect of knowledge sharing is the one emphasized by Kazuo Koike.[12] The experience-based knowledge shared by a team of workers on the shopfloor may be tacit and not readily transferable in the form of formal language, but is quite useful in identifying local emergencies, such as product defects and machine malfunctions, on the spot and solving them autonomously. Those workers nurtured in a wide range of skills may be able to understand, as individuals or as a collective, why defective products have increased, and may be able to devise and implement measures to cope with the situation and thus prevent the problem from recurring. This can be done without much, if any, "outside" help from specially designated craft workers, reliefmen, repairmen, and other specialists. Koike summarizes the point by saying that a wide range of job experiences helps develop workers' "intellectual skills to cope with irregular events" beyond the skills necessary for routine operating tasks. One may also say, from the perspective of the information system, that collective learning enhances

---

[12] K. Koike, "Skill formation system in the U.S. and Japan"; and "Skill formation in mass production: A Thai-Japan comparison," *Journal of the Japanese and International Economies*, 1 (1987), pp. 408–40.

workers' capacities for processing information relevant to shopfloor efficiency.

In fact, the J-firm has increasingly delegated work control to the shopfloor level since the mid-1960s and has encouraged workers to solve problems by themselves whenever possible. Individual workers are authorized to stop a production line when necessary. The number of specialists – such as repairmen, product inspectors, and technicians – has been reduced as much as possible, and, when necessary, their expertise is used to help shopfloor workers solve a particular problem; thus they act as consultants rather than performing a special function exclusively.

The main differences between the A-firm and the J-firm may be summarized as follows: The A-firm emphasizes efficiency attained through fine specialization and sharp job demarcation, whereas the J-firm emphasizes the capability of the workers' group to cope with local emergencies autonomously, which is developed through learning by doing and sharing knowledge on the shopfloor. In the former, the operating task is *separated* from the task of identifying and finding necessary expedients to overcome and prevent emergencies, whereas in the latter the two tend to be *integrated*.

The economists' claim that efficiency is increased through specialization has a long history, dating back at least to Adam Smith, and is said to apply universally. But the actual *extent* of specialization seems to be historically and culturally conditioned. It is well known that scientific management ideas in the United States crystallized in Taylorism around the turn of century, which attempted to minimize the need for communication between workers by segmenting the entire work process into a series of simple motions. The integration of finely divided jobs is the specialized task of the engineer cum manager. In part this idea may be thought of as a response to the situation prevailing then – the American factory was dominated by immigrant workers of diverse ethnic backgrounds, and there was no close cultural identity between management and workers. It is said that the foreign-born and native-born children of foreign-born parents constituted 71 percent of the male employees in the automotive manufacturing and repair industry in 1907–8; these percentages were also quite typical of other industries.[13] Despite the excessive zeal for specialization advocated by Frederick Taylor, however, the envisioned scheme was never adopted on a large scale, possibly because it failed to motivate workers and

[13] Cole, *Work, Mobility and Participation*, p. 228.

because in practice it was made clear that the breaking down of component tasks could disrupt the whole process very easily.

Job specialization on the shopfloor in the United States became formalized with the emergence of independent union power in the 1930s and the subsequent agreement between management and the union to introduce formal job evaluation procedures, which first appeared in the steel industry and then spread to other industries.[14] Under the job evaluation procedure, each job is given certain scores within a specific set of categories, which generally include characteristics relating to the job itself (skill, working condition, responsibility for equipment, responsibility for directing other workers, etc.) and characteristics pertaining to the individual holding the job (education, experience, and the like). Points are added across categories to determine point totals. These totals then serve as criteria for arranging jobs into pay grades. The A-firm and the union came to agree that promotion from one grade to the next in the job ranking, as well as demotion from one grade to a lower one in the event of a reduction in the work force, should be based on two criteria: the merit and the seniority of applicants. However, the seniority criterion is said to have prevailed in practice.

The job evaluation procedure was expected to serve as a restraint on the potentially abusive power of management by making the criteria for wage setting and promotional decisions more transparent and objective. In this way, the hazard of nepotism, favoritism, and arbitrary victimization by foremen and other lower management was expected to be curtailed. The industrial relation system developed under this arrangement may be called *job control unionism,* following Michael Piore.[15] But the job evaluation procedure was also intended to legitimize managerial control over jobs within the framework set out in the agreement between management and the union and to limit the involvement of workers in production decision making. The integration of specialized jobs itself had become a "specialized" function of management, which resulted in hierarchical control. Although significant variations emerged in the actual shopfloor labor–supervisor

---

[14] For a discussion of the emergence of independent union power and its impact on the development of the job evaluation scheme, see Katherine Stone, "The origins of job structures in the steel industry," in Richard Edwards, Michael Reich, and David Gordon (eds.), *Labor Market Segmentation,* D. C. Heath, 1975; and Richard Edwards, *Contested Terrain,* Basic Books, 1979.

[15] M. Piore, "American labor and the industrial crisis," *Challenge,* 25 (March–April, 1982), pp. 5–11; M. Piore and Charles F. Sabel, *The Second Industrial Divide,* Basic Books, 1984; Harry C. Katz, *Shifting Gears: Changing Labor Relations in the U.S. Automobile Industry,* MIT Press, 1985.

relations across plants and across work groups within a given plant, in general the relationship under job control unionism was marked by legalistic formality and unilateral decision making by management, which often produced an adversarial atmosphere when it came to interpreting and implementing an agreement.

The primary objective of the union in advancing job control unionism in the 1940s and early 1950s was, as pointed out above, to curtail the abusive exercise of managerial discretionary power and to lay down fair groundwork for competition among workers. This scheme operated fairly well in the period of stable economic growth in the 1950s and 1960s. Those were the years in which job classification was refined and became more detailed. As the economy entered a period of slower growth, industrial restructuring, and rapid technological change, however, clear-cut jurisdictional boundaries between jobs began to appear rigid and were felt to hamper the efficient internal reallocation of workers.

Meanwhile, the job classification scheme had become an instrument that the union used to protect members' jobs, particularly those of skilled production workers and craft workers. For example, even if production workers on the assembly line knew how to repair a broken machine, they were unwilling to help or to do the machinists' repair jobs, since doing so might have jeopardized the machinist's job security by making him appear redundant. Whereas the Japanese worker would consider it "immoral" to be idle while a fellow worker is sweating, the A-firm worker would say it is in perfect accord with the norm of respecting the prescribed duties and rights of one's fellow workers.

However, American unions and their rank and file are now becoming increasingly aware that in rapidly changing market and technological environments the rigid application of a job classification scheme threatens the competitive position of the employing firm, and thus ultimately their own job security. As a result, unions have begun to exhibit a more flexible attitude toward the actual application of the job classification scheme. For example, in some recent local agreements in t. automobile industry, production classifications have been broade. .d to include some minor machine maintenance, inspection, and housekeeping tasks previously performed by either craft workers or other production workers.

In the late 1970s General Motors even experimented with an operating team system at some nonunionized plants, mainly in the South, that collapsed all production worker classifications into one. In this system, skilled craft jobs were still classified, but a variety of job rotation schemes were tested in the operating work team, supplemented by a pay-for-knowledge system in which workers were paid according to a variety of job tasks that individuals could perform.[16] When those plants were later unionized, however, the team system was quickly replaced by the job classification scheme. Until New United Motor Manufacturing Incorporated (NUMMI), a new joint venture of Toyota and GM, introduced the more comprehensive team system in 1984, which I describe later in some detail, there had been no major experiment with the team system in unionized settings.

Even when a local agreement was reached to broaden the job classification and make job assignments flexible, it was often because of pressure from management to otherwise shift production to outsourcing. Although a variation of the Quality of Work Control (QWC) program was introduced by GM in the 1970s and 1980s to allow the work group to participate in identifying and solving workplace issues in a cooperative manner, a clear line was drawn between the participative program and job classification issues that fall in the domain of collective bargaining.[17]

The team approach, which allows workers to participate in problem solving and operating tasks to be integrated with the task of coping with local emergencies, would inevitably reduce the number of formal shopfloor rules and transfer a significant amount of regulatory authority from the written agreement to the work group. The foreman and other first-line supervisors often try to resist such a transfer because it will reduce their power, and their roles will become ambiguous as work group participation increases. For some workers, on the other hand, a relaxation of the formal rules pertaining to job assignment may imply less job security than is ensured under job control unionism, in part because some particular job categories will become redundant or the seniority right will be lost. Thus the insecurity both on the part of the supervisor and the worker seems to be a significant obstacle to fundamental change in the work organization of the A-firm.

But one may wonder why similar problems do not riddle the J-firm, which employs the less rigid job classification scheme. Even if the flexible job assignment and the practice of regular job rotation have developed autonomously from the shopfloor level, why has management of the J-firm allowed this to happen and even tried to make the best use of it, promoting the Quality Circle Movement based on the shopfloor work group? Has Japanese management not been threatened by the

---

[16] See Katz, *Shifting Gears*, pp. 88–104; and Thomas A. Cochan, Harry C. Katz and Robert B. McKersie, *The Transformation of American Industrial Relations*, Basic Books, 1986, chap. 8.
[17] For these developments see Katz, *Shifting Gears*, particularly chap. 4.

prospect of eventually losing control at the shopfloor by allowing the work group to have integrative autonomy? These questions cannot be fully answered without examining the "economic" incentive mechanism through which Japanese workers as individuals and as a collective body come to identify their self-interests with the objective of the firm more readily than under the job classification scheme, as well as the personnel administrative mechanism under which they comply with the "invisible" authority of management. Such mechanisms are dealt with in Chapters 3 and 5.

B.   *Centralized coordination versus the* kanban *system*

The contrast between the J-firm and the A-firm can be seen in intershop coordination as well as workshop organization. At the A-firm, job specialization on the shopfloor is coupled with the hierarchical coordination of shops by managers as specialists. At the J-firm, autonomous problem solving on the shopfloor is coupled with the mutual participation of shops in intershop coordination. In other words, both at the shopfloor level and the intershop level, coordinating task and operating task are clearly *separated* and specialized at the A-firm, whereas the two tend to be more *integrated* at the J-firm.

Because of the increasing diversity of consumers' preferences, which sophisticated engineering has made it possible to accommodate, the modern factory often produces hundreds, sometimes even thousands, of different varieties of goods in small and medium batches, using and assembling thousands of different materials, components, and half-products. For example, modern assembly lines of passenger cars specifically designed for the production of a particular model turn out thousands of varieties of cars, distinguished by different combinations of engine and transmission, color, body type, options, and so on. At the assembly factory of one Japanese manufacturer, 32,100 varieties of cars were produced in 1978, and the average amount of output per variety was only 11 in a three-month period. (This factory only produced 500 varieties in the mid-1960s.)[18] This kind of intensive product diversification and small-batch production is becoming an important feature of modern factories, if not to the same degree, even for systems traditionally characterized by mass production or continuous process technologies, which range from consumer products such as home entertainment electronics to industrial parts such as ball bearings, to material products such as steel and chemicals.

---

[18] Kazuichi Sakamoto (ed.), *Gijitsu Kakushin to Kigyo Kozo* (Technological innovation and the structure of the firm), Minerva Shobo, 1985, p. 117.

In response to evolving market demands for diverse products, the factory needs to determine not only the output quantity of each variety and the sequential order of production of various types, but also the coordinated supply of each of thousands of materials, parts, and half-products. Further, if a serious quality defect is found in half-products or parts at a midpoint of the production process and a batch has to be discarded, a chain of repercussions is bound to affect the productivity of the entire downstream process, and pressure will be placed on the shop with the problem to improve the quality of the products and to increase the quantity of production immediately so that the smooth operation of the entire process can be restored.

How is the necessary coordination between shops achieved when the inevitable unexpected event occurs, such as a change in final demand (demand shock), or an in-process shock arises in a particular shop or between particular shops and its repercussions go well beyond there (e.g., quality defects in parts production, malfunction of machines, breakdown in transportation of half-products)? Because of the "bounded rationality" of human beings, it is normally impossible to specify ex ante intershop transaction plans, each of which is contingent on the occurrence of a probable particular emergency, and thus such events often have to be dealt with ex post.

At the A-firm, the principle of specialization prevails in the sphere of coordination as well, with the result that intershop coordination becomes the specialized function of hierarchically ordered administrative offices. The central planning office of the production department makes the optimal plan of production for final outputs on the basis of the prediction of market demands or customers' actual orders over a certain period of time. The plan is then broken down successively into detailed accommodating plans for the final production sequence, supporting material requirements, inventory control, and so on, going down the ladder of the administrative hierarchy, and is given to the relevant shops. Actual flows of materials, parts, and semifinished products between shops are controlled centrally by the expediting office. At a certain interval, say, a week, the production and procurement planning schedule may be revised in response to the fluctuations in demand as well as to reviews of discrepancies between planned and actual performances of each shop. Although the continuing development of information technology tends to make the unit time interval for rescheduling shorter, unexpected events occurring during the interim period often have to be dealt with in the framework of the preset schedule. Inventory stocks of materials and in-process goods function as a shock buffer. The coordinating and operating functions are completely separated in this system; communications necessary for the coordinated adjustment of production operations of shops in reaction to uncertain market changes and in-process emergencies are channeled only through the central office or its subordinate section.

Similarly at the J-firm, the phenomena on the shopfloor – ambiguity and fluidity of jurisdiction – also appear in the sphere of intershop coordination. The centralized scheduling of production for a certain period of time only provides a general framework. As a supplement to the centralized plan, horizontal and direct dealing between interconnected shops for the actual transfer of materials, parts, and in-process products takes place within the period of implementation in order to fine-tune actual final output production to changing market conditions and in-process emergencies. The lack of a central office to control and expedite the flow of materials among shops is a conspicuous feature of the assembly factory of the J-firm.

The much-publicized *kanban* system at the Toyota factory provides an example of this arrangement. In this system, a tentative production schedule may be worked out by the central planning office on the basis of market forecasts at a regular interval – say, once every two weeks or every month – and every shop is informed of its production plan, just as in the centralized system. But this centralized schedule only provides each shop a general production guideline for that period. Information regarding actual customer demands for varieties of cars, which is transmitted by dealers to the marketing department, is used for fine-tuning the actual production schedule in a shorter time frame. The computer in the production planning office prepares a daily schedule for the sequence in which the various products are to roll off the assembly lines. This schedule is based on daily orders received from dealers a few days before and is transmitted to the computer terminal at the head of the assembly line just two days before the automobile rolls off the assembly line. In this way, the lead time can be as short as a week. The important point is that this up-to-date production schedule is only fed into the final assembly line, and communications necessary for fine-tuning production at upstream shops, to match the daily schedule of final outputs, need not be channeled through the administrative office because of the use of *kanban.*

The term *kanban* traditionally refers to a block of wood bearing the trademark of a merchant shop, but in the present context it refers to a card placed in a vinyl envelope. In implementing the daily production schedule, the final assembly line places a production-ordering *kanban* for each type of part or half-product (engine, transmission, body, head lamp, etc.) on a post adjacent to the relevant inventory store whenever it withdraws its inventory. This *kanban* specifies the kind and quantity of withdrawal as well as time of delivery for its replenishment. The upstream shop supplying the part or half-product collects the *kanban* from the post at regular intervals, say, a few times a day. This *kanban* functions as an ordering form and is returned to the inventory store together with actual delivery at a specified time. Thus the *kanban* plays the dual role of order form and delivery notice. The shop that receives the *kanban* from the final assembly line in turn dispatches its own *kanban* order forms to shops located immediately upstream, and, through the circular flow of *kanban,* the chain of bilateral order–delivery links between directly interconnected shops extends to the outside suppliers who are involved in long-term transactions with the final assembly manufacturer.

Upstream shops are supposed to adapt their production according to demands by their downstream shops, as indicated by the *kanban,* and are bound neither to respond to the predetermined command of the administrative office, which may become quickly outdated because of unexpected factors occurring during the interim period of planning, nor to smooth out their production streams according to their own convenience, nor to pursue the maximum use of their machines in isolation. In this sense, one of the important characteristics of the *kanban* system may be defined by saying that the downstream shop "pulls" the operation of the upstream shop rather than that the supply of the latter "pushes" the operation of the former. Through the chain of the circular flow of *kanban,* the entire system is made directly responsive to market demands. In contrast, the traditional approach of the American automobile industry has been to produce outputs according to a market "forecast" and then to adjust prices – by means of rebates, discounts, and options – to levels at which actual markets will absorb the outputs. In this system, clearly the supply side takes the lead.

In responding to market signals successively transmitted from downstream, each shop in the *kanban* system is required to adjust machine manning to make efficient use of manpower. The quantity and kinds of machines to be covered by a single worker are adjusted to minimize the idle time of workers, but not to make efficient use of local machines. Thus the multifunctionality of the worker is an essential ingredient of the *kanban* system. Any worker who is temporarily released from operational duty in the shop because production has slowed down may be assigned to a housekeeping job, retraining, or related jobs at another shop.

Another important function of the *kanban* system is quality control. The downstream shop can and should refuse to accept on the spot the delivery of any defective supply from the upstream shop. Quality checks can be made at each stage of the production stream rather than at an inspection post situated at the end of the assembly line, and a bug can be removed from the system quickly.

Although the *kanban* system may appear to be a rather crude information system, it is an effective mechanism that allows an intricate system of automobile production involving more than 20,000 component units to respond to unpredictable consumer demands for a variety of final outputs, while keeping the amount of in-process inventory as low as possible. Thus the *kanban* system is often referred to as the "zero inventory" method or the "just-in-time" method. However, it should be understood that this system introduces integrated control over production, inventory, and quality.

The *kanban* system was originally developed by Toyota industrial engineers from a careful study of the method used by American supermarkets to control the stock on their shelves. During the initial phase of the experiment, the labor union was opposed to introducing the multimachine manning that is indispensable to the operation of this system and staged a strike. Even when the *kanban* system was finally adopted, it was not without problems. It took Toyota almost 20 years from the initial experiment to achieve state-of-the-art operation and to surpass Western competitors with its remarkable productive efficiency. Now the *kanban* system has been adopted by many Japanese factories in assembly industries, and has been introduced to or is being tested by some American factories as well. In most cases, manufacturing costs have declined substantially since the adoption of the *kanban* system.

As already noted, an essential feature of the *kanban* system is that the fine-tuning of production is performed in response to evolving market conditions without the intermediation of the administrative offices above the operating units. Thus, this method of coordination may be considered a *horizontal* process as opposed to a centralized one, although a centralized production and material requirement plan must first be prepared to provide a framework for horizontal fine-tuning. As I explain later, the *kanban* system can be used only to control production processes with special technical characteristics. However, the system exhibits a generic element of a coordination pattern operating in the J-firm, the direct, horizontal coordination among operating units, which is often informal and bypasses hierarchically layered administrative offices. The statistical study by Lincoln et al. referred to earlier in the chapter has indirectly confirmed this horizontal tendency by showing that in Japanese plants, de facto responsibility averages more than one full level below the rank possessing formal authority and is notably lower than in U.S. plants.

However, if de facto decision making is delegated to lower levels and coordination between shops is entrusted to the shops themselves, there is obviously a danger that shops will haggle and misrepresent information in their bargaining. These problems may become particularly severe when teamwork within the shop is emphasized and the team develops a coherent collective interest in itself. In this context, the *kanban* system may be understood as a shrewd device to curb these problems by formalizing and automating horizontal coordination. Another possible way to cope with these problems is to rotate supervisors and senior workers among neighboring and technically related shops. This may serve to discourage shops from pushing their specific interests and may encourage shops to share knowledge and thereby prevent intershop haggling based on information misrepresentation.[19] As we have seen, the organization of shopfloor work in the A-firm and task coordination among shops are both based on the principle of "the right man in the right place" (economies of specialization). On the other hand, the approach that underlies these two processes in the J-firm is "integrative" in the sense that operating tasks are unified with in-process problem solving at the shopfloor and intershop coordination is done horizontally, on the basis of information sharing across jurisdictional boundaries.

In reality, the distinction between the specialization approach and

---

[19] In some cases, the transfer of workers may go beyond related shops. An unusual example of job rotation beyond the production department, yet one that is full of interesting implications for the issue at hand, may be found in the temporary dispatch of production workers to dealers adopted by Toyo Kogyo, the maker of Mazda, as an extraordinary measure during its business setback in the mid to late 1970s. At that time, the company was on the brink of bankruptcy, and as a countermeasure to the cutback of production and a measure to promote sales, a substantial number of production workers and white-collar employees were dispatched to its dealers. According to Richard Pascale and Thomas Rohlen, who did an interesting study of the Mazda turnabout, "in the first three years over 20 percent of Toyo Kogyo's employees were veterans of the sales experience" ["Mazda turnabout," *Journal of Japanese Studies,* 9 (1983), p. 34]. This extraordinary measure not only turned out to be effective in promoting sales, but in retrospect helped develop interdepartmental communications in the following sense.

Because product differentiation is highly developed in the automobile manufacturing industry, jurisdictional disputes and conflict between sales and production departments are not uncommon. The sales department, eager to accommodate consumers' evolving demands, tends to insist on flexible and speedier adaptation of the production schedule to meet these demands. On the other hand, the production department finds it easier to stick to a predetermined production schedule. The temporary dispatch of production workers to dealers in the present case turned out to be useful in easing the tension between the two departments. The workers temporarily dispatched were not only able to secure their jobs, but were also made aware of the vital need to adapt production to consumer demands, since the survival of the company and their jobs depended on it. Once transferred back to the shopfloor, they began to actively participate in Quality Control Circles set up to identify problems and opportunities for improving work processes as well as solving them autonomously.

the integrative approach should not be taken as absolute. In Japanese firms, horizontal communication functions in a framework that is shaped by overall administrative direction. At the same time, American firms have recently begun to place increasing emphasis on cross-jurisdictional, horizontal communications, implemented through cross-disciplinary project teams, less hierarchical small business divisions, and the like. According to a comprehensive comparative survey of major American and Japanese companies by Tadao Kagono et al., the degree of "formal" institutionalization of cross-jurisdictional relations appears to be much more developed among American companies, although for other indicators they exhibit much higher degrees of hierarchical centralization.[20] This finding may indicate that, whereas Japanese companies rely upon de facto, informal communications, U.S. companies may be moving toward a hybrid form of organization consisting of horizontal and centralized coordination through organizational designs. However, instead of speculating on this trend, in the next two sections I formulate two prototype models of the information structure of the firm: one features centralized hierarchical coordination based on the principle of specialization, and the other, decentralized horizontal coordination based on knowledge sharing. I then analyze the factors that determine the performance characteristics of these two models. In this way, I hope to identify some important issues that need to be considered in the development of a hybrid form.

2.   The traditional paradigm of the hierarchy

In order to assess the work organization and internal coordination mechanism of the J-firm vis-à-vis the A-firm, we must first distinguish between *strategic business* decision making and *operational* decision making. The former is concerned with those business decisions of the firm (corporate organization) that establish the basic framework of its operation. Decisions regarding investments in new equipment and buildings, the direction of research and development, diversification, and acquisition and divestiture fall into this category. Given these strategic business decisions, the firm must then adapt its operations to evolving technical and human emergencies (such as machine malfunc-

---

[20] Tadao Kagono, Yujiro Nonaka, Kiyonori Sakakibara, and Akihiro Okumura, *Strategic vs. Evolutionary Management: A U.S.–Japan Comparison of Strategy and Organization,* North-Holland, 1985, chap. 2. Their sample covers 227 American companies from the top 1,000 mining and manufacturing companies in the 1979 *Fortune* ranking and 291 Japanese companies from the 1,031 manufacturing companies listed on the Tokyo Stock Exchange.

tions, defective products, worker illness) as well as changing market circumstances. Such sequential adaptation consists, for example, of assigning specific tasks to each member of the work organization, making piecemeal improvements in the work process, and coordinating constituent work units (such as shops); I place this type of decision making under the second heading. In this and the following sections, I assume strategic business decision making as given and focus attention on the operational and adaptive attributes of the highly stylized J-firm in comparison with the conventional model of hierarchy. In Chapters 5 and 6 I consider interactive relations between the operational and business strategic decisions of the J-firm.

Let us imagine the production department of the A-firm to comprise many workshops engaged in specific operations. These shops lie at the base of a hierarchy built of layers of administrative offices. The adjustment of the target levels of various final outputs in response to *global* shocks (e.g., changing market circumstances) and concomitant adjustments of the flow of in-process products between shops are directed by the central office of production planning, possibly via intermediate coordinating offices. To implement the production directive, as well as respond to *local* shocks within the shop, the supervisor of each shop has been given discretionary power, within the limits set forth in the collective agreement on job classification, to specify a concrete operating task for each job and to coordinate different jobs. The repercussion of local shocks may be absorbed locally by changing the inventories of in-process products. Information regarding inventory changes will be used periodically by the central office of production planning in revising the production plan.

Abstracting further from the above basic feature of the A-firm, one may construct the formal model of hierarchy, as economists and organizational theorists conventionally do, in the following manner: The internal organization of the firm may be said to consist of many basic units crystallized around specific functions (operational and administrative), and, in any pair of units, one is superordinate/subordinate to the other (e.g., he/she is my boss) or else they are not comparable (I and a fellow worker in the same shop do not stand in any such relation). The superordinate directly or indirectly commands the operation of subordinates and the latter directly or indirectly reports to the former. The basic principle of this hierarchical coordination is characterized by the following two attributes:

1. Each constituent unit has no more than one direct superordinate and it does not communicate with other

constituent units (therefore any adjustment of operation between two incomparable units is done by a common direct superordinate).

2. Only one unit (the central office) is superordinate to any other unit.

The recent literature on hierarchies – which addresses such issues as the optimal design of hierarchical structure, the optimal assignment of managers with different capacities to offices in a hierarchy, and the relative efficiency of hierarchies in comparison with the competitive market mechanism[21] – seems to presuppose that the only viable alternative to the market mechanism, from the point of view of efficiency, is hierarchies. One notable exception to this view was presented by Oliver E. Williamson, who scrutinized the efficiency property of hierarchies relative to other modes of organizing production, such as the putting out system, the inside contracting system, and the radical ideal of worker communes.[22] According to Williamson, the hierarchical organization and coordination of work would reduce the costs involved in transactions between operating units relative to other modes of work and coordination for the following reasons:

[H.1] *Low buffer inventory cost:* A hierarchy can economize on buffer inventories and the expenses involved in intershop transportations by centralizing the coordination of material requirement planning.[23]

[H.2] *Economies of specialization:* The talents of employees are utilized most effectively when operating tasks are specialized and managerial and operating tasks are kept separate.

[H.3] *Economies of centralized handling of shocks:* A hierarchy responds best to global shocks because it is capable of opti-

---

[21] Williamson, *Markets and Hierarchies;* Jacque Cremer, "A partial theory of the optimal organization of a bureaucracy," *Bell Journal of Economics,* 11 (1980), pp. 683–93; John Geanakopolos and Paul Milgrom, "A theory of hierarchies based on limited managerial attention," mimeographed, 1985.
[22] O. E. Williamson, "The organization of work," *The Economic Institutions of Capitalism,* Free Press, 1985, chap. 9. The inside contracting system is the business organization in which the capitalist owner of capital equipment entrusts production tasks to the contractor who organizes and supervises workers. See also R. K. Sah and Joseph Stiglitz, "Human fallibility and economic organization," *American Economic Review,* 75 (1985), pp. 292–7.
[23] In relation to this, he also points to the following cost savings attributable to centralized monitoring: it discourages embezzlement and prevents production units from disguising the true quality of intermediate products.

mal planning owing to the centralization of all relevant information.[24]

However, Williamson admits that hierarchies may have a certain negative incentive attribute:

> [H.4] *Lack of work incentives:* Employees working under a hierarchy may not be motivated to work intensely and to improve local processes, because the link between reward and effort is not direct (the payment to employees is normally based on job titles). Also, they may be less responsive to local shocks because they are not authorized to respond to such shocks unless so directed by a supervisor, in accordance with the job classification scheme and hierarchical control.

But this disadvantage [H.4], Williamson has argued, may be outweighed by gains from the specialization of jobs and the centralization (hierarchical ordering) of information handling listed under [H.1] through [H.3]. In response to the radicals' claim that the hierarchy emerged as a dominant form of production organization in capitalist economies not because of its relative efficiency but because of capitalists' attempts to maintain control over workers in the workplace, Williamson argues: "Hostility to hierarchy thus lacks a comparative institutional foundation. There may be more or less preferred types of hierarchy; but hierarchy itself is unavoidable unless efficiency sacrifices are made."[25]

Although Williamson's point seems well taken where efficiency is concerned, the alternatives that he cites are either primitive production organizations, such as the putting out system and inside contracting, which historically preceded and were replaced by the hierarchical system, or idealized utopian systems such as the communes in which workers rotate various jobs regularly on the basis of common ownership of capital, which have never become viable on a large scale.

Williamson's analysis seems to presuppose market and technological environments in which scale economies are favored. Suppose that production is for mass markets in which standardized commodities are demanded by numerous anonymous consumers. In order to

---

[24] In relation to economies due to specialization and the centralized handling of systematic shocks, Williamson also points to the following advantage of the hierarchy in the reduction of uncertainty, i.e., innovation: The capacity of the hierarchy to recognize and implement system innovations is high because of the specialized contributions of engineers. I discuss this aspect of the hierarchy in Chapter 6.

[25] Williamson, *Economic Institutions of Capitalism,* p. 231.

exploit economies of scale in mass or large-batch production, a production process may be subdivided into multiple tasks, each of which may be performed with the aid of special-purpose machines (attribute [H.2] is relevant here). In addition, suppose that demand in these markets is more or less predictable, thanks to the law of large numbers, and that changing market circumstances may be adequately handled by regularly revising production planning at the central offices (attribute [H.3]). Interim adaptation may be handled by adjusting buffer inventories without rescheduling overall production (attribute [H.1]).

However, if, for some reason, scale merit is lost and if it becomes imperative to be flexible and to adapt quickly to local and global shocks in order to remain competitive, the advantages of hierarchical decision making and coordination may disappear. This point may be illustrated by an example. I have already pointed out that extensive product diversification and small- and medium-batch production are becoming important features of many modern factories. Through intensified competition among producers of different nations throughout the world, national markets are becoming more integrated into global markets, and, in order to capture a larger market share, each producer is forced to treat these markets more like "fashion markets," in which product life cycles are short, the shifts in demand from one variety of product to another are volatile, the batch of production is relatively small, and it is imperative to shorten the lead time from order to delivery. It seems that the economies of scale so effective in mass production are becoming less important in some industries because of this trend. In turn, the efficiency gains available from the hierarchical integration of specialization are losing some of their value for the reasons listed below:

> [N.1] *Increasing inventory cost:* As product diversification within a single manufacturing department is intensified, production coordination through buffer inventories may become very costly, because both the variety of final products and the number of parts, materials, and half-products to be integrated increase in great measure. Furthermore, the recent relative deflation in commodity prices and the slower increase in wholesale prices make the implicit interest cost of inventory higher than in a period of high inflation.

> [N.2] *The adaptive cost of specialization:* In order to adapt work organization to meet diverse and volatile market demands quickly and flexibly, rigid specialization based on a well-defined job classification scheme may not be condu-

cive to the efficient utilization of the work force. It may become necessary to assign diverse tasks to workers flexibly in order to respond to evolving circumstances.

Even if a multipurpose machine is used, the worker will not find it easy to make the frequent changes of jigs and tools necessary for small-batch production without broad knowledge of the production process. In order not to disrupt the smooth operation of an entire production process with small inventory stock, it may also be necessary to cope with local shocks quickly, without calling in the specialized help from outside the shop. However, doing so may require more versatile workers' skills (deeper and broader information-processing capacities), which have not been considered essential in traditional hierarchies.

[N.3] *Communication cost in hierarchies:* The central and middle coordinating offices may be limited in their capacity to understand and process information that they receive from subordinates and to make themselves understood by subordinates. Arm's-length communications and commands may be subject to noise disturbance and time-lag from the perception of in-process shocks to the implementation of an operating response to them. In addition, if in-process product flow is controlled centrally by the expediting office, valuable on-site information available at the interfaces of constituent units, such as information on the quality of intermediate products and emergencies affecting the timing of delivery, may remain unutilized.

[N.4] *The bargaining costs under specialization:* The negative incentive attribute of the hierarchy referred to [H.4] may be aggravated by the increasing need for flexible adaptation. Further, in order to extract more quasi rent available to the firm, specialized workers may take advantage of their monopolistic position and divert their attention and energy to unproductive activities to strengthen their bargaining power.

The costs that hierarchies incur owing to properties [N.1] and [N.3] have been relatively well understood, although it is not immediately clear whether an alternative system is available to avert those costs. Proposition [N.2] is a restatement of Adam Smith's dictum in the contemporary context: "The degree of specialization is limited by the extent of the market." Property [N.4] has been emphasized recently by

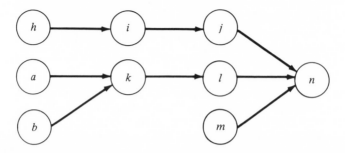

Figure 2.1. Tree structure.

John Roberts and Paul Milgrom.[26] Because of these negative attributes, hierarchical coordination based on the rigid separation of control and operation as well as the specialization of operating jobs may be losing some of the efficiency attributed to it by Williamson, particularly in those industries where product variety is great and the production process involves numerous steps. Is there an alternative mode of work organization and operating coordination that can respond to increasingly diverse market conditions and complex technological conditions more effectively?

3.   Horizontal information structure

Does the experience of the *kanban* system in the Japanese automobile industry suggest a new micro-micro informational structure for coordinating various manufacturing operations within the firm, alternative to the traditional hierarchical paradigm? Or is this system uniquely appropriate to the technological characteristics of the automobile production process? Is it effective only for a certain market environment but not for others? In this section I consider the technological and market conditions of the firm under which manufacturing operations can be coordinated in a nonhierarchical way for productive and informational efficiencies.

Suppose that the production process of the firm is such that shops are connected to each other through the input–output relationships depicted in Figure 2.1. In these input–output relationships, materials,

---

[26] P. Milgrom, "Quasi rents, influence and organization form," mimeographed, 1986; and J. Roberts and P. Milgrom, "Bargaining and influence costs and the organization of economic activity," mimeographed, 1987.

parts, and half-products flow in the direction of the arrow. Consider any pair of shops, say i and j. If i's output is utilized directly or indirectly by j, then we say that "j is downstream-situated from i (i is upstream-situated from j)." Otherwise they are not comparable.[27] The figure is drawn in such a way that if both i and j are downstream-situated from h, then i is downstream-situated from j, or j is downstream-situated from i. These characteristics may be put thus:

1. Each shop has no more than one direct downstream shop.
2. There is only one shop, denoted by n, that is downstream-situated to any other shop.

Such structure is (algebraically) referred to as a *tree*. The unit n in this input–output relationship is the shop that assembles all components and half-products into the final outputs.

Notice that this tree structure, which I have defined in terms of a technological input–output relationship, has exactly the same (algebraic) structure as the hierarchy defined in the previous section in terms of communication (command/report) relationship. The super/subordinate relationship parallels exactly the down/upstream relation here. Information on global shocks (i.e., the market signal) is fed into the most superordinate unit in the hierarchy (the equivalent of n here), which is the central administrative office, and after suitable processing and computation, first by the central office and then by the middle offices, that information is dissipated to every shop. Shops in the hierarchy are located at the end points of the information flow from the market.

If the only uncertain events to which the firm has to adapt are the fluctuations in final demand, quick communications may be made through the tree structure defined above. First, the market information may be processed by the central planning office, but it is transformed only into the corresponding plan of final products and fed only into the end unit n, which is the final assembly shop. Then sequential adjustments of production may be made toward successive upstream shops. Information flows "hierarchically" from the end unit (the final assembly shop) to upstream shops, but without intermediation by the administrative offices in the hierarchy that connect the central planning office to the shops. In this system of horizontal coordination, shops themselves are nodal points of the communication network, and it is the downstream shops that "command" upstream shops. (This

---

[27] We assume that this downstream relation has the algebraic properties of reflexibility, symmetry, and transitivity.

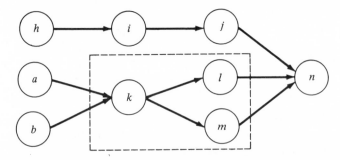

Figure 2.2. Quasi-tree structure.

corresponds to my previous characterization of the *kanban* system: The "supply" of an upstream shop is dictated by a "withdrawal" by its immediate upstream shop (see Section 2).

But let us note that for the workability of horizontal coordination and its possible informational efficiency relative to the hierarchy, we have assumed a simple tree structure for technology and a simple stochastic structure in which the only unexpected event is the market situation regarding final output. First, let us retain the second assumption concerning the stochastic structure, but suppose that technological structure is a little more complicated than that of a simple tree, yet satisfies the following two conditions:

1. Every two shops always have at least one common downstream shop, or one of them is situated downstream from the other. If there is more than one common downstream shop for two shops, then one shop in that group of common downstream shops is more immediately downstream-situated from the two than the others in the group.

2. However, any two downstream shops of any given shop may not be comparable in the sense that neither of them are downstream-situated from the other.

In Figure 2.2, shops *l* and *m* are downstream-situated from shop *k*, but they are not comparable. (For instance, both the transmission fabrication shop and the engine fabrication shop may be downstream-situated from the iron casting shop, but they are not comparable and the products of both shops may be assembled only at the final assembly shop.) However, the condition (1) ensures that only one shop, *n*, is downstream-situated from any other shop.

Although this is a more general technological structure, sequential adaptation may still be possible in principle if uncertain events only affect final demand. The assumption (1) of the existence of a most immediate common downstream shop for any group of shops implies that shops may be subgrouped in such a way that subgroups of shops form a tree structure, although within any subgroup member shops cannot be ordered by the down/upstream relation. In Figure 2.2, the subgrouping of shops indicated by the broken block generates the tree structure. Such a structure may be called a *quasi tree*. In this way, the complexity of organization may be localized.

The production structure of industry featuring the assembly of many component units may be regarded as approximating the quasi-tree structure. In such a manufacturing process, horizontal coordination between plants/shops can be designed, while containing possible non-tree structures within plans/shops on a manageable scale. This is probably one reason why Japanese firms in the automobile and electronic machinery industries rely extensively on semiautonomous subsidiaries and subcontractors as supply sources. The factory of the parent firm is organized with the final assembly shop and other essential component shops at the core, while retaining the simple tree relationship with many semiautonomous suppliers, to which it is connected in the *kanban* system. This arrangement simplifies the administrative structure of production coordination enormously. I return to this and other aspects of the subcontracting relations of the Japanese firm in Section 5.2.

As already discussed in Section 2, the function of the *kanban* system is to integrate production flow and information flow for the purpose of responding to market fluctuations with minimal inventories. If a product variety is limited or the market demand is very stable, however, the saving of inventory cost by fine-tuning final outputs in response to market signals through horizontal coordination may be trivial. On the other hand, the horizontal coordination without the centralization of information may not be effective for large changes in demand either. For instance, according to Toyota, demand variations of about 10 percent can be handled by changing only the frequency of *kanban* transfers, but larger seasonal changes in demand, or a larger change in actual monthly demand over the predetermined plan, requires that all of the production lines be rearranged administratively.[28] Furthermore, the absence of buffer inventories may make the horizontal system vulnerable to drastic shocks. The *kanban* system not only connects shops within a factory, but also the prime manufacturer

---

[28] Monden, *Toyota Production System,* p. 27.

and many suppliers. If they are geographically dispersed and if the transportation of materials and parts from a supplier to the prime manufacturer is disrupted by a large shock such as a natural disaster or a large-scale traffic accident, then the smooth operation of a whole system based on minimal inventories may become a problem.[29] A contingent production plan for large shocks is necessary.

We may thus posit:

> [I.1] *Savings on inventory cost:* If the process used to produce a variety of final outputs using a large number of components is organized in the (quasi-)tree structure, it can respond to continual market fluctuations with reduced in-process inventories through horizontal coordination. But it may be vulnerable to drastic shocks because of the reduction in buffer inventory.

The "zero inventory" requirement to dispense with buffer inventory necessitates the effective control of local shocks, such as the malfunction of machines, absenteeism of workers, and quality defects, in order to minimize their effect on the smooth operation of horizontal coordination. If small- and medium-batch production is to respond to the fluctuating demand for diverse products, each shop must be capable of performing with a considerable degree of flexibility and speed in adjusting the amount and variety of products needed. For example, it has to be able to change tools and jigs with speed and accuracy. To cope with irregularities at the shop level, workers may require a much higher degree of "intellectual skill" (Koike), or information-processing capacity than is necessary for running routine operations efficiently.

Such capacities may be developed and utilized through the flexible work organization as discussed in Section 1. Let us now reiterate the argument: The multifunctionality of workers fostered by a wide range of job experience (and job rotation in particular) may enable each shop to adjust job assignments flexibly in response to the requirements of the downstream operation. The worker may therefore be assigned to various combinations of different types of machines, depending on the changing composition and timing of outputs. The *kanban* system emphasizes the efficient utilization of manpower rather than the full utilization of machines, the result of which may be unneeded accu-

---

[29] On July 11, 1979, a large fire triggered by the collision of a few hundred cars in Nihonzaka Tunnel forced the Tomei Highway, the major highway connecting Tokyo and Nagoya, to close down for a few days. Some body assembly lines of a car manufacturer in the Tokai region were shut down in the afternoon of July 12 because of the delay in the delivery of parts from suppliers located in Tokyo.

mulations of in-process inventories. Multifunctional workers are also more effective in operating the multipurpose numerical-control machines that are replacing single-purpose machines as the emphasis shifts from economies of scale to repeated short-production runs of similar parts with short lead times. When the demand from the downstream shop slackens, idle workers are deployed in the maintenance of machines and other household jobs of the shop. Further, workers trained in a wide range of skills can better understand why more defective products are being produced and how to cope with the situation as well as prevent it from recurring. If horizontal coordination is to operate smoothly, product defects must be spotted in advance of the final inspection, namely, at the very place where the problem occurs, and remedial measures must be taken immediately.

The capacity of the worker to cope with changes in product composition and local emergencies may be specific to the global framework established through the strategic business decisions of top management, such as product mix and factory design. Such capacities may be effective to cope with continual and incremental changes within that framework, but not with drastic changes in the market and other conditions. It may be costly to develop versatility in workers to enable them to cope with a "very" wide range of changes, instead of recruiting specialists from markets as the need arises. On the other hand, if the market and other environments are very stable, workers' information-processing capacities may not be used effectively and may become redundant resources. Therefore the development of wide-ranged skills may be most effectively used for continual environmental changes.[30] In the longer run, however, when technological progress necessitates changes in the design of machinery and process, versatility and a deeper understanding of the technological process on the part of workers may help them adapt to a new process as well as start a new process without being interrupted by a reorganizational interim period (I dis-

---

[30] Hideshi Itoh confirmed this conjecture through the analysis of an interesting mathematical model of the two-level information structure of the firm, based on the theory of Baysian inference. Suppose that a strategic business decision is concerned with the top-level variable and the operating decision with the second-level variable. He summarized his analysis as follows: "The total [optimal] investment in the [shop-level] capacity increases either as a level of gradual changes [in the top-level state variable] increases, or as a level of drastic changes [in the top-level state variable] decreases except for the case that the variance of the top-level state variable is sufficiently low." H. Itoh, "Information processing capacities of the firm," *Journal of the Japanese and International Economies,* 1 (1987), pp. 299–326. See also M. Aoki, "The participatory generation of information rents and the theory of the firm," mimeographed, 1988.

cuss this aspect of versatility in more detail in the concluding section). Thus the following may be proposed:

[I.2] *Dynamic efficiency of flexible job demarcation:* Flexible job demarcation and the job rotation system at the shop level may sacrifice the static efficiency available in the specialization scheme in a stable market environment, but may contribute to the dynamic efficiency of horizontal coordination by encouraging workers to learn, which would enhance the capabilities of the work group at the shop level to adapt to continual changes in the market and other states and to cope with local emergencies autonomously. Also such capabilities may help the shop adapt to the new technology more smoothly.

As already discussed, if the production structure is of the quasi-tree type, the system shock can be absorbed and responded to "hierarchically" through the communication flow, which runs in the reverse order of the production flow. Shops can function as communication nodal points and there is no need to superimpose the administrative apparatus on top of the production structure for operational coordination. The superstructure of management may be used more for strategic business decision making and periodic production planning. Thus we may claim:

[I.3a] *Administrative efficiency of horizontal coordination:* If the production structure is of the quasi-tree type, the hierarchical layering of administrative offices specialized in operating coordination to adapt to market and other environmental fluctuations may be whittled down by horizontal coordination, that is, by the integration of manufacturing operation and coordination, which may lead to a substantial savings in administrative cost.

But what about local shock responsiveness? In [I.2] above, I argued that autonomous problem solving by a group of workers at the shop level may help contain the impact of local shocks within the shop. However, even if relevant shops attempt to absorb the local shocks semiautonomously, the repercussions may sometimes hit other shops as well. A breakdown in transportation between shops and the discovery of a large amount of defective in-process products after the delivery to the user shop may be cited as examples. In these cases, a local response to shocks by a relevant shop may trigger the need for further adjustments in the upstream direction as well as in the downstream direction. Furthermore, within a subgroup in the quasi-tree structure for which a simple tree structure is not defined, multidirectional adjustments may be necessary. Without at least the local centralization of information and rescheduling of the production plan by the concerned middle-level adminsitrative office, how can the horizontal coordination mechanism cope with such a situation?

Suppose that unexpected events occurring at an intermediate shop – say, k in Figure 2.2 – are dealt with locally without the administrative intermediary in such a way that local adjustments of production are made through multiple bilateral negotiations between shop k and other immediately neighboring shops, say, a, b, l, and m as needed (the ideal adjustment should proceed beyond shops in the immediate neighborhood, but let us ignore the possibility). It is an important characteristic of the J-firm that no manager exists who is specialized in intershop coordination and that the task of intershop adjustments that cannot be automated by regular *kanban* circulation is relegated to direct negotiation between foremen of relevant shops. Therefore the above assumption may be thought of as capturing an essential aspect of intershop coordination at the J-firm in the simplest form. Let us call it *localized horizontal coordination.*

A possible advantage of localized horizontal coordination vis-à-vis (localized) hierarchical coordination would be the savings of time needed for communications and computations via the administrative office and the quick use of on-the-spot information concerning emergent events. For instance, defects in in-process products, breakdowns in transportation, unusual depletion of inventory, and so on, are most likely to be recognized first by the directly relevant shops (the user shop of parts or the shipper of in-process products) and they can react or propose to react quickly. To the extent that shops understand the nature of their own work processes as well as those of neighboring shops, together they may be able to devise a good solution to emergent problems, at least from the local point of view, by making use of firsthand information about what is actually happening at the shop level.

To achieve a local optimal solution among concerned shops, however, it is necessary that individual shops internalize goals appropriately decomposed from the overall organizational goal (such as local cost minimization, if the overall objective is the minimization of total costs in the factory). Of course, it is not a trivial task to motivate them in that direction. As already noted, the communication of information pertaining to a problem, and the computation and implementation of local solutions consistent with the organizational goal may become difficult, particularly when the team approach is emphasized within each shop and each team develops its own goal. Inefficient bargaining costs similar to the one noted in [N.4] for hierarchies may arise. In [I.4] below I explain how this problem may be mitigated under a certain incentive scheme.

In addition, even if bargaining partners in localized horizontal coordination want to reach the best solution, they are prevented from doing so by the lack of centralized information and their limited problem-solving capacities at the shop level. The local problem-solving capacities will depend in part on the degree to which foremen and others engaged in bilateral negotiation understand the relevant technological processes. Here again, we see the importance of knowledge sharing (this time between neighboring shops). Senior workers are systematically rotated between related shops in the J-firm, a function of which is undoubtedly to facilitate knowledge sharing among shops so as to enhance local problem-solving capacities (and also to reduce inefficient haggling based on information misrepresentation). But learning to promote knowledge sharing may be costly in terms of time and initial efficiency losses.

Thus it may be summarized:

> [I.3b] *Informational efficiency and incompleteness of localized horizontal coordination:* Localized horizontal coordination to in-process shocks may be relatively swift and can make efficient use of on-site information, but it is incomplete because of the lack of centralized information and involves the cost to develop the problem-solving capacity at lower levels.

Thus the efficiency of hierarchical coordination and localized horizontal coordination in response to local shocks is a relative one. Now that we have made some basic observations, we can submit to a more technical analysis the question of which of the two coordination mechanisms is more effective in controlling the internal efficiency of the firm in various circumstances. I have already conducted such an analysis elsewhere[31] and now summarize some of the main results in nontechnical terms.

> [I.3b(1)] The relative efficiency of localized horizontal coordination increases as the information-processing capacity of the shopfloor work group to identify and solve emergent

---

[31] M. Aoki "Horizontal vs. vertical information structure of the firm," *American Economic Review,* 76 (December 1987), pp. 971–83.

local problems increases at a faster rate relative to the rate of obsolescence of engineering knowledge embodied in the design of a production process. However, learning by doing alone is not sufficient, and the initial educational level of the worker needed to identify and solve emergent local problems must be above a certain level to make localized horizontal coordination relatively more efficient than centralized hierarchical coordination.

[I.3b(2)] Given a production technology, centralized hierarchical control increases its relative efficiency as information regarding emergent events affecting shopfloor productivity is more precisely monitored and concomitant centralized solutions are more swiftly implemented at the shopfloor level without distortion.

[I.3b(3)] Localized horizontal coordination performs relatively better if shopfloor technology is subject to a relatively higher degree of diminishing returns (increasing costs) to scale. Centralized hierarchical coordination performs relatively better if capacity constraints of the shopfloor are less severe.

Proposition [I.3b(1)] indicates that the relative efficiency of the J-firm depends largely on the "grass-root" information-processing capacities of the worker at the shopfloor level to cope with uncertain events, determined by the initial educational level and experience, while proposition [I.3b(2)] indicates that the relative efficiency of the hierarchical system depends largely on the professional capability of its managers and the quality of its communication technology. A rigorous analysis can determine the relative advantage of the two in terms of the values of the parameters measuring those factors.

Although emphasis on on-the-job training is a well-known feature of the J-firm, increasing importance is also being attached to giving (selected) workers formal training at regular intervals (say, every several years) in the form of class room instruction and discussions, in order to formalize and systematize the knowledge and insights gained through experience.[32] In the light of proposition [I.3b(1)], it is suggested that such lifetime quasi schooling may be instrumental in the

---

[32] For the importance of formal off-the-job training in the Japanese context, see K. Koike, "Human resource development and labor–management relations," in Kozo Yamamura and Yasukichi Yasuba (eds.), *The Japanese Political Economy*, vol. 1, *The Domestic Transformation*, Stanford University Press, 1987, pp. 289–330.

efficient operation of horizontal coordination in an environment where technological progress is relatively fast, yet newly introduced machines and processes are related to older ones. Proposition [I.3b(2)] suggests that if the increasing size of the firm necessitates an increase in the scope of hierarchical control, its relative efficiency may start to deteriorate unless the information technology utilized is improved.

Proposition [I.3b(3)] implies that if local coordination is not based on centralized information, the local response may fluctuate "too much" from the viewpoint of the whole system unless there is some capacity constraint. In such a case, centralized hierarchical control may be favored to limit the local fluctuation within certain bounds.[33]

Finally, although the incentive aspect of the J-firm is the subject of subsequent chapters, in order to make the discussion here consistent with that in the previous section, I should briefly touch on the incentive property of the integrative approach, that is, shop participation in coordination and problem solving. My starting hypothesis is that worker's lifetime earnings involve an element of sharing of quasi rent made possible through the efficient operation of horizontal coordination in which their accumulated integrative skills are utilized. As has often been emphasized, workers' integrative skills can be nurtured by allowing them to learn a wide range of jobs on the shopfloor; in that sense, skills become truly firm-specific, not readily transferable through the market. Then workers as a collective can perhaps exercise effective bargaining power over the disposition of the quasi rent.

If the quasi rent is available to the firm because of its monopolistic position in the market, work groups might divert their energies and times to unproductive uses in order to enhance their bargaining position within the firm, and they can possibly afford to do so. But when the delay of response to global (market) and local shocks makes it possible for competitive firms to snatch away potential quasi rents from the employing firm, workers may be motivated to find an efficient solution to shocks without delay while agreeing on a stable distribution of the quasi rents. This conjecture has been, as discussed in Chapter 5, substantiated by recent contribution to game theory, which has shown

[33] This property is analogous to an analytical result of Weitzman's comparative study of price control and quantity control in the planned system. The decentralized coordination (through price signal in his model) is favored over the direct control of production quantity if the capacity constraint of each component unit of the system is sufficiently severe so that its cost function is sufficiently curved. See Martin Weitzman, "Prices vs. quantity," *Review of Economic Studies*, 41 (1974), pp. 471–91.

that such strategy is in fact the best one for the work group in such a situation.[34] Relegating a more detailed discussion of incentive issues to Chapters 3 and 5, let us hypothetically summarize the above argument as follows:

> [I.4] *Collective incentives to respond to shocks:* Workers as a collective body are likely to participate in the sharing of quasi rents available from the efficient operation of horizontal coordination and are thus motivated to contribute to local problem solving and to respond quickly to local and global shocks in order to enhance the amount of quasi rent that they share, provided that the market environment is competitive.

This incentive is of a collective nature. In spite of the provision of such a collective incentive, or rather because of its collective nature, individual workers may be motivated to shirk their work, because the effect of individual shirking on collective performance may be negligible. However, if everyone shirks on that assumption, the aggregate effect may make everyone worse off. This is the familiar free-rider problem. In Chapter 3 I discuss the individual incentive scheme the J-firm provides to curb such free-rider problems.

4.   Concluding remarks

In the two preceding sections, I compared performance characteristics of two prototype forms of information structure for coordinating operating activities of the firm: hierarchical and horizontal. Although stylized observations about the actual practice of the typical unionized American and Japanese firms have led to the formulation of these two models, they should be considered purely theoretical constructs. In actual practice, hierarchical and horizontal coordination are always used in combination. However, the essential difference in the micro-micro information structure between typical American firms and Japanese firms may be said to lie in the degree of emphasis on economies of specialization vis-à-vis (collective) learning by doing of workers to enhance their integrative skills. The analysis in the last two sections may help identify the strengths and weaknesses of the two.

We have seen that the relative advantages of the two prototype

---

[34] Ken Binmore, Ariel Rubinsterin, and Asher Wolinsky, "The Nash solution in economic modelling," *Rand Journal of Economics,* 17 (Summer 1986), pp. 176–88.

forms depend on various technological, market, and other environmental conditions. First of all, the technological structure must be of a quasi-tree type so that horizontal coordination can be utilized for adapting the production process to market fluctuations.[35] Given this structure, horizontal coordination may be more efficient than hierarchical coordination in the highly competitive market environment in which demand fluctuates continuously, but not drastically. It may also be efficient in the fairly complicated production process that involves a variety of products and numerous steps organized in a quasi-tree structure. On the other hand, hierarchical coordination may be more efficient in the market environment in which demand is very stable or changes drastically, as well as in the production process that involves smaller steps or continuous processing.[36]

[35] However, there are many important industries (particularly continuous process industries) for which the conditions of the tree structure do not hold. For example, modern integrated steel factories produce thousands of varieties of final outputs, differentiated by size, shape, thickness, amounts and kinds of other minerals to be blended, coating, etc., but the entire process starts with the production of a uniform steel ingot, which is gradually differentiated in the downstream processes, such as hot and cold rolling, billet casting, coating, and welding. Such continuous-process technologies do not exhibit a quasi-tree structure, and cannot be transformed into the tree structure even by subgrouping component operations.
A theorem of the algebraic theory, however, assures us that the structure characterized by a half-ordering relationship such as the down/upstream relationships can always be modified into the quasi-tree structure by establishing a fictitious common downstream unit to previously parallel shops. This corresponds to the establishment of a coordinating administrative office between them. By creating the coordinating administrative office, we introduce the essential element of hierarchical coordination. This possibility suggests that localized horizontal and hierarchical coordinations can be combined in the technological structure of non-quasi-tree type processes.

[36] The theoretical predictions regarding the relative advantage of horizontal/hierarchical coordination summarized here seems to be consistent with diverse empirical observations regarding the comparative competitiveness of Japanese companies. For example, Kagono et al. have identified the dominant adaptive behavioral mode of the American and the Japanese companies as *mechanical* and *organic,* respectively. The former is based on hierarchical coordination led by the innovative initiative of top management, whereas the latter relies on relatively informal and decentralized coordination based on the ample accumulation of organizational slack. In these terms, they have summarized one of their findings from the aforementioned questionnaire survey as follows: "One cannot say which of the two adaptive modes is superior to the other. It depends on various conditions. The organic adaptive mode recognized in Japanese companies fits changeable markets, while the mechanical mode recognized in American companies fits stable markets or drastically changing markets. In fact, those industries in which Japan has strong international competitiveness are in fields in which customers' preferences and technology have recently made diverse changes, such as automobile and electronics. . . . On the other hand, there are few Japanese companies of a world scale in stable market areas such as petroleum and food processing, (T. Kagono et al., *Nichibei Kigyo no Keiei Hikaku* (The comparison of Japanese and American management), Nihon Keizai Shinbunsha, 1983, p. 49).
Their focus is on market impacts on the relative competitiveness of the two modes.

The actual structure of a company is complex and, as indicated already, often mixes hierarchical control and horizontal coordination. Specifically, in the West, where hierarchy has been a dominant aspect of intrafirm coordination, there has recently been a trend toward incorporating elements of nonhierarchical communications. The matrix form management system in which cross-jurisdictional horizontal communications are interwoven with vertical hierarchical control, the hub system in which there are more than one interconnected communication centers, and networks in which component units communicate directly with each other as needs arise without the intermediation of a centralized information clearinghouse are some examples of experimental nonhierarchical communications. There has also been increasing reliance on the multidisciplinary team approach. This is particularly notable in development projects in the high-tech and architectural industries, where various disciplines like engineering, marketing, finance, and supply and procurement must interact and be integrated. The trend toward simplification of job classification schemes also seems to be inescapable.[37]

It is not clear yet whether this tendency in the West toward curbing the rigidity of hierarchy and job classification will generate a new hybrid form of informational structure. I discuss the feasibility of such a prospect in Chapter 8. It may be appropriate to point out here, however, that, if there is anything to be learned from the Japanese experience, it is probably that an important factor here is the integrative skills (information processing capacity) of workers, which enable them to utilize valuable on-site information effectively. Such utilization could be made possible by enhancing the job experiences of workers,

By focusing on technological impacts, James Abegglen and George Stalk, Jr., have presented the following observation based on their extensive consulting experiences: "The Japanese labor productivity advantage is enormous in high volume assembly processes where hundreds, even thousands, of interdependent steps must be coordinated. In simpler processes, such as foundry, where perhaps thirty operational steps are required, the Japanese advantage is slight, and sometimes non-existent. In process industries, such as paper, chemicals, and metal refining, Japanese labor productivity in comparable plants is no better than can be found in western plants. The same is true of other simple manufacturing" (J. Abegglen and G. Stalk, Jr., *Kaisha: The Japanese Corporation*, Basic Books, 1986, p. 61). The reason for this fact may not be intuitively obvious for those who still believe that the Japanese productivity advantage comes mainly from cheap or devoted labor or focused production. But the observation is clearly consistent with our theoretical prediction.

[37] There is much anecdotal evidence of this trend, but a true hybrid of the two Japanese and American giant firms, New United Motor Manufacturing Incorporated (NUMMI) founded in 1983 in Fremont, California, provides a particularly interesting example, in spite of its particularism, showing that the Japanese rotation scheme may be a viable alternative even in the U.S. union setting. I discuss this case in Chapter 8.

knowledge sharing among workers, and cross-jurisdictional communication at the operating level. No doubt these activities will be aided more and more by the fast-developing communication technology, but I submit that the human element cannot be dispensed with altogether.

Many Western firms have recently put considerable effort into reducing the layers of their hierarchies through the use of communication technology. Some of them regard the *kanban* system as simply a means of reducing hierarchical layers and buffer inventories. If the purpose of simplifying the hierarchy is only to simplify centralized coordination, however, it may be expected that management can be given additional leverage for controlling shopfloor events through robotics technology. It is in fact the long-standing hope of many engineers that the computer-aided control system of the factory will become available so that all the operating tasks can be performed by robots and can be coordinated by the computer network. There is no room for the human element in such a centralized system except for the engineer's sovereignty. If management feels insecure about the workers' capability to set the pace and intensity of work by themselves, it may try to retain or regain control over the shopfloor by implementing such a system.

But, paradoxically, it has been in Japan that robotics technology has spread at a faster rate. According to surveys by the Japan Industrial Robot Association and the Robotics Institute of America, the number of operating industrial robots (excluding fixed sequence robots) at the end of 1980 was 14,250 for Japan and 4,100 for the United States. By the end of 1984, these figures had risen to 67,300 for Japan and 14,500 for the United States.[38] Why have robots taken hold so rapidly in Japan, where much more emphasis is placed on integrative learning by the worker?

One type of robot used throughout Japan is designed with record-playback programming. This is the type in which operators on the shopfloor can program the robot by manually guiding its arms through the desired motions. These motions are automatically recorded and played back. It is obvious that the effectiveness of this type of machine depends on the acquired skills and the judgment of workers. In Japanese factories, this type of robot is widely used for spray painting and spot and arc welding of car bodies and any other tasks in which the control of three-dimensional movement is involved. In the United

---

[38] According to a survey by the Belgian Institute for Regulation and Automation, the numbers at the end of 1984 for West Germany, France, Sweden, and the United Kingdom were 6,600, 3,380, 2,400, and 2,623, respectively.

States, however, robots of the record-playback type had not been commercially promoted despite their technological potential, precisely because management was more interested in retaining control of production and is skeptical about giving workers control.[39] It was only after the Japanese had emerged as a challenger in the sphere of robotics technology that American management started to adopt this type of robot on a large scale.

Relatively easy-to-use, yet sophisticated, numerical controls for lathes, milling machines, and machining centers are also being introduced at a much faster rate in Japan by both large and medium to small firms.[40] These microprocessor-based machines feature programmable controllers and manual data input, so that operators on the shopfloor are able to program while machining a first part by simply storing instructions in the machine's memory as they proceed. Even if more sophisticated numerically controlled machines are employed, the programming of machines is not exclusively the job of programmers working outside the shopfloor of the J-firm. In order to program machines in an efficient way, programmers who lack shopfloor experience are required to consult and cooperate with skilled workers. Operators are also encouraged to debug and edit programs whenever they can, in response to programming errors, the wear of tools, subtle quality differences in operating objects, and so on. The spread of robots in Japan may thus be largely explained by the cooperative participation of robot operators in programming and the resulting reduction in programming costs, as well as prospective improvements in the operational efficiency over time through the operator's integrative learning.

It is widely believed that production processes consisting of numerous specialized jobs are more likely to become automated, and that in turn the tendency toward greater specialization will be reinforced when new technology is introduced. However, recent case studies in the United States have suggested that greater specialization is not necessarily the outcome of automation. In a case study of the banking industry, for example, Paul Adler finds that the introduction of the computer in this industry requires a broader knowledge of banking procedures on the side of employees. Barbara Baran's research on

---

[39] David E. Noble, *Forces of Production: A Social History of Industrial Automation,* Oxford University Press, 1984.

[40] In 1981, only about one out of every five NC tools made in Japan was sold to large firms. More than 25 percent were sold to shops with fewer than 10 employees (interview with the Robot Industrial Association). In the United States, a vast majority of NC machine tools are used by large firms. *American Machinist,* 1983, pp. 120–1.

insurance companies reveals that when computerization is introduced there, some companies have to expand job jurisdictions at the bottom of their hierarchies.[41]

These studies imply that the modern technology of robotics and communications can never completely substitute for human skills, since there will always be some useful unprogrammable knowledge at the operating level that can be utilized effectively in conjunction with modern technology. Even the most sophisticated computer-aided coordination system would not be able to cope with all the events that might occur, so that there will always be a need for human skills and wisdom. By paying sufficient attention to these human elements, we may find a way to utilize modern technology effectively.

[41] P. Adler, "New technologies, new skills," mimeographed, May 1984. B. Baran, "Office automation and women's work: the technological transformation of the insurance industry," in Manuel Castells (ed.), *High Technology, Space, and Society*, Sage, 1984.

CHAPTER 3

The ranking hierarchy of the J-firm as incentive scheme

In Chapter 2, I suggested that the internal efficiency of the J-firm, where it exists, may be largely due to the quality of the information structure institutionalized within it. That structure is characterized by rapid intrafirm communications, which are necessary for the coordinated adjustment of constituent operations in reaction to global (market) shocks as well as the decentralized handling of local shocks to minimize their impact on the system as a whole. Undoubtedly the quality of such an information system depends to a great extent on the information-processing capabilities (intellectual skills) of the workers who operate the system. I now turn to the problem of how such human resources can be accumulated and maintained within the firm. This is essentially a question of providing the employee of the J-firm with the incentive to develop the skills, knowledge, expertise, and cooperative attitude needed to effectively operate the horizontal informational structure.

This incentive problem has two aspects: the collective and the individual. The former provides appropriate incentives for firm-specific human resources as a whole, as distinguished from the firm's financial resources. I have already alluded to this aspect in Chapter 2 (Section 3) and will come back to it more fully in Chapter 5. This chapter deals with the latter aspect, that is, the way in which the J-firm provides its individual employees with an appropriate incentive package for competing in the development of skills, knowledge, and expertise useful to the firm, and for cooperating with one another when necessary.

From the discussion in Chapter 2, it is clear that the most effective worker on the J-firm shopfloor is the one who is skilled in a relatively wide range of jobs rather than merely a well-defined job in a narrow jurisdiction. A cooperative attitude, the ability to adapt to new tasks, the ability to communicate with other members on the work team and to take leadership in autonomous problem solving at the shopfloor level, and a willingness to help and teach relatively junior workers may also be considered important factors contributing to the enhancement of team productivity in the J-firm. A wide range of skills and the qualities of an effective team player may be developed over time by

49

actually experiencing various types of jobs in the context of teamwork. As we have seen, a worker's remuneration in the A-firm is defined by the particular job category to which he or she is assigned. When job demarcation is as fluid and ambiguous as it is in the J-firm, however, how is the worker paid? How is the worker motivated to develop a wide range of skills? What kind of incentive scheme is used to encourage the worker to become a team player over the long term?

Turning to the white-collar employees on the managerial track of the J-firm, we again observe that, to be effective in the horizontal coordination of operations, they must not only be able to handle a specialized task, but must also be able to bargain smoothly with their peers in interjurisdictional issues as well as skillfullly mediate between the conflicting demands of subordinates. Therefore, these employees need to develop an understanding of and insight into the full range of organizational activities in which they are directly or indirectly involved. Informal personal networking with colleagues across formal jurisdictional boundaries, which is often referred to as *jinmyaku* (human context), serves as a valuable asset as it allows the individual to collect information, identify problems, and reach agreements in the firm without putting too much time and effort into these tasks. Needless to say, such broad understanding and networking can be developed by experiencing various operational and managerial tasks within the context of a single firm.

One may therefore conclude that the J-firm assesses the value of an employee, both blue-collar and white-collar, by his or her *contextual skill,* which is developed over a relatively long period of time. By this I mean a relatively wide range of skills (integrative skills) that have been developed and are useful in the context of the nonhierarchical information structure described in Chapter 2. The J-firm has evolved a system of individual incentive schemes with which to evaluate and reward its employees over a long-term basis for competing in the development of such contextual skills, while using them cooperatively. Under such schemes, the firm can identify slow learning, low productivity, low motivation, and uncooperative workers by actual observation and differentiate them in pay and status over the long run, while attempting to lock in fast-learning, highly productive, highly motivated, cooperative workers by discouraging them from quitting in midcareer. This system has three important elements: (1) the wage system, which combines seniority and merit rating, (2) internal promotion discriminately applied to employees on the basis of merit rating, and (3) a lump sum payment at the time of (mandatory) separation *(taishokukin).*

The term *lifetime employment* is nothing but a somewhat exaggerated idealization of the relatively long job tenure at the J-firm, which is the result of this incentive system. The system is not "traditional" in the sense that it has been operating since the birth of capitalism in the last century, inheriting its commercial and other social customs in the Edo period. Rather, it evolved gradually – through the interaction of management, labor, and bureaucrats – since around the end of the Russo-Japanese War (1904–5) and came to be recognized as an established system only in the 1950s.[1] It is not a "paternalistic" system, either, in the sense that every employee is equally rewarded for his or her loyalty to the firm. Rather, it is a "competitive" system in that the competitive and cooperative performance of the worker is evaluated and rewarded differentially on a relatively long-term basis.

Personnel decisions that have long-term career implications for employees, such as promotions, transfers, layoffs, and discharges, are based on careful assessments of the individual's potential for developing contextual skills within the firm, although a certain limit is set on the range of managerial discretion because of the egalitarianism promoted by the enterprise-based union, which normally organizes all the nonmanagement employees. Since personal assessment is a standardized procedure and personnel files are kept and utilized centrally, the personnel department occupies a strategic position in the management of the J-firm. This is in sharp contrast to the secondary position of the personnel department in the American management structure. In the American system, such important personnel decisions as hirings, promotions, and discharges are largely entrusted to supervisors of functional hierarchies, although limits are usually set by collective agreement or a company rule to prevent arbitrary decisions. Managers assigned to the personnel department of the J-firm, whether for a limited period or permanently, are normally in one of the most promising career tracks within the firm. This is easy to comprehend when one recognizes that an essential managerial contextual skill is the ability to cultivate effective intrafirm personal networking.

The centralization of personnel administration in the J-firm in the sense of companywide administration, may explain why it is able to delegate more decision making authority to lower levels in operating and coordinating spheres. Although information processing and decision making are somewhat dispersed and decentralized in the J-firm, employees are monitored for the development of contextual skills over

---

[1] For this historical account, see Andrew Gordon, *The Evolution of Labor Relations in Japan: Heavy Industry, 1953–1955,* Harvard University Press, 1985.

their entire career in the firm, and their records are put into the organizational memory formally and informally. Those employees who have established a reputation over time for developing contextual skills, which they still appear capable of developing, may be given better opportunities for promotions and transfers within the firm, whereas those who fail to do so may be given fewer opportunities. Employee behavior is thus molded to be compliant with the organizational orientation in the long run.

In contrast, the A-firm is embedded in a societal framework that emphasizes egalitarianism, and consequently workers are more mobile, moving between firms in search of better individual opportunities. In this environment, management's authority is intrinsically insecure and may have to be reasserted through the institutionalization of a hierarchical information structure within the firm, with the threat of discharge as an important means of discipline for supervisors. Conversely, the development of a functional hierarchy based on fine job specialization and a well-defined classification of jobs has helped create standard job markets, external and internal to the firm, and has encouraged workers to become more mobile. We may refer to such a development as the decentralization of personnel administration.

In the J-firm, however, personnel administration needs to be centralized not only for purposes of control, but also for the efficient utilization of the contextual versatile skills of the worker nurtured in the nonhierarchical information structure. For example, in Chapter 2 I argued that the worker gains a better understanding of the technological process by doing a wide range of jobs and that this knowledge enables the worker to adapt to new technology such as robots (mechatronics) faster and to use this technology more effectively. In the discussion following proposition [I.3b(1)] I also indicated that, before workers can adapt to a new technology, they require formal training at regular intervals in a quasi-school environment that complements the informal training they receive on the job in order to systematize their experiences on the job. But how can a systematic in-house program of c er development be carried out and how can workers released from a abandoned work process be redeployed to a newly adopted work process without firmwide personnel administration?

Thus it appears that the decentralized approach to informational processing in the operational and coordinating sphere needs to be associated with, and complemented by, a centralized approach to personnel administration for purposes of organizational effectiveness (as in the case of Japan). Alternatively, the decentralized approach to human resource allocation needs to be associated with, and complemented by, the centralized, hierarchical control of organizational operations for the same purpose (as in the case of the United States). On the other hand, a centralized approach to both the information structure and personnel administration in an organization may be unnecessarily wasteful and too authoritarian. A centralized information structure is costly to run in terms of both the time and resources it takes to maintain communications in a changing environment. If it is not balanced by viable external opportunities for personnel, such a structure may give rise to further inefficiency because it suppresses individual initiative. We may therefore entertain the following proposition as a working hypothesis:

> [D1] *The duality principle:* If an organization is to be effective, it is necessary and sufficient that decentralization/centralization in the information structure of the organization be complemented by centralization/decentralization in its system of personnel administration.

This duality principle is one of the keys to understanding the Japanese system and will be a recurring theme throughout this book.

The structure of this chapter is as follows: Section 1 describes stylized facts about individual incentive packages offered by the J-firm. Section 2 analyzes the workings of the Japanese incentive structure in the framework of the growing incentive literature. The essential feature of the structure may best be captured by a notion of hierarchy as a system of ranks, with the remuneration paid to an employee depending upon the individual's rank and with internal promotion from lower to higher ranks. This hierarchy is distinct from that described in Chapter 2, namely, the centralized information structure.

The institutionalization of the ranking hierarchy within the J-firm as an incentive system that encourages the employee to develop contextual skills has two important consequences for labor markets in Japan. First, a market in which the demand for and supply of long-term employment prospects are transacted has developed alongside the market in which employment contracts of shorter duration for more specific jobs are transacted. Second, the market in which midcareer mobility is mediated has remained less formalized and unstructured until recently, although there are signs of change.

The terms of long-term employment bargained in the first market are extremely uncertain and incomplete. Although the expectation of lifetime employment is high, the actual duration of employment turns out to be substantially lower on the average than the expectation. Even if an employee is to remain with one employer, the probability of promotion is extremely uncertain, partly because the firm has no definite criterion, such as the seniority principle, to apply when deciding who is to be promoted or laid off, and partly because the performance of the firm over the lifetime of potential employees can at best be predicted by a wild guess. The long-term employment contract is thus bound to be far from complete.

This contractual incompleteness implies that the primary market for new entrants to the labor force functions as a mechanism for allocating potential human resources among firms, but the actual terms of employment throughout the course of individual career development within the firm must be determined sequentially, through implicit or explicit bargaining internal to the firm, as events evolve. This is the issue discussed in Section 3. A substantial part of this bargaining is to be mediated by the union specific to the firm. Section 3 discusses the role of the enterprise-based union, an institution unique to the J-firm. The discussion provides a logical transition from the topic of this chapter to that of Chapter 5, that is, from the individual aspect of the incentive problem to the collective aspect.

1.   Stylized facts

A.   *The pay structure and promotion scheme*

The J-firm employee on the career development track, blue-collar as well as white-collar, is paid a monthly salary and biannual bonuses. An hourly wage rate is applied only to the peripheral part-time job categories. Because of the identical treatment of all regular employees in this method of payment, the difference between the status of blue-collar and white-collar workers has become somewhat blurred in the J-firm. Although each firm designs its own payment scheme, the monthly earnings of the blue-collar and white-collar employee typically consist of three parts: a person-related payment *(honnin-kyu)*, a job-related payment *(shigoto-kyu)*, and various allowances for such things as housing, spouse and dependents, training, overtime, and commuting costs.

The person-related payment is, in principle, based on the employee's seniority and merit. Supervisors periodically (say, biannually) assess the individual employee's merit over a wide range of characteristics – such as acquired skills, motivation to learn, cooperativeness, and diligence – according to an elaborate evaluation scheme prepared centrally by the personnel department of the firm. The position of each blue-collar employee and of each white-collar employee in the respective ranking of basic pay grades is based on these merit assessments and seniority. Beyond the highest grade of blue-collar employees there are usually several classes of foreman, and beyond the highest white-collar positions there are ladders of managerial positions. Except in the foreman and management job categories, pay grades are not normally associated with a specific function, and higher grades simply mean higher status and higher annual increases in basic pay. An illustration of a pay-ranking system is provided in the appendix.

Foremen, of course, perform supervisory tasks at the shop they are responsible for, but their tasks often consist of providing leadership in teamwork rather than unidirectional supervisory control. Foremen are selected from among workers who have achieved the highest rank in the blue-collar job category because of their skills, leadership, and so on, and they maintain close identification with ordinary workers. Management jobs are also assigned to those who have been promoted through the ranking hierarchy for white-collar employees.

New entrants to the J-firm are placed at the lowest grade that corresponds to their years of schooling (see the appendix for an illustration). The collective agreement between the firm and the union normally specifies the maximum and minimum speeds of promotion from each grade to the next as well as the annual increases in basic pay for each grade in the ranking hierarchy. The basic pay according to rank may be supplemented further by a merit payment *(noryoku-kyu)*, which is normally an additional payment of a certain percentage of the basic pay, the percentage being determined by the supervisor's assessment of each employee, within a range agreed on in collective bargaining. Thus collective agreement limits the extent of the discretionary power of management, but within those limits the promotional and basic pay decisions may be based on the assessment of individual merits by supervisors. The relative weight placed on individual assessment in pay determination within the same grade differs from one firm to another. The union usually demands egalitarian treatment, and some firms have only a single basic pay rate for each grade. In depressed industries such as shipbuilding and iron and steel, however, a shift is taking place toward merit pay as a means of preventing wage costs due to the aging of average workers from increasing.

The merit assessment has somewhat more weight in the promotion decision. Therefore, some blue- (white-) collar employees may reach the highest grade in midcareer and then advance further to foreman (manager), whereas the least competent workers may reach the highest rank in the ordinary blue-collar job category only a few years before they retire. (The appendix provides an interesting case that illustrates the difference in promotional speed among blue-collar workers.) As a result of these differences, considerable disparity may develop over time in the basic pay of employees with the same tenure. Thus a seniority pay increase is automatic in a certain range, but it does not override the competition and differentiation among employees.

Although the J-firm has been stereotyped as a paternalistic and egalitarian organization, merit assessment *(satei)* by supervisors is an important determinant of an employee's earnings as it is the basis for promotion in the hierarchy of rank. This is one of the distinctive characteristics of the Japanese payment scheme and contrasts with that in the unionized A-firm, where managers have much less discretionary power over an individual's earnings, which instead depend on the job evaluation system (one single wage rate for one job) and the seniority rule.

One cannot deny that there is a danger of unfair treatment when supervisors assess the merit of subordinates. But, the union's monitoring and the centralization of personnel administration may mitigate this effect somewhat. To begin with, the merit assessment procedure is formalized and standardized by the personnel department to ensure that arbitrary decisions are not made by individual supervisors. Second, the average employee is assessed by many different supervisors during his or her career because jobs are rotated both at the supervisory and the subordinate level. Thus, over the long run, employees may expect fairly impartial treatment in the individual assessment. Third, many companies allow a discontented subordinate to appeal to the personnel department for transfer to another shop. In this way the personnel department can react to complaints by discontent employees as well as monitor the fairness and effectiveness of supervisory assessment. Fourth, the reputation of the supervisor among his or her subordinates has a direct effect on the career opportunity of the supervisor. In other words, the supervisor is subject to "informal" reciprocal monitoring by his or her subordinates.

The job-related payment *(shigoto-kyu),* which is offered in conjunction with the person-related payment, is determined in principle by the American type of job evaluation scheme. This scheme was introduced in the 1950s and 1960s and at the time was heralded by both management and the union as a transition from the "premodern" wage system, which was based on status differentiation by age and management discretion, to the more rational and fair wage scheme based on the principle of "equal pay for equal work." However, because job demarcation and assignments are rather fluid in the J-firm, the job classifications have remained rather ambiguous, and jobs tend to be evaluated on the basis of employees' skills and experiences in a very broad sense. As a result, there tends to be a high correlation between an individual's job-related pay and basic pay.[2] Yet, this scheme is thought to reward skilled young employees relatively more and has thus flattened the age profile of earnings.

The various allowances – for example, for spouse and dependents, housing, and commuting – are somewhat unique to the J-firm. They are reminiscent of the emergency measures taken immediately after World War II, when "payment according to need" was vital to the physical survival of employees and their families. Although that exigency has obviously diminished since then, the measure has survived, possibly because the dictum has remained appealing to the egalitarian ideal of unionism. It also helps management to elicit employee cooperativeness through the notion of "the firm as a family."

The sum of basic pay, merit- and job-related supplements, and various life-related allowances constitute the "contractually paid wages" to regular employees, according to official government statistics. There are no macro data regarding the relative composition of each except in case study examples (see the appendix).

In addition to the contractual payment, employees receive a 25 percent premiun for any overtime work and two bonuses a year. We will see later (Chapter 5) that both, particularly the former, are important for adjusting an employee's actual earnings according to the state of business cycle. There is some correlation between the profit of the firm and the average amount of bonuses paid (the profit-sharing aspect). But it should be noted that much of this bonus payment depends on the supervisor's assessment of merit and diligence, more so than in the case of a contractually paid salary.[3]

---

[2] This is pointed out by Ronald Dore, *British Factory – Japanese Factory: The Origins of National Diversity in Industrial Relations,* University of California Press, 1973, chap. 3.

[3] Between 1975 and 1985, the average amount of bonus earnings of regular employees fluctuated between 18 and 22 percent of total earnings. However, there are substantial differences in bonus payments depending on the size of the firm. In 1985, employees of firms with 500 or more employees received, on average, bonuses equivalent to 4.22 months of contractually paid salary, whereas employees of firms with 100–499 employees received 3.49 and those of firms with 30–99 employees received 2.68. On the other hand, firms of different sizes do not differ much in the amount of contractually paid earnings in the same age bracket, particularly in the young age bracket. For example, the average contractually paid monthly salary for male employees aged 20–24 at large firms in the manufacturing industry was ¥150.3 thousand in 1985, whereas it was ¥140.0 in medium-sized firms and ¥142.0 in small-sized firms (Ministry of Labor, *Monthly Labor Statistics*). The relatively wide differential of bonus payment suggests the possibility of employees' participation in the firm-specific quasi rent (profit sharing) in large firms. I come back to this aspect of bonus payment later.

One of the most important components of the lifetime earnings of the employee of the J-firm is the compensation paid at the time of separation *(taishokukin)*. The separation payment rises sharply with the years of service, but the amount also depends on whether the separation is for *jiko-tsugo* (private reasons) or *kaisha-tsugo* (company reasons). The latter include mandatory retirement (normally at age 60), transfers to related companies by order of the firm, discharges often disguised as "voluntary early retirement," and promotion to the board of directors. According to a 1982 model by Kansai Conference Board of Managers, the amounts paid to employees with college degrees in blue-collar and clerical categories who separate after 10, 20, and 30 years of service for private reasons were equivalent to 5.1, 15.9, and 31.6 months of contractually paid salary at the time of separation, respectively, but separation payment went up to 37.9 months in the case of mandatory retirement after 32 years of service. On the average, the separation payment at the time of mandatory retirement constitutes about 70 percent of the retirement benefits provided by companies surveyed in terms of present value, the rest being company-paid supplements to public pensions *(chosei nenkin)*.

This description suggests that the system of promotion and remuneration in the J-firm helps motivate its employees to develop their careers through long-term, if not lifetime, association with the firm. Successful career development within a firm is potentially very valuable to the employee, white-collar as well as blue-collar, because monthly pay and biannual bonus payments rise as one's position in the ranking hierarchy improves with seniority and the development of contextual skill. The separation payment can add a substantial amount of seniority premium at the time of retirement.

On the other hand, the midcareer separation, although not infrequent as we will see later, carries a financial penalty. The separation payment in the case of voluntary separation is less generous. Unless the employee possesses special skills that might be needed elsewhere, the value of those skills, accumulated in the context of teamwork and internal personal networking, would by and large be lost once he or she left the employing firm. Since precise information about the quality of midcareer job seekers is hard to come by and since voluntary midcareer separation may signal negative attributes (such as shirking or noncooperativeness), firms tend to rely on internal promotion based on the long-term assessment of their own employees to fill vacancies in the promotional ladder. Thus midcareer mobility does not generally provide better opportunities.

The impact of job tenure on the rising age-earnings profile has been studied from various angles by many authors. Of particular interest here are the results of a comparative econometric analysis performed by Masanori Hashimoto and John Raisian.[4] They found that the earnings, including bonuses, of the average male employee in a large firm in both Japan and the United States steadily increase with job tenure until the employee reaches a peak at about 27 years after entering the Japanese firm and 30 years after entering the American firm. But the peak percentage growth from initial earnings is 242.8 percent for the Japanese, and 109.7 for the American. Furthermore, controlling other factors such as total experience, schooling, and union affiliation, 205.2 percent of the earnings growth for the Japanese is attributable to continuing tenure with the current firm, whereas the same is true for only 52.6 percent of the American's earnings. In other words, if a Japanese male employee works for a large firm for 27 years, his earnings are likely to be almost three and a half times the initial earnings in real terms. But if he changes jobs at that time and his tenure at the original firm is not counted, his earnings would be a little less than half of what he currently gets. If the American male employee works for one large firm for 30 years, on the other hand, his earnings would only be doubled; however, if he separates from the firm at this point, only a quarter of his earnings would be sacrificed. The cross-national differential of job tenure effects on earnings may be further augmented by the institutional differences in the provision of postretirement benefits: The J-firm provides about 70 percent of its postretirement benefits in the form of lump-sum separation payments related to job tenure, whereas the American employee receives a large proportion of his or her retirement benefits in the form of portable pensions.

The rising age-earnings profile may be explained in large part by two alternative hypotheses, or by a combination of the two: the human capital theory approach and the incentive contract theory. According to the former, workers (and firms) invest resources during their early tenure to accumulate skills that will be used to enhance future output and therefore bring greater future rewards. Thus pay will rise with tenure as these skills are accumulated. The latter hypothesis posits that pay may rise even in the absence of productivity growth for a variety of incentive reasons, to be elaborated in the next section. Under such an arrangement, the worker is induced to work harder (or to work up

---

[4] M. Hashimoto and J. Raisian, "Employment tenure and earnings profiles in Japan and the United States," *American Economic Review*, 75 (September 1985), pp. 721–35. A more recent study in English may be found in Jacob Mincer and Yoshio Higuchi, "Wage structure and labor turnover in the U.S. and in Japan," *Journal of the Japanese and International Economies*, 2 (1988).

to the standard, whatever it is) to ensure durability of employment so that he or she can take advantage of the eventual high pay level.

The two hypotheses need not be exclusive; features of both may prevail. It would be interesting if the rising tenure-earnings profile could be decomposed into that part due to on-the-job training and that part due to incentive effects. Although such studies would undoubtedly provide a better understanding of the Japanese firm, as far as I know, none have yet been completed in this area.[5] The relatively large separation payment does suggest, however, that the Japanese employee has a substantial amount of incentive-based wealth at stake in the employing firm, because the sharp increase in payment at retirement cannot be considered to reflect a productivity increase toward the end of the worker's career. On the other hand, as I explain next, employees of large Japanese companies with less capacity for developing contextual skills are more likely to quit the employing firm in midcareer. They may leave voluntarily, because they do not think they can advance further in pay and status in the employing firm, or they may be ordered by the firm to transfer to relatively minor subsidiaries or related companies. As a result, the longer the job tenure of an employee, the more contextual skill he or she is likely to possess. Therefore, the human capital factor could not be ignored in an explanation of rising tenure-earnings profiles. In the next section, I attempt to relate the rising tenure-earnings profile of the employee of the J-firm to both human capital and incentives.

B.   The extent of lifetime employment

From the pay and promotion structure that I have described, one may infer that (1) the larger firm recruits new employees upon their graduation from high school or college and trains them in-house in contextual skills and (2) the majority of them are motivated to stay with the original firm until mandatory retirement, at which time a large separation payment is expected. This is what most foreign observers think the employment structure of the J-firm is like. The phenomenon of lifetime employment is generally considered to be the distinct and unique feature of the J-firm. Reality, however, is not that simple. For one thing, the phenomenon of near-lifetime employment among middle-aged and older workers, which is preceded by shopping for a job at

---

[5] For the United States, see Edward P. Lazear and Robert L. Moore, "Incentives, productivity, and labor contracts," *Quarterly Journal of Economics*, 99 (May 1984), pp. 275–95; James Medoff and Katherine Abraham, "Experience, performance, and earnings," *Quarterly Journal of Economics*, 97 (December 1982), pp. 716–24.

Table 3.1. *Estimates of the number of jobs held by males over a lifetime, Japan and the United States*

	OECD				Hashimoto-Raisian	
	All jobs		Jobs that last more than 2 years			
Age group (in years)	Japan 1977	United States 1981	Japan 1977	United States 1981	Japan 1977	United States 1978
16–19	0.54	1.07	0.19	0.13	0.72	2.00
20–24	1.19	2.54	0.84	0.58	2.06	4.40
25–19	1.54	3.69	1.22	1.04	2.71	6.15
30–34	1.75	4.57	1.42	1.42	3.11	7.40
35–39	1.92	5.35	1.59	1.74	3.46	8.30
40–44	2.05	5.98	1.73	2.01	4.21	10.25
45–49	2.15	6.45	1.86	2.25	4.91	10.95
50–54	2.26	6.90	1.97	2.48	—	11.15
55–64	2.62	7.50	2.33	2.75	—	11.16

Source: OECD Employment Outlook, September 1984, p. 63. M. Hashimoto and J. Raisian, "Employment tenure and earning profiles in Japan and the United States," *American Economic Review,* 75 (September 1985), p. 724.

a younger age, is widely observed in other industrial economies as well.[6] For another, it is actually a minority, even among male workers in large Japanese firms, who do not change jobs from graduation until mandatory retirement. The average Japanese male worker does change jobs in his lifetime, albeit not as often as his American counterpart. Thus the turnover of middle-aged employees of the J-firm is not negligible.

Table 3.1 provides two estimates of the number of jobs held by the average male over a lifetime in Japan and the United States. In both estimates, the annual number of new jobs started by the average person in each age group is first estimated using the tenure data for both countries. Then the average number of jobs held over a five-year span

---

[6] See Robert Hall, "The importance of lifetime jobs in the U.S. economy," *American Economic Review,* 72 (September 1982), pp. 716–24. He summarized one of his results of job tenure data analysis as follows: "Among workers aged 30 and above, about 40 percent are currently working in jobs which eventually will last twenty years or more" (p. 716). See also "The importance of long-term job attachment in OECD countries," in *OECD Employment Outlook,* 1984, pp. 55–68.

is calculated as five times the annual rate. The cumulative number of new jobs for any age provides the number of jobs held by the average male person of that age. This simple calculation yields the results shown in Table 3.1. The discrepancy between the two estimates results from different assumptions imposed by the authors to deal with definitional differences in the tenure data of the two countries. One may consider that the OECD estimate provides the lower bound of the turnover rates for the both countries, and that the estimate of Hashimoto and Raisian provides the upper bound for Japan.[7]

According to these estimates, the average male worker in Japan can expect to have 2.6 to 4.9 jobs in his lifetime. In both estimates, the Japanese worker has fewer jobs than the American worker, largely because Americans work in many jobs of short duration. If one counts only jobs that last more than two years, as the OECD report does, the number of jobs completed by the average American worker is about 2.8 over a lifetime, and that of the average Japanese male worker is 2.3 jobs. Thus the difference is considerably reduced.

When we compare the probability of leaving a job of short duration for the United States and Japan (see Table 3.2, column 1), we see a considerably higher turnover rate for Americans regardless of age, which no doubt contributes to the widely held notion that Americans are highly mobile. The relative importance of tenure effects is also clear, and the probability of quitting a job declines rapidly within a few years for all age groups in both countries. This is to be expected. But it is interesting that 30- to 39-year-old Japanese workers with 10 to 15 years of job tenure are more likely to leave their jobs than are 40- to 49-year-old Americans with 5 to 10 years job tenure. This runs counter to the widely held view. How does this phenomenon come about?

Tables 3.1 and 3.2 provide information on the behavior of the average worker, but do not take into account firm size. I now describe the

---

[7] The U.S. tenure data (Bureau of Labor Statistics) gives the number of workers who have tenure of six months or less, but the Japanese data *(Employment Status Survey)* only indicate the number of persons who changed jobs within the past year plus those who were not working a year ago, but are working now. The OECD estimate regards the stock of jobs in the 0–12 months tenure category for each age group as an estimate of the number of new jobs created over the year. By dividing the number by the population in that age group, we may calculate the average number of jobs started by the average person. This estimate considerably understates the number of new jobs, particularly for the United States, as some individuals may have changed jobs more than once during the year. Raisian and Hashimoto on the other hand assume that all Japanese workers in the 0–12 months tenure category have had tenure of 6 months or less, being actually in the 0–6 months category. The annual rate of new jobs in an age group is then twice the fraction of the age group in that category. The Hashimoto–Raisian estimate may thus have overestimated the turnover rate in Japan.

Table 3.2. *Probability of leaving a job, by age and tenure, Japan, United States, and United Kingdom*

Age of worker (in years)	Tenure interval			
	0–1 year over 1–2 years	0–5 years over 5–10 years	5–10 years over 10–15 years	10–15 years over 15–20 years
United States, 1981, all persons				
25–29	.54	.24	–	–
30–39	.52	.18	.09	–
40–49	.50	.15	.05	.07
50–59	.52	.12	.02	.05
Japan, 1977, all persons				
25–29	.28	.08	.06	.04
30–39	.35	.06	.04	.06
40–49	.26	.05	–	–
United Kingdom, 1979, all full-time workers				
25–29	.19	.10	–	–
30–39	.17	.10	.10	.11
40–49	.09	.07	.07	.09
50–59	.02	.01	.06	.08

Source: OECD Employment Outlook (September 1984), p. 59.

typical career of the male employee (blue-collar and white-collar) of the J-firm – that is, the representative large manufacturing firm – supplying supporting data as needed. (I discuss the female employee in the large Japanese firm in Section 5.3.)

A man may be employed by the J-firm immediately upon graduation from school (high school or technical school in the case of a blue-collar job and high school or college in the case of a white-collar job), or after a few years of job experience elsewhere. According to the *Employment Mobility Survey* conducted annually by the Ministry of Labor, about one-third of the newly employed "regular workers" at relatively large firms (1,000 employees) in 1980 were recruited directly from schools, and over half of them had previous job experience. These proportions change slightly from year to year depending upon business cycles, among other things, but have remained at that level since the 1960's. The definition of "regular workers" in this survey is too broad, however, as it includes those temporary workers whose employment contracts do not specify the length of employment or who have worked more than 18 days in the preceding 2 months. They may be referred to as semitemporary workers. Excluding these semitemporary workers from the regular workers, Koike has estimated that about half of the newly employed regular workers at large firms were new graduates.[8] The corresponding figures for white-collar employees may be higher. The new regular employee is placed at a lower grade on the basic pay scale, depending on his level of education, as already noted. Previous job experience does not normally count.

Besides regular workers, the J-firm employs temporary workers. The proportion of temporary workers among the newly employed in large firms fluctuates considerably with the business cycle. When the labor market tightens, the proportion drops, and vice versa. This indicates that most workers prefer the status of regular employee. The proportion declined somewhat in the early 1970s, but it climbed sharply after the 1975 depression and recovered to the 1960s level in the late 1970s. In the early 1980s, a little less than 30 percent of new entrants to large firms were in that category. Between the late 1960s and mid-1970s, temporary workers were closely monitored by foremen in the first few years of employment, and upon their recommendation could qualify for the entrance examination required to become a regular employee. Since the mid-1970s, however, a clear demarcation seems to have developed between the regular and temporary worker, and the status of temporary worker is no longer a stepping stone to regular employment.[9]

Contrary to popular belief, a relatively high separation rate is observed among young employees of large firms in Japan. Table 3.3, constructed by Kuramitsu Muramatsu from the Ministry of Labor's *Employment Mobility Survey* and *Basic Survey of Wage Structure*, provides information on the job separation rate by the duration of job and the size of the employing firm. Among those employed by firms with more than 1,000 employees, the separation rate, defined as the ratio of the number of separated employees during the year to the number of total employees at the beginning of the year, reached 82.5 percent in 1979 and 101.7 percent in 1980. These figures are even higher than the corresponding ones for smaller firms, possibly because the proportion of unstable temporary and semitemporary workers is higher at large firms. But it may still be the case that a fair number of regular employees quit jobs within a few years of employment to search for a better match, although the job search activity by young workers may not be as intense as in the United States.

[8] K. Koike, "Nihon kigyo no koyo to romu (Employment and personnel policy of the Japanese firm)," *Bijinesu Rebyu* (Business Review), 30, pp. 82–101.
[9] Koike, "Nihon kigyo."

Table 3.3. *Job separation rate by duration of job and employment size of the firm, male, 1978 and 1980 (unit %)*

Size of the firm	Duration of job (years)					
	Total	0–1	1–2	2–5	5–9	10–
1978						
1000 and more	6.1	82.5	10.8	8.7	3.9	3.9
100–999	10.4	57.7	17.6	12.5	6.5	5.2
5–99	13.4	50.6	23.4	14.3	7.9	4.9
Total	9.9	60.4	20.6	12.7	6.0	4.4
1980						
1000 and more	6.3	101.7	13.7	8.8	3.2	2.6
100–999	8.7	47.4	18.2	12.4	5.5	3.3
5–99	13.3	49.2	23.9	14.6	7.6	4.9
Total	9.8	61.3	22.6	13.9	5.7	3.4

Source: K. Muramatsu, "Rishoku kodo to rodo kumiai" (Separation behavior and the labor union), in Kazuo Koike (ed.), *Gendai no Shitsugyo* (Contemporary unemployment), Dobunsha, 1974, p. 170.

If an employee survives the initial career stage with the original employer, he tends to settle down and concentrate his efforts and energy on climbing up the firm's promotional ladder. Depending on his capability, learning speed, contribution to the organizational process, and reputation among supervisors and personnel department staff, his promotions may differ from those of his peers. If he scores well on these factors, by his late thirties he may be promoted to (sub)foremanship, in the case of a blue-collar employee, or to a lower management post, in the case of a white-collar employee. Then he is quite likely to pursue further career advancement in the present firm. If he does not score well, his promotion rate may start to slow down· at that stage of the life cycle, and it would gradually become clear that his future prospects in the firm are not bright. He may then consider an outside job opportunity seriously, if one becomes available, particularly if he cannot maintain good relations with his superiors and peers. But midcareer mobility may not improve the pay level very much, although it may provide better human relations, and work environments. According to the *Employment Mobility Survey,* after 1975 only 20 percent (19.8 percent in 1984) of voluntary midcareer job changers received salary offers more than 10 percent higher than their previous pay levels. Contrary to the widely held view that market environments are becoming more favorable to midcareer mobility, this ratio was much higher before 1974 (for example, 28.6 percent in 1971). As the separation payment is relatively low for voluntary separation, midcareer job changes, in general, carry a financial penalty for the employee.

For those who stay with the firm, competition for higher supervisory or managerial positions becomes keener. On the white-collar career track, only the most successful employees keep climbing the internal management promotional ladder. By their late forties and early fifties, many ordinary employees, as well as managers of various ranks, may be dispatched *(shukko)* by the parent firm to subsidiaries and related firms. According to a survey by the Central Labor Commission, 8.2 percent of the total employees of manufacturing firms with more than 1,000 employees were on *shukko* in June 1985.[10] This ratio is particularly high for depressed industries, such as the nonferrous metal industry (29.3 percent) and the chemical industry (14.1 percent). The *shukko* system is also used for positive purposes such as assisting the management of related firms and subsidiaries and facilitating the career development of promising young employees, but the quoted figures suggest that a significant portion of *shukko* is used as a method of employment restraint and selection at large firms, particularly for midcareer employees. If the parent company recuperates from business hardship or if a *shukko* employee proves to have valuable managerial or specialist ability, the employee may be recalled to the parent firm, but otherwise his employment contract will be formally switched to the *shukko* firm after two years. According to government statistics, between 1975 and 1978, 9.7 percent of the reduction in employment in manufacturing firms with more than 1,000 employees was due to *shukko*.[11]

---

[10] The Central Labor Commission, *1985 Survey of Separation Payment, Mandatory Retirement and Pensions*, 1985.

[11] Ministry of Labor, *Survey of Employment Fluctuation*, 1979. An econometric analysis by K. Muramatsu about the means of adjusting employment in Japanese manufacturing firms has found that the "net" rate of *shukko* did not have a statistically significant impact on the employment adjustment during the period, but the estimated result may have been affected by the specification of the model in which the size of the firm is not controlled. Obviously *shukko* as a means of employment adjustment can be used only by relatively larger firms. See K. Muramatsu, "Kaiko to sono daitai shudan: nihon no seizogyo no baai" (Discharge and its alternative means: the case of the Japanese manufacturing industry), in M. Mizuno, Y. Matsugi, and Th. Dams (eds.), *ME-ka to Koyo: Nichi-doku Hikaku* (Mechatronization and Employment: Japan–Germany comparison), Nagoya University Press, 1986, pp. 133–64. For *shukko*, see Giorgio Brunello, "Transfers of employees between Japanese manufacturing enterprises: some results from an inquiry on a small sample of large firms." *British Journal of Industrial Relations*, 26 (1988), pp. 119–32.

If persistent business setbacks require further employment adjustment, a firm may systematically introduce voluntary early retirement, – which is nothing more than an honorable discharge from the firm – and then outright discharges. Muramatsu has found that the rate of discharge starts to increase when a firm has to reduce more than 10 percent of its man-hours in response to a fall in demand or output.[12] When discharges occur, the most vulnerable are senior employees over the age of 45. According to the *Basic Survey of Employment Structure,* the age distribution of employees aged 45 or older was about 30 percent of the total labor force in 1979, but, among those separated by reason of discharge and liquidation of employing firms, about 46 percent came from that age group. There was no other age bracket for which the incidence of discharges fell more than proportionately to their share of employment.[13] This is in sharp contrast to the American situation, where the rate of unemployment is highly concentrated in the youth. No seniority rights regarding job security have been established for Japanese employees, as they have been for their American counterparts.

Thus, even among those who started their careers right after they graduated from school with the expectation of lifetime employment, only a minority may fulfill that expectation. Table 3.4 constructed from *The Basic Statistical Survey of Wage Structure* by the Ministry of Labor, shows the ratio of the number of male employees who have never changed employers to the total number of employees by age class, educational level, and industry. In the manufacturing industry, the ratio for high school graduates is as low as 65.6 percent in the 25–29 age category and indicates more frequent job search activity in the early career stage of this group. In the middle-age category, the ratio drops further, but not as significantly as among college graduates. One cannot immediately assess possible future job duration of employees from the cross-sectional data, but to the degree that the pattern is time invariant, these data suggest that high school graduates entering the manufacturing industry tend to settle down with their original employers if they find good matches. About half of those in the 50–54 age category have remained with their original employers. Also, the turnover of employees, particularly among high school graduates, is significantly higher in the retail, wholesale, and service industries, where the skills required may be more general and standardized than those required in manufacturing.

---

[12] Muramatsu, "Kaiko to sono daitai shudan."
[13] Koike, "Nihon kigyo."

Table 3.4. *Ratio of nonjob changers to total employees, male, 1980–5 (unit %)*

Age	Under 19	20–24	25–29	30–34	35–39	40–44	45–49	50–54	55–59	60–64	65–
High school graduates											
Manufacturing	100.0	73.1	65.6	61.0	57.4	53.8	49.3	45.6	25.7	4.6	1.5
Retail and wholesale	100.0	49.6	38.7	37.0	34.6	28.9	24.2	19.8	13.7	2.7	1.0
Services	100.0	53.0	37.6	33.6	29.3	22.7	21.5	16.2	9.4	1.9	0.4
College graduates											
Manufacturing	—	100.0	84.9	73.5	67.6	63.5	55.4	40.7	19.5	3.5	0.9
Retail and wholesale	—	100.0	73.9	73.1	65.7	53.5	33.1	30.6	14.7	2.2	2.2
Services	—	100.0	76.4	59.7	48.3	41.3	35.7	26.2	14.4	6.3	1.2

Source: Ministry of Labor, *Labor White Paper*, 1986 (constructed from *Basic Wage Survey*).

Most college graduates are engaged in white-collar jobs. The ratio of nonchangers in the 30–34 age category is 67.6 percent, which indicates less job hunting activity and higher expectations for long-term employment in the early career stage. The ratio declines at a faster rate, however, as one moves up in the age brackets than in the case of high school graduates. For the 50–54 age category, the ratio is 40.7 percent, which is lower than that among high school graduates. The conventional view that large firms offer the privilege of lifetime employment primarily to educated white-collar employees needs to be treated with caution. A substantial rate of separation, voluntary or involuntary, will occur even among this class of employees between midcareer and mandatory retirement age. Only a minority of employees seem to pursue lifetime employment up to mandatory retirement.

In sum, one may say that the screening of high-productivity types and the weeding out of low-productivity types by the J-firm is a very slow process, but that it exists nonetheless. The nature of the reward structure at the J-firm is not mere paternalism, and the competition among employees is no less keen than it is elsewhere. Its outcome, however, evolves slowly over the course of an entire career.

The questions is: Does the incentive structure of the J-firm, which motivates employees to compete over the long term for the acquisition of contextual skills within one firm, lead to an efficient outcome that is beneficial to both the employee and the employer? How is cooperation within the work group motivated in the face of such competition among individuals? Why are skilled senior workers most vulnerable to discharges when a reduction of employment becomes imperative? Is it not a waste of human resources to discharge senior workers, who may have developed more contextual skills than the junior workers? Or is there some efficiency reason for the J-firm to discharge them? I turn to these theoretical issues in the next section.

2.   The ranking hierarchy and reputation

Any large business organization faces at least two fundamental incentive problems. In this regard, even the J-firm is not an exception. They are

1. *Moral hazard problem:* How can the firm provide incentives that will discourage individual employees from shirking work under the condition of imperfect monitoring?
2. *Adverse selection problem:* How can the firm select employees who are highly productive and highly motivated from among

many candidates under the condition of asymmetric information regarding their attributes (i.e., the firm does not know as much about their attributes as they themselves do)?

As already mentioned in Chapter 2, the micro-micro information structure of the J-firm is heavily dependent on the information-processing capacities, or contextual skills that employees develop through integrative learning and dense communications among themselves, formal and informal. Therefore, the J-firm may have to give more conscious attention to the following incentive questions than do other firms:

3. How can it promote employees' integrative learning and discourage employees who have acquired (contextual) skills useful to the firm from quitting early?
4. How can it promote productive cooperative behavior in team production?

Many recent neoclassical studies have been concerned with the incentive nature of employment contracts in the framework of the "principal–agency" approach. The main issues addressed by the principal–agency theory are the first two cited above. This approach starts with the assumption that the objective of the employee (the agent) differs from that of the employer (the principal). For example, the employer would be better off when the level of profit is increased, whereas the employee would be better off if the effort expended was saved for a given level of compensation. Suppose that the agent's actions (say, effort supply) and uncertain uncontrollable events jointly determine outcomes, but that the agent's actions cannot be monitored perfectly by the principal. If the agent knows that the effects of his or her actions and uncertain events on outcomes are inseparable in the eyes of the principal, the agent would, given a compensation scheme, act (control his or her effect level) to his or her own advantage. This is the key moral hazard problem on the employee's side. What is essential to this problem is the asymmetry of information posterior to employment contracting.

In a situation involving moral hazard, what type of employment contract could at least mitigate the inefficiency stemming from the problem, if not make the first-best solution possible? Much of the principal–agent literature suggests that piece rates (output-dependent remuneration) could be used, but their exact form would depend on the precise circumstances of the two contracting parties – for example, their relative degree of risk aversion and the probability distribution of uncertain events. Although moral hazard is a potentially universal problem, the employment contract at the J-firm, as indicated in Section 1, does not specify remunerations to employees by piece rate, at least in the short run (one year). Bonus payments aside (I comment on these later), the firm promises the employee a remuneration fixed ex ante according to a rank.

One possible reason why the Japanese firm does not in general provide output-dependent remuneration to the employee in the short run may lie in the difficulty of measuring individual output according to objective criteria. Not only is individual output difficult to separate from that of the team, but the employee also may have to be judged in many dimensions, involving such diverse variables as the level of short-run output, the appropriateness of response to local emergencies, learning achievement, and contribution to and compliance with the collective mores of the shopfloor. How does the Japanese firm deal with the potential moral hazard problem in these wider dimensions?

Another important incentive issue arising in the study of employment contracts is that of adverse selection, which is caused by asymmetry in precontractual information. Potential employees may differ in their productivity, diligence, propensity to quit, learning capability, and other attributes relevant to the development of contextual skills such as leadership and harmonious character. Information concerning individual attributes may be known to potential employees themselves, but is not immediately available to employers at the time of hiring.

In this situation, if a uniform contract that suits the average worker is offered to workers with different attributes, those who are highly productive and have other favorable attributes would neither be satisfied with their job assignments nor rewarded properly for their productivity. Therefore their supply may be withdrawn from the market, while low-productivity types may disguise their own identity. Faced with this problem, the firm must devise a way to evaluate prospective employees. One such device is to screen potential employees by their educational credentials, but this is obviously an imperfect solution to the problem. The J-firm provides identical terms of employment to all new regular employees. How, then, does the J-firm deal with the adverse selection problem?

The third incentive issue concerns the provision of appropriate motivation for integrative learning on the job. The basic problems arising in this connection may be considered a subclass of the more general problems of moral hazard and adverse selection: How, for example, is the employee motivated not to shirk from developing his or her potential to its full extent? How can the firm select the most trainable employees who will not leave the firm after training? As already mentioned, however, these questions are particularly important for the J-firm in which the efficiency of the information structure depends on high employee integrative skills developed only in the context of the firm's organization. Therefore, some attention should be given to the problems specifically connected with learning.

The fourth question – that is, how to provide an incentive for cooperative behavior – has not been fully explored in the literature, but is obviously important to the J-firm and raises many interesting points. Suppose that production involves teamwork in the sense that if one shifts some effort to help someone else, it would increase the latter's output more than decrease one's own output. In such a setting, how is the individual motivated to help someone else, if the reward for doing so depends on his or her own output? Can this individual expect reciprocal help from the other? If so, under what reward system and intrafirm norm of behavior?

To see how the J-firm deals with these incentive issues, let us first formalize the essential feature of the reward structure of the J-firm, as described in Section 1. It may be captured by the notion of the hierarchy as a system of ranks, in which the remuneration paid to an employee depends on his or her rank and internal promotion from lower to higher ranks is based on a certain formalized standard. In this structure, ranks are not directly associated with particular jobs. Employees in the same rank may perform different tasks, and employees in different ranks may perform the same task. Thus rank ordering is not congruent with task assignments, as in the case of the A-firm. In this sense, it is quite misleading to refer to the internal organization of the J-firm as the "internal labor market," because remunerations to employees are associated primarily with their ranks as such, and not with jobs or individual output (except for minor payment by jobs and bonus payments, which may be related to output performance, as I will explain shortly). Therefore I refer to the internal system of ranking as *ranking hierarchy*.

Employment contracts offered to new entrants only specify the initial condition of employment, which is uniform for all entrants. They are placed at the bottom of the ranking hierarchy and remunerated uniformly regardless of their tasks and potential productivity at the time of entry. But the implicit understanding at the time of employment is that employees are to be selected for higher ranks according to their performance as observed by the firm over long periods, under the threat of costly separation in the case of misconduct.

To use more formal terms, let us distinguish between the *short run* and *long run* in which the ranking hierarchy operates. By the former I mean the period in which a definite pay rank is assigned to each employee and remains fixed. One may think of one year as the length of such a period. By the latter I mean the entire career of the employee, starting from entry to the firm and ending at the time of mandatory retirement. The *middle run* refers to a period longer than the short run, but shorter than the long run. In these terms, one may posit:

[R.1] In the short run, the employees' basic remunerations are fixed ex ante according to their rank, but are not directly related to their job or output performance.

[R.2] New entrants to the firm are placed in the bottom rank. However, they are promoted over certain periods on a rank-by-rank basis as their performances meet certain standards. In each period, they move up one rank, at most, but a differential arises among employees in the long run because of discriminatory treatment with respect to the speed of promotion, which results in substantial variation in one's lifetime earnings and separation payment.

[R.3] An employee whose performance does not meet the required standard of his or her rank is separated in midcareer and must find a job elsewhere.

The proposition [R.1] may seem to ignore the effects of bonus payment, the absolute level of which may be ex ante unfixed in the short run and may also be subject to a supervisor's evaluation of individual performance. However, I would argue that such bonus factors may be regarded as secondary. The level of bonus payment is determined by annual collective bargaining after the performance of the firm becomes known, but the ratio of the average amount of annual bonus relative to that of regularly paid remuneration is in general fairly stable over a period of time and is not as sensitive to the short-run performance of the business. In general, only after the business performance is extraordinarily good or bad beyond a period, can the ratio become variable.[14]

Bonus payments to individuals are often subject to supervisory assessment when individual performances are directly measurable by

---

[14] For example, according to an econometric study by Kazutoshi Koshiro, the changes in the bonus payment of major firms in the iron and steel and automobile industries can be explained by two variables: the profit per employee in the previous year (rather than in the current year) and the amount of bonus payments of the previous year. In these industries, the lagged profit elasticity of bonus payment is less than 10 percent and the regression coefficient of the amount of bonus in the previous year is about 80 percent, indicating a high degree of inertia in bonus payment and its lagged adjustment to current profits. K. Koshiro, "Labor market flexibility in Japan: with special reference to wage flexibility," mimeographed, 1986.

their contributions to the output of the firm. A good example is the bonus payment scheme to security company brokers. In this case, a substantial proportion of the individual bonus payment is linked to the amount of trade done in the period. But where it is difficult to distinguish the output of an individual employee from that of other employees involved in genuine teamwork, bonus payments cannot recognize individual employees' performance except to account for objective diligent factors such as days without absenteeism.[15]

Further, some supervisors are reluctant to treat their subordinates differently in assessing bonuses so as not to upset human relations. (It is also true that some enjoy treating their subordinates differently, however minute they may be.) Therefore, the relative differential of bonus payment among employees, particularly among blue-collar employees, may be regarded as approximately proportional to that of the contractually determined regular payment, although the absolute level may be adjusted over periods of time in response to the profit fluctuation.

There has been considerable debate as to whether the Japanese bonus system is a form of deferred wage payment or profit sharing. The deferred payment view emphasizes the short-run insensitivity of the bonus payment, whereas the profit-sharing view has come to emphasize the nonnegligible (lagged) elasticity of bonus payments with respect to profit. These two views may be reconciled to some extent by distinguishing between the short run and the middle run as follows:

> [R.1a] The bonus payment is fixed in the short run ex ante in a proportion to the contractually paid remuneration. However, it may be adjusted according to the business condition of the firm in the middle run.

I return to the profit-sharing and group incentive aspect of the bonus payment in Chapter 5. Although it cannot be denied that there is a short-run and individual incentive aspect to the bonus payment, I consider it to be of secondary importance and assume the above, which rationalizes the characterization [R.1] of the Japanese incentive system.

[15] In the operation of the *kanban* system, a mere increase in output volume is discouraged if it only contributes to the accumulation of in-process inventory that cannot be immediately absorbed by the downstream process. As discussed in Section 2.1, the emphasis is more on the coordinated production of a variety of outputs responding to the market situation rather than the single-minded pursuit of the maximization of output per machine. Under these conditions, the system of piece-rate payment and its variants (output-dependent bonus) do not provide appropriate incentives to employees.

The notion of a hierarchy as a system of rank characterized by [R.1] through [R.3] is obviously distinct from the notion of hierarchy as a vertical information structure presented in Section 2.2. In the latter case, lower ranks (subordinates) communicate with others only via higher ranks (superiors), and the superiors have authority over their subordinates in the sense that they give subordinates commands. This authority relationship is centralized in one office. In the former case, employees start out from the bottom of the structure and, as they realize their potential by developing their contextual skills to a sufficient degree, they are promoted to higher ranks. Joseph Stiglitz has introduced the terms *horizontal* and *vertical* hierarchy in order to distinguish the two. The former corresponds to the ranking hierarchy and the latter to the functional hierarchy.[16]

In the ranking hierarchy of blue-collar and white-collar employees at the J-firm, each rank is associated with a level of pay and standard of performance. If the employee meets a particular standard, then he or she may be promoted to one rank above. The working of this ranking hierarchy should not be confused with that of another type of rank ordering in which a predetermined number of slots is set up for each rank and employees are ordered according to their "relative" performance (vis-à-vis others) rather than according to an absolute standard. Competition in such a hierarchy has been labeled a rank-order tournament by economists such as E. Lazear and Sherwin Rosen, among others.[17] The difference between the two is neatly explained by Robert Drago and Geoffrey Turnbull: In the ranking hierarchy, "some firms may lead workers to perceive that there is always room at the top for a good performer," while in the rank-order tournament "there is always the possibility of outperforming others and making it to the top."[18] As already mentioned, the ranking hierarchy for blue-collar and white-collar employees in the J-firm may be considered more of a horizontal hierarchy, as characterized by [R.1] through [R.3]. Even for managers, when the economy allowed the J-firm to undergo steady growth in the 1960s and early 1970s, the J-firm created slots at various levels to which managers could be promoted if they qualified. As slow growth has made such flexible expansion of the promotional hierarchy difficult, the managerial ranking hierarchy seems to have become more

---

[16] J. Stiglitz, "Incentives, risks, and notes towards a theory of hierarchy," *Bell Journal of Economics*, 6 (Autumn 1975), p. 570.
[17] E. Lazear and S. Rosen, "Rank order tournament as optimum labor contracts," *Journal of Political Economy*, 89 (1981), pp. 814-64.
[18] R. Drago and G. K. Turnbull, "Competitive and noncompetitive incentives in team settings: notes toward a theory of promotion systems," mimeographed, 1987.

like the rank order tournament. We will see later how such an environmental change would affect the nature of incentives for managers and thereby their behavior.

After the above preparatory discussion, I now consider the theoretical question of how the ranking (horizontal) hierarchy copes with the incentive problems of the J-firm presented at the beginning of this section. The answer can be gleaned from the recent literature on incentives.

First, note that, alongside the labor market in which employment contracts for entry into the ranking hierarchy are transacted, there exist markets for fairly standardized jobs that do not require as much firm-specific skill. (In the next section I point out that new entry to the ranking hierarchy is about 30 to 40 percent of new jobs created yearly.) In these markets for standardized jobs, contracts provide less generous regular pay increases and separation payments, albeit possibly a higher starting pay. Such jobs are found more frequently in the service, retail, and wholesale industries, where the mobility of workers is naturally higher (see Table 3.4). Also, with the growing presence of Western multinational companies in Japan, there are now more alternative employment contracts for managerial and highly skilled white-collar employees that offer higher initial pay, but less job security.

Joanne and Steven Salop have proposed a model of self-selection relevant to such situation in which diverse contracts other than those for ranking hierarchy coexist.[19] Suppose that employers offer a range of contracts, some of which give high rewards to workers with high productivity (alternatively low propensity to quit) once they have proven themselves, but severely penalize those who turn out to be low-productivity types (who tend to be more mobile), whereas other contracts penalize low productivity (high mobility) less severely. In that way, workers may be induced to reveal information about their attributes. Applicants hoping to enter the ranking hierarchy of the J-firm characterized by the relatively low initial pay and the relatively higher intrafirm upward mobility reveal themselves to be of the type who are willing to endure the long training needed to accumulate contextual skills and willing to wait for the financial returns, which are realizable only after long periods. Once revealed, that information can be used both to provide appropriate rewards and to assign employees to appropriate tasks, including costly training. Thus the coexistence of employment contracts for relatively standardized jobs alongside those for

[19] J. Salop and S. Salop, "Self-selection and turnover in the labor market," *Quarterly Journal of Economics*, 90 (November 1976), pp. 619–27.

entry to the ranking hierarchy functions as a "self-selection" mechanism to cope with the adverse selection problem.

Second, note that characterization [R.3] imposes substantial costs on employees who do not meet the performance standards of any given rank. The separation does not have to be an outright firing. Although appearing to be voluntary, it may actually be imposed through pressure from the supervisor and peer group, or both. In any case, midcareer separation involves a financial penalty because of the disadvantageous treatment in the separation payment. Furthermore, because of adverse selection, potential employers may judge the attributes of midcareer job changers by their personal job history. The fact that they were separated from their internal promotional mechanism in midcareer may suggest that they did not perform satisfactorily in their previous ranks. Because of this "reputation" effect, they may only get jobs of lower rank and their lifetime perspectives may be lower than if they had advanced within the promotional hierarchies of their original firm. The cost of midcareer separation therefore functions as a device for enforcing discipline on employees after entry.

The idea that dismissal costs deter shirking has appeared in a number of recent studies on incentives. Guillermo Calvo, Carl Shapiro, and Joseph Stiglitz, and others have argued that the presence of involuntary unemployment serves that role.[20] With employment, a worker has no incentive to shirk, for, if she or he is detected shirking (with a positive, but less than one probability because of imperfect monitoring by the employer) and is fired, the individual will not be able to obtain another job immediately, the probability depending on the size of unemployment. The equilibrium unemployment rate must be sufficiently large to make long-term cost (human capital loss) from the possibility of being caught shirking and unemployed greater than the

[20] G. Calvo, "Quasi-Walrasian theories of unemployment," *American Economic Review Proceedings,* 69 (May 1979), pp. 102–6. C. Shapiro and J. Stiglitz, "Equilibrium unemployment as a worker discipline device," *American Economic Review,* 74 (June 1984), pp. 443–4. Also see Herbert Gintis and Tsuneo Ishikawa, "Work intensity and unemployment," *Journal of the Japanese and International Economies,* 1 (1987), pp. 195–228; and Masahiro Okuno-Fujiwara, "Monitoring cost, agency relationship, and equilibrium modes of labor contract," *Journal of the Japanese Economy and International Economies,* 1 (1987), pp. 147–67. In the papers by Calvo and by Shapiro and Stiglitz, the worker who shirks is spotted and discharged by the employer with an exogenously given probability. In the paper by Okuno-Fujiwara, the probability is a function of resource input allocated to the monitoring of workers by the employer. In other words, the monitoring of technology is treated as endogenous. The Okuno-Fujiwara paper may be more relevant to an understanding of the Japanese economy as it discusses the implications of the coexistence of long-term contracts and short-term contracts.

immediate gains from shirking. Stiglitz and Shapiro have solved their general equilibrium model for the equilibrium unemployment rate and have interpreted the efficiency losses associated with it as the social monitoring cost. In the Japanese model, the loss of the separation payment or the demotion potential in the ranking hierarchy after separation plays the same role as the threat of unemployment does for the Stiglitz and Shapiro model.

In Lazear's view, the scheme of raising the seniority wages of employees who have not been found shirking is a form of performance bond.[21] This scheme is equivalent to giving the employee a constant wage in the absence of learning, but taking back part of his earlier payments as a bond, which is later returned to him. Since the payment inclusive of bond recovery would exceed the employee's productivity in the later stage of his or her career, there is no incentive for senior employees to quit voluntarily. This also explains, Lazear argues, why there is madatory retirement. Thus, one aspect of the Japanese seniority payment and separation payment may be understood in terms of performance bonds.

Lazear's model suggests another fundamental incentive issue in the employment relation, that is, the moral hazard on the employer's side. The firm would have an incentive to claim that employees shirked, even if they did not, when they are about to enter the "payoff" period in which they recover their bonds so that the firm could appropriate the bond. Or the firm may be induced to lay off senior employees rather than junior employees when it is necessary to reduce employment so that the firm can save on seniority payments. This is again equivalent to the firm simply appropriating the bond. As Lazear has pointed out, however, the firm's reputation as an honest employer may solve this problem. The employer is implicitly penalized in the long run for firing a senior worker because this would make it more difficult for the firm to attract prospective employees in the future. (Later I explain how the Japanese firm can be caught in a serious dilemma, during a prolonged state of business depression, between the long-run reputational concern and the midrun efficiency requirement.)

An unsatisfactory feature of Lazear's model is that the performance of the employee is rated either satisfactory or unsatisfactory. Because there are no degress of satisfaction, the optimal contract is indeterminate. One way to solve this problem is to rank employees according to standards with certain ranges. Consider, for example, the elegant

[21] E. Lazear, "Why is there mandatory retirement?" *Journal of Political Economy,* 89 (1979), pp. 841–64.

model by Bentley MacLeod and James M. Malcomson in that direction.[22] They suggest that a hierarchical rank can be defined by the wage to be paid and the performance level below which the employee is dismissed by the firm. The output of individual employees need not be measured precisely. If an employee is dismissed, he or she will then be assigned by the new employer to a position one rank below his or her previous one, because the new employer believes that the ability of the dismissed employee fits a lower rank than the one occupied before the separation. Their model of a hierarchy thus corresponds to our formulation of the reward structure at the J-firm as the ranking (horizontal) hierarchy.

In order that the ranking hierarchy results from labor market competition, it must be incentive-compatible in both of the following senses: First, it must be in the interest of the firm not to terminate the contract, provided the employee performs at the required level or higher; that is, the required level of performance at each rank must yield output greater than the level of pay associated with the rank. Second, given the potential for dismissal involving costs from the loss of reputation, it must be in the interest of employees at each level to perform at the required level, provided that the firm continues to offer the associated pay; in other words, given an ability, the discounted value of future utilities from remaining at a rank must be greater than the short-run benefit from shirking plus the discounted value of default utilities from the next period on. MacLeod and Malcomson have shown that the equilibrium number of rankings is endogenously determined for a given distribution of ability and that it is finite even if ability is a continuous variable. The reason for this is that a finite cost of demotion needs to be imposed on those who shirk. In equilibrium, no midcareer mobility will actually occur, although the threat of potential dismissal functions as a deterrent to shirking.

In the equilibrium, employees of different ability are placed in different ranks corresponding to their abilities. But because of asymmetric information, the ability of potential employees is not known prior to contracting, and the firm cannot place them in the appropriate rank directly. Employees will not select the appropriate rank themselves. It is to their advantage to choose the rank with the highest pay at entry and, if their ability is actually too low for the position, to shirk and get

---

[22] W. Bentley MacLeod and James M. Malcomson, "Reputation and hierarchy in dynamic models of employment," *Journal of Political Economy,* in press. See also Yashitsugu Kanemoto and W. B. McLeod, "Long-term contracts with team production: towards a theory of the Japanese firm," mimeographed.

dismissed. A selection mechanism to cope with this adverse selection is necessary. MacLeod and Malcomson have proposed that the promotion mechanism serves that purpose. Although all employees are placed at the bottom of the ranking hierarchy upon entering the firm, they will be promoted one rank in each period if they perform at or above the level required for promotion. MacLeod and Malcomson have shown that there exists an equilibrium promotion scheme in which it is in the interest of employees in any rank below that appropriate for their ability to perform at the required level for promotion, but it is not in the interest of those already in the appropriate rank because it involves excessive effort relative to their abilities. The employees in this model self-select their appropriate ranks.

The self-selection in the MacLeod and Malcomson model takes time since employees move up at most one rank in each period. Until new entrants reach an appropriate rank for their ability, the economic rent arising from the difference between their productivity and pay is captured by the firm, or the employees may shirk up to the minimum performance level required for promotion while they are working to be promoted. This inefficiency phenomenon arises when the ability of employees is exogenously determined prior to contracting. But the discussion in Chapter 2 and Section 1 of this chapter indicates that the ability of the employee at the J-firm with regard to productivity (conceptualized as contextual skills) can build up over periods of time through learning by doing. Can the hierarchy also be understood as an incentive device for motivating such learning?

Lorne Carmichael has proposed a model of promotional hierarchy in which inefficient quitting and firing of trained workers are controlled by an appropriate design of ranking hierarchy.[23] Workers join a firm for one period of training, after which their firm-specific productivity may be increased. After two periods, the worker is made to retire. In the first period the worker bears the cost of training in the form of a lower wage relative to the prevailing rate in the external market. If the person is not fired at the end of the first period for failing to achieve sufficient training, she or he gets the competitive wage in the second period. Sometime in the second period, the person is promoted to a still higher pay rank purely on the basis of seniority and recovers the investment cost of training and its return, although there is no productivity increase in the post-training second period. Such contracts maximize the ex ante joint wealth of the worker and the firm under asymmetric information, in which only the employer is able to know

[23] L. Carmichael, "Firm-specific human capital and promotion ladders," *Bell Journal of Economics,* 14 (October 1979), pp. 251–8.

the true productivity of workers ex post and only the worker is able to know the implicit utility cost of work. Since a definite number of slots in the highest rank must be filled on the basis of seniority, the firm does not gain from firing a senior worker with qualified skill. Thus the moral hazard problem on the side of the firm can be avoided. The firm discharges a worker only when his or her productivity gain through training is revealed to be too low at the end of the first period, even if this information is available only to the firm.

On the other hand, if the expected earnings in the second period are lower in relation to the job satisfaction level revealed to him or her at the end of the first period, the worker may then quit. If that happens, however, the worker receives an exogenously determined lower wage, and this limits the extent of costly post-training exits. One can imagine the situation in which the outsider cannot distinguish between those fired and those quitting voluntarily, so that voluntary quitting damages the reputation of a worker, even that of the high-productivity type. There is a gap between the level of pay and the worker's marginal productivity at the senior level, which may account for the existence of mandatory retirement, just as in Lazear's model.

Basically, Carmichael interprets the ranking hierarchy as a device for promoting learning and preserving costly skills within the firm (the human capital approach), whereas proponents of the agency-approach theory interpret it as a device for dealing with moral hazard and adverse selection. One way that the two approaches might be synthesized is suggested by the following scenario. Suppose that the current productivities of the new entrants to the ranking hierarchy are indistinguishable and that all are placed at the bottom, but that they differ in potential ability, which may be realized only through learning. However, the employer has no information regarding their potential ability to learn at the time of hiring (adverse selection). As learning accumulates, the potential is gradually realized, but learning involves costs to the employee in terms of time and effort. At the same time, those who fail to develop their potential incur costs in that they sacrifice the higher lifetime earnings associated with higher ranks or they risk being discharged in midcareer. Employees may be motivated to develop their potential, striking a balance between the cost of shirking learning and the benefits of promotion. There may well be an equilibrium promotion scheme under which employees of different potential endeavor to achieve a rate of promotion that corresponds to their potential in the long run. This idea still needs to be worked out formally, but it may be that a dynamic extension of the MacLeod and Malcomson model will yield such a scenario.

Another important factor to consider is the nature of the ranking hierarchy as a device for promoting cooperative behavior. Some interesting pioneering work has been done in this area by Drago and Turnbull.[24] They started out with an observation that conforms to the description of the micro-micro structure of the J-firm presented in Chapter 2, namely, that workers typically perform their duties at the same location and may require help from one another. In other words, Drago and Turnbull examine situations in which it is efficient for employees to engage in two types of effort: work that increases one's own output and work that increases someone else's output. That is, shifting some effort to helping others would increase other's output more than decrease one's own output. However, if the ranking hierarchy is of the competitive type (i.e., rank-order tournament), there is no incentive for individuals to help someone else, because it is costly to oneself in terms of one's own output while contributing to the other's output, and thereby hurts one's own chances of promotion. Developing mere reciprocity in the workplace would not help either, because in this case workers would collude not to work.

In the horizontal hierarchy as opposed to competitive hierarchy (rank-tournament), there will be no help if individuals behave independently (in the Cournot sense that each individual does not take into account the effect of his or her own behavior on the behavior of others) and if they are not altruistic (in the sense that they do not derive positive utilities from someone else's promotion). In this situation, helping someone else may enhance that person's promotability (to which I may be indifferent), but would decrease my promotability because I would be neglecting my own work. But Drago and Turnbull have shown that if the principle of reciprocity develops under the horizontal hierarchy so that my help is reciprocated by other's help, an efficient mix of my own and helping efforts would occur. And, under a relatively wide range of situations, it is expected that everyone will be better off under the horizontal hierarchy than under the competitive hierarchy. Thus the horizontal hierarchy at the J-firm may act as an incentive for promoting efficient cooperation.

This completes our theoretical discussion of the incentive characteristics of the ranking (horizontal) hierarchy, as revealed by the recent incentive literature. We have seen that a concern with reputation plays an important role in helping both the employer and employee cope with the moral hazard problem and in restraining the premature quitting of trained employees. Before concluding this section, I should mention two important points regarding the role of reputation in the

[24] Drago and Turnbull, "Competitive and noncompetitive incentives."

J-firm: The first deals with the reputation of employees who quit after training and the reputation of the firm that then employs them; and the second deals with the reputation of the firm that lays off senior employees because of bad business conditions.

In discussing the role of proposition [R.3], I pointed out that because of adverse selection, employees who quit spoil their reputation and incur a high separation cost. Outsiders who reemploy them also treat them as low-productivity, low-motivation types. This property [R.3] is an indispensable element of the ranking hierarchy, not only for discouraging employees from shirking, but also for controlling the departure of trained employees. In reality, however, even the J-firm will have employees whose skills may be highly useful to other firms (i.e., where the purely "contextual" element of the skill is relatively unimportant), such as engineers and researchers in basic disciplines, financial specialists, and the like; and it is not difficult for other firms to identify their true productivity. I submit, however, that Japanese firms, particularly large and established ones, have bound themselves to an implicit code of not hiring former employees of other firms, particularly skilled ones, so that ranking hierarchy at each firm can function effectively as an incentive to discourage skilled employees from quitting. If each firm defaults on such an implicit agreement by recruiting specialists from other firms with better terms of employment, the workings of the ranking hierarchy as an incentive scheme may be put in jeopardy. In order to avoid such a "prisoner's dilemma" type of situation, Japanese firms have implicitly agreed to maintain reputation among themselves.

But there are signs that this mechanism is losing its force because a growing number of new firms are not abiding by this implicit agreement. These include many subsidiaries and branches of Western multinational firms, particularly in financial industries, and relatively small entrepreneurial firms in the high-tech industry, newly set up or already established but entering new business lines by applying the technological expertise that they have developed in their traditional business lines. The terms of employment they offer to ready-made specialists are significantly better than the current pay level in the J-firm. Also, as already mentioned, the slower growth of the J-firm has made the nature of promotional hierarchy for specialists and managers more competitive rather than horizontal, and lowered their chances of promotion. Some of those who would have been qualified for promotion to managerial positions in previous years may no longer have the opportunity. They may therefore be motivated to find better opportunities outside the firm.

Those specialists and managers who quit, however, may yet incur separation costs of various types. If a worker quits at midcareer, the separation payment is so high that returns to training costs must be reaped from yet-to-be earned compensation. Multinationals tend to evaluate employees in terms of relatively short-run, competitive performances, and the future of an entrepreneurial firm in a high-tech industry is highly uncertain. As a result, new jobs carry less security. Midcareer mobility may give workers the reputation of being high-mobility types, and may thus limit their future job opportunities. Therefore the potential quitter must weigh the benefit of short-run gains against the risk of such long-run costs. I suspect that a great majority of Japanese employees, even the highly skilled type, regard the costs of midcareer mobility as relatively high. As a consequence, although there will be growing varieties of contracts in the midcareer mobility market, the basic structure and working of the ranking hierarchy at the J-firm will persist for years to come.

Consider next the reputation problem associated with layoff decisions of the firm. I argue that in implementing this decision the J-firm is faced with a serious dilemma involving the efficiency requirement and reputation maintenance. If workers who have been laid off can be recalled or if new workers can be hired without any loss in efficiency due to the standardization of job skills, layoffs may be a cost-saving reaction to a depressed state of demand, at least from the viewpoint of the firm. But if productivity on the shopfloor depends on the contextual skills that employees have developed over a period of time and that are useful only in specific contexts of the work team or internal organization, a move to sever employees from those contexts, even if temporarily, may reduce the capital value of such skills. This may be due in part to the fact that the differential treatment of employees at the time of layoff may impair future communicability among team members on the shopfloor. Layoffs also mean the loss of on-the-job training needed for the development of contextual skills. When demand conditions improve, the resulting productivity loss may be relatively higher than the current loss from hoarding redundant employees while providing them with training.

Therefore, the first measure that the J-firm takes in reaction to temporary setbacks in demand is to shorten work hours so that team members may share the burden. Another measure is to assign some employees to training programs or to different divisions that have not been hit so hard by the downturn in demand. When the setback in demand is expected to last a long time or even permanently, however, the accumulated costs from hoarding redundant employees will exceed the potential benefits from preserving, or investing in, the stock of contextual skills, and layoffs become inevitable even for the J-firm. There are no definite criteria to indicate who should be laid off first at the J-firm. As pointed out in Section 1, however, the more senior employees are the ones most vulnerable to layoffs.

If the seniority payment is considered a performance bond, laying off senior employees may be interpreted as a default on a contractual agreement by the firm. Further, if contextual skills can only be developed over many periods, it appears inefficient to lay off the more productive senior employees. In spite of these problems, why does the J-firm tend to lay off senior employees?

To anlayze these problems, consider the very simple two-period, two-state model formulated by L. Carmichael.[25] Suppose that the physical marginal product of the unskilled worker in his or her first period at the firm is MP_u, but that it will be raised to MP_s in the second period because of the development of contextual skills. The product price is p_+ in the good state and p_- in the bad state. If the senior worker is laid off in this period because of the bad state, the current value loss is $p_- \times MP_s$. If the junior worker is laid off instead, then the current value loss is $p_- \times MP_u$ and is certainly smaller than in the first case, because $MP_s > MP_u$. But if the junior worker is laid off, their contextual skills will not be developed, and when the worker returns to his job in the next period, he or she will still need to develop contextual skills. Assuming that the bad state and the good state arise with equal probability in the next period, the expected value loss due to missing the training opportunity in the first period will be

$$\frac{1}{2}(p_- + p_+) \times (MP_s - MP_u).$$

If we suppose that there is no discounting on future value, this capital loss is greater than the net current loss from laying off more productive senior workers, since $p_+ > p_-$.

As Carmichael has pointed out, a layoff reduces the total working lifetime of a worker, but does not shorten his or her training period. Therefore the productivity loss always pertains to experienced workers. For young workers, however, this lost output is evaluated at an average level of prices in the next period, whereas for experienced workers it is evaluated at the current low price. Of course, if the future value of product loss from the postponement of training of junior workers is discounted, the argument will be weakened, but if the dis-

---

[25] L. Carmichael, "Does rising productivity explain seniority rules for layoffs?" *American Economic Review,* 73 (1983), pp. 1127–31.

count rate is not too great, it still remains relatively efficient for the firm to lay off senior workers close to mandatory retirement. Actually doing so, however, may jeopardize the reputation of the firm, which puts it in a serious dilemma. As is often observed, Japanese firms that have to resort to layoffs in depressed times but hope to recuperate in the future (so that their discount rate is not too high) offer additional separation payments to senior employees who are willing to "retire" early. This may be interpreted as an attempt to salvage the reputation of the firm in a difficult time by returning at least a part of the retained bond.

3.   Contractual incompleteness and enterprise unionism

Section 2 indicates that the individual who is potentially capable, as well as willing, to endure long-term training cooperatively and the J-firm have a mutual interest in establishing and maintaining the long-term association. Job duration in the J-firm can therefore be expected to be relatively long. Although the conventional view that the majority of Japanese workers are employed for life immediately after leaving school is too simplistic a generalization, it is reasonable to assume that employment contracts transacted in a core part of the labor market involve the mutual expectation of long-term association. In this section, I discuss the nature of these contracts.

Firms of all sizes except for the marginal ones are on the demand side of the core market. Evidence suggests that (1) average job tenure at small and medium firms is relatively shorter than at large firms, but is not negligible, and (2) the view that jobs of long duration are limited to large firms is mistaken.[26] Also, experienced blue-collar workers in small- and medium-sized firms are often promoted to white-collar jobs, but this type of mobility is often recorded as a change of job in official statistics, so that the long-term association with small- and medium-sized firms may easily be underestimated.

A considerable proportion of fresh college graduates as well as fresh high school graduates, screened by school credentials, are on the supply side of the core market. Traditionally, entry to this market has been predominantly male. With the enactment of the Equal Employment Opportunity Act in 1986 and the gradual change in social attitudes toward career women, I expect that the gender barrier will be gradually

---

[26] See K. Koike, "Workers in small firms and women in industry," in T. Shirai (ed.), *Contemporary Industrial Relations in Japan,* University of Wisconsin Press, 1983, pp. 89–115.

Table 3.5. *New jobholders by background and sex, 1962–82*

	1962–5			1968–71			1977–82		
	Total	Male	Female	Total	Male	Female	Total	Male	Female
Total of new job holders	4.68	2.88	7.05	4.50	2.90	7.08	5.79	3.54	9.44
Before entry to job									
Schooling	3.20	2.21	4.32	2.69	2.14	3.57	1.89	1.50	2.43
Householding	0.75	0.03	1.94	1.11	0.05	2.83	1.96	0.07	4.12

Note: The ratio of new jobholders to the total number employed at the end of the previous year.
Source: Management and Coordination Agency, *Basic Survey of Employment Structure.*

weakened, if not removed completely, in the near future. The number of recent graduates among new male job entrants was on the average 1.50 percent of the total stock of male employees in 1977–82 (Table 3.5). About half of these fresh graduates can be expected to remain with their original employers after 10 years (see Table 3.4) and therefore can be considered a crude estimate of the supply to the core market from school. There is an additional supply of previous jobholders to long-term employment. According to a rough estimate by Koike (see Section 3.1), the proportion of new graduates and of previous jobholders who were newly employed "regular" workers at large firms was about the same in 1980, although this estimate of previous jobholders may be too high for white-collar jobs and may be too low for small- and medium-sized firms. Therefore, roughly speaking, the supply of male labor to the core market every year may be estimated as somewhere between 1 percent and 1.5 percent of the total stock of males employed and between 30 percent (= 1.00/3.54) and 40 percent (= 1.5/3.54) of all new jobs.

How are the terms of potential lifetime employment determined in the core markets? No explicit clause regarding the "lifetimeness" of employment is actually contained in the contract. There is only an implicit understanding between the potential employer and the potential employee that an employment relation, if initiated, will continue, unless there arises a reasonable cause for either side to terminate it at an unforeseen future date. We can refer to such employment relations as *quasi-permanent employment.*

The only objective data available to potential employees for a decision to accept or reject a quasi-permanent employment offer are the current pay schedule of the potential employer and the past history of its managerial policy. Theoretically, the potential employee may be considered, as neoclassical economists would argue, superrational, so as to calculate his subjective probability of promotion speed based on his own assessment of his relative merit and his expectations of the growth of the firm. Then he may be able to calculate the expected lifetime earnings from permanent employment at the firm. Neoclassicists would say that what is transacted at the core market is the "implicit contract" of expected terms of employment over the entire course of the employment relationship. But I submit that postulating such hyperrationality of an individual does not shed light on the nature of the core labor markets nor on that of the J-firm.

First of all, the uncertainty involved in contracting quasi-permanent employment in the core market is considerably higher than that normally presupposed for the theory of implicit employment contracts, as developed by Costas Azariades and others.[27] In this theory, the length of an employment contract may be considered to be a few years, corresponding to the normal length of collective bargaining agreements in the United States. Further, contracted jobs would be standardized under job control unionism so that fixing the wage rate for the contract period with some objective probability of a layoff becomes feasible in practice and efficient in theory for the risk-neutral employer and risk-averse employee. However, lifetime employment may extend to almost 40 years, and the employment status of the potential employee during that period may vary because of many uncertain factors beyond the capability of rational calculation of any individual. Even if the individual is exceptionally talented and motivated, will elements of pure luck not play some role if he or she is to become president of the company? Will his or her tenure with the company not terminate at some unknown future date because of unexpected illness or bankruptcy of the company? Will the currently prosperous company continue to grow 40 years from now and guarantee the employee a handsome separation payment? And so on.

Further, one of the very reasons for the emergence of quasi-permanent employment is that the employer can rate an employee's productivity and motivation with much richer language and can reward the employee accordingly at a later date. Using educational credentials and other signals, the firm certainly screens its job candidates, but a candidate's potential and promotability cannot be assessed precisely because of adverse selection. Nor is this necessary. If the correspon-

[27] C. Azariades, "Implicit contracts and underemployment equilibria," *Journal of Political Economy,* 83 (1975), pp. 1183–202.

dence between productivity and reward is ensured ex post through long-term experience rating, it will suffice. Rather, lifetime employment is a rational adaptation to the "bounded rationality" of economic agents facing adverse selection, and therefore assuming superrationality for the analysis of this institution seems to miss the point.

Another important factor that argues against introducing the concept of implicit contracts to the analysis of the core market of quasi-permanent employment is that the probability of future promotion, layoff, early "voluntary" retirement, and so on will not be determined objectively, independently of future managerial policies and the cooperativeness of other employees not involved in the current transactions in the core market. Therefore, the objective implicit contract cannot be drawn up without binding management to a certain policy stance and involving incumbent and new employees in a mutual cooperative agreement.

Some might argue that although such multilateral, multipurpose agreements may be beyond the rationality of human beings, past behavioral patterns of a company can lead one to form reasonable expectations concerning the managerial policy stance of the company and its employees' attitudes and that such predictable patterns may be called "corporate culture." No doubt, corporate culture does play a role in a job candidate's assessment of future possibilities, yet it only provides a general framework for the behavior of participants in the firm. Concrete managerial actions, as well as employees' collective behavior, which affect individual earnings and promotability in actual situations, are yet to be specified sequentially as events evolve.

One may then characterize the nature of the core market as follows. It mediates the transaction of potential lifetime employment agreements subject to the implicit understanding that the employment relation may be terminated before the mandatory retirement age if the need arises on either side. The firm, on the demand side, does not make different offers to potential employees, but offers each an identical starting salary. The current pay structure agreed on with the enterprise-based union, as well as its corporate culture, however, provides general information regarding future possibilities for potential job applicants. Potential job applicants use this information and, together with their subjective assessment of their own relative merits, form general expectations regarding lifetime opportunities at the firm, however subjective and ambiguous they may be. If the general expectation of a potential applicant exceeds his or her reservation level, he or she will consider a career opportunity in the firm. The firm evaluates candidates according to their educational credentials and other available information. If there is a match, a contract of quasi-permanent employment is agreed upon.

This matching does not yet specify the terms of employment in the future. The revision of pay scale and the speed of individual advancements in salary and ranking have to be determined sequentially as events evolve. Thus we may posit that

> [U.1] The quasi-permanent employment contract in the core labor market is fundamentally incomplete and has to be supplemented by sequential bargaining internal to the firm.

What is the nature of this sequential internal bargaining? As already pointed out, job security and advancement opportunities for employees depend not only on the general state of the business environment, but also on the managerial policy (strategic business decisions) and the cooperativeness and motivation of employees. For instance, employees may have a better promotional opportunity if management pursues growth of the firm beyond the level that profit maximization would warrant. Also, employees may be committed to diligence if they are assured of job security beyond the level that profit maximization would warrant. Further, they may be more cooperative if they can expect some fairness in the differential treatment of employees in matters pertaining to pay schedules, layoffs, promotional opportunities, and so on.

However, bargaining over managerial policy and the fair treatment of diverse employees are, needless to say, beyond individual capacity. Because of the cost of quitting a promotional hierarchy in midcareer, the threat of departure (quit) cannot be an effective and credible means of having individual preferences heard within the firm. Yet the body of employees as a whole has considerable potential bargaining power over the determination of general pay level as well as other managerial policy matters relevant to the welfare of employees, since the cooperation of employees is vital to the efficient operation of the integrative information structure, as discussed in Chapter 2. This is the positive side of the situation. The normative side of it is that since the collectivity of employees embodying contextual skills becomes a set of truly firm-specific assets, this body has a legitimate claim on the distribution of quasi rents accruing to the firm. Before the body of employees can represent their preference concerning the general pay level and other managerial policy matters relevant to their well-being and can bargain with management effectively, collective bargaining needs to take place right at the level of the enterprise. This is why the enterprise-based union plays an important role in the J-firm: It represents the collective interest of incumbent employees and mediates it into decisions on intrafirm distribution and other managerial policies.[28]

The enterprise-based union of the J-firm normally organizes all regular nonmanagerial employees of the firm, both blue-collar and white-collar. This unique institution was not created directly by statutory provision, but rather evolved from the post–World War II industrial relational process (I deal with this historical process in Section 5.3). Section 5 of the Labor Union Act stipulates that a union can be protected by this act only if it has been recognized as an independent union by the neutral Labor Commission after scrutiny of its rule book. Since the right to organize a union is interpreted legally as a derivative of the fundamental human right to organize guaranteed in Article 28 of the Constitution, once it is recognized as an independent organization, any organization of employees or its agent has the right to bargain with management, however small its membership may be. Therefore, theoretically it is possible for the employees of one firm to be represented separately by rival unions or by an industrial union.

This legal framework differs significantly from the one in the United States, in which majority support by members of a bargaining unit in official balloting administered by the National Labor Relation Board endows the local chapter of an industrial union the exclusive right to represent the unit and to bargain with management. In the conventional view, the major difference in the collective bargaining framework in the United States and Japan is that the bargaining agent is the "industrial" union in the former and the "enterprise-based" union in the latter. But this distinction is not enlightening, because even in the United States the great majority of collective bargaining agreements in the manufacturing industry are made at the *enterprise* level,[29] whereas in Japan enterprise-level bargaining in one industry is often coordinated by an industrial federation of enterprise-based unions.

In my opinion, a greater difference can be found in the ways that preferences of different constituent members of a union within one enterprise are aggregated and represented vis-à-vis management.[30] In

[28] For the enterprise-based union, refer to Taishiro Shirai, "A theory of enterprise union," in Taishiro Shirai (ed.), *Industrial Relations in Japan,* University of Wisconsin Press, 1984, pp. 117–43.

[29] According to the 1976 Bureau of Labor Statistics survey of collective agreements covering 1,000 or more workers, 2.8 million workers in manufacturing are covered by agreements with single employers, while only 0.6 million workers are covered by agreements with multiemployers.

[30] For a comparison of legal frameworks between Japanese enterprise-based unionism and Western unionism and its economic efficiency implications, see M. Aoki, *The Cooperative Game Theory of the Firm,* Oxford University Press, 1984, chap. 9–11.

the United States the best strategy that the industrial union can follow to secure the majority support of its constituent members is to represent the preference of the median voter on relevant issues. This probably explains why the American union is more concerned with wage issues than job security issues, unless the job security of the majority of members is threatened by the closure of a factory and the like. Under the seniority rule of job security, workers who are most vulnerable to layoff are marginal young voters, and the median voter on the issue would be the one in the middle of the seniority order who is most likely protected from the threat of layoff in a normal situation.

Although the Japanese legal framework allows different interest groups of employees at one firm to be represented by separate organizations, the leadership of a union would prefer to represent all employees of the firm so that it can be an effective bargaining agent vis-à-vis management. The emergence of a rival union would certainly spoil the bargaining strength of a union. However, since majority support does not guarantee exclusive representation rights, as in the United States, union leadership must rely on consensus building to gain the support of different constituent members. Otherwise, the consistent negligence of minority interests may lead to the formation of a rival organization that represents those interests. Therefore the leadership of the enterprise-based union takes great pains to strike a balance between the interests of different groups: blue-collar and white-collar, senior and junior, male and female, and so on. Needless to say, this requires, great political skills on the part of union leaders.

It is quite natural, then, for leaders of the enterprise-based union to be mainly employees of the firm on leave from the payroll rather than professional bargainers versed in legal technicalities, and to have developed personal networks within the firm. It is also interesting to note that former officials of the enterprise-based union often have a good chance of being selected to the board of the firm because of their expertise in arbitration and the personal networks that they have built up during and after their tenure as union officials. According to a survey conducted by Nikkeiren (the Japan Management Association) in 1978, out of 6,457 directors of 352 respondent companies, 1,012 (15.7 percent) directors were former members of executive committees of their enterprise-based unions. But this practice seems to be gradually falling off because of the increasing bureaucratization of management and union structures in large firms.

In the normal course of affairs, in which the firm steadily grows, the aggregation of interest among different constituent groups through consensus is not impossible, although complicated. This consensus-building process within the union appears to be opaque for outside observers, and seems both complex and informal. However, when some important issue arises that would affect a segment of employees severely, such as large-scale discharges, it may be impossible to reach a consensus, and conflicts may become open and visible and may lead to the formation of a rival organization, customarily called the "second union." Disputes between rival unions formed under such circumstances are so bitter that communications among constituent members of different organizations can become impaired and can spoil the efficiency of the internal information-production system of the firm. It is only after the decisive weakening of one organization that the firm can implement the desired managerial decision that triggered the turmoil.

This observation may be taken to prove that the smooth mediation and representation of diverse interests among employees by a single enterprise-based union is crucial for the efficient working of the information-production system of the J-firm. Therefore we posit that

> [U.2] The enterprise-based union is a substructure of the J-firm through which the diverse interests of the quasi-permanent employees are mediated and represented as a collective interest vis-à-vis management.

The enterprise-based union not only negotiates with management about traditional bargainable subjects such as revising the annual pay scale, the average level of annual bonus payment, and general personnel policy (e.g., promotional criteria), but it is also briefed and consulted regularly by management about important strategic business decisions and their implementation (e.g., a layoff or the relocation of a factory) as well as the general state of business of the firm. Most top managers are not likely to make any important managerial decisions without first giving thought to the possible reactions of the enterprise-based union.

Thus, once the diverse preferences of the firm's employees are successfully aggregated through the intermediary of the enterprise-based union, the body of employees as a whole seems to have nonnegligible impact on managerial policy relevant to the well-being of the quasi-permanent employees. But the explicit and implicit collective bargaining done by the enterprise-based union only provides the general framework for individual competitions for the intrafirm careers that do not violate the common feeling of fairness among members. The sequential specification of individual terms of employment must be determined within that framework on the basis of the official evaluations of supervisors and the personnel department. Since contextual skill is to be specific to the organization, each individual may be considered to have potential bargaining power over the evaluation through the potential threat of noncooperation. In other words, implicit in the sequential specification of individual terms of employment over the course of entire careers may be individual bargaining complementing collective bargaining.

To summarize the argument in this section, it can be said that the incompleteness of the quasi-permanent contract transacted in the core labor market is closed by subsequent intrafirm bargaining, collective as well as individual. How then does such intrafirm bargaining affect the behavior of the J-firm? Is there anything in the behavior of the J-firm that is different from the neoclassical profit-maximizing firm, which is constrained only by labor market conditions (or collective bargaining agreements determined at a suprafirm level)? Do the fundamental incompleteness of quasi-permanent employment contracts and the emerging importance of intrafirm bargaining modify the nature of the J-firm from the neoclassical ideal type in any important way? We turn to these issues in Chapter 5.

Appendix.   An illustration of ranking hierarchy

This appendix illustrates the stylized structure of the pay ranking and promotion scheme of the J-firm, as described in Section 3.1, through the example of a case study drawn from the practices at Hitachi Manufacturing Co., which is one of the largest manufacturers of electric machinery in Japan and was the subject of a now classical comparative study, with a British company, made by Ronald Dore in the early 1970s.[31] All employees of Hitachi except for those engaged in managerial, engineering, and other specialist (research, design, and instruction) jobs are placed in one of the following job categories: (A1-3) planning jobs, which involve job planning and supervising its implementation; (B1-8) clerical jobs, which consist primarily of desk work; (C1-8) technician jobs, which consist of direct productive tasks, such as machining, assembling, finishing, welding, founding; (D1-8) nondirect productive tasks such as transportation, packaging, driving; and (F1-3) supervisory jobs such as that of foreman. The planning job categories have three basic pay ranks, the clerical and technician job categories have eight each, and the supervisory job categories have four. These ranks represent only the status differentiation and accompanying pay gradation, but not functional demarcation.

---

[31] Dore, *British Factory – Japanese Factory*.

Rank

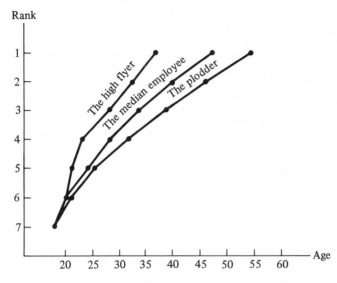

Figure 3.1. Promotion pattern for technical and clerical employees at Hitachi.

New entrants out of school are placed either into the clerical or tech-nician job categories, depending on their blue-collar or white-collar status. In the case of white-collar employees, junior high school grad-uates start their careers at the bottom eighth rank of the clerical job category, high school graduates at the seventh, technical school grad-uates at the sixth, college graduates at the fifth, and master's degree holders at the fourth. A similar arrangement applies to technician jobs, although very few college graduates are in this job category.

Promotion for high school graduates in the technician and clerical job categories roughly follows the pattern depicted in Figure 3.1. Beyond the first rank, the high-flyer clerical and technical job catego-ries may be advanced to the planning job and the supervisory (fore-men) categories, respectively. There are special titles at the top of each of these categories. In the case of the technician job category, there are first- and second-rank craftsmen *(kosho)* and master craftsmen *(koshi)*. Hitachi has about 30,000 employees in blue-collar jobs, and about 6,000 of these are in the first rank of the technician job category, 1,000 in the supervisory job category, and about 40 are master craftsmen. Master craftsmen have a prestigious position among blue-collar employees at Hitachi, and their status is symbolized by monthly din-ner meetings with the president of Hitachi.

At the top of the supervisory and planning job categories, we find

Table 3.6. *Pay increase by rank at Hitachi, 1986*

	Basic pay (yen)		Additional payments (%)	
	Average	Minimum	Average	Minimum
Planning job category				
Rank 1	4,700	2,820	55	47
Rank 2	3,900	2,340	49	42
Rank 3	3,300	2,050	43	37
Supervisory job category				
Rank 1	3,800	2,280	53	45
Rank 2	3,700	2,260	52	44
Rank 3	3,300	2,050	49	42
Rank 4	3,100	1,950	41	35
Clerical and technician job categories				
Rank 1	3,300	1,980	44	38
Rank 2	3,100	1,890	42	36
Rank 3	2,900	1,830	38	33
Rank 4	2,700	1,730	31	27
Rank 5	2,500	1,630	25	22
Rank 6	2,300	1,500	21	18
Rank 7	2,100	1,370	17	15
Rank 8	1,900	1,240	13	12

four special titles: *assistant sanji, associate sanji, sanji,* and *sanyo.* (These titles may vary from one company to another. Some companies have no such title system except for managerial positions.) Managerial positions, such as section directors *(ka-cho),* directors-general of a division *(bu-cho),* and plant managers *(jigyosho-cho)* are chosen from these titleholders. Therefore, theoretically there is a possibility, albeit slim, that blue-collar workers will be promoted to managerial positions via supervisory jobs. This "blue sky ceiling" arrangement (meaning no upper ceiling for promotion) was introduced after a tumultuous labor dispute in 1950. Hitachi offers no special allowance for managerial jobs as such. The basic salaries of managers are determined entirely by their titles. On the other hand, there are titleholders who do not hold any managerial position.

Based on the collective agreement reached between Hitachi and the Hitachi Labor Union in the Spring Offensive of 1986, the average and minimum basic pay *(kihon-kyu)* increase for each rank in various job categories and the average and minimum percentages of additional payments *(kakyu)* made according to individual merit assessment are shown in Table 3.6. An employee's basic pay and merit supplement increase every year because of two factors: the negotiated "base up" in the basic salary in each rank, as shown in Table 3.6, and personal advancement, if any, in rank. According to Table 3.6, there are non-negligible differences between the average and minimum figures; these indicate a fair amount of room for supervisory merit assessment. But it is said that the merit assessment is emphasized more at Hitachi than at other comparable companies.

At Hitachi, the basic pay and the additional merit payment are supplemented by the job-related payment *(shokumukyu)*, which is based in principle on the American-style job evaluation scheme. But as already noted, because of the fluidity and ambiguity of job classifications, job evaluation at Hitachi is in practice the disguised evaluation of personal attributes. As a consequence, individual positions on the job payment scale and the basic pay scale are highly correlated. Further, there are considerably fewer job classifications at Hitachi than at unionized American companies. There are only 9 job classes in the technician job category. (There can be more than 100 blue-collar job titles at a unionized electric machinery company in the United States.) The job-related payment differential between the lowest job class in the technician job category (blue-collar job category) and the highest job class in the supervisory job category (foremen category) is only 169 percent, a considerably lower figure than observed in typical American companies.

On the average, 36.5 percent of the monthly earnings of Hitachi employees are paid in the form of basic pay, 27.0 percent in merit supplement, 29.2 percent in job-related supplement, and the rest (7.2 percent) in various allowances. In addition to the monthly earnings thus determined, Hitachi and its labor union agreed at the end of 1985 to give regular employees bonus payments equivalent on the average to 5.34 months of earnings, to be paid in two installments, in December 1985 and June 1986. This amount is much higher than the national average. Individual payment of a bonus is the total of two components: two months' equivalent of the job-related payment plus a multiple of one month's basic pay. The multiplier is composed of two parts: an evaluation parameter determined individually by the supervisory merit assessment and a diligence parameter objectivly formulated on the basis of the days of work. The average and minimum values of the evaluation parameter for each pay rank are determined in the collective agreement, thus limiting the range of supervisory discretion to some extent. The value of the evaluation parameter goes up fairly sharply, as the pay rank (accordingly years of employment) progresses. For instance, the negotiated average parameter value for the first-rank employees in the clerical and technical job categories was

486, that for the fourth rank was 290, and that for the eighth rank was 178. The differential between the average and minimum for each pay rank is also great. The negotiated minimum values of the evaluation parameter for the first, fourth, and eighth ranks were 152, 51, and 12, respectively. Thus, in the bonus payment a much wider differential can be created among employees in different ranks as well as in the same rank.

The amount of separation pay at mandatory retirement at Hitachi is basically determined by three factors: the amount of basic pay at the time of retirement, the years of employment, and the nature of retirement (whether it is mandatory or not). For example, a second-rank craftsman who retires at the age of 55 after 25, 30, 35 years of service at Hitachi receives 8.6 million yen, 11.7 million yen, and 12.4 million yen, respectively, as the separation payment, about 70 percent of which is paid in a lump sum at the time of retirement and the rest as supplementary contributions to the national pension. No direct merit assessment by the supervisor is involved in the calculation of separation payments, but since the amount of basic pay at the time of separation is determined by the terminal rank that the retiree has achieved, in retrospect the cumulative assessment over an employee's entire career at Hitachi indirectly affects the amount of separation payment.

CHAPTER 4

Corporate finance, stockholding returns, and corporate governance structure

In Chapter 2, we saw that the A-firm relies on economies of speciali-zation. This characteristic has generated two important consequences: the development of well-organized markets external to the firm for standardized jobs; and the emergence of job-control unionism, under which jobs are allocated and paid within the firm according to the well-articulated job-evaluation scheme. Economists have come to call this intrafirm job allocation mechanism the internal labor market. The widely accepted neoclassical notion of the firm has been formulated to reflect such developments. The basic rates of pay for all employees of the firm, including managers, are determined in the external and inter-nal labor markets, and the residual of revenue after all contractual pay-ment is made – that is, the quasi rent in economic terminology – is accruable to the ultimate controller of the firm. This ultimate control-ler cum residual claimant is identified with the body of stockholders. This body exercises, or should be made to exercise if it does not or is prevented from doing so, ultimate control over the business and affairs of the firm by selecting the board of directors, which is in turn respon-sible for selecting the executive management responsible for the hier-archical control of the internal labor market.

On the other hand, a reasonable impression for the reader to have gained so far may be that the quasi-permanent employee of the J-firm has achieved a clear status in the firm that does not dissolve in the market mechanism. In contrast, the position of the stockholder of the J-firm may appear to be rather weak at first glance. The board of direc-tors of the J-firm is essentially a meeting of senior managers of the firm promoted from within, sprinkled with only a few outsiders represent-ing close business partners, such as banks. The chief executive officer, *shacho,* is normally appointed by the retiring predecessor, and the stockholders' meeting has very limited de facto power over selecting, supervising, or monitoring management of the firm. The threat of unfriendly takeover can scarcely be exercised either, because of an effective insulative measure (which I discuss later) mutually taken by managements of a group of firms. According to some people, further

99

evidence of the weak position of stockholders, although it is not well founded on economic theory, is the fact that the average rate of dividends per share is very low relative to price.

From these developments, a rather unique common sense notion of firm membership has arisen in Japan. In casual conversation, the Japanese word, *shain* (member of the firm), is used to refer to the quasi-permanent employee of the corporate firm, although it means the stockholder of the corporation in the legal definition given in the Commercial Code (Corporate Law). This schism between the common sense notion and the legal definition poses some interesting questions: Which of the two may be considered to provide a more reasonable concept of the J-firm from the viewpoint of economics? Has the legal definition of firm members become a mere fiction in legal documents in Japan, and has the J-firm in effect come to be taken over by, and controlled on behalf of, its quasi-permanent employee? Or is this merely a superficial view, and does the neoclassical doctrine of stockholder sovereignty – which assumes share price maximization as a dynamic analogue of profit maximization – have universal scientific validity, in spite of the apparently unique organization of the Japanese corporate firm?

Most econometric research on corporate behavior by the Japanese seems to have accepted the neoclassical doctrine of share price maximization without careful scrutiny. The weak explanatory power of such a hypothesis is dealt with by adding ad hoc assumptions, such as, flexible employment adjustment by the firm is not costless. However, in-depth neoclassical inquiry into the role of the stock market as a management-disciplinary mechansim and into the principal–agent relation between stockholders and management has not been attempted in the context of the Japanese institution. The reason, I suspect, is that it seems intuitively odd and unrealistic to pose such questions in the Japanese setting.

On the other hand, the view that the J-firm is actually controlled by and managed on the behalf of its employees has recently been gaining some authoritative support. Ryutaro Komiya, one of the leading neoclassical economists in Japan, has been converted to such a view. He has argued that "management is to be characterized as the representative of the employee group. This is something unique to Japanese firms with practically no parallels in other countries. A manager who makes light of employees' interests cannot retain his position, or rather, cannot achieve such a status," although Komiya cautions that "the striking weakness of Japanese stockholders' control over the management of the firm . . . does not imply that their interests are neglected."[1] Abegglen, who is a foremost Western authority on Japanese management, and Stalk have devoted an entire chapter to the question of "Who owns the *kaisha*?"[2] They have argued that "the shareholder in the *kaisha* is in the position of an investor, but is in no operational sense in control of the company" (p. 191). Further, "the *kaisha* becomes in a real sense the property of the people who make it up. It will not be sold, in whole or in part, without the specific approval of all of its directors, acting on behalf of its employees. Earnings of the company go first as a return to investors, with the entire balance going to ensure the company's future and thus ensure the future of its employees" (pp. 207–8). Thus the employee of the *kaisha* is looked upon as the ultimate controller cum residual claimant. The neoclassical notion of the firm is completely reversed here.

However, my immediate reactions to this characterization of the J-firm *(kaisha)* are as follows: If the *kaisha* is really owned by quasi-permanent employees, why does the body of employees not have the power to regain more explicit control over the firm in the event of bankruptcy? Why are employees susceptible to discharges at their own cost? Why are senior employees the ones most vulnerable to layoff? Are they not in the strongest position with respect to the property ownership of the firm, by virtue of their seniority?

In Chapter 5, I present an alternative hypothesis: that the J-firm is a *coalition* of the body of stockholders and the body of employees, integrated and mediated by management, which acts to strike a balance between the interests of both sides. This hypothesis may appear eclectic at first, but its implications can be worked out in a rigorous analytical framework of bargaining game theory to provide a rather rich theoretical explanation for the apparently unique structure and behavior of the J-firm. Chapter 3 has provided a preliminary step toward that hypothesis in dealing with the human side of the J-firm. This chapter takes the next step and deals with the capital side.

Section 1 provides stylized facts about the stockholding structure and corporate finance of the J-firm. Three major types of stockholders are identified: the bank stockholder, nonfinancial corporate stockholder, and individual stockholder. Although the position of the individual stockholder appears to have declined somewhat, the J-firm has

---

[1] R. Komiya, "Japanese firms, Chinese firms: problems for economic reforms in China. Part I," *Journal of the Japanese and International Economies,* 1 (March 1987), pp. 41, 43.

[2] J. Abegglen and G. Stakes, Jr., *Kaisha: The Japanese Corporation,* Basic Books, 1986.

clearly delivered rates of return to individual stockholders that are at least comparable to those from the A-firm. Evidence is also presented to show that equity financing has become the dominant means of investment financing since the mid-1970s and that bank financing has fallen off.

Section 2 deals with theoretical issues concerning the dual role of the bank as stockholder cum lender: What is the motive of the bank to hold stock of the J-firm? Is there any conflict of interest between the individual investor and the bank in their capacity as stockholders? Why has the bank's role in corporate financing become less important recently? Is it because the rate of investment has declined, or is there some other reason? What implication does the declining role of the bank have for the position of the individual stockholder in particular and for the direction of strategic business decision making of the J-firm in general?

Using the data in Section 1 and the theoretical analysis in Section 2, I then discuss the position of the individual stockholder in the corporate governance structure of the J-firm. I argue that the individual stockholder of the J-firm is neither in a commanding position, as the neoclassical paradigm would suggest, nor in the position of an outcast dominated by the body of employees. Rather, the stockholder is part of a stable constituent body of the J-firm. The discussion in the concluding section paves the way for the construction of the bargaining game–theoretic model of the J-firm in Chapter 5.

1.   Stylized facts

A.   Corporate finance

Once established by the capital contribution of the initial stockholder, the firm may raise additional financial resources by issuing new equity, incurring long-term (fixed) debt, and retaining profits (by the long term I mean a period not shorter than one year). As is well known, in the idealized neoclassical world envisioned by Franco Modigliani and Merton Miller, in which the frictionless perfectly competitive market operates and no tax disturbs its working, it does not matter to the firm which means of financing is chosen. They serve the interests of the stockholder of the firm equally. Needless to say, however, the real economy in which we live has inescapable traces of a host of taxes levied on corporations and individuals, as well as the interposition of gigantic financial intermediaries between the wealthholder and the firm. Depending on the characteristics of tax schemes and financial institutions, as well as the regulatory mechanism surrounding financial intermediaries, a distinct pattern of corporate finance will emerge.

Let us denote the amount of paid-in capital, the amount of long-term debt, and the accumulated amount of retained profits at time T by $K(T)$, $D(T)$, and $R(T)$, respectively. The sum of $K(T)$ and $R(T)$ is called stockholder equity capital $E(T)$, implying that it is the contribution by stockholders. As time passes, some original stockholders may sell their shares in the market and other investors may purchase them and/or subscribe to new stock issues. Let us call a collectivity of stockholders at any point in time the body of stockholders. In the J-firm, as we see in detail in the next subsection, this body is composed of three major groups: banks and other financial institutions, nonfinancial business corporations, and individual investors. Their interests need not be the same. (I discuss the motives of stockholding for different groups in the next section.)

Long-term debt of the J-firm at any time T, $D(T)$, is roughly composed of long-term borrowing from banks and other financial intermediaries such as insurance companies and agricultural cooperatives, $DB(T)$; long-term bonds, $B(T)$; and reserves for employees' separation payment, $SP(T)$. The last item that appears in the balance sheet of the J-firm represents the funds actually accumulated and reserved within the firm according to a tax rule described later, not to be confused with unfunded pension liabilities of the A-firm.[3]

The J-firm also incurs current liabilities while running its business. The current liabilities at time T, $CL(T)$, are roughly composed of short-term borrowings from banks and trade accounts and notes payable. Some portion of short-term debt is often rolled over beyond a contractual loan period so that it is actually a disguised long-term liability. In addition, the current portion of long-term debt to be payable within a year is recorded as short-term debt. The sum of current liabilities and long-term debt is simply called liabilities $L(T)$ [$= CL(T) + D(T)$].

Figure 4.1 depicts the time series of the average composition of equity capital and liabilities of 865 manufacturing companies listed on the Tokyo Stock Exchange continuously over the period March 1966 through March 1987. Let us assume that the average figures from various financial data for these companies, compiled by the Nikkei Eco-

---

[3] In addition, before the revision of the Commercial Code in October 1982, Japanese companies were allowed to accumulate various nontaxable reserves to protect against price fluctuation, overseas market development, losses due to exchange rate fluctuation, etc., and record them as long-term liabilities. They were de facto retained profits and have been included in equity capital since 1983.

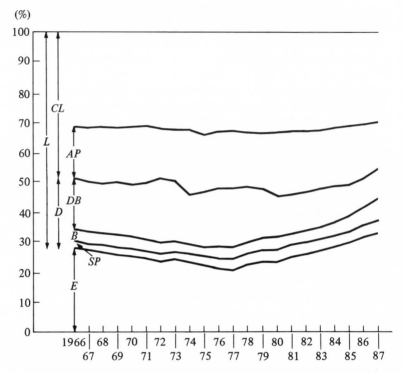

Figure 4.1. The relative composition of liabilities and equity capital of all listed manufacturing companies, 1966–87 (end of March). Key: L = ratio of liabilities to total assets, CL = ratio of current liabilities to total assets, AP = ratio of trade accounts and notes payable to total assets, D = ratio of long-term debt to total assets, DB = ratio of long-term borrowings to total assets, B = ratio of long-term bonds to total assets, SP = ratio of reserves for separation payment to total assets, E = ratio of equity capital plus legal specific reserves other than SP to total assets. *Source:* NEEDS.

nomic Electronic Data System (NEEDS), provide the corresponding financial status for our stylized construct, the J-firm. A quick glance at Figure 4.1 suggests that the J-firm incurs high liabilities relative to its own equity capital. For example, the average ratio of total liabilities L = $CL + D$ to the sum of liabilities and equity capital (the debt/asset ratio = $L/(L + E)$) for the 865 manufacturing companies was 68.4 percent at the end of March 1986 (66.9 percent at the end of March 1987). The equivalent ratio for all American manufacturing companies with assets of more than \$250 million was 55.5 percent at the end of the first quarter of 1986, according to the *Quarterly Report* of the Federal Trade Commission (hereafter I refer to this survey as the *FTC Report*). This difference is often casually quoted to indicate the heavy dependence of the J-firm on debt financing. I submit that such a straightforward comparison and casually derived implication are misleading, because of differences in accounting practices between the two countries and the unique organizational and transactional characteristics of the J-firm.

The total financial resources of the J-firm raised by contributions of the body of stockholders (equity capital) and the current as well as long-term liabilities are allocated between current assets, $CA(T)$, and fixed assets, $FA(T)$, at time T. By the accounting identity,

$$CA(T) + FA(T) = L(T) + E(T).$$

Current assets include cash and deposits, short-term securities, trade accounts, and notes receivable, as well as physical inventories of materials and products. Fixed assets include tangible assets such as land, machines, equipment, and buildings, as well as nontangible assets such as investments in subsidiaries and securities intended to be held for a long term.

Figure 4.2 depicts the time series of composition of assets for the 865 companies described earlier. Parallel to the high ratio of current liabilities relative to the total of equity capital and liabilities, we observe here the high ratio of current assets relative to the total assets (59.9 percent at the end of March 1986 and 59.0 percent at the end of March 1987). According to the *FTC Report,* a comparable figure for the American companies was on average 34.7 percent at the end of March 1986. The relatively higher ratio for the J-firm is also often quoted as evidence of the inefficiency of financial management in the J-firm. There may be some element of truth in this claim, but again we need to take into account the different accounting, organizational, and transactional practices in the two countries.

Consider now some of these factors that contribute to the apparently high ratio of liabilities (current assets) to total assets at the J-firm. First, fixed assets are normally recorded at their acquisition value in the balance sheet of the J-firm, and there is a large gap between the book value of fixed assets and their actual value. In other words, the J-firm has accumulated a substantial amount of off-balance sheet assets, *fukumi-shisan,* in the form of capital gains. This can be inferred from one statistic: The price index of land for industrial use constructed by the Institute of Real Estate Research was 3,877 at the end of March 1986, whereas it was 911 at the end of March 1965 (100 at the end of March

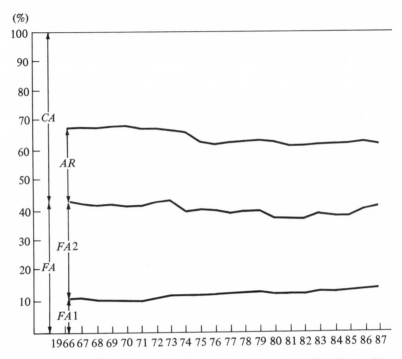

Figure 4.2. The relative composition of assets of all listed manufacturing companies, 1966–87 (end of March). Key: *CA* = ratio of current assets to total assets, *AR* = ratio of trade accounts and notes receivable to total assets, *FA* = ratio of fixed assets to total assets, *FA2* = ratio of investment in tangible and intangible fixed assets to total assets, *FA1* = ratio of long-term investments in subsidiaries and other related firms to total assets. *Source:* NEEDS.

1955). The price of land more than quadrupled in that period. Since banks normally require companies to place collateral, particularly in the form of real estate, against long-term loans, the distortion of the degree of indebtedness of the J-firm due to the lack of asset revaluation should be corrected in order to gain a real picture of the financial position of the J-firm.

According to the aggregated balance sheet of the 865 manufacturing companies in question, the proportions of land value and long-term investments in subsidiaries and other related companies relative to total assets were 4.0 and 8.5 percent, respectively, at the end of 1985. However, the ratio of market value of land owned by the nonfinancial companies as a whole to the total value of assets net of intercorporate stockholding (estimated by the Economic Planning Agency and reported in the *National Accounts*) was 24.7 percent at the end of 1984. If we make a bold assumption that the 865 companies held exactly the same proportion of their assets (net of investment in other companies) in the form of land at the end of March 1985 as the nonfinancial companies as a whole did at the end of 1984, we estimate that those companies had off-balance sheet assets in the form of land equivalent to 18.6 percent of their total assets. When this estimated capital gains from landholding accrues to the value of equity capital, the relative ratio of liabilities to the total assets goes down from 70.5 to 59.4 percent.[4] A similar adjustment is needed for other fixed assets as well, although this is not attempted here.[5]

Second, the proportion of short-term borrowing from banks and other financial institutions relative to total assets was on average 12.1 percent during the period April 1, 1981, to March 31, 1985, for the 865 companies; this figure is very high in comparision with that for American firms (3.2 percent at the end of March 1985 in the *FTC Report*). This comparatively high ratio of short-term borrowing is paralleled by a high ratio of cash and deposits on the asset side. The latter ratio was on the average 11.5 percent during the same period for the Japanese companies (2.0 percent for the American companies mentioned in the *FTC Quarterly Report*). Initially, it may be thought that, since the figures are aggregated ones, some Japanese companies borrow short, whereas others lend short. But in fact many companies, except for a few excellent companies, borrow short and at the same time hold nonnegligible portions of their assets in the form of cash and deposits.[6]

The consistently high ratio of cash to assets observed for companies incurring relatively high short-term and long-term bank debt appears

---

[4] By the assumption, the percentage ratio x of capital gains in landholding to total assets of those companies in 1985 is given by $[x + 4.0]/[100.0 - 8.5] = 0.247$. Solving this, we get $x = 18.6$. Then the revised liabilities/asset ratio would be $70.5/[100.0 + 18.6] = 59.4$.

[5] For the reevaluation of depreciable physical assets for inflation, see Albert Ando and Alan Auerbach, "The corporate cost of capital in Japan and the U. S.: a comparison," mimeographed, *National Bureau of Economic Research Working Paper, No. 1762*, 1985.

[6] The cash (including deposits)/assets ratio is volatile and erratic for those excellent companies with no debt, such as Toyota and Matsushita (for example, it was 3.1 percent for Matsushita at the end of March 1985 and 5.5 percent for Toyota at the end of March 1981, but the ratio sometimes exceeded 15 percent). This volatility is explained by the fact that there have emerged high-yield short-term money assets, such as the unregulated certificate of deposit (CD), as a result of financial deregulation, and those companies have been shifting the forms of their current asset holdings flexibly between those money assets and other liquid assets, such as short-term securities, as a part of financial management known as *zai-teku* in Japan.

to be an effect of the practice of "compensating balance" between the bank and its customer company. When the former extends credit to the latter, the latter is normally required to set aside a certain portion of the borrowed amount and retain it as a compensating deposit. The rate of retention is determined by bilateral negotiation between the bank and the borrower. This is where the relative bargaining power of the two parties as well as the general condition of the credit market comes into play. As long as the retention rate is positive, the borrowing company must borrow in excess of its actual needs and the amount appears on both the liability and asset sides of its balance sheet, making the debt/equity ratio seem higher. Also, the higher the retention ratio, the higher the effective interest rate on the borrowed funds at the disposal of the borrower. In spite of the apparent rigidity of the contractual interest rate on the long-term loan, the bank can adjust its effective rate flexibly, over time as well as across borrowers, to the extent that the bank can control the retention ratio.

The practice of the "compensating balance" developed originally from the bank's desire to maintain the customer's relation (relational contracting) with the borrowing company, but its implementability was derived from the bank's traditionally strong bargaining power vis-à-vis the borrower owing to the scarcity of other financial instruments, such as bonds issued in the home market and abroad. However, the practice is said to have been weakened recently, particularly for large companies, by the liberalization of the financial market, relatively easy monetary supply, and more efficient portfolio management of the J-firm.[7]

The third factor contributing to the high debt/asset ratio of the J-firm is the relatively high number of trade accounts and notes payable. The average proportion of these to total assets for the 865 companies was 21.3 percent at the end of March 1985. This figure is more than twice as large as that of their American counterparts (7.5 percent at the end of March 1985 in the *FTC Report*). Again, this comparably high

---

[7] For example, at the end of March 1974 when credit was tightened and the official discount rate was set at 9 percent, Nippon Steel had cash and deposits equivalent to 20.3 percent of total short-term and long-term borrowing, but at the end of March 1984 when the discount rate was lowered to 5 percent, the ratio of cash to total borrowings outstanding was lowered to 18.0 percent. During this period, Nippon Steel also shifted the source of long-term debt from bank borrowing to long-term bond issues. At the end of March 1974, its long-term borrowings outstanding were 5.8 times as much as bonds outstanding, but only 2.3 times at the end of March 1984, indicating less dependence on banks. But for 59 listed companies in the textile industry, the ratio of cash to total borrowing outstanding was 40.2 percent at the end of 1974 and remained at 39.1 percent at the end of 1984, indicating their much weaker bargaining power vis-à-vis banks.

ratio is paralleled by the high ratio of trade accounts and notes receivable on the asset side of the balance sheet, which was 24.1 percent at the end of March 1985 (13.4 percent at the end of 1980 for the *FTC Survey*). The J-firm relies heavily on trade credits because of the following industrial organizational characteristics (to be discussed in more detail in Chapter 6).

Japanese manufacturing companies tend to keep their size relatively small in terms of their own operations (as measured by number of employees) by spinning off upstream processes as partly owned subsidiaries or by relying on supply firms on a long-term basis in which they often have minority interests. Although the payments for transactions with those partly owned and related suppliers are normally in the form of trade credits, those transactions should be regarded as (quasi-) internal transactions.[8] The large manufacturing companies can usually write off their trade debts to smaller suppliers in relational contracting if they wish, but the latter prefer to sell on short-term credit, because the notes issued by the major companies are brought to banks for discount and "signal" the creditworthiness of the suppliers. This helps them to raise long-term funds for investment from the bank without much ado. The evidence of relational contracting with major companies serves the same role as a high credit rating in the American bond market.

Another factor to consider is the nature of the reserves used for employee separation pay, *SP,* in the J-firm and its implications for corporate finance in the J-firm. Japanese companies are allowed to set aside tax-free a fixed percentage, α (50 percent up to 1979 and 40 percent thereafter, with some transitory adjustment), of the total hypothetical obligation of separation payments at the end of each accounting year under the assumption that all employees retire at that time. The separation payment actually made during the accounting year should be charged against these reserves, and the difference between the tax-free limit and the remaining balance of the reserves at the end of the accounting year can be charged as an expense. The payment is fully deductible for corporate income purposes. The firm may reserve more than the tax-free limit, but the accumulation of an additional

---

[8] For example, for Matsushita, of trade debts amounting to 17.2 percent of its assets existing at the end of November 1984, 6.4 percent was with consolidated subsidiaries and 1.1 percent was with unconsolidated subsidiaries and related companies, where a subsidiary means a company of which majority shares are owned by a parent company and a related company means a company of which more than 20 percent of stock is owned by a parent company. For Toyota, out of trade debts amounting to 11.6 percent of its assets existing at the end of December 1985, 6.6 percent was with subsidiaries and related companies.

amount would be subject to normal corporate income tax. Although the reserves are listed as long-term debts of the firm, if one considers the nature of quasi-permanent membership of the employee in the firm, it is apparent that they are considerably different from other liabilities. Rather, they may be understood as de facto capital contributions by the quasi-permanent employee. As noted in Chapter 3, the quasi-permanent employee can be said to be purchasing a membership in the J-firm by bearing the cost of accumulating contextual skill as well as posting incentive bond. A part of the returns to this investment in training (not paid in the form of seniority premium during the tenure) and bond is contributed to the capital formation of the J-firm. When employees terminate their membership (mandatory retirement), they recover their contribution, which is returned in the form of the separation payment.

As employees are legally entitled to receive full separation payments before any other corporate liabilities are taken into account in the case of corporate reorganization, the body of employees may be considered to have de facto property rights in corporate assets equal to 100 percent of the total separation pay claims; and actual stockholders' equity may accordingly be reduced by the amount equal to the unfunded amount of separation payment obligations. If the firm accumulates and reports only the legal tax-free limit, then the employees' de facto contributions to the capital formation of the employing firm would be $SP(T) \times [100/\alpha]$. Then the ratio

$$\{SP(T) \times [100/\alpha]\}/\{SP(T) + E(T)\}$$

represents the potential maximum proportion of employees' contributions in the "own" capital of the firm, when they are regarded as constituent members of the firm. Table 4.1 provides the ratio of "reported" reserves for separation payment to the sum of equity capital and all tax-free reserves, $SP(T)/\{SP(T) + E(T)\}$, and the above defined ratio for the 865 listed manufacturing companies. The actual rate is somewhere between the reported ratio and the potential maximum. Note that the degree of employees' contributions increased from the 1960s to the late 1970s and is currently somewhere between 10 and 26 percent.

We have seen that the degree of indebtedness of the J-firm is over-represented in the official balance sheet of the J-firm for a variety of reasons. Let us now examine how much the J-firm relies on debt for its investment financing in flow terms. For any variable, $X(T)$, so far defined, denote the increment, $X(T) - X(T - 1)$, by $dX(T)$. For instance $dFA(T)$ implies the net increase in fixed assets in the period

Table 4.1. *Employees' relative contribution to capital formation in all listed manufacturing companies, 1969–87 (end of March)*

	Reported	Potential maximum
1969	0.083	0.166
1974	0.109	0.218
1979	0.141	0.282
1984	0.115	0.288
1987	0.104	0.260

Note: The reported numbers refer to the ratio of reported reserves for separation payments to the sum of equity capital and all tax-free reserves. The potential maxima refer to the reported numbers times the inverse of the legally set percentage ratio of tax-free reserves to the total separation payment obligations (50% before 1979 and 40% thereafter).
Source: NEEDS.

ending at T. Figure 4.3 provides various aggregate ratios for the sources of investment financing (financing for fixed assets) of the 865 manufacturing companies. The ratios, $dE(T)/dFA(T)$ roughly indicates how the magnitude of the net accumulation of stockholder equity and new equity issues in those companies have changed over time relative to the amount of net investments in fixed assets. The ratios, $dB(T)/dFA(T)$ and $dDB(T)/dFA(T)$ indicate the portions of fixed asset investment financed by new bond issue and new borrowing. The figure shows that in the period 1966–75 the accumulation of stockholder equity fell short of one-half of the amount of investment in fixed assets. Specifically, new stock issues provided funds covering only about 10 percent of new capital expenditures in fixed assets. Those companies were able to cover the rest of the cost of fixed investment by incurring various long-term liabilities, specifically borrowings from banks.

After the mid-1970s, the financial situation of those companies changed dramatically. Stockholder equity accumulated faster than fixed investments. Companies also shifted their source of long-term liabilities from banks to bond markets. Utilizing new opportunities for bond issues, home and abroad, and relying on improved profitabilities, those companies have reduced the amount of long-term debt from banks even in absolute amounts. Thus the commonplace view that the

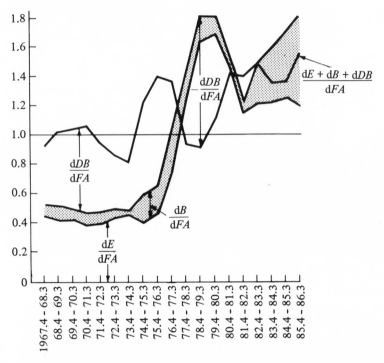

Figure 4.3. The ratios of sources of long-term funds to investments in fixed assets, 1967–86 (three-year moving average). Key: dE/dFA = ratio of increase in equity capital to investment in fixed asset, dDB/dFA = ratio of long-term bond issues to investment in fixed asset, dB/dFA = ratio of increase (decrease) in long-term borrowing to investment in fixed assets. *Source:* NEEDS.

J-firm is able to grow faster because it can raise investible funds at low cost from banks does not seem to provide a precise picture of the recent corporate finance of the J-firm.[9]

---

[9] When the "cost of capital" is compared across countries, the weighted sum of the interest rate and the rate of return to stockholding is used, with weights being given by $L/(L + E)$ and $E/(L + E)$, respectively. Some authors, such as G. N. Hatsopoulos and Ralph Landau, have argued that the cost of capital is much lower in Japan, using such a construct. If the rate of interest is lower than the rate of return to stockholding, then a higher weight on the former leads to a lower estimate of the cost of capital. As argued in this section, the unadjusted ratio, $L/(L + E)$, calculated from the financial statements of Japanese companies is much too high to represent the real indebtness of those companies. Further, the effective interest rate borne by those companies may be higher than the nominal rate of lending, as customarily used in the calculation of the cost of

B.   *Returns to stockholding*

Consider the structure of returns to stockholding. Suppose that time consists of periods of equal duration, denoted by $T = 0, 1, 2, \ldots$. $T = 0$ is the time of the initial incorporation of the firm. Suppose for simplicity's sake that there is no new stock issue after the initial incorporation. Let us denote the value of total stock at the beginning of period T by $V(T)$. The J-firm normally determines the amount in dividends $d(T)$ at the end of period T in reference to the value of $V(0)$, that is, the par value of stock. It maintains annual dividend payments as a fixed percentage of the par value, usually somewhere between 10 and 15 percent of the par value of stock. This proportion may change, depending on the level of current profits, but with considerable inertia. When an operating loss is incurred in the current year, the J-firm first tries to make it up by realizing capital gains from stockholding or landholding in order to deliver the conventional rate of dividends. However, if losses continue beyond the current period, then dividends may be lowered. In an extreme case, $d(T) = 0$. Because of this practice, the proportion of dividend payouts to before-tax earnings in the entire corporate sector is on the average only about 10 percent in the past several years. U.S. and European dividends tend to be more flexibly adjusted in relation to current corporate earnings, usually about half of earnings.

Suppose that the profit in the T-th period is $P(T)$, the corporate tax rate applicable to retained profit is t_c, and the rate applicable to distributed profit t_{cd}. Then

$$E(T) - E(T - 1) = P(T)(1 - t_c) - d(T)(1 - t_c + t_{cd}).$$

Suppose further that the book value of fixed assets differs from the actual value at the end of the period T by $OB(T)$. Such off-balance sheet assets can be created if the market values of land and securities owned by the firm appreciate over time while the balance sheet records only those acquisition values, a common practice at the J-firm. If the

capital, because of the practice of compensating balance. On the other hand, there is no convincing reason to believe that the average rate of returns to stockholding in Japan is lower than elsewhere. See the next section for a discussion of this. Finally, the cost of capital which is relevant to investment decisions should be the marginal rate rather than the average rate as calculated above. G. N. Hatsopoulos and R. Landau, "Capital formation in the United States and Japan," in R. Landau and Nathan Rosenberg (eds.), *A Positive Sum Strategy,* National Academy Press, 1986, pp. 583–606. See also G. N. Hatsopoulos and S. H. Brooks, "The gap in the cost of capital: causes, effects and remedies," in R. Landau and D. W. Jorgenson, (eds.), *Technology and Economic Policy,* Ballinger, 1986.

market is rational in the sense that the market value of stock at the beginning of the $T + 1$ period reflects the sum of the book value of stockholder equity and the off-balance sheet assets at the end of the period T precisely so that

$$V(T + 1) = E(T) + OB(T),$$

then

$$dV(T) = P(T)(1 - t_c) - d(T)(1 - t_c + t_{cd}) + dOB(T),$$

where

$$dV(T) = V(T + 1) - V(T) \text{ and } dOB(T) = OB(T) - OB(T - 1).$$

Market gains from stockholding for one period consist of two parts: capital gains $dV(T)$ and dividends $d(T)$. Suppose that the tax rate applicable to capital gains is t_g and the tax rate applicable to dividends is t_d. Then the market rate of after-tax returns from stockholding from the beginning of period T to the beginning of the next period is given by

$$\frac{dV(T)(1 - t_g)}{V(T)} + \frac{d(T)(1 - t_d)}{V(T)}. \tag{S.R}$$

From the above two formulas, if $(1 - t_g)(1 - t_c + t_{cd}) > (1 - t_d)$, the stockholder is better off if the firm reduces the dividend payout and delivers its earnings to stockholders in the form of capital gains, and vice versa.

Applicable tax rates differ depending on the characteristics of a stockholder. If he/she is an individual investor, his/her capital gains are not taxable ($t_g = 0$) and his/her dividends are taxed at source at 20 percent if the amount of dividend income per stock is less than ¥100 thousand, 35 percent otherwise. Corporate tax rates are $t_c = 0.433$ and $t_{cb} = 0.333$ in 1986. He/she clearly prefers profit to be retained to dividend payout. If a stockholder is a corporation, one-fourth of the difference between dividend income and its imputed acquisition cost is taxed at the ordinary corporate tax rate t_c, so that the effective rate t_d is relatively lower than the corporate tax rate, while the realized capital gains are added to corporate earnings subject to the ordinary corporate tax rate t_c. Therefore, unless the corporation reports a negative profit, it prefers dividends to capital gains.

At the end of 1980, the relative share of individual stockholding in the total listed stock was 29.2 percent and individual shares in total stock sales during 1981 were 41.5 percent. On the other hand, the relative share of bank stockholding was 17.9 percent, and that of sales was only 3.1 percent. This contrasting behavioral pattern of individuals and banks is consistent with the above observation.

Table 4.2. *Annual after-tax market rate of return to individual stockholding, 1963–86 (percent)*

Year	(1) d/V	(2) dV/V	(3) 1 − t	(4) (1) × (3)	(5) (2) + (4)	(6) dP/P	(7) (5) − (6)
1963	5.6	13.6	90	5.0	18.6	6.1	12.5
1964	5.2	−9.0	90	4.7	−4.3	4.7	−9.0
1965	5.8	−0.1	95	5.6	5.4	6.4	−1.0
1966	5.6	22.7	95	5.3	28.0	4.2	23.8
1967	4.9	1.2	85	4.2	5.4	5.8	−0.4
1968	5.2	11.0	85	4.4	15.4	3.8	11.6
1969	4.9	32.5	80	4.0	36.4	6.3	30.1
1970	4.1	8.2	80	3.3	11.5	7.9	3.6
1971	4.4	15.4	80	3.5	19.0	4.6	14.4
1972	3.6	68.6	80	2.9	71.5	5.3	66.2
1973	2.4	28.0	80	1.9	29.9	19.2	10.2
1974	2.1	−13.5	75	1.6	−11.9	21.9	−33.8
1975	2.4	3.7	75	1.8	5.5	7.8	−2.3
1976	2.4	13.9	75	1.8	15.7	10.4	5.3
1977	2.2	9.6	70	1.5	11.1	4.8	6.3
1978	2.2	12.9	65	1.4	14.3	3.6	10.7
1979	1.8	9.0	65	1.2	10.2	5.7	4.5
1980	1.7	6.7	65	1.1	7.8	7.1	0.7
1981	1.5	19.3	65	1.0	20.3	4.3	16.0
1982	1.5	0.6	65	1.0	1.6	1.8	−0.3
1983	1.5	21.5	65	1.0	22.5	1.8	20.7
1984	1.5	27.9	65	1.0	28.9	2.6	26.3
1985	1.3	25.7	65	0.8	26.5	1.8	24.7
1986	1.0	39.0	65	0.7	39.7	−0.3	40.0
Average	3.1	15.4		2.5	17.9		11.7
Standard error							18.5

Note: Stocks traded on the Tokyo Exchange, 1st section. d/V = dividend-price ratio (Japan Securities Research Institute estimate); dV/V = capital gain rate (Japan Securities Research Institute estimate); t = maximal separate tax rate on dividend incomes; dP/P = the rate of increase in consumer price index (Office of the Prime Minister, Bureau of Statistics).

Table 4.2 shows the time series of aggregate annual rates, $d(T)/V(T)$ and $dV(T)/V(T)$, computed for all listed nonfinancial companies on the Tokyo Stock Exchange, and the after-tax market rate of returns from stockholding to the individual investor subject to the higher dividends income tax rate at source. Because of the dividends policy mentioned above, there is a steady decline in the ratio $d(T)/V(T)$, which recently dropped to a low of 1 percent after tax. But it is quite erroneous to conclude from this, as some casual observers do, that the interests of individual stockholders are neglected by the J-firm. On the contrary, the dividend policy of the J-firm may be interpreted as quite a rational strategy from the individual stockholders' viewpoint. Rather, the high dividend payout ratio of the A-firm under the favorable tax treatment of capital gains has perplexed economists and has raised the question of why the corporation pays dividends, which has not yet been resolved satisfactorily.

As Table 4.2 indicates, individual investors in the J-firm have, on the average, enjoyed a reasonably high after-tax market rate of return – 17.9 percent in nominal terms and 11.7 percent in real terms, over the past two decades – precisely because of high capital gains made possible by the restraint of dividend payout. In the light of other studies, this rate is not inferior to that of representative Western companies.[10]

C.   Stockholding structure

As indicated already, there are three major types of stockholders in the J-firm: individual stockholders, financial-institutional stockholders, and other corporate stockholders. Figure 4.4 depicts the time-series change since the reopening of the Tokyo Stock Exchange in 1949 in the relative composition of stockholding by each type of stockholder in the stocks of all nonfinancial companies listed on the Tokyo Stock Exchange and other stock exchanges.[11] A glance at the figure will reveal

---

[10] For example, Table 8 in Ando and Auerbach, "The corporate cost of capital," indicates a much higher median value of the market rate for their sample Japanese companies (13.6 percent) in comparison with that of the sample American companies (2.2 percent). But they comment: "We do not wish to assert here, on the basis of information presented in Table 8a and 8j, that the required rate of return on equity has been this much higher in Japan than in the U.S. On the other hand, even a much smaller revision in this direction of the after-tax costs of equity reported earlier would be sufficient to nullify any apparent difference in overall returns to capital in the two countries. Given all the evidence presented in this paper, therefore there does not seem to be any ground to conclude that the cost of capital in Japan was significantly lower than in the U.S. for the period covered."

J. Abegglen, in his studies of 30 major Japanese, American, and European companies in the electrical industry (in which Japan demonstrates high growth and competitive strength) and the chemical industry (in which it does not), also found that "dividend income is low in Japan, but the gains resulting from high levels of re-investment and therefore high rates of growth have over the past ten years provided a higher return both pre-tax and after-tax for the shareholder in a Japanese company than for a shareholder in a competing U.S. company." J. Abegglen, "Profitability analysis of Japanese, American and European firms," unpublished manuscript, 1986.

[11] Relative shares are measured in terms of par value, but those in terms of market values available for recent years exhibit almost the same pattern.

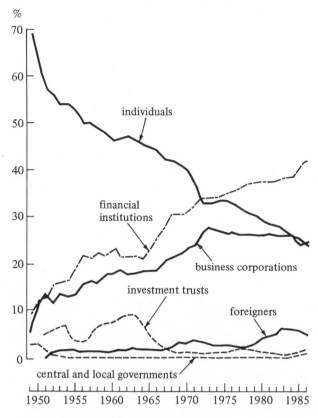

Figure 4.4. Distribution of stockholding in all listed nonfinancial companies by type of investor, 1949–86.

five conspicuous phenomena about the stockholding structure of the J-firm conceived as the average of the listed companies:

1. The relative share of individual stockholding has been steadily declining, from 69.1 percent at the end of 1949 to 23.9 percent at the end of 1986.
2. The relative share of stockholding by financial institutions – including banks, trust banks, and insurance companies – has been steadily increasing, from 9.9 percent at the end of 1949 to 41.7 percent at the end of 1986.
3. The relative share of corporate stockholding has been steadily increasing, from 5.6 percent at the end of 1949 to 24.5 percent at the end of 1986.

4. The relative share of investment trust (mutual funds) increased to nearly 10 percent in the early 1960s, but declined sharply in the aftermath of 1964–5 stock market crash and remained at a low level throughout the 1970s and early 1980s.

5. The relative share of foreign corporations and individuals has risen to a nonnegligible extent (it was at 4.7 percent at the end of 1986) after the liberalization of international capital transactions in 1980.[12]

As a result of these time-series changes, the current relative share of individual stockholding in the J-firm (23.9 percent at the end of 1986 and 29.2 percent in 1980) is considerably lower than that in American companies (51.1 percent in 1980 according to the Securities Exchange Commission).[13] Also noteworthy is the dominating size of holdings by financial institutions and business corporations. The combined share of financial institutions and non-financial corporations in the stock of the J-firm was 15 percent in 1949, but passed the 50 percent mark in 1968 and has now reached almost two-thirds of total stock traded in the 1980s.

Banks hold a dominant position among financial institutions. According to a 1986 survey by the National Conference Board of Securities Exchanges, nearly half of the stockholdings of financial institutions (21.4 percent of total stocks) are those of banks (city, local, and trust banks). Life insurance companies (13.3 percent) and casualty insurance companies (4.4 percent) follow. Whereas U.S. banks are not

---

[12] According to the revised Law for the Control of Foreign Exchange of 1980, a foreign person, legal and natural, can own up to 10 percent of the stock of any company for portfolio purposes without any restrictions.

[13] See Securities Exchange Commission Table 350. The SEC report nets out the intercorporate stockholding from the total value of stocks outstanding. The quoted share in the text is recalculated for the total value including intercorporate holdings to make it comparable with Japanese data. Also note that the relative share is calculated by the SEC for all stocks including over-the-counter (OTC) stocks and all closely held stocks. The relative proportions of OTC stocks and closely held stocks in total corporate stocks were 19.8 percent and 14.4 percent, respectively, in 1980. The proportion of U.S. individual stockholding may be biased somewhat upward for the comparison, because those types of stocks are more likely to be owned by individuals such as founders of companies and their associates. Yet a relatively smaller proportion of individual stockholding remains to be a comparatively significant feature of Japanese companies.

The institutional stockholding in the United States is scattered among private pension funds (11.1 percent of total domestic stock excluding intercorporate holdings in 1980), personal trust funds (8.4 percent), state and local retirement funds (2.9 percent), foundations and other educational endowments (2.7 percent), insurance companies (3.8 percent), and investment companies (2.7). Unfortunately, the SEC stopped collecting this valuable data concerning relative shares of various types of stockholders as of 1980 because of budget cuts.

allowed to hold stocks of other nonfinancial companies on their own account,[14] banks in Japan are allowed to do so up to the 5 percent limit imposed by the Anti-Monopoly Law. On the other hand, city and local banks do not in general engage in trust management pursuant to administrative guidance by the Ministry of Finance. Pension funds and trust funds are managed by trust banks and insurance companies. But, as pointed out in Chapter 3, separation pay is still the dominant form of postretirement benefits provided by Japanese companies, and pension funds are still in an early stage of development. Further, pension funds are managed according to a strict Prudent Man's Rule and their portfolios do not include as many stocks as their American counterparts. The share of pension funds managed by trust banks in the stockholdings of listed companies still remained at 0.9% in 1986, although it is expected to grow in the future. Thus a predominantly large proportion of stock is held by financial institutions on their own accounts.

The importance of bank holdings needs to be seen in a broader perspective of intercorporate stockholding involving nonfinancial corporations as well. Article 9 of the Anti-Monopoly Law makes it illegal to establish a holding company whose "principal business is to control . . . the business activities of other companies." However, a large nonfinancial corporation may hold stocks of other corporations where the effect is not "substantially to restrain competition," and only to the extent that the acquisition value of those stocks does not exceed the value of its own net assets. Even this limitation may be lifted in some cases, for example, when a joint venture is set up with a foreign person (natural or legal) or when a company spins off a part of its business as a fully owned subsidiary.

Intercorporate stockholding permissible under such a statutory framework has given rise to two types of corporate grouping, the functions of which I discuss in Chapter 6. One type is the so-called former *zaibatsu* corporate group or financial *keiretsu*. The other type of corporate grouping is the subsidiary grouping, or capital *keiretsu*. Zai-

[14] However, many pension and trust funds in the United States are not self-administered but are managed by trust departments of banks and insurance companies. According to a 1977 study of the Subcommittee on Reports, Accounting, and Management chaired by the late Senator Metcalf, 25.2 percent of the stock voting authority in the largest 122 corporations in the United States is vested in banks and 4.3 percent in insurance companies (the market value of common stocks of these corporations amounted to 41 percent of the total market value of all outstanding common stock). In spite of such concentration of trust assets in banks, however, the trust manager legally owes fiduciary duties to beneficial owners of pension and trust funds, and those funds are managed, at least theoretically, independently of the interests of commercial banking departments of banks.

batsu refers to the conglomerate corporate group that existed until the post–World War II reform. These groups were controlled by holding companies exclusively owned by founding families such as Iwasaki (Mitsubishi), Mitusi, Sumitomo, and Yasuda. Post–World War II corporate groups, or financial *keiretsu*, are no longer consolidated by single holding companies, but are loosely formed through mutual stockholding along the lines of old *zaibatsu* connections, or with a bank as the nucleus. In the subsidiary grouping (capital *keiretsu*), on the other hand, a dominant parent company consolidates its own subsidiaries through full or partial stockholding and vertical technological relations.

Former *zaibatsu* groups and financial *keiretsu* can be identified by Presidents' Clubs, which meet regularly. There are six such major groups, as indicated in Table 4.3 The member companies of such a group are normally engaged in noncompeting lines of business and relate to other member companies only loosely in terms of business relations, if any. But each group includes (at least) one city bank, one trust bank, and one trading company, and they have acted as major, albeit not exclusive, financial intermediaries and trading agents to member companies, as indicated in Table 4.3. The Presidents' Club functions as an information club and has neither a de facto nor de juer commanding position in the corporate group. Nor do any of the member companies do all or most of the group stockholding. Rather, the intragroup stockholding takes in a number of member companies, each with a relatively small number of shares. However, not only does the member bank hold shares of member companies, often to the legal limit, but also certain shares of the bank's stock are reciprocally held by member companies. From the extent of aggregate mutual stockholding it can be easily seen that outsiders would have little hope of taking over a member of those corporate groups through open market bids if the members acted against such a move in concert.

As I point out in Chapter 6, the coherence of the former *zaibatsu* or financial *keiretsu* group is visibly in eclipse, but since the mid-1970s there has been an increasing tendency for major companies, whether member companies of financial *keiretsu* or not, to spin off subsidiaries or to acquire existing companies as partly owned *keiretsu* firms, as indicated in Table 4.4.[15] Here a subsidiary means a company of which

---

[15] *A Survey of Corporate Group 1985* by the *Oriental Economist* alternatively defines group member of a subsidiary group (or capital *keiretsu*) as those companies of which more than 10 percent of the stock is owned by the apex company as the first or second largest stockholders, or of which more than 20 percent of the stock is owned by other member firms as the first largest stockholders. The *Survey* identified the number of member firms of subsidiary groupings headed by such major companies as Toyota, Hitachi, Nihon Steel, and Matsushita as 64, 190, 151, and 611, respectively.

Table 4.3. *Six major corporate groups, 1985*

	Mitsui	Mitsubishi	Sumitomo	Sanwa	Fuyo	DKB	Total
Number of Corporations in Presidents' Club	24	28	21	44	29	47	188
Intra-group Shareholdings (%)	17.9	25.2	25.0	16.8	15.8	13.3	
Intra-group bank finance (%)	21.2	22.4	27.7	20.3	18.4	12.1	
Weight of Groups in the entire non-financial sector							
in terms of assets	2.20	2.36	1.36	2.93	2.55	4.19	14.24
in terms of profits (%)	5.07	3.07	1.42	3.03	3.59	3.29	17.16
in terms of employees (%)	0.69	0.69	0.38	1.16	0.96	1.92	4.54

Source: The Oriental Economist, *Kigyo Keiretsu Soran, 1987.* Since there are several corporations which belong to two groups, the numbers of six presidents' clubs do not add up to the total number of corporations which belong to at least one of the six groups.

Table 4.4. *Ratio of investment in
subsidiaries and related companies
to total assets by all listed
manufacturing companies, 1967–
87 (end of March) (percent)*

1967	4.5
72	4.0
77	4.9
82	6.7
87	9.0

Source: NEEDS.

majority shares are owned by a parent company, and a related company means a company in which more than 20 percent of the stock is owned. Some of the partly owned subsidiaries and related companies of subsidiaries are themselves listed and traded on the Tokyo Stock Exchange. Therefore the tendency toward increasing subsidiarization of the Japanese companies is one of the factors contributing to the decline in the relative share of individual stockholding.[16]

As for individual portfolios, according to the *National Accounts* by the Economic Planning Agency, stockholding (including holdings of shares in investment funds) comprised only 11.2 percent of the total financial assets of households at the end of 1984, whereas deposits and similar assets comprised 60.5 percent, the rest being mostly insurance-related savings. It is estimated that only 16.9 percent of all households include stocks in their portfolios. Note, however, that the aggregate of individual holders of all stocks listed on the stock exchanges has been increasing recently. It was 4 million in 1949, but reached a record high of 17.6 million in 1986. This suggests that diversified stockholding is

---

[16] For example, suppose that company A, worth ¥110 billion, spins off its division B, worth ¥2 billion, as a subsidiary and issues new equity worth ¥1 billion for the new subsidiary to the public. Imagine that the individual stockholder who had owned half of the stock of company A adds this newly issued equity in his/her portfolio. The individual's stockholding has increased from ¥5 billion to ¥6 billion, and the relative share of the individual stockholding in total stock outstanding net of parential stockholding has risen to 54.5 percent (= [5 + 1]/[10 + 1]). But the relative share of the individual would decrease to 46.1 percent (= [5 + 1]/[10 + 3]) from 50 percent by this subsidiarization operation, if the value of the holding in the subsidiary B by the parent company A is included, as it is in the calculation used as the basis of Figure 4.4, in the value of total stock outstanding.

becoming a more common feature of the financial portfolios of some individuals.

One possible reason why stockholding has not become a more important means of storing individual assets in Japan is presumably the high risk cost and high transaction cost involved in holding and trading a small number of shares. As indicated by Table 4.2, the standard error of the annual market rate of returns to stockholding over the period 1962–86 was 18.5 percent, whereas the average rate was 11.7 percent. Therefore, assuming a normal distribution of stockholding returns, there was on average about a 25 percent chance that individual investors would incur a loss from holding portfolios proportional to the market portfolios over a year, and this ratio may go up for individual stockholders for whom the possibility of diversification may be limited by the size of investible wealth. Another deterrence to individual stockholding is the high broker's fee charged by securities companies for trading shares, which is regulated and highly regressive in Japan.[17] Further, dividend income is subject to income tax, although capital gains are not, and the deposit rate was certain, although it is low relative to the expected market rate of returns to stockholding, and not taxable for small savers.[18] Therefore it seems reasonable to assume that, when the level of accumulation of financial assets is low, investors tend to allocate a relatively larger proportion of their assets to safe forms such as bank deposits, to avoid risk and transaction costs.

According to a recent Bank of Japan estimate, in spite of the high personal saving rate, the assets of most Japanese households are still in the form of land, houses, and other fixed assets (63.4 percent of total assets in 1982). The relative share of financial assets was only 33.4 percent at the end of 1982, whereas in the United State 64.1 percent of individual assets are in the form of financial assets (24.1 percent in fixed assets).[19] This comparision may be somewhat deceptive, however, as the quasi-permanent employees of the J-firm have latent financial assets in the form of future claims on separation pay reserved in their employing firms. But this wealth is realized only at the time of retirement and is not currently salable. This nonsalability limits the possibility of risk diversification for preretired individuals, making

---

[17] The rate for brokering transactions not exceeding ¥1 million in value per stock is as high as 1.25 percent of the value of transaction, whereas the rate for transactions of more than ¥100 million is 0.55 percent.

[18] According to the scheme of preferential treatment of small amount savings, individual interest incomes from bank deposits and postal savings, each not exceeding ¥3 million, were not taxable up to 1987.

[19] Bank of Japan, *Monthly Report,* February 1984, p 6.

them behave relatively prudently in their portfolio selections. After the receipt of separation payment, the retired quasi-permanent employee seems to participate in the stock market more actively. For the household headed by a person aged 60 or older, the relative proportion of stockholding in the asset portfolio exceeded 15 percent in comparison with an average 11.4 percent in 1986.[20] Note that the ranking hierarchy as an incentive device at the J-firm has far-reaching repercussions on the stockholding structure of the J-firm by affecting individual portfolio behavior.

Even if we accept the hypothesis that the relative insignificance of stockholding in individual assets in Japan is partly attributable to the lower level of financial accumulation by the typical Japanese household, two questions remain. First, why, then, was the relative proportion of individual stockholding so high at the time that the Tokyo Stock Exchange opened in 1949, when the level of financial accumulation by individuals was much lower? Second, why, except for a brief surge in the early 1960s, have investment trusts (Japanese-style mutual funds) not developed in Japan for overcoming the risk and transaction costs associated with small-scale stockholding? These questions can be dealt with historically. In doing so, we can also trace major historical events leading to the formation of corporate groups in particular and the increase in financial and other corporate holdings in general.

D.   A historical note on stockholding structure

The large share of individual stockholding in 1949 was the direct outcome of the *zaibatsu* dissolution directed by the Supreme Commander for the Allied Powers (SCAP). This operation was also responsible for dismantling the traditional system – by removing Japanese companies from the control of capitalist families – and establishing managerial control. Between August 1946 and August 1947, 83 companies were designated holding companies by the government, at the instruction of SCAP, and in 1947 10 families were designated *zaibatsu* families in control of those holding and other companies. Most of the shares of the holding companies and *zaibatsu* families were transferred to the Holding Companies Liquidation Commission. The total value of shares transferred under this operation, combined with those transferred to the government as a means of tax payments, amounted to ¥118.4 billion, which was about two-fifths of the total value of stocks outstanding at that time.

[20] Management and Coordination Agency, *1986 Family Saving Survey*.

Those shares were sold by the Security Liquidation Coordination Council in the absence of an open stock exchange. The council adopted two noteworthy policies for the purpose of liquidation: (1) the priority purchase of liquidated shares at the sales price set by the council was given to the employees of the respective companies and then to the residents of localities in which the companies resided; and (2) no individual was allowed to acquire more than 1 percent of any company in this liquidation operation.[21] As a result of this policy, shares purchased by employees amounted to 38.5 percent of the total liquidation, and 29.3 percent of employees of the affected companies purchased some shares of their employing companies. This is why individual holdings topped nearly 70 percent of total stock outstanding of all listed companies at the end of 1949. Thus the family control that had governed many strategic companies through holding companies was effectively removed.

The Anti-Monopoly Law of 1947 outlawed holding companies outright and no subsequent attempt was made to revise this provision. However, the regulatory framework provided by the law did not prevent the gradual reformation of corporate grouping initiated by the bank. Although banks had been allowed to hold stock in nonfinancial companies in Japan from the pre-war period, city banks did not become the target of *zaibatsu* dissolution. A 5 percent ceiling was imposed on the holdings of city banks for any stock of a single company by the Anti-Monopoly Law of 1947, but this ceiling was quickly raised to 10 percent in 1953. Bank holdings of stocks of listed companies were at 9.9 percent by the end of fiscal 1949, and then increased to more than 20 percent by the end of 1956.

Intercorporate stockholding also increased from 5.6 percent in 1949 to 15.7 percent in 1956. Intercorporate stockholding was virtually prohibited by the Anti-Monopoly Law of 1947 except for single-layer holdings of technologically related subsidiaries, but this stringent restriction was also swiftly repealed in 1949. Through the liquidation operation by the Holding Companies Liquidation Commission, a substantial number of shares were purchased by securities companies and eventually resold to city banks and other companies. Further, the preemptive right of existing stockholders to subscribe to newly issued shares was not established statutorily, and a substantial portion of new stock issues of major companies was subscribed mutually among companies related to each other through old *zaibatsu* connections or the intermediaries of city banks.

---

[21] Holding Companies Liquidation Committee, *Nihon Zaibatsu to sono Kaitai* (Japanese *zaibatsu* and their dissolution), chap. 7, 1951.

Meanwhile, investment trusts experienced a surge after the 1950s, as the economic recovery accrued increasing financial wealth to some individuals. At the end of 1963, 11.9 percent of households owned shares in investment trusts and 20.3 percent held stock. The relative proportion of stockholding by investment trusts increased from 3.9 percent in 1956 to 9.5 percent in 1963. Investment trusts were managed by 14 investment trust companies controlled by major securities companies. After the relatively minor stock crash in 1961, however, securities companies borrowed heavily from the calls market, the Japan Security Finance Corporation, city banks, and the like, and incurred high financial costs. In order to maintain the prices of securities, which were apt to tumble, major securities companies utilized their controlling power over portfolio selections of investment trusts and traded between themselves. This only made the impact of the following security crash in 1964–5 worse. Most investment trusts suffered from heavy capital losses and many contracts were canceled by panicking individual investors. As a result, the proportion of households that held shares of investment trusts dropped to 4.8 percent in 1967.

This crash had two important enduring effects. First, investment trusts declined. Resentful small investors lost trust in security companies and became extremely skeptical about the wisdom of investing in stock in general. The newly created Securities Department of the Ministry of Finance (MOF) tightened regulations, and entry into the security industry became tightly controlled. Thus the number of securities companies decreased sharply from 484 to 277 between September 1965 and April 1968. Under the administrative guidance of MOF, portfolios of investment trusts were made to include substantial amounts of national bonds, long-term bonds issued by long-term credit banks, public utility companies, and the like. Thus shares in investment trusts were not particularly appealing investments for individuals until the recent fierce competition in the development of new financial commodities began to take place.

Another important consequence of the 1964–5 crash – which nearly drove one of the security companies, Yamaichi Shoken, into bankruptcy – was the acceleration of corporate holdings. In reaction to the crash, the Shoken Hoyu Kumiai (Security Holding Union) and Nihon Kyodo Shoken (Japan Cooperative Securities) were created with the backing of the government. To stabilize market prices, these organizations purchased securities from the market and security companies as well as from ailing investment trusts. Subsequently, these shares were to be liquidated in the market. At this time, however, Japan was internationally liberalizing its capital market and managers who feared possible unfriendly takeovers by foreign investors tried to counteract any such threat through mutual stockholding. This was called the "Stockholder Stabilization Operation."

As a result of this operation, by the end of 1968 stockholding by financial institutions had climbed to 30.3 percent of the total stocks outstanding of all listed companies, and stockholding by other business corporations rose to 21.4 percent. I discuss other aspects of intercorporate stockholding later, but it is important to note here that the management of the typical large Japanese companies in effect became insulated from outside takeovers as a consequence of the development of intercorporate stockholding.

2.   Debt versus equity financing

We have seen that the Japanese bank plays a dual role in corporate finance: It acts as a major long-term and short-term lender, as well as a major stockholder. The main bank of the J-firm normally owns stock in its client company up to the ceiling limit of 5 percent. The proportion of stock of a listed manufacturing company owned by all banks combined was on average 19.2 percent at the end of 1980. At the same time, the bank supplied long-term credits to the J-firm (conceptualized as the average image of 865 manufacturing companies listed since 1966) amounting to about 46.6 percent of its total investment in fixed assets during the period March 1966 to March 1975. But after March 1977 the amount of the J-firm's long-term borrowing outstanding started to decline; and the amount at the end of March 1985 was less than that at the end of March 1975. In retrospect, the mid-1970s were indeed a very important watershed.

These observations raise a host of theoretical and empirical questions: What is the bank's motive in holding the stock of a client company? Does it do so simply to obtain higher returns, or to maintain a good customer relationship with portfolio companies and to reserve the right to influence, if necessary, their policy decisions? Is there a conflict of interest, or an absence of unanimity, between the individual stockholder and the bank cum stockholder regarding the corporate finance policy to be adopted by their company?

These questions are not easy to answer without analyzing the interactions between the individual stockholder and the bank through financial markets and the corporate governance structure of the J-firm. I have attempted such an analysis elsewhere using a simple financial general equilibrium model and I describe some of the main results below.[22] Let us assume that the economy is simply composed of the household sector, called the individual investor; the banking sector, called the bank; the nonfinancial corporate sector, called the J-firm; and the Bank of Japan, denoted as the BOJ. In the model, there are only two types of assets: stock of the J-firm and credits intermediated by the bank (I assume that the stock of the bank is not tradable).

We assume that the economy is insulated from the international financial market and that neither the government nor the bond market exists. Thus, we actually assume away some very important features of Japanese financial markets since the mid-1970s and should consider this a highly abstract model of the Japanese financial system before the mid-1970s that highlights the dual role of the bank. With the aid of this model, I hope to pinpoint how the eventual deregulation of international financial transactions, the accumulation of national bonds, and the change in the BOJ's policy stance have altered the nature of the Japanese financial system and contributed to a significant modification of the relationship between the J-firm and the bank.[23]

We simplify matters by positing that the savings decision of the individual investor as well as the investment decision of the J-firm has been predetermined outside the model and by considering only the portfolio selections of the individual investor and of the bank under the influence of the BOJ. Investment by the J-firm is financed either through the internal retention of profit (by the reduction of dividends) or through bank loans; no new stock is issued by the J-firm. Time consists of an infinite series of periods of equal duration, and at the beginning of each period, the stock market opens and the contract of individual deposits as well as bank loans to the J-firm is drawn. The duration of the deposit and loan is one period.

At the beginning of the current period, T, the individual investor

---

[22] M. Aoki, "Shareholders' non-unanimity on investment financing: banks vs. individual investores," in M. Aoki (ed.), *The Economic Analysis of the Japanese Firm*, North-Holland, 1984, pp. 193–224.

[23] The Japanese government started to finance its budget deficits by issuing national bonds on a large scale in 1975, and the accumulated stock of national bonds since then was bound to have profound effects on the workings of financial markets, such as the development of unregulated open money markets and bond markets. After the transition to the flexible exchange system in 1973, incentives and pressure for the liberalization of international transactions mounted. Since 1977 deregulation started to proceed in this sphere and the revision of the Law for Controlling Foreign Exchange and Foreign Trade (abbreviated hereafter as the Foreign Exchange Law) in 1980 liberalized international transactions in principle. Further, as we shall see later, fundamental policy stance of the BOJ was revised around 1975.

renews his/her portfolio between stockholding and deposit so as to maximize his/her expected utility derived from after-tax returns within the constraint of its predetermined wealth W:

$$BD + k_i V = W, \tag{B.I}$$

where BD = bank deposit; k_i = individual demand for shares in the stock of the J-firm; and V = share price.

The interest rate, r_i for deposit is assumed to be a policy parameter.[24] There is no tax on interest incomes from deposits.[25] The algebra of expected after-tax returns from stockholding is given by the formula (S.R) on page 114 where capital gains, $dV(T)$, and dividends, $d(T)$, are uncertain variables at the time of portfolio selection. Therefore, portfolio selection by the individual investor, (BD,k_i), depends not only on the deposit rate, r_i, and current share price, V, but also on the probability distribution of capital gains and dividends (which are assumed to be distributed normally and time independently), as well as the risk attitude of the individual investor. At the subjective optimal portfolio selection of the individual investor,

> The expected market rate of after-tax return from stockholding less the individual risk cost from stockholding must be equal to the deposit rate (ignoring the possibility of a corner solution). (E.I)

Needless to say, the more risk-averse the individual investor is, the larger the proportion of his/her saving that is held in the form of deposit.

Suppose that the level of demand for the stock of capital by the J-firm is K and that a proportion, α, of it is to be financed by bank loan.

---

[24] Until 1970 interest rates for deposits of various duration were set by the Temporary Council of Money Rates Adjustment chaired by the president of the BOJ. Since then the rates have been regulated by the posting of a BOJ guideline within the maximum set by the council. City banks have followed the guideline. In 1979, the certificate of deposit (CD) was introduced for deposits more than ¥1 billion for which the interest rate became unregulated. In October 1985, interest rates for deposits more than ¥100 million (¥50 million after April 1986) became unregulated.

[25] By the system of favorable tax treatment for small savers, interest incomes from bank deposits and postal savings, each not more than ¥3 million per person, were not taxable until 1988. Since monitoring on this restriction by the Tax Authority was rather lukewarm and banks and post offices were not positively compliant with the restriction, many savers were able to evade taxes on interest incomes by having multiple accounts with various banks, post offices, and other financial institutions. It is estimated that about 60 percent of total deposits and postal savings by individuals in the mid-1980s were treated as not taxable.

Suppose that the rate of retention of loan for the compensating balance is β. Then in order for the demand for debt to be met, it must hold that

$$\alpha K + \beta L = L, \tag{M.L}$$

where L = the amount of bank loan to the J-firm. Considering the loan practice prevailing before the mid-1970s, it may be regarded as more realistic to assume that the lending rate r_L and the interest rate on the compensating balance r_C are exogenously fixed by the regulatory mechanism.[26] Even though the contractual rate is exogenously determined, however, if the bank can require the compensating balance, βL, whenever it makes loan, L, to the J-firm, the net gain to the bank in interest receipts is $[r_L - \beta r_C]L$, and the opportunity cost of the loan in terms of foregone investment in stock is $[1 - \beta]L$. Therefore

$$r = \text{the effective bank loan rate} = \frac{[r_L - \beta r_C]}{1 - \beta}. \tag{M.R}$$

By adjusting the retention rate, β, the bank can adjust the effective lending rate, r, flexibly in spite of the apparent rigidity of nominal lending rate, r_L. Therefore we assume that the effective lending rate, r, is to be determined endogenously in the model.

The bank is obliged to lodge with the BOJ legal reserve deposits in an amount equal to outstanding deposits times a reserve rate specified by the BOJ. The BOJ also provides credits to the bank by lending up to a credit line at the official discount rate. Should there be any shortage in reserve deposits, a penal rate higher than the official discount

[26] Lending rates for short-term loans (one year or less) have been bounded by the minimum "standard" rate and the maximum ceiling rate announced pursuant to the Temporary Money Rate Adjustment Act. Between 1959 and 1975, the standard rate, equivalent to the American prime rate, is the rate applicable to loans and discounting of commercial bills issued by highly rated companies, and between 1959 and 1975 it was fixed at a level 0.25 percent higher than the official discount rate by agreement of the National Banking Association. In 1975 this agreement was abolished formally, and since then banks have adjusted the rate voluntarily (at a level 0.5 percent higher than the discount rate since 1981) under the price leadership of the bank in charge of the office of presidency of the National Banking Association. Under this arrangement, city banks can choose appropriate rates, depending on the credit rating of borrowers and their own bargaining power vis-à-vis borrowers. There is no maximum long-term rate based on the act, but the preferred rate applicable to loans made to public utilities companies, which is set by long-term credit banks after consultation with the BOJ, has served as the de facto standard rate; and loans to other companies have been made by adding conventional rates of premiums, depending on the borrower's credit rating, on top of the standard rate.

rate will be imposed on the amount of the shortage.[27] We assume that the bank's marginal cost of incurring net debt, $MC(BB - R)$, to the BOJ is nondecreasing, where R = reserve deposit of the bank and BB = borrowing from BOJ.

Suppose that the bank's equity capital is E_b at the beginning of period T. Then the bank's asset portfolio selection between reserve deposits, loan to the J-firm, and stockholding is constrained by the following balance sheet constraint:

$$R + L + k_b V = BD + \beta L + BB + E_b, \qquad \text{(B.B)}$$

where k_b = the bank's demand for shares in the stock of the J-firm.

In selecting the demand for stock, k_b, the bank is under some legal and institutional constraints. A ceiling is set on bank stockholding by the Anti-Monopoly Law.[28] Therefore we require $k_b < k_b^{max}$ for some k_b^{max}. On the other hand, the bank may be required to hold a minimum number of shares of the J-firm in order to maintain a stable customer relationship with the latter and/or to control its corporate finance. Therefore we assume $k_b > k_b^{min}$ for some k_b^{min}.

The bank selects the portfolio $(L - \beta L, k_b, R - BB)$ to maximize its profit net of risk cost subject to the supply of money to the bank and the institutional constraints just mentioned. The algebra of expected market rate of after-tax return from stockholding is given again by the formula (S.R) on page 114 although tax rates applicable to the bank differ from those to individual investors, as noted there. At the subjective optimal portfolio selection,

> The expected market rate of after-tax return from stockholding minus the bank's risk cost from stockholding (which depend on the bank's risk attitude and expectation) is equal to the effective lending rate (ignoring the possibility of a corner solution). (E.B-1)

The profit from lending net of the cost of money supply, $r(1 - \beta)L - r_i BD - C(BB - R)$, is taxable at the corporate income tax rate, if it is

---

[27] As we shall see presently, in actuality, the BOJ has also been able to affect the reserve position of the banking sector by operating in money markets that are not explicitly recognized in our model. This activity has become much more important relative to direct lending since the mid-1970s. But in order to capture the essence of the BOJ's role in corporate finance, it suffices to assume for now that the BOJ can affect the bank's reserve position only through direct lending.

[28] The ceiling is 10 percent of the total stock of any single company until 1987 and 5 percent thereafter.

positive, where $C(BB - R)$ is the cost of incurring net debt from the BOJ. At the equilibrium,

The marginal cost of borrowing from the BOJ, $MC(BB - R)$, is equal to the effective lending rate r.   (E.B-2)

The demand for shares of the J-firm by the bank and by the individual investor must be equal to the total supply and, since there is no new stock issue in the period, the stock market clearing condition is given by

$$k_i + k_b = \hat{k}$$ (M.K)

where $\hat{k}$ = the existing number of shares of the J-firm.

There are eight variables in each period: the individual portfolio selections, k_i and BD; the bank's portfolio selections, k_b, L, βL, $BB - R$; and the market determined effective loan rate, r, and stock price, V. There are eight equilibrium conditions in each period: the balance sheet constraints for the individual investor (B.I) and for the bank (B.B); three market equilibrium conditions, (M.L), (M.R), and (M.K); and one marginal condition for the optimal portfolio selection for the individual investors (E.I) and two marginal conditions for the optimal selection for the bank (E.B-1) and (E.B-2). Once the rate of debt financing, α, and the (common) expectation regarding the future returns to stockholding are given, all the endogenous variables can be determined. But adding the balance sheet constants, (B.I) and (B.B), and the market clearing conditions, (M.K) and (M.L), it must hold at equilibrium that

$$\alpha K + \hat{k} V = W + E_b + BB - R.$$

This condition implies that, assuming that capital gains are offset by the corresponding adjustment in wealth, an increase in debt financing must be accommodated by a corresponding increase in the credit provision of the BOJ net of reserve deposits:

$$d\alpha K = d(BB - R),$$

where $d\alpha K$ and $d(BB - R)$ denoted changes in αK and $BB - R$, respectively, which is equivalent to saying that

net increase in debt financing by the J-firm
= net increase in BOJ credit provision
−net increase in reserve deposits of the bank.   (BJ-1)

The left-hand side corresponds to what the BOJ calls the "shortage of funds" in the private sector in our simple model. Such a shortage tends to decrease reserve deposits, if the credit extension by the BOJ to the bank remains unchanged. In order to facilitate the debt financing by the bank without restraining its reserve position, the BOJ has to adapt its credit provision to the shortage of funds in the short run.[29] [However, in the longer than short run the BOJ can affect the behavior of the bank by changing the condition of its own credit provision. This can be done either through the direct rationing of lending (the so-called "window guidance") or by indirectly affecting the cost of borrowing by the bank through money markets.[30] Regulating the amount of lending by the banking sector to the private sector (in practice the nonfinancial corporate sector) through such policy instruments was in fact regarded as the BOJ's "operating" target up to 1975 for realizing the "ultimate" target of the economic policy of the time: growth with external balance and price stability.[31] I discuss this and related issues shortly.]

For a given choice of α by the J-firm and the accommodating credit provision, $BB - R$, of the BOJ under a certain condition affecting the cost of bank borrowing, there corresponds a set of equilibrium values of endogenous variables of the model. In order to answer the questions posed at the beginning of this section – that is, the (im-)possibility of unanimity between the individual investor and the bank – consider the following experiment: Suppose that at equilibrium the J-firm weighs the implications of modifying its financial policy so as to increase the degree of reliance on debt financing, α, by 1 percent in the current period. How will such perturbation of corporate finance policy affect the financial returns net of risk costs to the individual investor and the bank?

If the J-firm increases borrowing by ¥1 in order to finance a predetermined level of investment, it can increase dividend payout by the same amount, which results in an increase in after-tax income of the

---

[29] Bank of Japan, *Waga Kuni no Kinyu Seido* (Financial Institutions in Japan), 8th ed., 1977, p. 101.

[30] City banks that have been major lenders to the corporate sectors have been able to borrow surplus funds from local banks, farmers cooperatives, and other financial institutions through interbank money markets. Therefore, the BOJ can affect the borrowing costs of city banks by intervening in these interbank money markets and influencing the money rate prevailing there. For instance, the BOJ purchases private commercial bills and sells self-addressed bills of exchange at the call market and the bill market. Since 1963 the BOJ has also bought securities (in practice, 10-year government bonds) possessed by banks at a free rate determined by auction in order to supply "growth money." However, since the bill market and call market were relatively less developed and the rates prevailing there normally exceeded the official discount rate in the period of high economic growth, there was always a tendency for the bank to rely upon the BOJ's lending up to a credit line to meet the shortage of funds. This is what was called the "over-loan" by the BOJ.

[31] Bank of Japan, *Waga Kuni,* rev. ed., 1986, pp. 459–61.

individual investor in the current period by $¥(1 - t_d)$, where t_d is the tax rate applicable to dividend income. If the individual investor is to maintain the same consumption level as before the perturbation in corporate financial policy, he/she can increase the portfolio balance by the same amount. At equilibrium, he/she is equally better off by increasing either the deposit or stockholding. Suppose that he/she increases stockholding. Then the expected gain in the next period will be $¥(1 - t_d)$ times the expected after-tax market rate of return to individual stockholding. However, in order to fulfill the increased interest payment obligation incurred by the perturbation of the investment financing in the next period, the J-firm will have to reduce its dividend payment in the next period by the amount $¥[1 + (1 - t_c)r]$, where t_c is the corporate income tax, and the interest payment by the J-firm is assumed to be tax deductible. The after-tax dividend reduction to the individual investor, then, is this amount times $(1 - t_d)$. Comparing the marginal after-tax benefit and the cost, the individual investor is better off by the perturbation of corporate finance policy of the J-firm if $(1 - t_c)r$ is less than the expected after-tax market rate of return to stockholding minus risk cost and vice versa.

It can be proved for our model that the share price appreciates or depreciates by an incremental debt financing of the J-firm, according to whether the marginal after-tax benefit of the policy to the individual investor exceeds or falls short of the marginal after-tax cost.[32] We therefore claim

> [F1] The individual investor's utility (expected financial returns net of risk cost) is maximized when share price V is maximized.[33]

Next, suppose the situation in which the J-firm has chosen the share price-maximizing debt ratio, α^*, but considers increasing its debt-financing further. A somewhat elaborate calculation, which is not repeated here, can show that the following adjustment will occur: The general equilibrium solution of the effective loan rate will go up. The profit from this rise in the equilibrium effective loan rate is more than enough to offset the capital loss of the bank due to the nonshare price-maximizing policy of the J-firm.[34]

The situation is depicted in Figure 4.5. The horizontal axis represents the ratio of debt financing, α, by the J-firm. At the point α^*, the

---

[32] See Aoki, "Shareholders' non-unanimity," pp. 204–8.
[33] This is not necessarily true for models in which there are many individuals whose risk attitudes and expectations are different.
[34] M. Aoki, "Shareholders' non-unanimity."

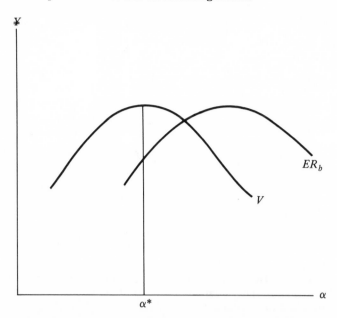

Figure 4.5. Nonunanimity of interests between the individual investor and the bank.

share price V is maximized. However, at that point expected financial returns to the bank net of risk cost, ER_b, are rising. Therefore we posit that

> [F2] The bank wants its portfolio firm to rely upon debt financing beyond the level warranted by the share price maximization as long as the BOJ provides accommodating credits.

Thus there does not seem to exist the unanimity of interest between the individual investor and the bank regarding the extent of reliance on debt-financing. Suppose that the degree of debt financing is determined by management of the J-firm that strikes the balance of interest between the two types of stockholders. From the reasoning above, the deviation from the share price maximization, or, equivalently, the degree of "overborrowing" from the viewpoint of the individual stockholder, may be measured by the difference between the marginal cost of the deviation, $(1 - t_c)r$, and its marginal benefit, that is, the expected market rate of return to individual stockholding minus risk cost. Remembering that, by the condition of optimal portfolio selec-

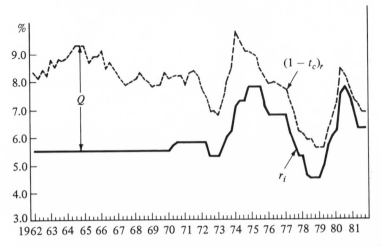

Figure 4.6. Decline of "overborrowing" by the J-firm measured by Q. *Source:* M. Aoki, "Shareholder's nonunamity on investment financing: banks vs. individual investors," in M. Aoki. *The Economic Analysis of the Japanese Firm,* North-Holland, 1984. p. 212.

vidual investor, the expected market rate of returns minus the risk cost of individual stockholding is equal to the deposit rate, r_i, at equilibrium, the measure may be written as

$$Q = (1 - t_c)r - r_i.$$

As pointed out, Q becomes zero when the share price is maximized. In contrast, if this measure is sufficiently large, it suggests that the bank's interests dominate the corporate finance policy of the J-firm. The bank derives high utility from the rising effective loan rate and it owns stock of the J-firm only in order to influence its corporate finance policy to its own advantage, rather than purely for the income-generating purpose. (This implies that the lower-bound constraint on bank stockholding is binding.)

Figure 4.6 depicts the movement of $(1 - t_c)r$ and r_i as well as Q, where r is represented by the estimate of an effective one-year loan rate and r_i by a one-year deposit rate, both at the beginning of each quarter. We see that the deviation from share price maximization has narrowed down considerably since the mid-1970s, indicating the decline of bank influence. In fact, the reliance of Japanese manufacturing companies on debt financing by banks has decreased considerably since then, as we have already seen in the previous section.

One may argue that the decline in bank borrowing since the mid-1970s is mainly the result of the decline in the level of current investment by the J-firm, rather than the decline in the influence of banks. However, as Table 4.2 showed, the ratio of dividend per share has also declined considerably since the mid-1970s. This suggests that if the J-firm had to pay out the same rate of dividend per share price in this period as in the 1960s, it would have had to rely more heavily on borrowing in order to finance its current investment. The fact that it actually did not suggests that the possible decline of banking influence may also be responsible for the relative independence of the J-firm from the bank in the recent period. On the other hand, if the J-firm has had the power to increase internal financing by reducing the dividend payout in the interest of individual stockholders in the 1960s to the same level as in the post-1975 period, the degree of dependence on debt financing might have been lower.

I have done a statistical analysis on how the recent tendency of the J-firm to rely less on long-term bank borrowing for financing investment in long-term assets is decomposable into the effect of the decline in the level of investment and in banking power (the deviation from share price maximization) as measured by Q, controlling for the measure of internal efficiency of the J-firm. The measure Q declined by 1.15 percentage points on average from the period 1961–1972 to the period 1973–82, whereas the relative dependence of long-term investment on long-term borrowing from the bank has declined from 16.0 percent in the period 1966–72 to 10.5 percent in the period 1973–80. According to the statistical analysis I conducted, if banking power as measured by Q had remained at the same level in the period 1973–80 as in the period 1961–72, the magnitude of decrease in long-term borrowing between the two periods might have been smaller by half. On the other hand, if the banking power in the period 1966–72 was at the same level as in the period 1973–82, long-term borrowing in that period might have been smaller by one-third.[35] Thus the high degree of reliance on bank financing by the J-firm in the 1960s and the early 1970s seems to be at least partly explained by the deviation from the share price maximization norm and the so-called over-borrowing of the J-firm may have really existed then from the viewpoint of the individual investor.

The diminished reliance on bank financing and the increased availability of internal funds to the J-firm in the post-1975 period were brought about partly as an unplanned result of the apparently peculiar dividend practice of the J-firm referred to in the last section: That is,

[35] Ibid., pp. 210–9.

the J-firm sets the dividend payout ratio as a stable percentage of the par value of the stock, not of profit. However, since economic returns from stockholding are higher for the bank if the J-firm distributes its profit rather than retains it (see Section 1.B), the bank would have pressed the J-firm to increase dividends as profits increased, if it could. The fact that it has not been able to do so indicates that the relative bargaining power of the bank vis-à-vis the management of well-run companies has visibly declined in the post-1975 period and that management of the J-firm shifted its corporate financial policy, consciously or unconsciously, in the direction consistent with the interests of individual stockholders in spite of the decline in their relative share in the stockownership structure.

I conclude this section by briefly reviewing the main factors contributing to the disappearance of the overborrowing of the J-firm from the bank. First, during the pre-1975 period the J-firm had few alternative means to raise external funds other than bank borrowing. The issue of corporate bonds was more strictly regulated then. Long-term credit banks and public utilities companies aside, only highly rated privately owned companies were able to issue bonds on rotation, placing tangible assets, such as land and buildings, as collateral. Issuing companies had to pay annual fees to banks or securities companies responsible for monitoring the security of collateral, adding nonnegligible financial costs to bond issues. With the underdeveloped condition of the security market, a large proportion of new issues had to be accepted by financial institutions, mostly by banks. Bond issues in foreign markets and borrowing in foreign currency were also regulated before the revision of the Foreign Exchange Law in 1980. The lack of alternative means doubtlessly endowed the bank with strong bargaining power. Afraid of severing relational contracting, Japanese companies had to overborrow under the pressure of the bank to finance excessive compensating balance, speculative investment in lands directly unrelated to their line of business, and the like.

The large-scale issues of national bonds by the government beginning in 1975 and the subsequent liberalization of bank dealing in national bonds in 1978 had a great impact on the growth of the previously undeveloped securities markets. The market yields of national bonds came to represent the long-term rate and made the market evaluation of other long-term securities easier. This development had inevitable repercussions on the issuance market as well, making the regulation of the conditions of bond issues increasingly outdated. A new opportunity also opened for highly rated companies to issue bonds abroad, denominated in both yen and foreign currency, without the requirement of collateral, and this doubtlessly increased competitive pressure on the domestic issuance market.

As a result, the J-firm has increasingly substituted bond issues, including convertible bonds, for long-term borrowing from the bank. According to NEEDS, of the 865 manufacturing companies listed on Tokyo Exchange, the ratio of bond issues outstanding with more than one year maturity to long-term borrowing with more than one year maturity rose from 17.2 percent at the end of March 1975 and 30.2 percent at the end of March 1980 to 60.5 percent at the end of March 1985. The increased marketability of securities has made corporate bonds more attractive financial assets for a wide range of investors, including individual investors, business corporations, and foreigners. In 1984, 57.5 percent of new domestic issues of corporate bonds were purchased by individual investors.[36] The issue of bonds abroad has also been steadily increasing since 1975. The ratio of bond issues in foreign currency denominated to total bond issues was 49.2 percent in 1986.[37] These phenomena of de-intermediation have doubtlessly diminished the relative bargaining power of the bank vis-à-vis the J-firm and contributed to the reduction of overborrowing of the latter.

There is also a supply-side factor to consider in the reduction of the overborrowing. It is related to the situation that developed following the large-scale issue of national bonds that the government introduced in 1975.[38] The private banking sector in Japan accepted the large proportion of national bond issues. Therefore, during the first stage of the large-scale national bond issue, reserves of the banking sector would decrease by the amount of its national bonds purchase. But during the second stage, when proceeds from national bonds issue are used for the purchase of goods and services by the government, the nonfinancial private sector supplying those goods and services would increase its assets in the form of cash and deposits by the amount of government payments. In the banking sector, this increased money supply would replete reserves diminished in the first step. But since the money supply has increased by the amount of the government deficit, reserves are now in shortage if there is no accommodating increase in BOJ credit provisions or decrease in reserve equipments. This can be seen by modifying equation (BJ-1) so as to incorporate the government sector. The shortage of funds, now the sum of the increase in debt

---

[36] *Monthly Report of Public and Corporate Bonds* by the Public and Corporate Bonds Acceptance Association.

[37] *Asahi Shinbun,* September 14, 1987.

[38] Bank of Japan, *Waga Kuni,* pp. 472–9.

financing and the increase in payments by the government, must be met as follows:

net increase in debt financing of J-firm's investment
+ net increase in payments of the government
= net increase in BOJ credit provision
− net increase in reserve deposits of the bank.   (BJ-2)

If the BOJ had followed the policy stance described in the model of this section, it might have responded to the fund shortage by a net increase in payments of the government by providing additional credits. By the mid-1970s the BOJ accommodated the lending propensity of the banking sector as far as it judged necessary for economic growth with price stability and external balance. But in the aftermath of the great 1973–4 inflation, the BOJ has decisively changed its policy stance, shifting the focus of its operating target of monetary policy from the level of bank lending to the money supply. In the late 1970s to the early 1980s, the BOJ did not increase its supply of base money in response to an increase in the form of cash and deposits by the private sector, because it was concerned about price stability, and committed to a supply of base money with a constant rate of growth. Then simply assuming that there is no provision of BOJ credit in addition to a steady-state rate and that there is a fixed reserve requirement to be met, it must hold that

net increase in debt financing of the J-firm's investment
+ net increase in government payments
= a predetermined constant.   (BJ-3)

That is, the banking sector had to offset the relative shortage of reserves created by the increase in government expenditure through restraint in its lending to the nonfinancial corporate sector and through the resale of national bonds to the market. Thus, by abandoning accommodating policy, the BOJ eased the bank pressure on the J-firm for overborrowing.

Note in passing that a new situation created in the mid-1980s has made the BOJ's commitment to a constant rate of money supply untenable because of a change in the international environment. Incorporating the foreign sector, the fund shortage equation stands as

shortage of funds
= net increase in debt financing of J-firm's investment
+ net increase in payments of the government
− net increase in payments of foreigners.   (BJ-4)

Because of Japan's increasing trade surplus, the third term became substantially large in the mid-1980s and the private sector increased its assets in the form of cash and deposits. This increase of money supply in the private sector had the effect of reserves surplus in the banking sector. The BOJ was alarmed by its consequence on price stability, but mounting international pressure was placed on Japan to stimulate domestic demand as a remedy for the trade imbalance, and it became difficult for the BOJ to tighten the provision of credit in order to offset the external imbalance. The J-firm was induced to bear out the BOJ's easened stance and the result was that bank borrowing by the J-firm increased sharply relative to its investment. This increase in borrowing is of quite a different nature from the increase observed up to 1972 (but rather close to the one observed in 1973) in that it occurred when the J-firm generated ample equity capital for investing in fixed assets and that the surplus of funds was directed toward short-term financial market operations (the so-called *zaiteku*) and speculative investment in real estate.

When all these developments are combined, it is easy to see that a significant change has occurred in the relationship between the bank and the J-firm. But it should be added that, although the J-firm now depends less on the bank for investment financing and the bank has less direct influence over the J-firm's corporate finance policy, this does not by any means imply that the banking business has become unprofitable or weakened under the emerging condition. Well-run banks have expanded their sphere of activities in response to the changing environment, beyond the traditional sphere of financial intermediation between the household sector and the domestic corporate sector. City and local banks now hold a larger proportion of their assets in the form of national and corporate bonds on their accounts (from 12.1 percent at the end of 1975 to 13.8 percent at the end of 1985). Since the liberalization of bank dealing in national bonds in 1977, banks have been actively involved in security markets. They have also expanded their scope of activity internationally. The contributions that international business sections of city banks make to their gross profits have increased from 8 percent in 1977 to 14 percent in 1984.[39] The experience that banks have accumulated in international financial transactions and their international information networks may change the nature of bank services to the J-firm considerably from that observed up to the mid-1970s.

What implications does this changing relationship between the bank and the J-firm have with respect to the nature of corporate governance

[39] Ibid., p. 75.

of the J-firm? If management of the J-firm is now more free from the dominating influence of the bank than it was in the pre-1975 period, to whom is it accountable? Is the individual stockholder gaining the power to supervise management of the J-firm through the stock market or otherwise? Or can management of the J-firm, by being freed from the pressure of the bank, pursue its own objective? I begin to consider these issues in the next section and continue the discussion in chapters 5 and 6.

3.   The bank as a monitoring agent

This section is about the stockholder's capability to control strategic business decisions of the portfolio company in its own interests. Sections 1 and 2 have pointed out that under the current tax system the interests of the bank stockholder and those of the individual stockholder may diverge with respect to corporate finance and dividend policy. Therefore we cannot rigorously talk about the control of management by *the* stockholder. Thus I pose the present question in terms of the possibility of controlling management in the interests of the individual stockholder. From this perspective, I also ask whether there is any possibility of an agency relationship between the individual stockholder and the bank stockholder, even though their interests diverge in certain strategic business decisions (corporate finance policy).

As already stated in the introduction to this chapter, the prevailing view is that the individual stockholder has a weak position in the corporate governance structure of the J-firm. According to this view, stockholders' interests are overridden by those of other constituents of the J-firm – namely, the employee and/or management and possibly the firm's main bank. The reasons normally given to support this proposition are as follows:

1. The J-firm can raise investment funds by borrowing from the bank at a low cost and does not have to rely on equity financing. Therefore its strategic business decision (corporate policy) can be made free of the interest of individual stockholders.
2. Individual stockholders of the J-firm are underprivileged in the sharing of economic returns to the J-firm, as they receive only a very small fraction of profit as dividends.
3. The position of individual stockholders in the corporate governance structure of the J-firm is almost nonexistent. The board of directors is nothing but a self-perpetuating body of senior managers promoted from within the rank of quasi-

permanent employees, not the organ through which the
surveillance of stockholders over the business and affairs of
the company is exercised.

4. Since interlocking corporate stockholding has developed to
such a degree that the takeover of the J-firm through open bids
is virtually impossible, management of the J-firm is free from
the discipline exercised by stockholders through the stock
market.

In the first two sections of this chapter I have argued that evidence
does not support (the first half of) contention 1 and that the reasoning
behind contention 2 is not well grounded. It has been argued that
equity financing is becoming a more and more important means of
corporate financing in the J-firm, freeing the J-firm from overreliance
on the bank; and that individual stockholders of the J-firm have been
enjoying on average a reasonable rate of return over time, precisely
because of the substitution of retained profits for dividend by the J-
firm. Yet one may still argue that the position of the individual stockholder is that of a passive investor because of the reasons stated in
contentions 3 and 4 above. There are some elements of truth to this
claim, but I contend that management of the J-firm may not yet be
completely free of the stockholders' surveillance, although management is certainly not an agent to stockholders, as envisioned in neoclassical economics.

In the legal framework of corporate law, the stockholders' general
meeting is empowered to select the board of directors *(torishimariyaku
kai)* of the J-firm, whose function is to make corporate decisions except
for those reserved for the general meeting (such as those concerning
fundamental changes in corporate character, dividend payments,
directors' bonus payments, etc.), just as in American corporate law or
British company law.[40] However, under the provision that the stockholder meeting can remove directors with or without a cause by a more
than two-thirds vote of the stockholders general meeting, the stockholder of the J-firm appears to have potentially greater power than
under American law, which stipulates that the board of directors cannot normally be replaced without a cause for the period of their terms.

The board of directors is in turn empowered to choose one or more
representative director(s) *(daihyo torishimariyaku)* to represent the
company vis-à-vis third parties and to be responsible for the execution

---

[40] For the difference and similarity between American corporate law, the British Companies Law, the German Codetermination Act, and the Japanese Commercial Code
regarding the corporate governance structure, see Aoki, *The Cooperative Game Theory of the Firm,* chaps. 10 and 11.

of corporate decisions. One of the representative directors is normally assigned the title of *shacho* (the chief of company), as mandated by a company bylaw. Furthermore, the Commercial Code does not prevent companies from setting up a substructure of the board by bylaw to which the function of the board is delegatable, except for matters specified by the code as belonging to the entire board (e.g., the election of representative directors and decisions on new share issues within the limit of authorized capital). Such a substructure, normally called the board of full-time directors *(jyomu torishimariyaku kai),* is composed of representative directors and a few other senior directors.

In practice, most "plain" directors *(hira torishimariyaku)* in the board are, with a few outside directors from the main bank and business partners aside, responsible for the main business divisions of the company, the personnel department, the corporate finance department, the central research laboratory, and managers of major factories. Thus, in one sense, the board of directors is a coalition of various internal interest groups. On the other hand, unless the company is ridden with serious internal fractional disputes or business difficulties necessitating outside help from the bank and business partners, the *shacho* is normally chosen by the retiring predecessor and given rather strong discretion in choosing permanent directors by promoting candidates from among the plain directors. Thus, in practice, the relationship between the representative directors and the board of directors, as well as the board of permanent directors and the board of directors, is the reverse of the statutory arrangement. In the normal course of affairs the board of directors functions as a de facto substructure of the management system subordinate to the representative (and permanent) directors.

Since the board of directors does not serve as a source of independent supervision, as it does in the United States, Japanese lawmakers recognized the need for an independent organ to watch executive directors. The revised Commercial Code 1982 stipulates that the general meeting of stockholders must elect more than one auditor for the purpose of auditing management. The auditors have a wide range of auditing authority, which extends to accounts, but they cannot interfere with directors' decisions involving discretion. However, in order to prevent the board of directors from making an illegal or seriously unjust decision, auditors have the right to attend board meetings and be heard. When they find a serious wrongdoing, the auditors can initiate a derivative suit for injunction without putting up securities for expenses.

In theory, then, the office of auditor can be a powerful check on the directors of the J-firm. However, its effectiveness is not ensured unless the auditors are competent and independent of management. The original draft of the Revised Code prepared by the Ministry of Justice included a clause specifying that at least one of the auditors must be an "outsider" who has not been either a director or an employee of the company for a certain period of time before assuming the office of auditor. However, this clause was dropped from the final draft, owing to strong opposition from the business community. Without it, however, there is a danger that auditors will face an extremely difficult task in acting as a watchdog over their senior collegues.

The general meeting of the stockholders does not seem to provide a forum for their opinions to be heard or management policy to be communicated in sincerity to stockholders. One Japanese practice frequently referred to in this connection is the activity of the so-called *sokaiya* (professional general meeting attendants). The *sokaiya* hold a very small share of the company and are actively engaged in monitoring the business and affairs of the company as well as the private lives of directors. Any company normally has a few incidents, sometimes serious and sometimes only anecdotal, that it does not want made public in order to preserve its reputation. The company is often trapped into bribing those *sokaiya* with a dubious social background who have access to information regarding such incidents; in return, *sokaiya* cooperate with management at the general meeting to protect management from potentially embarrassing situations. The revised Commercial Code 1982 made payments to *sokaiya* subject to severe punishment, but some *sokaiya* are still said to be engaged in trouble shooting for the company, although they are thought to be disguised – for example, as subcontractors of the company – in order to receive payment.[41]

How about stock market discipline? If individual stockholders become disenchanted with management, then, even though their voice in the corporate governance structure is weak, they may be able to exit from it by selling their shares in the stock market. The neoclassical parable tells us that, if it occurs on a large scale, it will affect the share price substantially and result in a takeover raid by a person or company that intends to acquire a sufficient number of shares to be able to

[41] I would like to add one remark concerning the role of *sokaiya* to avoid a misunderstanding. The existence of *sokaiya* does not imply that management of the J-firm can cover up any wrongdoing by simply bribing them. For management, *sokaiya* are a convenient instrument with which to handle its mischief behind the scenes, but it is always humiliating and potentially dangerous for any decent management to rely on them. The fact that *sokaiya* are very shrewd in information gathering and that they are not necessarily credible as allies is one factor that prompts management to behave ethically.

replace the existing management, to realize capital gains, or to amalgamate with other companies controlled by the raider. If the share price drops too low, the existing stockholders may be induced to sell their shares to the raider at an offer price that is usually better than the market price. Thus management tries to make sure that the share price is kept high. Therefore, we are told by neoclassicists, the potential transferability of shares by individual stockholders can serve as an effective disciplinary device.

As noted already, however, the phenomenon of intercorporate stockholding serves to insulate the management of member companies from the threat of a takeover raid. In addition, it is very hard (albeit not impossible) and time-consuming to amalgamate internal organizations of unrelated Japanese companies, even in the case of horizontal mergers. As discussed in Chapter 2, the quasi-permanent employee endeavors to develop his/her personal network as a valuable asset within the internal organization that he/she serves. When two companies merge, however, those informal networks do not easily mesh beyond the boundary of the former formal organizations because of the inertia of human contacts. This is a serious drawback for the horizontal information structure, as discussed in Chapter 2, if it is to operate effectively. After Fuji Steel and Yahata Steel merged to become the world's largest steelmaker, Nippon Steel, and Daiichi Bank and Kangyo Bank merged into the largest bank in Japan in terms of its assets in the early 1970s, both companies took great pains to mesh premerger organizations by such means as alternating the complementary positions of chief and subchief of every section and department between persons from both merged companies. Yet it is said to have taken a decade for employees to stop being concerned about the former identity of their colleagues. The potential loss of information efficiency due to the mechanical consolidation of separate organizations may provide another explanation for the scarcity of takeovers in Japan.

Thus, on the surface, the position of individual stockholders in the J-firm appears to be hopeless. Management of the J-firm seems to be unaccountable. Yet this impression may be substantiated only from the viewpoint of the hard-boiled neoclassical paradigm, which regards the firm as the property of stockholders and its management as an agent of the stockholder. As already indicated in the introduction to this chapter, I submit that the J-firm is a much more complex organization than this, and that its management is accordingly placed in an institutional milieu of complex monitoring devices other than takeover. This viewpoint is developed in Chapters 5 and 6; in the remainder of this section, I merely present two preliminary points in that direction.

First, I submit that the takeover discipline is double-edged for the purpose of disciplining management. That mechanism may serve as the last resort to replace management who seriously damage the stockholders' interests. But "short-run" share price maximization, as defined shortly, does not necessarily lead to internal efficiency of the firm viewed as a coalition of the body of stockholders and the body of quasi-permanent employees.

If all other resources of the firm, other than equity capital, can be mobilized from competitive markets and priced there, share price maximization against market-determined costs will ensure internal efficiency. However, if human resources of the firm have come to be internalized, as discussed in Chapter 3, the well-being of the quasi-permanent employee will also depend on various corporate policies such as investment, employment, and the like, which would affect their career opportunities and job security. In this situation, choosing strategic business policy to maximize share price subject to the pay level of the quasi-permanent employees – predetermined either through collective bargaining or markets – would not lead to internally efficient decision making. This is easily seen as follows: If two agents, A and B, bargain over the trade of good x for good y, the Pareto-efficient outcome is guaranteed only if the amounts x and y are chosen conjunctionally so that the marginal rates of substitution between the two goods are equalized for the two agents. If the choice x is agreed upon between two agents first, and then y is chosen to maximize A's utility subject to the chosen level of x, A would choose the amount of y for which the marginal rate of substitution of y for x is zero for him. But if B derives utility from good y, his marginal rate of substitution at the choice dictated by A would not be zero. There is room for Pareto-improving modifications of this choice. One can substitute the body of stockholders for A and the body of employees for B as well as the pay level of the body of employees for x and any strategic business policy variable relevant to the welfare of the quasi-permanent employee for y.

As this simple apparatus makes clear, share price maximization subject to the employment costs narrowly defined in terms of the pay level would not be internally efficient. Rather, the choice of pay level and strategic business decision making have to be coordinated. In other words, share price has to be maximized vis-à-vis a given level of well-being (utility) of the quasi-permanent employee, which depends on pay level as well as other strategic business decision variables of the firm of high relevancy. Therefore, pressing management continuously for unilateral share price maximization posterior to collective bargaining in which the pay level is fixed would not be wise. Such share price maximization may be referred to as "short-run" share price maximization. The supremacy of takeover discipline may be warranted only for cases in which managerial efficiency is seriously damaged beyond the short run.

Second, although the management of the J-firm may be insulated from the discipline exercised through the stock market, it is placed under close monitoring by financial intermediaries, particularly when it has to rely on borrowing from the bank for financing investment. The so-called "main bank" of a company, which is a major stockholder of the company and serves as an organizer of long-term loan consortiums to the company on a regular basis, plays an especially strategic role in monitoring. The main bank is in the position of being briefed about the company's general business and affairs in the capacity of a major stockholder and is able to scrutinize the company's strategic investment plan in the capacity of a major lender. It often sends its representative to the company's board of directors. Thus the main bank cum major stockholder has considerable ability to closely monitor its customer companies. However, does it exercise its expertise and informational advantage only for its own gain?

One possible scenario is as follows: In the normal course of affairs and business of the portfolio company, the individual stockholder, obviously disadvantaged in his/her capacity to gather information and monitor management, may feel more secure if the main bank closely and responsibly monitors management of the company to reduce bankruptcy risk. One may thus say that the individual stockholder is willing to delegate the monitoring function to the main bank cum major stockholder. The deviation from share price maximization by the company at the sacrifice of individual stockholders and the phenomenon of overborrowing in the interests of the bank may in part be thought of as serving as the "agency fee" paid by individual stockholders to the bank for that service.

If the above scenario is correct, then it is vital for the main bank to maintain its reputation as a competent and responsible monitor. This may explain an aspect of the rescue operation put forth by a main bank when it discovers serious financial difficulties in a customer company, yet judges that the ailing company has a chance to recuperate. A rescue package may call for reduced interest rates and compensating balances, and sometimes an interest moratorium. The bank may also persuade the ailing company to sell its assets and to transfer some employees to related companies. When such a rescue package is introduced, the main bank often takes over mangement of the ailing company, through persuasion. In this connection, the provision of the Commercial Code that any director can be replaced at any time by a two-thirds vote of the stockholder general meeting is of crucial importance. By virtue of its position as an influential stock voter, the main bank can take the initiative in calling an emergency stockholder meeting and have its takeover of management approved by coordinating both lenders and stockholders in rescue strategies. When the company has recuperated under the leadership of an emergent management team organized by the main bank, however, management is often turned over again to managers promoted from within the internal main organization of the company.[42]

The main bank's direct purpose in rescue operations is, needless to say, to secure its own loans, but the main bank often bears a more than proportionate burden of rescuing costs in comparison with other minor lenders. This indicates that what is at stake when a customer company fails is the main bank's reputation as a responsible monitor, and the cost bearing may be understood as a price for the misjudgment that led to the financial trouble of the customer company. As long as the main bank tries to secure its long-run interests through the recuperation of the ailing company rather than by liquidating it, individual stockholders may also benefit from escaping the casualty of bankruptcy.

However, as the J-firm becomes less dependent on the bank in its corporate financing, the monitoring capability of the bank starts to weaken. Whether the individual stockholders exercise their own monitoring through the corporate governance structure of the J-firm or the stock market, or whether management of the J-firm is comfortably left in a vacuum of effective monitoring remains to be seen. For the next step of the discussion here, I assume that management of the J-firm has not and is not completely negligent of the stockholder's interests in corporate decision making, even though it does not act as an exclusive agent of the body of stockholders. As supporting evidence I quote the already mentioned stylized fact that the J-firm has delivered a rate of return to stockholders comparable to rates that well-run Western companies have delivered.

---

[42] For a case study of such a process, see R. Pascale and T. Rohlen, "Mazda turnabout," *Journal of Japanese Studies,* 9 (1983).

CHAPTER 5

Bargaining game at the J-firm

So far I have treated the human resources and the financial resources of the J-firm separately. I have also emphasized the competitive aspect of individual incentives and the possible conflict of interests between different types of stockholders. In this chapter, I deal with the collective interests of quasi-permanent employees and stockholders and analyze the way they interact at the J-firm with the mediation of management. It is assumed that various interests of quasi-permanent employees are aggregated and represented by the enterprise-based union. The possible deviation from share price maximization on behalf of the bank stockholder may be regarded as the agency fee that individual stockholders pay the bank for its monitoring function, although I do not deal with this cost explicitly here. I assume that the body of stockholders is interested in share price maximization.

These two bodies are considered to be integral elements of the J-firm. The efficiency of the decentralized micro-micro information structure of the J-firm as discussed in Chapter 2 depends on the information-processing capabilities of the quasi-permanent employees who participate in it; and information that is generated, processed, and developed within the structure is accumulated and shared among them. They even contribute to a nonnegligible portion of the capital of the J-firm in the form of the accumulated claims for separation payment and future seniority premiums. On the other hand, the body of stockholders contributes an increasing amount of equity capital to the J-firm that is transformed into physical assets that are not readily malleable. Both the body of quasi-permanent employees and the body of stockholders are inseparable and indispensable constituencies of the J-firm as an ongoing organization.

The economic rewards that either group receives for participating in the J-firm are not altogether contractually determined. On one hand, the speed of promotion, the separation payment, and other life-time benefits from the ranking hierarchy that may accrue to each employee

150

are subject to the sequential interactions of managerial policy, employees' collective efforts, and various exogenous factors over the course of their careers. On the other hand, despite the J-firm's peculiar practice of maintaining the rate of dividends as a fixed percentage of the par value of stock irrelevant of short-run business performance, the body of stockholders also receives performance-dependent returns in the form of capital gains.

Thus, neither the employees nor the stockholders can be said to be the sole residual claimant at the J-firm, where residual refers to the remainder of the firm's revenue after all contractual payments have been made. Rather, they seem to participate in sharing the uncertain outcome of the J-firm's business through bargaining internal to the firm. The bearing of business risk is not taken to be the specialized social function of the investor; the quasi-permanent employee also bears the risk associated with the firm's performance in the form of fluctuating bonuses, uncertain opportunity for promotion, and uncertain separation payment (which he/she may not even be able to receive fully in the case of bankruptcy).

In proposition [I.4] in Chapter 1.3, I hypothesized that one essential aspect of Japanese remuneration is its sharing scheme. Martin Weitzman, in his widely discussed book, *The Share Economy*,[1] also argued that the Japanese economy is "the only industrial economy in the world with anything remotely resembling a share system." Later, in his preface to the Japanese edition, Weitzman added that Korea and Taiwan also exhibit characteristics of the profit-sharing system and that "because of the flexible compensation scheme, these countries have been able to maintain high, stable rates of employment and production, while steering through business cycles. In these countries, governments have been able to afford to combat inflation without causing unemployment."[2]

I support his contention that "the principal economic problems of our day have at their core not *macro* but profoundly *micro* behaviors, institutions, and politics. The war against stagflation cannot be won at the lofty antiseptic plane of pure macroeconomic management.... What is most desperately needed is an improved framework of incentives to induce better output, employment, and pricing decisions at the

---

[1] M. Weitzman, *The Share Economy*, Harvard University Press, 1984, p. 76.
[2] The Japanese preface to *Shea Ekonomi* (The share economy), Iwanami Shoten, 1985, p. vii.

level of the firm."[3] Although I concur with his basic premise, I submit that the resemblance between his purely theoretical model of the share system and the Japanese system itself may be rather superficial. Nonetheless, by examining the two we may be able to clarify the nature of the Japanese sharing scheme, as I perceive it, and its implications for the industrial structure, as well as macro performance, of the Japanese economy.

The essence of Weitzman's share system is that the employer and the union representing the employees agree on a share parameter, say $\alpha < 1$ (or possibly the employer unilaterally announces the parameter), according to which revenue net of material costs and depreciation charges of the firm can be divided between the body of employees and the firm (profit earner). This parameter is fixed for a certain period of time, during which the employer has the *unilateral* power to set the level of employment according to the profit-maximizing motive. In other words, in the Weitzman share scheme only the share parameter is a bargainable variable. Under this scheme, the marginal cost, MC, of additional labor is always smaller than the marginal revenue product, MR, of additional labor, because the former equals the share parameter fraction of the latter; that is, $MC = \alpha MR < MR$. Therefore, the employer is always motivated to expand the output and employment.

Within the monopolistic competition framework à la Chamberlain, given a downward sloping demand function of a firm's output and a fixed labor-output ratio, revenue per worker declines as the level of output increases. Therefore, the firm would reduce the level of pay to workers in the short run by expanding the output. In essence, "[a] share contract, then, can generally be defined as any payment mechanism where, throughout the life of the contract, worker remuneration varies inversely with firm's employment level, all other things being held constant."[4]

If one accepts Weitzman's design of a share contract, then the perpetual short-run demands for additional employment may seem an inescapable logical conclusion. However, I find it quite unrealistic to

---

[3] Weitzman, *The Share Economy*, p. 3. In my book (*The Cooperative Game Theory of the Firm*, Oxford University Press, 1984) published in the same year as the Weitzman's book, I stated: "In my assessment, an out-of-proportional attention has been given to the monetary aspect of the recent stagflationary phenomenon. However, it is at the level of enterprises that prices of products, wages of various jobs, amount of employment, and so on are actually determined. Is there not an internal driving force within the firm to generate such a phenomenon?" (p. 6). From this perspective, I tried to offer a microeconomic explanation of stagflation in the cooperative game (bargaining game) theoretic framework. See chaps. 5 and 7 of that book.

[4] Weitzman, *The Share Economy*, p. 84.

imagine that the union will fail to recognize the subsequent outcome of agreeing with Weitzman's share contract, namely that the union loses control over the remuneration per worker. Weitzman is careful to qualify his argument by referring to the eventual long-run macro outcome: "As each firm expands, its new workers spend their wages on the products of other firms, creating new demands,"[5] and this multiplier effect would bring up workers' compensation to the level consistent with the optimal allocation of resources. But I doubt that the union, or at least the Japanese enterprise-based union, is that farsighted. I am also uncertain that the union is altruistic enough to accept the managerial discretionary power to add new employment at the sacrifice of the level of pay to the incumbent employees, even in the short run.

The controversy as to whether Weitzman's share model captures the essential feature of the Japanese system has centered around the issue of whether the Japanese bonus system is a variant of a profit-sharing scheme or a form of deferred wage payment. This issue needs to be settled empirically, but for now I am willing to adopt as a working hypothesis the view that there is an element of sharing in the Japanese bonus scheme, with the qualification that bonus adjustments in response to the fluctuation of the firm's revenue may be made only in the middle run (see Section 3.2).

My critical point is that Weitzman's system does not live up to the full expectation provoked by the attractive name "share." In his system, decisions on strategic management variables crucial to the wellbeing of employees, such as employment, are not shared by the employer and the union, either explicitly or implicitly, but are exclusively in the realm of managerial prerogatives. In contrast, I submit that the Japanese enterprise-based union has acquired implicit bargaining power over such strategic managerial issues as employment and relocation, which are of vital concern to its members, in exchange for its own commitment to a certain level of effort expenditure (and wage restraint, if necessary). It is a very important feature of the J-firm, in my view, that considerably wide issues are subject to explicit and implicit consensus making.

The implicit or explicit consensus making over managerial issues may not necessarily lead to outcomes pleasant to "outsiders," as we shall see later. However, viewing the Japanese sharing system as covering a wide range of issues beyond the traditional wage issue seems to explain some industrial organizational and macroeconomic features of

[5] Ibid., p. 5.

the Japanese economy better than Weitzman's paradigm. But how can we formulate such a sharing scheme and analyze its implications? This is the task that we are about to tackle here.

Section 1 formalizes the hypothesis that the J-firm is a coalition of the body of quasi-permanent employees and the body of stockholders and that the behavioral characteristics of the J-firm are understood as the equilibrium outcome of the interaction between the two. I formulate the interaction between them as a bargaining game and examine the implications of various hypoptheses concerning the nature of bargaining. I draw on some interesting recent achievements of bargaining game theory to explain the interrelatedness of collective bargaining involving the enterprise-based union, managerial discretionary decision making on strategic management issues, and the implicit commitment to the cooperative effort by the body of employees.

In Section 2 I discuss various behavioral characteristics of the J-firm as the bargaining outcome that is efficient, free of strategic disturbance, and fair to the constituent bodies. These characteristics include the J-firm's tendency to pursue higher growth than the level that the share price-maximizing norm would warrant, to restrain the size of quasi-permanent employment through the adoption of capital-intensive technology and outsourcing (subcontracting and subsidiarization), to rely on the "gift exchange" of high effort expenditure by the worker and the assurance of job security by management, and to prefer work sharing over layoffs as a response to adverse business conditions.

On the basis of the theoretical analysis in Section 1, Section 3 examines the various facets of management of the J-firm and relates them to a series of events in the post–World War II period.

1.   The structure of the bargaining game

In the introduction to this chapter, I argued that the body of stockholders and the body of quasi-permanent employees are essentially in a symmetrical position within the J-firm. Both contribute indispensable informational and financial assets to the J-firm, and they share uncertain returns produced by the combined commitment of these assets. In this sense, one may say that the firm is a *coalition of the two constituent bodies*. This view of the firm is different from the neoclassical one in which the body of stockholders is the owner of the firm and an exclusive residual claimant (risk taker).

Let us call the revenue of the firm, after all market-determined payments are made, *organizational quasi rent*. The constituent bodies of the J-firm compete with each other in the sharing of the organizational quasi rent generated by the J-firm. It is to be divided into remuneration to the quasi-permanent employees, dividends to the stockholders, and incremental accumulation of corporate assets (recorded as equity capital and reserves for separation payments for accounting purposes) to finance the growth of the firm. But in order to generate the organizational quasi rent, both bodies need each other's commitment to the accumulation of financial and human assets. If the body of stockholders is not assured a satisfying rate of return on their investment, it may withhold the additional supply of financial capital. If the body of employees is not assured a satisfying reward and career advancement, it may withhold its efforts to accumulate and efficiently use the stock of knowledge.

Obviously such noncooperative behavior does not benefit either side, because it allows the competitive position of the firm to be encroached upon by other competitive firms and thus cause the organizational quasi rent to dwindle over time. Both constituent bodies have an interest in avoiding conflict situations and seeking an accord with respect to the rate at which they should aim to produce the organizational quasi rent and how they should share the outcome of their cooperative effort, while committing themselves to certain behavioral standards that will enable them to sustain and expand the production of the organizational quasi rent. This is a typical bargaining game situation.

Let us now describe the general structure of a bargaining game in somewhat formal language and then see how the characteristics of the bargaining situation at the J-firm can be expressed in those terms. Let *bargainable subjects* or *bargainable variables* be defined as those variables that are relevant to the payoff to the body of stockholders (share price) and to the payoff to the quasi-permanent employees (as represented by the collective objective function of the enterprise-based union) and on which decisions are made by an explicit or implicit agreement (consensus making) among participants of the firm. The bargainable subjects certainly include such traditional collective bargaining issues as employee pay. In addition, depending on the decision-making structure of the firm, the strategic managerial variables – such as investment, employment, and relocation of a factory, which traditionally belong to the managerial prerogative – may also become explicit or implicit bargainable subjects. Even the effort level controlled by the quasi-permanent employee may become an implicit bargainable subject in exchange for the inclusion of strategic managerial variables in the set of bargainable subjects.

The set of payoff pairs feasible under admissible value combinations of bargainable variables is called the set of attainable *outcomes*. The choice of an attainable outcome by an implicit/explicit agreement between the constituent bodies of the firm through a complex intrafirm decision-making process is called a *bargain outcome*. If a consensus cannot be reached on bargainable subjects, the constituent bodies are assumed to receive a fixed pair of payoffs, which is called the *conflict outcome*. There is an attainable outcome in which both bodies are better off than the conflict outcome. Therefore, if both constituent bodies are rational, they are mutually interested in finding an outcome better than the conflict outcome.

A bargaining game situation may be regarded as a universal phenomenon at the modern firm. But is there anything distinctive about the bargaining structure at the J-firm? I submit the following characterizations of the bargaining game at the J-firm for examination:

1. *A wide range of bargainable subjects:* Bargainable subjects at the J-firm extend to a relatively wide range of issues beyond conventional collective bargaining subjects such as remuneration to the quasi-permanent employee and other conditions of employment. Strategic decision variables of high relevance to the welfare of quasi-permanent employees, as well as their standard effort level to accumulate and efficiently use contextual skills, are included (implicitly) as bargainable subjects.

2. *Implicit commitment:* The agreement regarding some variables defining a bargain outcome may not be written in an explicit and enforceable contract, but may be understood only as implicit commitment.

3. *Mediating role of mangement:* The major role of management in the bargaining game is that of a mediator who formulates strategic management decisions agreeable to both the body of stockholders and the body of quasi-permanent employees by committing itself to a certain neutral policy-making standard.

As we have seen, in the J-firm quasi-permanent employees are given incentives to develop the contextual skills needed for effective horizontal coordination of operating tasks and autonomous problem solving over time. If their career development is suspended because of layoffs or discharges necessitated by the loss of competitiveness of the employing firm, future returns to employee's learning effort that would otherwise be available in the form of a seniority premium and separation payment are sacrificed. Conversely, if the firm keeps expanding, it opens better career prospects for incumbent employees in the form of better chances of future promotion and the increased earnings associated with promotion.

Thus the utility function of the quasi-permanent employee includes not only conventional variables such as the current level of earnings and effort level, but also strategic management decision variables of the firm, such as the level of employment (which may affect the job security of quasi-permanent employees), the investment rate (which may imply the rate of expansion of the horizontal hierarchy), and so on. The collective objective function of, or equivalently the payoff to, the enterprise-based union would reflect such fundamental characteristics of the individual member's utility function, whatever the method of aggregation may be. On the other hand, the effort level of the quasi-permanent employee would, together with conventional strategic management decision variables, affect the share price through the output level of the organizational quasi rent.

In this situation, then, as discussed at the end of Chapter 4, it is not internally efficient that only the pay level is codetermined by collective bargaining and that strategic management decisions are made unilaterally by share price-maximizing management posterior to wage bargaining, while employees unilaterally control the level of their effort to their own advantage. Efficient decision making in the usual Pareto sense cannot be achieved unless both the strategic management decision variables and the effort variable are included with the conventional distributional variables in the domain of bargainable subjects, and trade among the three sets of variables becomes facilitated.

To realize efficient trade over such wide-ranging bargainable variables may seem a formidable task. Under a certain regularity condition, however, it can be shown that efficient trade and the choice of an efficient "bargain" may become possible by decomposing decision making over different kinds of bargainable subjects into separate spheres: Let distribution variables (pay level) be decided in collective bargaining between management and the enterprise-based union, while making management and the quasi-permanent employee mutually committed to a certain "nonprofit-maximizing" managerial decision-making "rule" and a certain norm of collective effort expenditure, respectively. In this scheme, an agreement on strategic management decision variables and the effort level variable is only implicit and enforced by mutual concerns with reputation. Although this decomposition may seem ad hoc, if rules for management decision making and effort expenditure are properly designed, the outcome in this scheme turns out to be "fair," "power balancing," and "equilibriating" at the same time, each in a well-defined sense. However, seeing this requires some roundabout logical thinking.

First, let us begin by considering the following thought experiment: What kind of bargaining outcome is likely to emerge under each of the following bargaining schemes and what is the mutual relation among those outcomes?

(A) Management acts as a benevolent arbiter between the body of stockholders and the body of quasi-permanent employees and adjudicates on bargainable variables according to a certain "fairness" rule.

(B) Management acts as a neutral referee between the two competing constituent bodies and dictates a certain outcome by striking a balance between bargaining powers of the two bodies.

(C) Management acts solely as an agent of the body of stockholders and is engaged in strategic bargaining with the enterprise-based union.

In each case, assume that the bargainable subjects cover all relevant distributional, strategic managerial, and effort variables, and that the "bargain outcome" in each scheme is enforceable. The only difference between the schemes is in the nature of the decision-making process as specified; the payoff functions of the two constituent bodies and all other data defining the bargaining situation are exactly the same. Of course, outcomes in each scheme would be different depending on the notion of "fairness," the concept of "power balance," and the procedural nature of the collective bargaining institution. Once these issues are settled, however, one may expect the outcome to differ from one scheme to another. Somewhat suprisingly, however, recent developments in bargaining game theory have shown that the outcomes of these schemes tend to become qualitatively the same and to approximate the so-called Nash bargaining solution under certain conditions.

Scheme (A) may be identified with Ronald Dore's view of Japanese management as "hierarchical corporatism",[6] and its logical modeling

---

[6] "What one might call the 'corporatist' view of the firm are ideas (essential parts of the Japanese management ideology): 1 that 'the company' as a collectivity corporate, can be said to have interests in much the same way as one talks of the 'national interest' – either as something 'over and above' sectional interests, or as the sum of those interests. . . . [This] Japanese solution . . . is to see the managers as the benevolent guardians of the interest of the company as a whole (including the interests of workers as well as shareholders). Their 'broader' view, and more long-term view, entitles them to adjudicate the claims put to them by individuals or various interest groups within the company. One might call this 'hierarchical corporatism.'" Ronald Dore, *British Factor –Japanese Factory: The Origins of National Diversity in Industrial Relations*, University of California Press, 1985, p. 364.

may be given by John Nash's seminal axiomatic model. Nash has formulated a set of axioms that a reasonable outcome in a two-person bargaining game should satisfy.[7] These are, roughly speaking, the requirements of efficiency in the sense of Pareto, fairness, and some kind of informational economy in decision making. This set of axioms may be said to provide an instruction manual for the neutral arbiter. As weak as the requirements may appear, Nash showed that only one outcome satisfies his set of axioms. It is the one that maximizes the product of payoff gains to both players from cooperation. That is, if the payoff to each partner is represented by u and v defined over a set of bargainable variables $\mathbf{x}$, and its value at the conflict situation is represented by $\hat{u}$ and $\hat{v}$, the Nash solution is the one at which the product

$$[u(\mathbf{x}) - \hat{u}][v(\mathbf{x}) - \hat{v}]$$

is maximized.

The axiom of fairness as formulated by Nash in the context of a pure distribution game goes roughly as follows: The bargain outcome should be independent of the labels of players who play the game, and if they interchange playing positions the outcome should remain unchanged for each position. It may not appear so easy, however, to find an appropriate institutional interpretation of this requirement in the context of the bargaining between the body of stockholders and the body of quasi-permanent employees whose payoff structures are very different.

But note that the maximization of the Nash product is also implied by the following condition (those readers who are unacquainted with the mathematical technicalities will find that they can manage quite well by ignoring them): Suppose that a bargainable variable (a vector) $\mathbf{x}$ affects the payoffs u and v, and that their derivatives (gradients) with respect to $\mathbf{x}$ are represented by $\nabla u_{\mathbf{x}}$ and $\nabla v_{\mathbf{x}}$; then $\mathbf{x}$ ought to be adjusted in the direction in which the value

$$\nabla u_{\mathbf{x}}/[u(\mathbf{x}) - \hat{u}] + \nabla v_{\mathbf{x}}/]v(\mathbf{x}) - \hat{v}]$$

is increased. If this condition is satisfied, I say the adjustment is Nash improving. Each term represents the percentage payoff gain for the relevant party (or loss, if negative) with respect to the marginal change in the variable $\mathbf{x}$ relative to the total gain from cooperation. If the efficiency requirement is satisfied in the usual Pareto sense, then a marginal change in the variable makes one party better off (the corresponding term is positive) and another worse off (negative). Therefore, the above condition is interpreted by saying that bargainable variable(s)

---

[7] J. Nash, "The bargaining problem," *Econometrica,* 18 (1950), pp. 155–62.

should be adjusted as far as the percentage gain for one party is greater than the percentage loss for another party and that the adjustment should stop at the point where the percentage loss for one party is just matched by the percentage gain by another party.[8] This equality represents the notion of fairness.

I have explored a model of scheme (B) in the context of the bargaining situation involving a wide range of bargainable subjects by using the so-called Zeuthen principle.[9] Suppose that each bargaining partner has to risk the retaliatory withdrawal of cooperation by the other side when he/she makes an excessive additional demand with respect to a bargainable variable $\mathbf{x}$. How much risk (the maximum probability of the withdrawal of cooperation) he/she can dare to take depends on his/her risk attitude (i.e., the curvature of u or v) and his/her attained gains from cooperation (i.e., $u(\mathbf{x}) - \hat{u}$ or $v(\mathbf{x}) - \hat{v}$). When there is an additional demand $\mathbf{h}$, the body of quasi employees must consider its subjective estimate of the probability of the other party's withdrawal of cooperation, q. The employees' expected gain from making an additional demand h is $(1 - q)[u(\mathbf{x} + \mathbf{h}) - u(\mathbf{x})]$, and the expected loss is $q[u(\mathbf{x}) - \hat{u}]$. In order for the demand to be worthwhile, the former must be greater than the latter. Therefore the maximum probability of breakdown of cooperation per additional demand the body can tolerate would be the one that would equate the two: $q^{\max}\mathbf{h}^{-1} = \{[u(\mathbf{x} + \mathbf{h}) - u(\mathbf{x})]/\mathbf{h}[u(\mathbf{x} + \mathbf{h}) - \hat{u}]\}$. By making $\mathbf{h}$ approach zero, the ratio approaches

$$\nabla u_x/[u(\mathbf{x}) - \hat{u}].$$

This maximum probability of conflict may be taken to represent the party's "willingness" to take the risk of demanding the infinitesimally small change in $\mathbf{x}$ and may be called "boldness" following Robert Aumann and Mordecai Kurz.[10] Symmetrically, for an infinitesimally small change, $-\mathbf{h}$, the boldness of the body of stockholders may be defined as

$$-\nabla v_x/[v(\mathbf{x}) - \hat{v}].$$

---

[8] It is known that this adjustment rule leads to the (local) maximization of the Nash product, even if the set of possible bargain outcomes does not satisfy the regular convexity condition, as in the original formulation of Nash's model. That is, phenomena of increasing returns and external economies in underlying technology may be permitted. See M. Aoki, "An incentive-compatible approximation of Nash-like solution under nonclassical environments," in Theodore Groves, Roy Radner, and Stanley Reiter (eds.), *Information, Incentives and Economic Mechanisms: Essays in Honor of Leonid Hurwicz,* University of Minnesota Press and Basil Balckwell, 1987, pp. 295–307.

[9] See Aoki, *The Cooperative Game Theory,* pt. II.

[10] R. Aumann and M. Kurz, "Power and taxes," *Econometrica,* 45 (1977), pp. 137–60.

The boldness measure is equal to the percentage gain from the marginal increase in x relative to the total acquired gain from cooperation. As a party gains more in the variable x, he/she becomes less bold in bargaining for an additional change in x for fear of losing the acquired gain, as well as the diminishing marginal utility from an additional gain.

The Zeuthen principle, as formulated by John Harsanyi, dictates that the equilibrium of bargaining process is achieved at the point where boldness is equalized for both bargaining partners with respect to all relevant bargainable variables.[11] At this point, both parties' willingness to risk the conflict situation is just equalized and the equilibrium of the bargaining process will be reached. Alternatively, one may imagine a situation in which management strikes a balance in its decision making between the interests of the two constituent bodies of the firm, taking boldness as the measure of local bargaining power of each bargaining partner. It is immediately clear that the equilibrium according to the Zeuthen principle is identical with the above Nash condition of fairness.

Scheme (C) reflects the conventional adversarial view of neoclassical economics. Noteworthy progress has been made along this line of thought recently by important contributions by Ariel Rubinstein and associates. Rubinstein formulated a bargaining process for a simple pure distribution game in which bargaining partners alternate offers and counteroffers at equal intervals in a strategic manner until either party accepts an offer by the other, at which time the game ends.[12]

Rubinstein gave a severe interpretation to the rationality requirement by investigating "perfect equilibria." To be a perfect equilibrium, it is not sufficient for a pair of planned strategies chosen at the beginning of the game to be the best choice for each player in the sense that given the other's choice there is no other strategy for him/her that would yield a better outcome. But also the planned strategies must form an equilibrium in each round of the game after all possible histories (otherwise the proposal of any Pareto-efficient division and its acceptance can be an equilibrium). In particular, the following conditions must be met at any bargaining turn, following a sequence of offers and rejections: (1) the player whose turn is to make an offer has no superior alternative to offering what his/her strategy prescribes; and (2) the other player, if he/she plans to accept (reject) at time t, cannot do better by rejecting (accepting) it.

[11] J. Harsanyi, *Rational Behaviour and Bargaining Equilibrium in Games and Social Situations,* Cambridge University Press, 1977.
[12] A. Rubinstein, "Perfect equilibrium in a bargaining model," *Econometrica,* 50 (1981), pp. 97–110.

In Rubinstein's model, the risk of breakdown of cooperation is exogenous, rather than the outcome of the players' decision to withdraw their cooperation. For example, the firm and the enterprise-based union bargain over the quasi rent that they cannot realize until reaching an agreement, but in the meantime this rent opportunity might be snatched away by a rival firm, and this probability is a constant parameter per time. Another interpretation of his model is that the outcomes $\hat{u}$ and $\hat{v}$ are the status quo payoffs. If both parties reach an accord, then the rent possibility is increased, but they discount future payoffs at a constant rate of time discount. In other words, they are time impatient and interested in reaching an accord earlier than later.

In this situation, Rubinstein has proved that there is a unique perfect equilibrium in which an offer of the first mover is accepted and the game ends there. Intuitively speaking, the equilibrium strategies would be such that the first mover would extract the premium attached to avoiding the risk of a breakdown in cooperation (or the time discount premium) during the interval between offers and counteroffers. The first mover is always at an advantage, because the other party is risk averse or time impatient and would rather yield to less payoff than wait until its turn of offer. But Ken Binmore, A. Rubinstein, and Asher Wolinsky have proved recently that, if bargaining partners are time efficient in the sense that the interval between offers and counteroffers is infinitesimally small, then the perfect equilibrium of the strategic two-person bargaining game converges on the Nash solution.[13]

Actual bargain outcomes under the three institutional schemes may be different, depending on the corresponding disagreement outcomes $\hat{u}$ and $\hat{v}$ and other parameters. But the proof of the qualitative equivalence of bargain outcomes under the three schemes is a remarkable theoretical result. It may allow us to regard qualitative characteristics of Nash bargaining solution invariant to the choice of disagreement outcome as reflecting the nature of bargain outcome that is robust with respect to the variations of institutional interpretation of the bargaining situation facing the J-firm, listed as (A) through (C) earlier in this section. As I have discussed elsewhere, variations in the scope of bargainable subjects in different bargaining institutions may be more responsible for generating divergent outcomes than differences in the bargaining scheme itself.[14]

If we accept the qualitative equivalence of bargain outcomes under the three institutional schemes and assume that bargainable subjects

[13] K. Binmore, A. Rubinstein and A. Wolinsky, "The Nash bargaining solution in economic modelling," *Rand Journal of Economics*, 17 (Summer 1986), pp. 176–88.
[14] M. Aoki, *The Cooperative Game Theory*, pt. III

cover a wide range of distributional, effort, and strategic managerial variables, the next logical step is to find an appropriate combination of institutional schemes that may simplify the achievement of Nash solution (I assume that a disagreement outcome is the one available to both parties in the absence of a cooperative agreement). Under a certain regularity condition, we can trichotomize the decision in the following way[15]:

[B.1] *Bargaining over distributive share:* Management and the enterprise-based union should agree on a share parameter through collective bargaining, according to which the cost of growth and the organizational quasi rent after the payment for the cost of growth should be distributed between the body of stockholders and the body of employees.

[B.2] *Commitment of effort by the employee:* The quasi-permanent employee should commit himself/herself to the level of effort at which the marginal organization quasi rent with respect to effort is equal to the marginal value disutility of effort.

[B.3] *Strategic management decision making based on the weighting rule:* The choice of strategic managerial variables should be made by management, responding to changing market environments, by weighting the choices optimal to constituent bodies with their respective shares as weights.

Let the share parameter of the body of stockholders and that of quasi-permanent employees determined by [B.1] be α and $1 - \alpha$, respectively. The weighting rule [B.3] implies the following: Suppose that the marginal benefit with respect to a certain strategic managerial variable, x, for the stockholder is given by MB_x^s and that for the

---

[15] Under a certain regularity condition, relative bargaining power may be measured by the ratio of "pure boldness" of both the constituent bodies. As already defined, the boldness of each constituent body normally declines as the level of payoff increases, because the denominator [the difference, $u(\mathbf{x}) - \hat{u}$ or $v(\mathbf{x}) - \hat{v}$, between the acquired payoff and the conflict payoff] increases, and the numerator (the marginal utility ∇u_x or ∇v_x) decreases. The boldness thus measures the degree of willingness to bargain in the neighborhood of the achieved position. In order to get the measure of willingness to bargain at large, one must eliminate the component that measures its attitude toward small gains. This can be done by dividing the boldness by the measure of absolute risk aversion in the small due to Pratt and Arrow. If the payoff indicies u and v belong to a simple class of utility function, the pure boldness derived in this way becomes a constant regardless of the level of payoff and is considered to represent global bargaining power of the player in the game. Then the following trichotomization becomes possible. See Aoki, *The Cooperative Game Theory*, pp. 74–80.

employee is by MB_x^e; then the condition for fair and equilibrating strategic managerial decision is given by

$$\alpha MB_x^s + (1 - \alpha)MB_x^e = MC_x, \tag{5.1}$$

where MC_x is the marginal cost of the strategic management decision variable, x. In the next section, I explore some implications of the weighting rule for behavioral characteristics of the J-firm.

2.   Some behavioral implications of bargain outcome in the J-firm

A.   Growth-seeking behavior

Suppose that the strategic management decision variable, x, represents the rate of growth of the firm's value-added. If the wage bill is determined by collective bargaining and a growth rate can be chosen by management posterior to the collective bargaining agreement in order to maximize share price on behalf of the body of stockholders, management ought to follow the rule: $MB_x^s = MC_x^s$, where the left-hand term represents the percentage increase in capital gain due to one extra percent growth and the right-hand term represents the percentage decrease in current dividend in order to finance the extra percent growth (see Appendix 5.1 for the derivation of equations in this subsection). This corresponds to what we called short-run share price maximization in Section 4.3. Suppose that α is the stockholder share of the current value-added; then the above condition may be rewritten (as Appendix 5.1 shows) as

$$\alpha MB_x^s = MC_x, \tag{5.2}$$

where MC_x is the percentage decrease in current value-added in order to finance an extra percent of growth and may be interpreted as the marginal cost of growth of the firm as a coalition of the body of stockholders and the body of employees who participate jointly in the sharing of value-added.

Symmetrically, consider a twin firm whose technological and market conditions are exactly the same as the above stockholder-controlled firm, but assume that the firm is obligated to pay a certain fixed amount of dividend to the body of stockholders, while its management can choose a rate of growth to maximize the lifetime utility of the representative employee. The representative employee is assumed to derive utility from a positive rate of growth of the firm due to enhanced promotability and the prospect of increased separation payment, but at a diminishing marginal rate with respect to an increase in the growth rate.[16] For this employee-controlled firm, management ought to choose the growth rate according to the rule $MB_x^e = MC_x^e$, where the left-hand term represents the percentage increase in employee's benefits in present value from an extra percent growth of the firm and the right-hand term represents the percentage decrease in current earnings of the employee in order to finance an extra percent of growth. Supposing that $1 - \alpha$ is the employees' share in current value-added, this condition can be rewritten as

$$(1 - \alpha)MB_x^e = MC_x. \tag{5.3}$$

Compare these two equations, (5.2) and (5.3), with the condition for the Nash bargain outcome, (5.1). As far as MB_x^e is strictly positive – that is, as far as the representative employee derives positive utility from the growth of the firm – the growth rate, x^*, to be chosen by the coalitional firm according to (5.1) is higher than the growth rate, x^s, to be chosen by the short-run share price-maximizing firm according to (5.2) [and the growth rate, x^e, chosen by the employees' utility-maximizing firm according to (5.3)]. Figure 5.1 depicts the situation. The area of the shaded region ABCD represents the additional growth cost necessary for financing extra growth, $x^* - x^s$, for the benefit of employees beyond the level, x^s, that short-run share price maximization would warrant. Even if this portion of growth cost is financed by the firm's retained earnings and recorded as equity capital for accounting purposes, it is de facto seized by the body of employees. To the extent that this is true, the assumption stated in Section 4.1, that retained profits will be fully reflected in the share price, needs to be modified. We summarize:

[B.4] *Pursuit of higher growth:* The coalitional firm pursues a higher growth rate than the level that short-run share price maximization would warrant to deliver extra benefits to the quasi-permanent employee in the form of enhanced promotability and better prospects for a separation payment.

As yet I am unable to present solid econometric support for this theoretical proposition, but it appears that Japanese firms on the average have grown faster ex post than corresponding American firms, which presumably are more constrained by stronger stockholder pressure for short-run share price maximization. If this hypothesis is indeed correct, then the J-firm deviates from the share price-maximization norm

[16] For this see ibid., chap. 7.

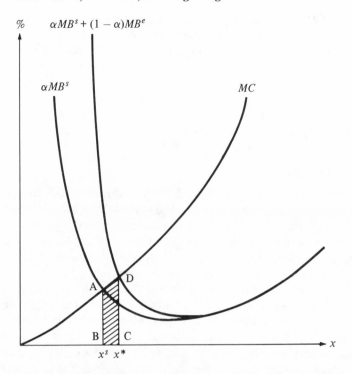

Figure 5.1. Equilibrium growth of the coalitional firm.

in a dual sense: It exhibits higher-than-share price-maximizing growth on behalf of the quasi-permanent employee and higher-than-share price-maximizing debt on behalf of the bank at the expense of individual stockholders.[17]

B.   Dilemma of industrial democracy

As hinted at in the preceding section, the weighting rule [B.3] for strategic managerial decision making includes as a special case the profit-maximizing rule in which the weight given to the body of employees is null. This corresponds to the case in which employees do not possess any firm-specific contextual skills and receive market-determined remuneration. As the relative bargaining power of the body of quasi-

---

[17] In ibid., pp. 85–8, I have also shown that debt financing is preferred to internal financing by the employee even with perfect capital markets and no tax. Therefore the Modigliani–Miller theorem does not hold for the coalitional firm.

permanent employees increases, the weight given to the strategic managerial decision making optimal to employees increases from zero to one, at which point the body of stockholders ceases to be anything more than rentiers. Therefore one can possibly predict the effect of a change in the relative bargaining power between the two constituent bodies on strategic managerial decision making by examining qualitative and quantitative differences in decisions optimal to each of them.

Let us compare the preferences of both bodies for growth. First, assume that the firm is controlled by the body of stockholders, who unanimously support the maximization of share price. If they wish, existing stockholders can opt for monopolizing gains from growth among themselves in the form of capital gains, while they bear all the cost of growth among themselves in the form of retention of profit. When they opt for making new members bear a part of the growth cost in the form of a new equity issue, capital gains accruable to themselves are reduced by exactly the same amount as the total value of new equity issues under the assumption of a perfectly competitive financial market and no taxes.[18]

Imagine next the twin firm that is controlled fully by the body of homogeneous incumbent employees, but is otherwise identical to the stockholder-controlled firm. Suppose that in order to finance growth, incumbent employees have to sacrifice current earnings in the form of the retention of revenue by the firm. The growth would normally entail the expansion of the work force, unless labor-saving technology was introduced. In this situation, incumbent employees, while bearing the cost of growth, cannot monopolize the benefits from extra growth, as the stockholder does, because the newly employed would eventually participate in returns from growth. The possibility of external debt financing would mitigate this effect to some extent, as it would shift some portion of the growth cost to incoming employees, but not completely. It may also be argued that status differentiation can be created between senior employees and new employees so that the latter bear the cost of growth in the form of lower starting earnings and the former reap the benefit from growth in the form of a seniority premium and separation payments. It is, however, unlikely that the newly employed workers are initially endowed with sufficient capital, both human and financial, to finance growth of the firm equivalent to the share price-maximizing rate of the stockholder-controlled firm.

From this thought experiment, one can predict that the firm would

---

[18] This is an implication of the Modigliani–Miller theorem.

choose lower investment, or, when it invests, it would choose more labor-saving technology, if the relative bargaining power is tilted in favor of the employees. Also, as Hajime Miyazaki has shown in his elegant model, when the future risk of layoff is involved, the firm would choose the lower level of employment so that the probability of layoff of the incumbent employees would be reduced.[19] Thus we can posit:

> [B.5] *The restraint of employment:* The J-firm, in comparison with the share price-maximizing firm, tends to restrain the size of employment relative to the growth of value-added by adopting capital-intensive technology in order to secure the vested interests of incumbent employees.

This proposition provides a clue to a puzzle posted by an elaborate comparison of productivity growth among industries in the United States and Japan by Dale Jorgenson, Masahiro Kuroda, and Keiko Nishimizu.[20] The average growth rates of output, capital, labor, and intermediate inputs over 1960–79 that they have estimated for selected industries are shown in Table 5.1. It is evident that Japanese industries have grown much faster than their American counterparts, but on average have done so with more intensive doses of capital. For all industries, the growth of capital input is 3.67 times as high as the labor input in Japanese industries, whereas in the United States the ratio is 2.62, although in the motor vehicle and electric machinery industries, the American firms have adopted slightly more capital-intensive methods.

This result is not surprising, if the rate of increase in capital cost is relatively lower than that in wages in Japan during the period in question. Jorgenson and his colleagues do not give the rates of increase in the "factor prices," but they have estimated the Japanese capital and labor price indeces transformed by purchasing power parity at 1970 and have found that "the hourly wage in Japan was less than 30 percent of that in the U.S. On the other hand, the purchasing parities for capital input show that the cost of capital in Japan was about 80 percent of that in the U.S." If growth rates of factor inputs in that year were the same as the average observed for the entire period, Japanese

[19] See Aoki, *The Cooperative Game Theory,* especially p. 112; Hajime Miyazaki, "Internal bargaining, labor contracts, and a Marshallian theory of the firm," *American Economic Review,* 74 (1984), pp. 381–93.

[20] D. Jorgenson, M. Kuroda, and K. Nishimizu, "U.S.–Japan Industry-level comparison of productivity change," *Journal of the Japanese and International Economies,* 1 (*March*) 1987.

Table 5.1. *Average growth rates of output, inputs, and technological progress for selected industries in the United States and Japan, 1960–79*

Industry	United States					Japan				
	Productivity	Output	Capital	Labor	Intermediate	Productivity	Output	Capital	Labor	Intermediate
Textiles	2.12	3.93	2.81	-0.03	2.44	0.29	3.44	5.28	-1.68	3.18
Chemicals	0.91	5.35	4.73	1.93	5.24	2.45	10.16	10.09	1.60	8.08
Iron, steel	-0.44	2.48	1.45	0.76	3.86	0.90	9.07	11.62	0.68	8.20
Electrical machinery	1.99	5.75	5.76	2.13	4.67	3.28	13.28	12.37	4.90	10.67
Motor vehicles	0.84	4.28	4.62	1.78	3.95	0.59	11.82	14.06	6.81	11.78
Average	0.26	3.48	3.75	1.43	4.08	1.12	8.46	9.96	2.71	8.50

Source: K. Jorgenson, M. Kuroda, and M. Nishimizu, "Japan–U.S. industry level productivity comparisons, 1960–79," *Journal of the Japanese and International Economies,* 1(1987), pp. 14–15.

Table 5.2. *Rate of increase in employment relative to real rate of increase in product sales in major manufacturing firms, 1966–86*

	All listed f. ns	Toyota Motors	Matsushita Electric	Hitachi Manufacturing	Nippon Steel
1966–71	—	0.301	0.209	0.207	0.043
1971–6	—	0.274	−0.562	1.470	−0.894
1976–81	−0.837	0.289	−0.536	−0.061	−0.943
1981–6	0.101	0.365	0.190	0.162	0.596

Source: NEEDS. Sales are normalized by NEEDS annual wholesale price index.

industries added comparatively more capital-intensive methods then in spite of the relatively higher cost of capital. This conclusion is not consistent with the neoclassical paradigm, which predicts that a firm will choose the cost-minimizing technology, and that both capital and labor will be taken as exogenous factors of production supplied through markets.[21] The study by Jorgenson et al. is industry based so that it does not provide a precise picture of technological adoption at the micro level and does not directly support proposition [B.5], but may suggest the usefulness of further empirical studies along the lines of the nonneoclassical reasoning developed in this chapter.

The reasoning leading to [B.5] also indicates that the strengthening of incumbent employees' power within the coalitional firm may have an adverse effect on the firm's demand for new employment. In an earlier work I called this adversarial effect of increasing employees' voice within the firm on new employment "a dilemma of industrial democracy."[22] The evidence is not inconsistent with the hypothesis that the Japanese industry is not free of this dilemma. Since the 1974–5 depression, when the Japanese economy recorded the first negative growth in the post–World War II period, large Japanese firms have limited the expansion of the work force considerably. Table 5.2 shows the ratio of the rate of increase in employment (decrease if negative) at major manufacturing firms relative to the rate of expansion of their operations measured by (real) product sales.

Large Japanese firms have thus been trying hard to reduce the size of their work force relative to their sales rather than woo new workers

---

[21] However, the estimate by Jorgenson et al, is explicitly based on the neoclassical modeling of profit-maximizing firms.
[22] See Aoki, *The Cooperative Game Theory*, chap. 4

at the risk of reducing the earning level of the incumbent employees, as Weitzman's model of the share scheme would predict. However, if Japanese firms wish to restrain new employment relative to sales, why has the dilemma of industrial democracy not manifested itself at the macroeconomic level in the form of unemployment? In fact, unemployment in Japan has been rather low, and was still not above 3 percent by the end of 1986. Some, like Koji Taira, consider Japan's low level of unemployment to be a statistical artifact, but even when the data are adjusted in the light of the American definition of unemployment this does not seem to narrow down the difference between the two countries.[23]

One reason that restraining employment at large firms does not cause massive unemployment is that there are alternative ways to absorb employment. First, leaving aside the effect of labor-saving technology and organizational innovation, as described in Chapter 2, the large firms have been able to reduce employment by simplifying the hierarchical layers, hiving off subsidiaries (see Section 3.1C), and relying on subcontracting (outsourcing). Controlling for other factors that may affect the labor input requirement, I estimate that the hiving off of subsidiaries alone contributed to the 3.5 to 4.5 percent per annum growth in sales in real terms without any increase in the work force at listed firms in the electric machinery and electronics industry over the period 1973–82.[24] Through subsidiarization and outsourcing, large Japanese firms have been able to create differential employment conditions that presumably contribute to the semimonopolization of growth benefits by their incumbent quasi-permanent employees. (I discuss this mechanism in more detail in Chapter 6.)

Second, the low level of unemployment may be partly attributable to the absorption of the potentially unemployed into other categories of disadvantaged workers. In the great surges of growth after 1955 large firms hired many of their new workers on temporary contracts of three months to one year, which could be renewed at management's discretion. Whereas regular workers were provided with a considerable degree of job security and other benefits such as retirement compensation, bonuses, and so on, temporary workers were vulnerable and

[23] Koji Taira, "Japan's low unemployment: economic miracle or statistical artifact," *Monthly Labor Review*, July 1983, pp. 3–10. T. Ito, "Why is the unemployment rate so much lower in Japan than in the U. S.?" mimeographed, University of Minnesota, 1984.

[24] M. Aoki, "Innovative adaptation through quasi-tree structure: an emerging aspect of Japanese entrepreneurship," *Zeitschrift für Nationalökonomie*, 1984 supplement, pp. 177–98. The autonomous rate of labor savings per sales due to internal organizational and technological innovation is estimated to be as high as 10.0 percent per annum.

underprivileged, although they were actually employed on a more or less permanent basis as long as business conditions of the firm permitted. Around 1960 these temporary workers reached their peak numbers, accounting for roughly 12 percent of all workers employed by firms with 500 or more employees in manufacturing industries.

The Income Doubling Plan of 1960 declared that the removal of this dual employment structure – that is, the segmentation of the work force into a class of privileged quasi-permanent employees and a class of disadvantaged temporary workers – should be high on the modernization agenda. During the high growth of the 1960s, the labor shortage became acute, and even enterprise unionism based on incumbent regular workers was able to absorb the aspiration of temporary workers to attain more secure membership in employing firms without forcing the regular workers to make a sacrifice. Many temporary workers at large firms were either promoted to the status of regular workers or quit voluntarily to seek relatively better-paid jobs at other firms (not rarely at small firms). By the early 1970s, the use of temporary workers as a ploy to maintain a buffer group of long-term but lower-paid workers had largely disappeared.

Recently, however, a new category of workers who are employed for relatively shorter periods has arisen: these are part-time workers, predominantly middle-aged females, whose total annual working days amount to less than 200 or who work less than 35 hours a week. When the part-time job category was first mentioned in the yearly *Labor White Paper* by the Ministry of Labor in 1967, the main reason cited for the employment of part-timers was the scarcity of people willing to work full time. However, since the mid-1970s this category of workers has been used on a larger scale, particularly in relatively smaller firms in the service, wholesale, and retail industries, because of the low cost and the relative ease of terminating employment. In 1984, however, the number of part-time workers even in manufacturing industries rose to about 7.5 percent of total employees (see Table 5.3). About half (43 percent) of female part-time workers are aged 35–44.[25]

Traditionally, when the labor demand slackened, a large proportion of female workers who failed to find a job were discouraged from continuing their search and retired from the labor market.[26] But recent studies suggest that the effect of "discouragement" is becoming weaker

[25] Prime Minister's Office, *Special Survey of Labor Force*, 1981.
[26] For example, Akira Ono has estimated the proportion of discouraged workers who were not in the labor force in Japan to be 8.9 percent in 1978, and that in the United States to be 1.4 percent. In that year the official unemployment rate was 2.2. percent in Japan, and 6.0 percent in the United States.

Table 5.3. *Composition of part-time workers in total employment by industry and by employment size of the firm, 1976–84*

	76	77	78	79	80	81	82	83	84
Total	3.5	4.2	4.7	6.0	5.8	6.0	6.9	7.1	7.6
Mining	0.3	0.1	0.3	0.2	0.2	0.3	0.1	0.6	0.3
Manufacturing	3.4	4.1	4.4	5.5	5.3	5.8	7.2	7.2	7.5
Transportation,									
communication	0.9	0.9	0.5	1.4	1.0	1.3	1.0	1.3	0.9
Utility	0.2	0.2	0.2	0.2	0.1	0.2	0.1	0.1	0.3
Trade	5.6	7.1	8.3	10.1	11.2	10.6	12.0	12.3	13.9
Wholesale	2.3	1.7	2.3	2.1	2.6	2.5	3.9	3.2	5.0
Retail	8.5	12.5	13.4	17.1	18.1	18.0	19.0	21.3	21.4
Finance	0.7	0.9	1.1	1.0	0.7	0.9	1.2	1.3	1.4
Real estate	2.4	2.7	0.8	1.2	1.6	5.0	4.4	3.9	3.9
Services	4.2	4.1	4.9	6.2	5.3	5.5	5.6	5.6	5.9
Firm size									
above 1,000	2.2	3.1	3.1	2.9	3.8	3.9	5.2	5.7	5.3
300–999	3.1	3.8	3.5	4.8	6.3	5.0	6.2	5.4	6.0
100–299	4.1	4.1	5.1	6.0	6.8	5.9	6.2	6.6	6.9
30–99	4.2	4.9	5.4	7.3	6.7	7.6	8.6	8.9	11.2
5–29	4.8	6.0	7.0	9.8	7.9	8.8	9.6	9.7	10.0

Source: Ministry of Labour, *Employment Mobility Survey.*

and the phenomenon of "involuntary" part-time workers has become more common.[27] There is a growing tendency among female workers to prefer working to leisure,[28] and to stay in the labor market in order to seek an alternative job even if the prospects are not bright. Some may remain unemployed, but many are likely to be absorbed in part-time jobs as (subjectively) transitory measures.

According to the *Survey of Job Seeker's Situation* by the Ministry of Labor in 1984, a great majority of female part-time job seekers aged 30 to 44 quoted as motives for entry into the part-time job market such factors as the flexibility of working hours, the difficulty of working full time because of child-rearing duties, health, and housekeeping. However, about 6.1 percent responded that they entered the market involuntarily because full-time jobs were unavailable. An estimate by Wakisaka based on the official *Labor Force Survey* has given a still higher

---

[27] See, for instance, A. Wakisaka, "Seriousness of female unemployment: a study of the Employment Status Survey," a report to the Ministry of Labor, 1986.
[28] See Y. Higuchi, "Kikon jyosei no roudou kyoukyu koudo" (labor supply behavior of married women: cross-section, time-series and pooled data), *Mita Shogaku Kenkyu,* 25 (1982), pp. 28–59.

figure for female involuntary part-time workers: 46 percent in 1982. However, his definition of involuntary part-time workers is broader and includes those who are seeking full-time jobs, additional hours, or alternative jobs.[29] In any event, this figure indicates that women who interrupt their careers by getting married and raising children are at a disadvantage.

In many cases part-timers do not qualify for the bonus payment, separation payment, paid vacation, and/or an automatic annual increase in the hourly pay rate, although the job sometimes lasts more than one year. The increasingly widespread use of part-time workers without benefits may be considered one conspicuous manifestation of the dilemma of industrial democracy in Japan and is becoming a focal point of labor policy of the Ministry of Labor as well as that of the organizing drive of industrial unions such as *Zensen Domei* (which used to be an industrial union for female textile workers).

C.   Gift exchange of higher effort and job security

In Appendix 5.2, the complete conditions for the Nash bargaining outcome are derived when the probability of layoffs is involved. They are

[B.1*] The employed worker receives his/her marginal value product *plus* a portion of surplus determined by his/her relative bargaining power where the surplus is defined as the difference between the average value product and his/her marginal value product.

[B.2*] The marginal value product with respect to effort is to be equated with the marginal value disutility of effort by the employed worker.

[B.3*] The level of employment is to be set at the level at which the marginal value product of an additional worker is equal to the worker's earnings minus the marginal rate of risk premium of unemployment.

When the possibility of layoffs is involved, the regularity condition for the trichotomization of decision making is not assured and these three equations must be solved simultaneously for the equilibrium values of three bargainable variables: worker's earnings when employed, the level of worker's effort (working hour), and the rate of employment (the probability of layoffs). The level of utility of unemployed workers is exogenously given by earnings at alternative jobs or unemployment

---

[29] Wakisaka, "Seriousness of female unemployment."

compensation. When the equilibrium values of these bargain variables are solved for, the level of earnings may be written into the collective bargain agreement, but the other two may remain implicit mutual commitments of the worker and management.

Condition [B.2*] requires a higher expenditure of effort on the side of the employed worker than when the marginal value disutility of effort is equal to the wage rate per unit effort (which is but a portion of the value-added of the firm). Condition [B.3*], on the other hand, requires management to hire more employees than the case under the short-run profit-maximizing rule posterior to wage determination (which only requires that the marginal value product be equal to the wage rate). What is involved here is the "partial gift exchange" of higher effort and higher job security between the worker and management à la Akerlof.[30] Although the result of bargaining over the earnings of the employed worker may be enforceable, the agreement of this gift exchange is only implicit, and both effort and employment decisions may be controllable by the worker and management posterior to the agreement on the earnings. Then they may be motivated to default on the implicit agreements on those variables to their own advantage. What makes them bind themselves to the commitment of gift exchange?

Suppose that, given the contracted earnings of the worker and an effort level chosen by the employed worker posterior to the collective bargaining, management defaults on rule [B.3*] and chooses the profit-maximizing employment level. The lower the ex post effort level of the worker, the lower the employment level. Suppose further that, knowing this reaction of management, the worker defaults on commitment [B.2*] and chooses the effort level that maximizes his/her utility given the contracted earning level. Management responds to this choice according to the above-mentioned profit-maximizing rule. A new noncooperative pair of effort and employment levels results. If, under this post-bargain noncooperative equilibrium combined with contracted earnings, both parties are worse off, there would be mutual incentives for both parties to abide by the bargain solution. Commitment would become self-binding.

However, depending on parameter values of the model, it is conceivable that the case arises in which management as a profit maximizer becomes better off under the noncooperative equilibrium than by binding itself with rule [B.3*]. This possibility is examined in

---

[30] G. Akerlof, "Labor contracts as partial gift exchange," *Quarterly Journal of Economics,* 97 (1982), pp. 543–69.

Appendix 5.2. Roughly speaking, it corresponds to the case in which the worker's boldness in the determination of effort level at the risk of layoffs is relatively weak. In this situation, the worker's fear of unemployment is so large that management can elicit higher effort expenditure from the worker without sticking to the promise of job security.

But even in this case, the short-run gain of management from the default of rule [B.3*] may be offset by the long-run loss. Management of the J-firm and the enterprise-based union representing the interest of quasi-permanent employees will meet repeatedly in future bargaining, and management's loss of reputation as a good employer resulting from the default on the implicit promise of job security will have negative impacts on future bargain outcomes. That is, the achievement of the Nash bargain outcome over the comprehensive range of bargainable subjects, including effort and job security, will become difficult because of the loss of trust in management by the enterprise-based union. Assuming that management is reasonably farsighted, it is to the benefit of both parties to avoid such a conflict situation. Thus we may claim:

> [B.6] *Gift exchange:* There are likely to be self-enforcing gift exchanges of higher effort expenditure by the quasi-permanent employee and the assurance of higher job security by management at the J-firm than are possible under the neoclassical profit-maximizing firm that employs the wage-surplus (wage less disutility from work) maximizing worker through the market.

D.   *Flexibility of earnings and work sharing*

Economists appear to have two conflicting views about the flexibility of the Japanese wage system. According to one school of thought – as represented by Jeffrey Sachs, Kazutoshi Koshiro, and Fumio Ohtake, among others – the Japanese wage is relatively downward rigid, and possibly results in a profit squeeze.[31] The other school of thought – as represented by Robert Gordon, Richard Freeman and Martin Weitzman, Ryutaro Komiya and K. Yasui, Masaru Yoshitomi, and Yoichi Shinkai, among others – has emphasized the flexibility of wage adjust-

---

[31] J. Sachs, "Wages, profits, and macroeconomic adjustment: a comparative study," *Brookings Papers on Economic Activity,* 2 (1979), pp. 269–332; Kazutoshi Koshiro, "Labor market flexibility in Japan with special reference to wage flexibility," mimeographed, 1987; F. Ohtake, "Jishitsu chingin no shinshikusei ni tsuite" (On the flexibility of real wages), mimeographed, 1986.

ment in Japan, referring to the unique institutional settings such as annual wage bargaining called *shunto* (spring offensive), the bonus system, and cooperative industrial relations.[32]

The first view generally regards the neoclassical market adjustment mechanisms as the norm and any persistent deviation of the actual adjustment of wages and employment from it as a sign of rigidity. For example, Sachs has started out by estimating an aggregate production function and regarding the derivative with respect to labor input at the full employment level as the warranted wage. Since energy is explicitly counted as one of the inputs in the production function in his study, an increase in energy prices would reduce the level of warranted wage. Sachs has shown that the gap between the observed wage rate and the warranted wage rate widened after the first oil shock in Japan and has suggested the possibility of the profit squeeze phenomenon. But the applicability of the neoclassical norm of flexibility may be questioned. We have assumed that the J-firm is coalitional and that its behavior is understood as an equilibrium bargain outcome over a wide range of subjects rather than as a result of single-minded short-run profit maximization. From this point of view, the finding of the rigidity of the Japanese wage in the neoclassical sense is not particularly surprising. It may be interpreted as supporting the view that there is an aspect of the Japanese system that cannot be understood by neoclassical modeling.

The second view focuses on the flexibility of wage adjustment at the micro level of the firm.[33] Gordon and Freeman and Weitzman have emphasized the role of the bonus system as a source of wage flexibility.

---

[32] R. Freeman and M. Weitzman, "Bonuses and employment in Japan," *Journal of the Japanese and International Economies,* 1 (1987), pp. 168–94; R. Gordon, "Why U.S. wage and employment behaviour differs from that in Britain and Japan," *Economic Journal,* 92 (1982), pp. 13–44; R. Komiya and K. Yasui, "Japan's macroeconomic performance since the First Oil Crisis: review and prospect," in *Journal of Macroeconomics,* 20 (1984), suppl., pp. 69–114; John Taylor, "Differences in economic fluctuations in Japan, the U. S. and Europe: the role of nominal rigidity," mimeographed, Stanford University, 1987: Yoichi Shinkai, *Gendai Makuro Keizai no Kaimei* (Analysis of the contemporary macroeconomy), Toyo Keizai Shinpo-sha, 1982; M. Yoshitomi, *Nihon Keizai* (The Japanese economy), Toyo Keizai Shinpo-sha, 1981.

[33] There is also a view that finds the flexibility of wage adjustment in Japan based on the estimation of the macro Phillips curve. See, for example, D. Grubb, R. Jackman and R. Layard, "Wage rigidities and unemployment in OECD countries," *European Economic Review,* 21 (1983), pp. 11–39. In this type of study, if a change in the wage rate is sensitive to the rate of unemployment, wage flexibility is concluded. But an estimated unemployment coefficient may be biased if an economy does not have a sizable movement in the rate of unemployment. See T. Tachinbanaki, "Labor market flexibility in Japan in comparison with Europe and the U.S.," *European Economic Review,* in press.

Gordon and Komiya and Yasui, along with Taylor, Shinkai, Yoshi-tomi, and others, have found that the wage changes flexibly in response to changes in terms of trade and productivities. According to Shinkai, such flexibility occurs because the enterprise-based union makes its annual wage demand in the framework of *shunto*, and takes the employing firm's ability to pay into consideration. For example, in 1978 the steel union leadership proposed the so-called "macro-consistent wage demand tactics" which were based on their assessment of the impact of high wage hikes in the midst of the great inflation in 1974, after the first oil shock: namely the business slowdown and the reduction of employment. Their proposal first met with a storm of criticism from the rank and file members, but the leadership succeeded in persuading the unionists to adopt the tactics for the 1980 collective bargaining after the second oil shock. Major steel unions demanded a relatively lower wage increase consistent with the security of jobs, based on the prediction of a fairly sophisticated macroeconometric model. At that time steel unions still had pattern-setting power over collective bargaining in other industries and these macro-consistent wage demand tactics are thought to have had considerable macroeconomic impact on relative employment stability.

It is true that the bonus system contributes to the relative flexibility of employees' earnings to some extent. But, as Asao Mizuno, J. Taylor, and others have rightly pointed out, the major source of flexibility may be found in the regular earnings, made possible in particular by regular annual wage revision through the *shunto*.[34] In addition to the annual wage adjustment, the flexible adjustment of working hours through overtime and work sharing adds another source of flexibility, expecially at large firms. Table 5.4 provides estimated standard deviations of the rate of change in output, employment, and working hours calculated by Y. Higuchi, A. Seike, and H. Hayami. It appears that Japan shows the highest deviation in the adjustment of working hours and the lowest in that of employment among the major industrialized

---

[34] A. Mizuno, "Wage flexibility and employment changes," *Japanese Economic Studies,* 16, (1987–8), pp. 38–73. The proportion of bonus payments to total earnings is at most 25 percent, and it has been declining lately. Mizuno has estimated that the relative contribution of flexibility of bonus payments to that of total wage payments was only about 10 percent during the period 1960–83. Koshiro has found that the profit elasticity of negotiated wage increase between 1970 and 1984 was about 0.229 for the total industries, which is considerably higher than that of changes in bonus payment (0.058). Therefore, if the annual bargaining concerns the distribution of incremental value-added, the major source of flexibility of employees' earnings seems to be found in regular earnings (K. Koshiro, "Labor market flexibility in Japan"). Taylor has also found that the bonus system does not increase nominal wage flexibility by very much and explains a relatively small part of the difference between Japan and the U.S. wage flexibility (Taylor, "Differences in economic fluctuations").

Table 5.4. *Standard deviations of the rate of change in output, employment, and working hours for selected countries, manufacturing, 1970–83*

	Production	Employment	Hours
Japan	6.509	2.089	1.903
United States	6.963	4.376	1.447
United Kingdom	4.635	2.409	1.508
Federal Republic of Germany	4.014	2.325	1.509
France	5.368	—	0.728

Source: Yoshio Higuchi, Atushi Seike, and Hitoshi Hayami, "Rodo shijyo: Danjyo rōdoryokuno shugyo kōdono henka" (Labor markets: changes in male and female labor participation behavior), in Koich Hamada, Masahiro Kuroda, and Akiyoshi Horiuchi (eds.), *Nihon Keizaino Makuro Bunseki* (Macro Analysis of the Japanese economy), University of Tokyo Press, 1987, p. 265. Original data source: Bank of Japan, *International Statistics.*

economies. In other words, the brunt of the business cycle seems to be borne more by the adjustment of working hours (work sharing) than the adjustment of employment. The overtime premium is 25 percent in Japan as well as in the United Kingdom and Federal Republic of Germany, whereas it is 50 percent in the United States. Thus there does not seem to be any particularly high incentive for Japanese firms to utilize overtime hours by the international standard from the profit-maximizing point of view. Can this somewhat unique behavior by Japanese firms regarding the adjustment of work hours and the resulting flexibility of employees' earnings be explained by our bargaining model?

The upward rigidity of employment (the use of overtime hours) may be explained by the general tendency of the coalitional firm to restrain the size of employment, as already explained. In order to see the downward rigidity of employment – that is, the preference for work sharing rather than layoffs – as an equilibrium bargain outcome, first combine propositions [B.2*] and [B.3*] as follows (seeAppendix 5.2 for a proof):

wage elasticity of effort supply

$$= \frac{1}{1 - \dfrac{\text{marginal risk premium of unemployment}}{\text{total earnings}}}.$$

This contrasts with the condition of the equality of wage elasticity of effort supply to one, customarily referred to as the "Solow condition," which is the profit-maximizing wage-setting condition for the firm that can employ all the labor it wants at the wage it chooses.[35] Suppose now that the effort level is measured by working hours with homogeneous intensity. Further assume that the wage elasticity of the supply of working hours is diminishing from a sufficiently high value to zero as working hours increase over a relevant range of working hours. Then our condition implies that the higher the marginal risk premium of unemployment associated with the worker, the shorter the working hours and the lower individual earnings should be in comparison with the level dictated by the Solow condition. This, together with condition [B.3*] above, in turn implies a higher employment level than the profit-maximizing Solow condition implies. Thus we may summarize the above argument as follows:

> [B.7] If the risk premium of unemployment associated with the worker is high, there would be agreement between the worker and management to prefer work sharing to layoffs.

Of course, the use of work sharing as an alternative to layoffs is not limitless. As already emphasized in Section 3.1, if bad times persist, layoffs become inevitable. As also noted there, Muramatsu has found that when a firm has to reduce more than 10 percent of its man-hours in response to a fall in demand or output, the probability of discharge becomes higher.[36] The probability of layoffs would also depend on the nature of the contraction of business opportunities of the firm. If the adverse business condition of the firm is due to the general business cycle condition, then the prospect of alternative earnings becomes simultaneously worse, and accordingly the risk premium of unemployment attached to the worker becomes higher. Under these circumstances, the firm would try to absorb more of the brunt of the business cycle condition by work sharing. But if the adverse business condition of the firm is firm specific or industry specific, then the prospect of alternative earnings may remain fairly constant. In that case, the bargain outcome may result in the use of layoffs rather than work sharing.

Finally, there may be one pitfall in using work sharing. If the adverse business condition of the firm is expected to be temporary, then work sharing can be an efficient bargain outcome in the Pareto sense. Such

[35] Robert Solow, "Another possible source of wage stickness," *Journal of Macroeconomics*, 1 (1979), pp. 79–82.
[36] K. Muramatsu, "Kaiko to sono daitai shudan: nihon no seizogyo no baai" (Discharge and its alternative means: the case of the Japanese manufacturing industry), in M. Mizuno, Y. Matsugi, and Th. Dams (eds.), *Me-ka to Koyo: Nichi-doku Hikaku* (Mechanization and employment: Japan–Germany comparison), Nagoya University Press, 1986.

was indeed the expectation held by the steel and shipbuilding industries in the early 1980s. Major firms adopted a wide range of work-sharing measures to preserve the employment of the quasi-permanent employees. For example, many firms in these industries kept operating old, less efficient plants that were located in the so-called company castle town, while cutting down the operating level of their more efficient plants.[37] Since the appreciation of the yen in the mid-1980s, however, it has become evident that both industries had lost substantial competitiveness to Koreans and others because they had paid out relatively high wages. The steel industry, which had produced 120 million tons of steel in 1973, has been forced to cut down its capacity to the level of 90 to 85 million tons geared toward high value-added products in the late 1980s and thus is expected to reduce work force by at least one-third. Large-scale permanent layoffs have already begun to take place. Both industries are now paying a high price for work sharing based on a misjudgment of their own future competitiveness.

3.   Historical formation of Japanese management

Corresponding to the trichotomy of the bargaining game at the J-firm, as developed in Section 2, management is conceived of as playing three complementary roles:

[B.1**] *Bargaining agent vis-à-vis the enterprise-based union:* Management is engaged in collective bargaining vis-à-vis the enterprise-based union regarding the disposition of the organizational quasi rent to ensure a satisfactory return to stockholders, as well as an adequate addition to the physical assets of the company.

[B.2**] *Administrator in ranking hierarchy:* Management monitors quasi-permanent employees to ensure that they fulfill their commitments to exercise sufficient effort for the maximized organizational quasi rent net of the cost of their effort. It can do so by providing the quasi-permanent employee with the pay and promotional structure described in Chapter 3 as an incentive scheme and admistering it centrally.

[B.3**] *Arbitrative strategic managerial decision maker:* Management is engaged in making strategic managerial deci-

---

[37] One of the major shipbuilding companies, IHI, even closed the most efficient Chita shipyard in the 1978 depression, while maintaining old Aioi and Kure yards.

sions so as to balance the interests of the constituent bodies of the firm by following the weighting rule.

One caveat is necessary with respect to [B.3**]. This characterization by no means implies, as a casual reading might erroneously suggest, that Japanese management is a passive agent that merely reconciles partly conflicting, partly harmonizing claims put forth by the two constituent bodies. In order to make efficient mediation according to the weighting rule, management must account for the benefit from the growth of the firm accruable to the quasi-permanent employee in the form of better promotional prospects in addition to that accruable to the stockholder in the form of capital gains. And, in the world of uncertainty, the growth possibility of the firm is never exogenously given, but must be explored by the use of considerable corporate assets, financial and human, as well as entrepreneurial spirit. If management can organize the activities of the firm in such a way as to realize a higher growth for the organizational quasi rent at a lower cost, it will improve the promotional opportunity for the quasi-permanent employee within the firm as well as increase capital gains for the stockholder. This will enhance the legitimacy of the manager and his or her reputation.

Therefore, efficient management in its arbitrative role ought to be aggressive and growth exploring rather than passive and conciliatory. This consideration suggests the fourth characteristic of Japanese management, that is, the *entrepreneurial* spirit that pursues the growth of the firm by exploring new business opportunities through innovation. I return to this aspect in Chapter 6 after discussing the recent innovative activity of the J-firm.

The first and second faces of management described earlier are rather familiar ones in mainstream neoclassical economics. But the third notion – that Japanese management acts as an arbitrator between the body of stockholders and the body of employees, rather than as an agent of the former – is an unorthodox one. Is arbitrative management the outcome of a long evolutionary process unique to Japan? Is it a result of extraordinary shocks external to the economic process? Or is it indicative of some general trend in the industrialized economy? To deal with these questions fully is beyond the scope of this book, which is primarily concerned with modeling contemporary economic systems in Japan, but let me briefly review some important post–World War II events that may have considerable bearing on those questions.

Before arbitrative management could become viable and replace the neoclassical type of management acting in the sole interest of the body of stockholders and facing the union in an adversarial manner, at least three conditions had to be met: (1) management had to be freed from the institutional setup underlying classical capitalist control as well as its supporting ideology that management should act as an agent serving the sole interest of the owner; (2) the collective bargaining framework had to be developed in a direction that would foster mutually beneficial exchange, implicit or explicit, between the current pay level and managerial policy choices highly relevant to the welfare of the employee, and the ideological stance supporting this framework had to be adopted by both sides participating with bargaining; and (3) management had to be protected, to a certain extent, from the unilateral pressure of the "short-run" share price maximization exercised by stockholders through the market.

The first, and probably most important, impetus for the formation of arbitrative management was given by the post–World War II reforms directed by the Supreme Commander for the Allied Powers (SCAP), especially the *zaibatsu* dissolution and the liberalization of union activity. I described *zaibatsu* dissolution in Section 4.1, where I noted that about 40 percent of the shares previously owned by *zaibatsu* families, directly or indirectly through their holding companies, were transferred to employees of the companies that those stocks represented. Undoubtedly, this shift fundamentally changed the nature of control exercised by stockholders on management.

Parallel to the *zaibatsu* dissolution, executive officers of two hundred important companies during the war period were purged by the Memorandum Concerning Purges of Politically and Economically Important Positions issued by the government under the direction of the SCAP in November 1946. In addition, the Law for Removing Control Power of *zaibatsu* families enacted in January 1948 banned all the members of 10 *zaibatsu* families and the high-ranking directors of 240 related companies from assuming directorships of related companies for 10 years. As a result of these two measures, more than 3,600 business leaders were expelled from the business community.[38]

Thus the eventual economic recovery and high growth was led by two new types of management. One was the younger generation of managers promoted from the internal hierarchy of employees at former *zaibatsu*-related companies and left in a vacuum insulated from effective capitalist control, and the other was those founder cum managers who had arisen outside the realm of *zaibatsu* in the turmoil at

[38] For a detailed description of the *zaibatsu* dissolution, see Eleanor Hadley, *Anti Trust in Japan*, Princeton University Press, 1970.

the end of the war by their extraordinary entrepreneurial abilities.[39] There were certain attitudinal differences between these two types of managers in the early period. Briefly, the latter were generally more technologically innovative and growth oriented than the career managers in the former *zaibatsu* companies, who tended to be more cautious about entering new lines of business.

Nothwithstanding these differences, however, it is important to recognize that founder cum managers have never developed into controlling families of the old *zaibatsu* type. The companies founded by them have eventually developed a ranking hierarchy from which succeeding managers have come to be chosen. The difference between the manager of a former *zaibatsu* company and of the successor to a founder has tended to be blurred. Of course, this does not mean that every firm gives stockholders' and employees' interests equal weight. In firms where founder cum managers have presided or still exercise influence and employees are relatively younger because of the firm's shorter history, the weight is likely to be less in favor of employees. I would contend that this difference in the relative weighting is, however, a quantitative rather than a qualitative matter.

But is the emergence of arbitrative management an accidental outcome of the *zaibatsu* dissolution, which was directed by the idealist zeal of New Dealers under the authority of the SCAP? Note that the eclipse of *zaibatsu* control had already begun before the reform. As early as the 1920s the closed form of holding companies was found to be inadequate for the large capital requirements of the emerging heavy industries. In the late 1920s and early 1930s the old *zaibatsu* was challenged by the so-called new *zaibatsu,* which grew on the basis of open stock market operations. But this challenge was a rather short-lived episode. In order to funnel the flow of investible funds to strategic industries, the government began to play an active role and had great impact on the financial system through the late 1930s up to the end of World War II. It introduced stringent regulations over dividend payments as well as taxation on capital incomes in the late 1930s, and the stock market was finally closed in 1945. In place of the stifled capital market, the government tried to develop and strengthen its direct reign over the flow of investible funds through financial intermediaries by drastically reducing the number of banks by administrative guidance, developing the tax-free postal saving system, relying on BOJ deficit

---

[39] Konosuke Matsushita of Matsushita-Panasonic, Soichiro Honda of Honda Motor Co., and Dai Ibuka of Sony were among those entrepreneurial founders.

financing, introducing a series of ever-tightening ordinances for regulating funds flow, and so on.

In the early 1930s, home-made *zaibatsu* reform was tried, particularly at Mitsui, in response to the situation in which the misery of poverty in the rural areas had given some credibility to the anticapitalist agitation by the leftists as well as the populist rightists. Between 1931 and 1936, under the leadership of reform-minded Seihin Ikeda, who became a full-time director of Mitusi Partners (the holding company of Mitsui), all of the family members were retired from directorships and positions of executive officers of all Mitsui-related companies except for Mitsui Partners. Also between 1933 and 1934, stocks of important Mitsui member companies, such as Ohji Pulp and Toyo Rayon, were made public.[40]

But these developments before the end of World War II were at best evolutionary. The removal of classical *zaibatsu* family control and the dispersal of stock ownership to employees through the *zaibatsu* dissolution, combined with the complete overhaul of management by the promotion of younger employees free from psychological subordination to the *zaibatsu* families, decisively accelerated and condensed the evolutionary process; the outcome of those measures may be aptly described as the "managerial revolution from above." But, precisely because this "revolution" was on the extention of the evolutionary process, no serious attempt has ever been made to resurrect classical capitalist control since then. The Anti-Monopoly Law of 1947 outlawed holding companies outright, but a revision on this provision was never proposed or attempted. On the other hand, the restriction on banks' stockholding in the law was quickly relaxed, as already described in Section 4.1, since it was out of line with the change that had already occurred before and during World War II.

Although capitalist control over management was removed in the *zaibatsu* dissolution, the new and inexperienced management were immediately faced with a challenge from the other side – that is, from the militant union movements. After union activity was legalized as an important component of the post–World War II democratization of Japan directed by the SCAP, unionization began to proceed at remarkable speed. In December 1945 Japan's 509 unions had 380,000 members, but by June 1946 there were 12,000 unions and membership had swelled to 3,680,000. An interesting aspect of this rapid unioni-

[40] Mitsui Partner itself merged with Mitsui Trading Company in 1940 and was made an independent stock company in 1944.

zation that had considerable bearing on the later development of arbitrative management was that the unionization, particularly at the larger firms, took the form of enterprise-based organization encompassing all employees, blue-collar and white-collar, rather than industrial or craft organizations. Even the Communist Party, which exercised a dominant influence on the union movement at that time, did not object to this organizational form because of its own interest in union control of enterprises.

For this organizational form, too, there had been a historical precedent. After the independent labor union movement was crushed by adversarial management and ruthless police in the 1930s, the military regime initiated its own effort at organizing branches of the Industrial Patriotic Society at all industrial establishments and localities. Although the principal purpose of the society was to promote employee morale and thus to enhance industrial production, the activities of its branches at the enterprise and plant level had an aspect of forced egalitarianism amidst the scarcity of goods, in assisting families of conscripted employees, functioning as a mechanism to ration limited consumer goods, and so on.

When the war ended, the society was outlawed. Its leaders at the branch level, except for a few who openly converted and were accepted, were defamed and banned from active social life. But the experience of this large-scale corporative organization encompassing all employees gave impetus to the rapid formation of an independent union under new militant leadership. Without the organizational experience of the massive Patriotic Industrial Society, the rapid unionization after World War II would probably have been unimaginable. The situation is somewhat analogous to that in the United States in the early 1930s, when the newly organized United Steel Workers rapidly expanded its organizational basis by capturing management-sponsored electorates of the company union that had developed in the 1920s.

The labor dispute immediately after World War II centered around critical issues for the mere physical survival of employees and their families, such as wage demands in the midst of hyperinflation exceeding the annual rate of 500 percent in 1946 and job security during the drastic downscaling of production due to the destruction of productive capital assets and the shortage of raw materials and power (the production index by the Economic Planning Agency was 39.2 percent of the 1934–35 level in 1946, and 76.7 percent in 1949). It was at this time that the person-related pay system was introduced in collective bargaining in the public utility industry and began to spread to other industries. It was the only conceivable pay system that could satisfy the critical subsistence needs of employees, depending on their age and family composition, from limited wage funds. In view of this situation, the enterprise-based organization was also the most natural form to emerge, at least at relatively large firms, because employees could not possibly secure their jobs, except to defend their current jobs at the employing firms, and because bargain outcomes depended largely on the company's ability to pay. This also turned out to be the most effective form when it came to protecting and bargaining for employees' interests, even after subsistence ceased to be the critical issue. As discussed in Section 2.3, enterprise-based bargaining is the most appropriate form for negotiating firm-specific distribution of the organizational quasi rent and associated management issues at a firm in which ranking hierarchy is highly developed.

In general, it is at the developmental stage – in which the firm-size distribution of the industry becomes uneven because of the emergence of a few monopolistic firms – that the most relevant bargaining is likely to take place at the enterprise (or plant) level. If the pay level is set too high at the industrial level, many of the small firms will not be able to survive. On the other hand, if the industrial-level bargain set only the minimum or the safety net, skilled workers at large firms would not be content, and monopolistic firms would be willing to bargain with them for supplementary payments in order to run their own personnel management.[41]

Nevertheless, in Europe supra-enterprise bargaining is still dominant, partly because of worker solidarity (as in Sweden), unionists' traditional suspicion of syndicalism (as in West Germany), or ideological cleavage leading to weaker grass-roots union organizations (as in France). But the main reason for the persistence of supra-enterprise bargaining is historical inertia, as typified by the case of England. In England the apparatus for supra-enterprise bargaining was firmly established as early as the 1870s, when the firm-specific employment structure was still underdeveloped and workers were still mobile between firms in particular localities. As the firm-specific employment structure developed, supra-enterprise industrial collective agreements tended to be supplemented by sporadic and informal wage bargaining at the workshop level (1950–60s). But after it was seen that unofficial

---

[41] According to an unofficial estimate by a researcher at SAF (Swedish Employers Association), even in Sweden, where the industrial level bargaining is considered to be most developed, the yearly average negotiated wage increase between 1970 and 1984 was 5.6 percent, whereas that of the wage drift (the wage increase due to supplemental bargaining at the enterprise/plant level) was 4.5 percent. Ulf Jakobsson, "A Note on income policy from a Swedish perspective," SAF Document no. 1410, June 1984.

bargaining generated inflationary pressure known as "wage drift," more formalized enterprise-level bargaining came to be considered a necessity and in fact started to spread in the 1970s. But the shift has not been smooth, precisely because of the institutional inertia of the apparatus adapted to supra-enterprise bargaining.[42]

The situation was somewhat different in the U.S. manufacturing industry, where large-scale unionism started in the 1930s when monopolistic firms had already been firmly established. Thus in the United States bargaining between the *single employer* and the *local* of a trade union that had its basis on the enterprise or plant level became the dominant pattern. Prominent labor specialists of a few decades ago, like Derek Bok and Sumner Slichter, used to consider enterprise-level bargaining the most distinctive institutional characteristic of the American collective bargain vis-à-vis the European.[43]

In the 1960s, when stable economic growth was expected and realized, there was a tendency in the United States for enterprise agreements among leading firms in an industry to be uniform. The development of the cost-of-living adjustment (COLA) and annual improvement factor (AIF), which automatically adjusted the annual wage in response to the rate of inflation and productivity growth, fostered this tendency. But, even in the auto industry, where the COLA and AIF were most fully developed, when the competitiveness of the industry was challenged by foreign manufacturers, the COLA and AIF clauses were quickly modified or suspended. The automatic pay increase according to the predetermined formula was partly replaced by various profit-sharing schemes in the 1982 and 1985 agreements entered by major manufactureres.[44] Of course, the profit-sharing scheme generates an enterprise-specific outcome, depending on the business performance of the employing firm. Thus the American collective bargaining framework unlike the European, still accommodates enterprise-specific agreement.

Japan probably benefited even more from the "late development effect" (R. Dore) than the United States.[45] In Japan it was only after the end of World War II that the large-scale union movement resumed, and because of the vacuum created by the war, there was no institutional inertia to hamper the formation of enterprise-based

[42] I discussed this issue in more detail in *The Cooperative Game Theory*, chap. 8.
[43] D. Bok, "Reflections on the distinctive character of American labor laws," *Harvard Law Review*, 84 (1971), pp. 1394–1463.
[44] Harry C. Katz, *Shifting Gears: Changing Labor Relations in the U. S. Automobile Industry*, MIT Press, 1985.
[45] Dore, *British Factory–Japanese Factory*.

unions. There had even been a large-scale organizational experience at the Patriotic Industrial Society, which paved the way for the enterprise-based organization.

Of course, enterprise-based unionism itself did not guarantee the cooperativeness of the union. In fact, immediately after World War II, the enterprise-based union was quite militant in its efforts to ensure subsistence for its members. At some important factories, unions even controlled production by replacing incompetent and disarrayed management. It was only after the management offensive of the Red Purge swept ruthlessly through the union leaders and union ranks with the strong backing of the SCAP that the revolutionary zeal subsided and that the leadership of the enterprise-based organizations was taken over by more moderate unionists, or the "second union" led by such unionists superseded more militant organizations through intrafirm union rivalries.

However, even in the 1950s, a series of serious labor disputes still arose over discharges.[46] One of the most notable was the 193-day strike at Muroran Steel Mill of Nihon Seiko (Nikko Muroran), which ended with the discharge of 662 workers out of 3,742 employed and the formation of a second union by one-third of the employees. The discharge costs amounted to almost twice the company's capital. This dispute made it clear to management that attempts to discharge would be met with determined worker resistance, even under the most moderate leadership, and could be very costly. Thus the Nikko Muroran dispute contributed to the subsequent establishment of the de facto right of the regular worker to obtain permanent employment at the J-firm.

Another important labor dispute was the strike lockout at the Miike Mine of Mitsui Mining Company in 1960, which lasted more than 300 days. The union had defeated an attempted large-scale discharge in 1953, but because the coal industry was in decline management found it imperative to repeat the attempt. The Miike dispute occurred at the same time that political turmoil was developing over the renewal of the U.S.–Japan Security Treaty and thus had a deep impact throughout the nation. It was during this dispute that the Ikeda cabinet took office with "politics of tolerance and conciliation" as its slogan; its first act was to mediate the dispute.

Two years after the settlement, a disastrous blast in the Miike mine took the lives of 458 miners. Many attributed this disaster in part to the low morale and poor safety provisions that remained after the

---

[46] One of those disputes, the one at Nissan Motor Co., has been recently described by a competent journalist, although the roles of individuals are overwritten. See D. Halberstam, *Reckoning,* Morrow, 1986, pt. 3.

adversarial confrontation. By the time the incident occurred, most Japanese managers had accepted the philosophy of cooperative and conciliatory industrial relations for productive efficiency at the shop-floor level. The government had also ceased to be overtly adversarial toward labor.

Another important event that marked the transition to the new era of cooperative enterprise unionism was the defeat of a three-month strike led by leftist leaders in the steel industry in 1959. In the aftermath of the steel strike, the militant leaders were replaced by a more moderate slate in the following union election, and the new leadership created a bargaining framework in which single-offer bargaining *(ippatsu kaito)* among five major companies and their enterprise-based unions in the steel industry set a pattern for wage settlements elsewhere every spring. This new approach came to be called *shunto* (spring offensive). Single-offer bargaining has forced both bargaining partners to make as clear as possible the objective situations that would influence the bargain outcome, such as the ability of the company to pay and the union's willingness to compromise. A clear understanding of these situations helps partners find a stable bargain outcome.

Behind the fanfare of the annual spring offensive of the 1960s, enterprise-based unionism firmly established its roots at various levels of the firm. At the shopfloor level, the work team gained more autonomy over job assignments under the leadership of a foreman who was himself a unionist, and this gave rise to the egalitarian job-rotation scheme. In the period of high growth in the 1960s, many large-scale plants were built in newly developed industrial parks along the coastline and masses of workers were transferred from old plants to the new. The enterprise-based union was briefed, consulted, and formally negotiated with regarding the conditions of transfer.

In the late 1970s, the enterprise-based union succeeded in securing the commitment of management to maximum job security in exchange for wage restraint. As noted earlier, the union's "macro-consistent" tactics were formulated after members witnessed the adverse impact of aggressive wage demands on employment in the wake of the first oil shock. However, as noted already the restraint of layoffs and work sharing introduced between the late 1970s and early 1980s have led to dynamic inefficiency in some industries, such as steel and ship-building, which have retained inefficient production facilities through a miscalculation of future business prospectives.

To summarize, the prevailing conventional view that cooperative industrial relations at the J-firm are intrinsic is not quite right. As we

have observed, the fact that Japan had no history of industrial unionism played a decisive role in the establishment of the enterprise-based
bargaining framework. The cooperative relations that facilitated the
emergence of an arbitrative management have been shaped and have
evolved only gradually by trial and error on both sides of the partner-
ship. They might be subjected to another test if the whole industry was
hit by adversity.

Let us now turn to the third historical condition for the formation
of arbitrative management. I have already explained how corporate
grouping developed as a means of insulating management from taking
threats (see Section 4.1). This freed management from the pressure of
short-run share price maximization. By short-run share price maximization I imply unilateral share price maximization posterior to wage
agreement, as described in Section 4.3, which is equivalent to assigning
a zero value to the weight $1 - \alpha$ attached to the employees' interests
in the formula of the weighting rule (5.1). Such behavior is inefficient,
as I have emphasized throughout this discussion. But if management
is always pressed for share price maximization in its management decision making out of a fear of takeover, while the pay level is fixed, management may be forced to ignore and forgo the interests of the body of
employees.

The strategy of insulating management from market discipline is
double-edged, however. Freed from effective monitoring by stockholders, management may pursue its own interests in income, prestige, and
power, using the firm as a vehicle for achieving its objectives. Alternatively, there is the danger that management might join forces with
the enterprise-based union, to the detriment of stockholders' interests
and might gradually prevent the firm from sustaining growth by
endangering the accumulation of financial assets. These possibilities
again draw attention to the question of monitoring management,
which I take up in Chapter 6.

I hope that this brief sketch on the historical background of arbitrative management in Japan has made it clear that, as drastic and decisive as the SCAP postwar reform may have been, the overhauling of
capitalist control and the emergence of enterprise based unionism were
not entirely accidental to the evolutionary process of the Japanese
economy. I have not answered directly, however, the question of
whether the Japanese experience is unique. It is yet too early to ascer-
tain whether stable institutional stockholding in the place of classical
individual ownership in Japan is indicative of a general trend. Law
and regulation in the security market in general have great impact on
the pattern of stockholdings. But, in the United States and elsewhere,

the growth of pension funds and various experiments with employees' (or unions') stock ownership plans may have some important features in common with the Japanese system. In the United States, pension funds now own about one-quarter of corporate equity, and by the year 2000 that share could climb to 50 percent, according to the Federal Reserve Board. Institutional pools of money have grown so large that it is said that they cannot easily be shifted from one stock to another. As a consequence, longer-term dialogue between management and large institutional stockholders is being sought.[47] I have also emphasized that the focal point of effective collective bargaining has been shifting toward the enterprise level everywhere. On this point I would argue with more confidence that Japan, benefiting from late development, may be setting the pace in establishing a highly effective collective bargaining framework at the enterprise level.

Appendix 1.   Growth-seeking behavior: an illustration of the weighting rule

The behavior of the J-firm as a coalition of the body of quasi-permanent employees and the body of stockholders is somewhat different from what the neoclassical theory of the stockholders' controlled firm would predict. Since I have already presented a bargaining game-theoretic analysis of the coalitional firm elsewhere, I restrict my discussion here to the main results that I have obtained, by way of illustration. These results pertain to the growth-seeking behavior of the coalitional firm and show that an application of the weighting rule [B.3] would dictate the pursuit of growth at a higher rate than the short-run share price-maximizing rule.

Suppose that time consists of an infinite series of periods of equal duration and that at the beginning of the current period, the share price of the firm is V. Suppose that there is no tax, no uncertainty, and no imperfection in financial markets. Let d be dividend per share in the current period. Management is expected to pursue the steady state growth of the firm at rate g, so that capital gains at the end of the current period equal gV. Then the total rate of returns from stockholding to ex post stockholders (i.e., stockholders after the opening of the stock market) is $d + gV$. If the interest rate prevailing in the alternative bond market is r, by arbitrage it must hold that

$$d + gV = rV.$$

---

[47] See the cover story, "Corporate control: shareholders vs. managers," *Business Week,* May 18, 1987. Also see my *The Cooperative Game Theory,* pp. 46–8 and chap. 11 for implications of the growth of institutional shareholders.

In other words, the equilibrium share price will satisfy

$$V = \frac{d}{r - g}.$$

Suppose that ex ante stockholders (i.e., the existing stockholders before the opening of the share market in the current period) are interested in letting management maximize the share price. What growth rate is to be chosen for this purpose? Steady state growth of the firm is not costless. The firm must expend funds for new equipment, sales organization, advertisement, training of personnel, research and development, and so on. It may be reasonable to assume that, as the firm intends to grow faster, this expenditure should increase more than proportionally, because external (market) or internal (organizational) constraints on growth become more apparent. Suppose that the firm must expend $f(g)$ percent of its current revenue, R, in each period in order to sustain steady state growth at the rate, g, where $f(.)$ is a monotonic increasing, differentiable convex function; that is $f'(g) > 0$ and $f''(g) > 0$ for all $g \geqq 0$. Further let us denote the share of wage bill, w, in value-added net of growth cost by $(1 - \alpha)$; that is,

$$w = (1 - \alpha)R[1 - f(g)].$$

By accounting identity,

$$d = \alpha R[1 - f(g)].$$

Substituting these two relations into the above formula V, we have

$$V = \frac{R[1 - f(g)] - w}{r - g}.$$

This formula clearly demonstrates two opposing effects of an increase in the target growth rate g on the share price V. The denominator shows that an increase in g will decrease the effective discount rate, $r - g$, through its capital gains effect. The numerator represents the cost effect of growth as discussed above. The maximization of the share price, given a wage bill, is arrived at where the marginal effects of these opposing effects just offset each other. Formally, differentiating V with respect to g and equating the result to zero, we have the following maximization condition:

$$\frac{1}{r - g^s} = \frac{Rf'(g^s)}{R[1 - f(g^s)] - w},$$

where g^s denotes the value-maximizing growth rate of the firm, which is controlled by the body of stockholders.

The left-hand side of the formula represents the percentage gain in capital value due to a decrease in the effective discount rate, $r - g$, when the target growth rate is increased by 1 percent, and may be called the marginal rate of growth benefit to the body of stockholders (MB^s). The right-hand side represents the percentage decrease in dividends when the target growth is increased by 1 percent, and may be termed the marginal rate of growth costs to the body of stockholders (MC^s).

The above result, albeit elementary, already captures the essential logic of share price maximization; the dynamic analogue of profit maximization. However, in order to prepare a framework for the behavior of the coalitional firm, substitute the definition of $1 - \alpha = w/R[1 - f(g)]$ into the maximization condition and get

$$\alpha \frac{1}{r - g^s} = \frac{f'(g^s)}{1 - f(g^s)},$$

which requires that MB^s times the share of stockholders in the net revenue is equal to the percentage decrease in the net revenue after the growth expenditure due to an additional percent of growth. The latter may be termed the marginal rate of growth cost to the firm (MC). Obviously MC is smaller than MC^s. Figure 5.1 depicts the graphs of αMB^s and MC. Needless to say, the abscissa of the intersection of the two curves corresponds to the value-maximizing growth rate g^s.

The above analysis does not take into account the employees' interests, except implicitly, in that their current remunerations are assumed to be exogenously given. But if employees are quasi-permanently employed by the firm, as assumed for the J-firm, they may also derive some benefits from the growth of the firm. If one takes two firms, there may not be a large difference in the level of salary for comparable positions in the two. If one firm grows faster than the other, however, the former creates more positions at higher ranks, and, given the practice of internal promotion in the ranking hierarchy, this implies higher promotability for the quasi-permanent employee. In addition, as the amount of separation pay at mandatory retirement is determined in reference to the level of salary at the end of an employee's career, the difference in the growth of the firms will create a potentially large differential in lifetime earnings for representative quasi-permanent employees.

One caveat is necessary. As emphasized, growth is not possible without costs. If the body of stockholders has a constant share in the net revenue after financing growth costs, the body of employees cannot enhance their higher promotability without sharing the cost of growth, namely by sacrificing the current level of earnings. This trade-off between future earnings and current earnings may be formulated symmetrically to the share price-maximizing case.

Assume that the present value W of the total lifetime earnings of the representative quasi-permanent employee is the current bill w times a certain multiplier, depending on the growth of the firm:

$$W = wH(g),$$

where $H(g)$ is a monotonic increasing, differentiable concave function; that is, $H'(g) > 0$ and $H''(g) < 0$ for $g > 0$. The functional form depends on various factors: for example, the nature of hierarchical design such as the span of hierarchical control (as measured by the average number of subordinates that a superordinate supervises) and the degree of salary graduation between different ranks, the discount rate that employees use to evaluate the present value of their future earnings, and the age composition of incumbent employees.

Suppose that the firm is run on behalf of the incumbent employee and that management seeks to maximize the value of W. In doing so, suppose that management is constrained to deliver the minimum amount of divident d to the body of stockholders in the current period. Therefore,

$$W = \{R[1 - f(g)] - d\}H(g).$$

Maximization of W with respect to g yields the condition:

$$\frac{H'(g^e)}{H(g^e)} = \frac{Rf'(g^e)}{R[1 - f(g^e)] - d}.$$

The left-hand side represents the percentage increase in the present sum of lifetime earnings of the representative employee due to an additional percent of growth of the firm and may be termed the marginal rate of growth benefit to the body of quasi-permanent employees (MG^e). The right-hand side represents the percentage decrease in the level of the current wage bill caused by financing an additional percent of growth, while maintaining the level of dividends at d, and may be termed the marginal rate of growth cost to the body of quasi-permanent employees (MC^e). The condition of the equality of marginal rate of growth benefit with the marginal rate of growth cost gives the optimal solution for the growth rate g^e of the employee-controlled firm. Using the share parameter α as defined before, the condition may be alternatively written as

$$(1 - \alpha)\frac{H'(g^e)}{H(g^e)} = \frac{f'(g^e)}{1 - f(g^e)}.$$

This optimal condition for the employee-controlled firm is symmetric to the condition for the stockholder-controlled firm. The marginal rate of growth cost to the controlling body (MB^e) multiplied by its share in the revenue net growth cost is equated to the marginal rate of growth cost to the firm as a whole (MC). However, the managerial growth policies prescribed by the two conditions are both "short-sighted" in the following sense: Both policies are arrived at by maximizing the long-term benefit accruing to the controlling body, while neglecting the long-term benefit potentially accruable to the other body. The stockholder-controlled firm, in maximizing the wealth of ex ante stockholders, duly accounts for the demands of the employees regarding their current earnings but ignores their future welfare. The employee-controlled firm, in maximizing the lifetime welfare of quasi-permanent employees, duly accounts for the demands of stockholders regarding current dividends but ignores their capital gains.

The employee-controlled firm may increase both the employees' lifetime welfare and the stockholders' wealth at the same time by delivering more capital gains to the stockholders by growing faster than the rate g^e, while transferring some current revenue from the stockholders to the employees. The stockholder-controlled firm may do so too by delivering more promotional opportunities to the quasi-permanent employee by growing faster than the rate g^s, while transferring some of current revenue from employees to stockholders.

In fact, the bargaining game approach shows that the growth rate g^* that satisfies the following condition is more efficient than either g^s or g^e; and, further, that given the distributive shares α and $1 - \alpha$ no other growth rate is more efficient (in the Pareto sense) than g^*:

$$\alpha \frac{1}{r - g^*} + (1 - \alpha) \frac{H'(g^*)}{H(g^*)} = \frac{f'(g^*)}{1 - f(g^*)}.$$

The growth rate is to be chosen in such a way that the weighted sum of MG^s and MG^e is equated to the marginal rate of growth cost of the firm, MC. The distributive shares can be predetermined through internal balancing of power between the two constituent bodies; management can use these distributive shares as parametric weights on constituents' interests to determine the managerial growth policy of the coalitional firm. In the text, I termed such a decision-making rule the "weighted rule." This rule characterizes the bargaining outcome for the coalitional firm, which is fair, power-balancing, and equilibrating in the sense described in Section 1.

Figure 5.1 depicts the situation, with x substituted for g. The bargaining game solution g^* is obviously greater than the optimal growth rate for the stockholder-controlled firm and that of the employee-controlled firm. The area of the shaded region ABCD is

$$\int_{g^s}^{g^*} \frac{f'(g)\, dg}{1 - f(g)} = \ln \frac{1 - f(g^s)}{1 - f(g^*)},$$

which represents the logarithm of the ratio of revenue available to current distribution at the stockholder-controlled firm to that at the coalitional firm. Namely, the coalitional firm retains more earnings for financing a higher growth rate than the stockholder-controlled firm. This additional savings by the coalitional firm is more than necessary for the maximization of stockholders' wealth when the current wage bill to the body of employees is given, but delivers additional benefits of promotability to employees. In that sense, this part of retained earnings, albeit recorded as stockholders' equity for accounting purposes, may be considered to be de facto seized by the body of employees. To the extent that this is true, the proposition stated earlier – that retained profits will be fully reflected in the stock price – needs to be modified.

Appendix 2.   Gift exchange of effort and job security

Section 5.1 has shown that whether the constituent bodies of the coalitional firm are noncooperative strategists or are arbitrated by a neutral manager, the possible bargaining outcome is likely to be characterized by the Nash solution. However, whether each constituent body of the firm voluntarily complies with the Nash solution posterior to the agreement is another matter. In particular, under the situation in which an explicit contractual agreement can be written only on a partial set of bargainable variables mutually relevant to the constituent bodies, but the agreement on the remaining variables cannot be contractually enforceable and each of those variables may be controlled by either of the constituent bodies, they may be mutually motivated to default on the implicit agreement on those controllable variables to their own advantage. Whether such mutual manipulation would lead to an actual improvement in the utility of either body or a prisoner's dilemma–like situation in which both parties are worse off depends on the parameter values of the model. In this appendix I illustrate the possibility of both cases in the context of a plausible collective bargaining framework, focusing on employee commitment to the work norm and management commitment to the job security favorable to employees.

Let the objective of management be to maximize the profit:

$$P = R(eL) - wL,$$

where $R(.)$ is the value production function, e is the level of effort by employed workers, and L and w are bargainable employment and earnings, respectively. Suppose that the employment L is taken out of the firm-specific labor pool of size N, and that the objective of the union is to maximize the expected utility of union members in the pool:

$$Eu = [L/N]u(w - h(e)) + [1 - (L/N)] \, \hat{u},$$

where $u(.)$ is the von Neuman–Morgenstern utility function of the representative workers in the pool, $h(.)$ is a concave function representing the disutility of effort expenditure measured in terms of monetary value, and $\hat{u}$ is the utility level of the representative worker when unemployed from the firm.

Assuming that the profit level in the event of breakdown of cooperation is zero and that management is risk-neutral, the Nash bargaining solution (w^*, L^*, e^*) can be characterized by the following three conditions:

(1) $w^* = R'(e^*L^*)e^* + \frac{1}{2}[R(e^*L^*)/L^* - R'(e^*L^*)e^*];$

(2) $R'(e^*L^*) = h'(e^*);$

(3) $R'(e^*L^*)e^* = w^* - \dfrac{u(w^* - h(e^*)) - \hat{u}}{u'(w^* - h(e^*))}.$

The first condition states that a worker's earning consists of his/her marginal value product plus his/her share in surplus, defined as the difference between total revenue and the workers' total productivity, where at equilibrium (Nash solution) the workers' total share in the surplus is exactly one-half.[48] The second condition dictates that the effort expenditure of the employee be at the level at which the marginal disutility cost of effort is equal to the value product of marginal effort expenditure. The third condition dictates that the level of employment be set at the level where the marginal value product of an additional worker is equal to the worker's earnings minus the marginal risk premium of unemployment.[49] Therefore, given diminishing returns to

[48] This rule of equal division obtains because we do not explicitly introduce the collective objective function of the union. In general, the division is determined by the relative bargaining power between the employer and the union. See *The Cooperative Game Theory*, chap. 6.

[49] If the probability of unemployment is p, the risk premium s of unemployment at the equilibrium is defined as satisfying the following condition:

$$(1 - p)u(w^* + s - h(e^*)) + p\hat{u} = u(w^* - h(e^*)).$$

Expanding $u(w^* + s - h(e^*))$ around $w^* - h(e^*)$, neglecting terms of order higher than the first, solving for s/p, and letting p approach zero, the ratio approaches the second term on the right-hand side of the equation.

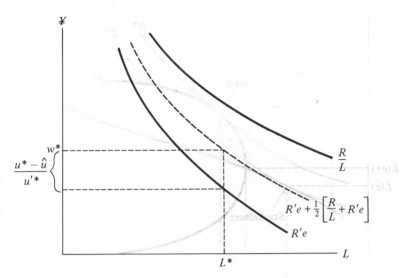

Figure 5.2. Gift exchange of higher job security and lower wage.

scale, the level of employment is higher than the level that a profit-maximizing firm will offer and the wage level is higher than the marginal value product of a worker (see Figure 5.2).

It is known that a profit-maximizing firm that can employ all the labor it wants at the wage it chooses to offer will offer the wage satisfying the Solow condition: the elasticity of effort with respect to the wage is unity. From (2) and (3), however, we can derive

$$1 = \frac{w^*}{h'(e^*)e^*}\left(1 - \frac{u(w^* - h(e^*))}{w^*u'(w^* - h(e^*))}\right).$$

That is, the wage is set at the level at which the elasticity of effort with respect to wage times a factor less than one (one minus the ratio of risk premium of unemployment to the wage) is unity. This condition is interpreted in Chapter 5.2.D in terms of work sharing (see proposition [B.7]).

Suppose now that only the negotiated earning w^* can be written into an enforceable contract, but that the agreement on the level of employment and the level of effort remains implicit. Suppose further that the workers can control the post-agreement effort level, while management can manipulate the level of employment, responding to workers' choice. Under this circumstance, are they motivated to keep the mutual commitments of gift exchange or to default on them? Imagine that, given the equilibrium negotiated earning level, w^*, and a level of

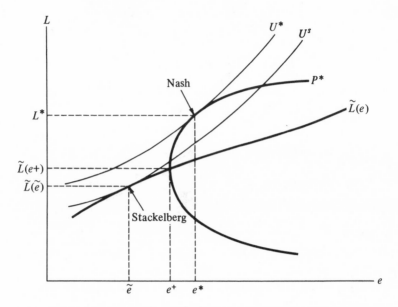

Figure 5.3. The Nash solution and the Stackelberg post-bargain equilibrium (Case I).

effort, e, chosen by employed workers posterior to bargaining (e may be equal to e^*), management is motivated to choose the profit-maximizing level of employment, $\tilde{L}$, satisfying the condition of the equality of marginal revenue and the bargain wage:

(4) $w^* = R'(e\tilde{L})e.$

We assume that the employer can meter the marginal revenue product of an additional worker precisely. As noted already, for the contractual wage w^* and the implicitly agreed-upon effort level e^*, the implicitly agreed-upon employment L^* involves redundant employment from the profit-maximizing point of view. Differentiating (4) with respect to e, we have

$$\tilde{L}'(e) = -\tilde{L}[1 + \frac{R'(e\tilde{L})}{e\tilde{L}R''(e\tilde{L})}.$$

Provided that $0 > e\tilde{L}R''/R' > -1$, $\tilde{L}'(e) > 0$; that is, higher the effort level, the higher the level of employment (see Figure 5.3).

Given contractural earnings and given a certain level of employment, the employed worker is always motivated to shirk. But suppose that the workers' shirking would trigger noncooperative behavior on the side of management such that employment would be reduced from an agreed-upon bargain solution to the profit-maximizing level corresponding to the chosen effort level. By knowing this reaction of management, the worker would choose the level of effort e, which would maximize the post-bargain expected utility:

$$\tilde{E}u = [\tilde{L}(e)/L^*]\, u(w^* - h(e)) + [1 - (\tilde{L}(e)/L^*)]\hat{u},$$

where $\tilde{L}(e)$ is the level of employment chosen by management according to (4) in reaction to the workers' choice of effort level, and $\tilde{L}(e)/L^*$ is the probability of employment posterior to wage bargaining. Technically, the worker is assumed to be the Stackelberg leader. The maximization of expected utility subject to (4) requires that the marginal opportunity of employment due to additional expenditure of effort, $\tilde{L}'(e)$ be equal to to the marginal utility rate of substitutions between the effort expenditure and employment:

$$(5) \qquad \tilde{L}'(e) = \frac{u'(w^* - h(e))h'(e)}{u(w^* - h(e)) - \hat{u}}\, \tilde{L}(e).$$

Write

$$\frac{u'(w^* - h(e))h'(e)}{u(w^* - h(e)) - \hat{u}} = B_u(e),$$

which is equal to the maximum risk (probability) of unemployment induced by the marginal reduction of effort that the worker can tolerate and may be interpreted as the post-bargain worker's "boldness" in determining the effort level facing the risk of unemployment.[50] On the other hand, the percentage ratio $\tilde{L}'(e)/\tilde{L}(e)$ may be interpreted as representing the sensitivity of employment adjustment by management. Therefore condition (5) can be read as the equality of the sensitivity of employment adjustment to the worker's boldness in determining the effort level.

The 3-tuple, $(w^*, \tilde{L}(\tilde{e}), \tilde{e})$ satisfying (4) and (5), would characterize the equilibrium post-bargaining Stackelberg outcome when each party defaults on that part of the Nash bargain outcome only implicitly

---

[50] This can be seen as follows: If the probability of unemployment induced by reducing the level of effort by s from e is p, the worker's expected marginal net benefit from doing so is

$$(1 - p)[u(w^* - h(e - s)) - u(w^* - h(e))] - p[u(w^* - h(e)) - \hat{u}].$$

Setting this equal to zero, solving the equation for p/s after the Taylor expansion of $u(w^* - h(e - s))$ around e, and making s approach zero, we can obtain the right-hand side of (5).

agreed upon and manipulable by itself. Since the efficient solution must always satisfy the conditions (1) and (3), this post-bargain Stackelberg equilibrium is not efficient, so that both parties cannot be better off at the same time; the question is whether either of the parties would benefit from defaulting on the implicit agreement or whether both parties would be worse off.

In order to see this, first consider all possible combinations of (e, L) that satisfy the relation

$$R(eL) - w^*L = R(e^*L(e^*)) - w^*L^*.$$

The set of such (e, L) depicts the iso-profit curve P^*, on which any point yields the same profit level as the Nash bargain outcome. It is easy to check that the iso-profit curve is convex toward the west direction and has its peak at the intersection point with the $\tilde{L}(e)$ curve as depicted in Figure 5.3. Denote the intersecting point $(e^+, \tilde{L}(e^+))$. Also consider all possible combinations of (e, L) that satisfy the relation:

$$L[u(w^* - h(e)) - \hat{u}] = L^*[u(w^* - h(e^*)) - \hat{u}].$$

The set of such (e, L) depicts the indifference map U^*, on which any point yields the same utility level as the Nash bargain solution. It is easy to check that the indifference map is convex toward the south east direction (see Figure 5.3).

At the Nash bargaining outcome (e^*, L^*), the indifference map and the iso-profit curve are tangent to each other, since it is Pareto efficient. Therefore, from Figure 5.3, it is clear that any point on the $\tilde{L}(e)$ curve is outside the region enclosed by the indifference map U^*. This implies that at post-bargain Stackelberg equilibrium (which is on the $\tilde{L}(e)$ curve), the worker can never be better off than at the Nash bargain outcome. This observation leaves us with the following two cases:

Case 1: $\tilde{L}'(e^+)/\tilde{L}(e^+) < B_u(e^+).$

At the critical level e^+, management's sensitivity in employment adjustment is less than worker's boldness. This case is illustrated in Figure 5.3. In this case the post-bargain Stackelberg equilibrium would entail a lower effort level $\tilde{e}$ than e^+ and, as a result, both the worker and the profit earner are worse off by mutually breaching the implicit agreement of the Nash bargain solution. Therefore there would be mutual incentives for both parties to bind themselves to the Nash bargain outcome (e^*, L^*) and sustain mutual exchange of gifts of higher job security and higher effort level.

Case 2: $\tilde{L}'(e^+)/\tilde{L}(e^+) > B_u(e^+).$

At the critical level e^+, sensitivity of employment adjustment is greater than worker boldness. The post-bargaining Stackelberg equilibrium would entail a higher effort level $\hat{e}$ than e^+ and thus higher profit, but lower expected utility for the workers than at the Nash bargain solution. Therefore, there is an incentive for the workers to commit themselves to the agreed-upon (but unenforceable) effort level, e^*, so as not to trigger management's retailiation of employment reduction. But the situation is not symmetrical for management, and there may be no incentive for management to honor the gift exchange in the short-run in which the worker's earning is fixed at w^*. This is so because the worker's fear of unemployment is so large that management can elicit a relatively higher effort level from the worker to its advantage without holding to its promise of job security at the level L^*.

However, the manipulation of employment level posterior to the contractual wage agreement according to the short-run profit motive may trigger the retaliation of the worker in the next round of wage bargaining. By knowing that management is not to be trusted, the gift exchange of lower wage and higher effort for job security may be declined by the disenchanted worker. The Nash bargain solution over a range of wage, job security, and effort level would then fail to be achieved and both sides would be stuck in a nonefficient outcome. If long-run losses from such a noncooperative, inefficient situation are reckoned to be greater than the short-run gain, however, management may still abide by the Nash bargain outcome. Such a possibility must be analyzed in the framework of a multiperiod model in which the rate of discount of future gains/loss by the employer would enter as an essential factor in the determination of bargain outcome.

CHAPTER 6

The changing nature of industrial organization

In Section 4.1, we saw that predominant intercorporate stockholdings in Japan have given rise to two types of corporate groups: capital-*keiretsu*, or subsidiary groups; and former *zaibatsu*, or financial *keiretsu*. In this chapter, I focus on the transactional aspects of these two groups. In dealing with the first type, however, I concentrate on a special class of capital-*keiretsu* characterized by a particular transactional feature, that is, the subcontracting group, which is a stratified, quasi-permanent group of suppliers subcontracting to a major manufacturer.

The bargaining game analysis in Chapter 5 suggested that the coalitional firm tends to limit the size of its employment in order to protect the vested interests of its incumbent employees. I have called this phenomenon the "dilemma of industrial democracy," because the voice of incumbent employees is enhanced within the firm to the detriment of outsiders' interests. I have argued that this dilemma is manifested in the J-firm in the form of differential employment status (such as that of part-time workers) and have hinted that, to some extent, the increasing hiving off of subsidiaries and reliance on subcontractors by the J-firm may be a similar phenomenon. This may sound like the old dual-structure hypothesis: Large Japanese firms exploit their monopsonic positions to make use of smaller subcontracting suppliers as a business cycle buffer.

But the subcontracting group formed by the major contracting firm and its satellite supplier firms is a complex economic institution. Suppliers are stratified within the subcontracting group, and transactions among them are perpetual, or relational, in economic terminology. For example, in the automobile industry, which is where these relations are most developed, the major manufacturers normally maintain direct first-tier relations with about a hundred suppliers organized into exclusive cooperative associations, which in turn have second-tier relations with still smaller subcontractors, and so on. According to a survey by the Agency for Small- and Medium-Sized Enterprises conducted in 1977, an unnamed prime manufacturer of automobiles (possibly Toyota) had direct relations with 122 first-tier suppliers and indirect relations with 5,437 second-tier suppliers and 41,703 third-tier suppliers.

After we adjust for double counting, we find that this manufacturer stood at the apex of a stratified group with a membership of 35,768 suppliers.[1] The relationship between the prime manufacturer and first-tier suppliers, like the relationship between the J-firm and the quasi-permanent employee, is quasi-permanent. Between 1973 and 1984, only three firms exited from the association of first-tier Toyota suppliers, whereas 21 firms entered.[2]

The subcontracting grouping does not seem to be just a device to deliver a monopsonic rent to the prime contracting firm, but seems to exist for reasons of productive and informational efficiency, which give rise to the quasi rent unique to the relationship between the prime contracting firm and subcontractors. Some upper-tier subcontractors and their employees seem to have considerable bargaining power over the sharing of such quasi rent. In Section 1, I describe the generic mode of transactions within the subcontracting group, analyze its sharing and incentive aspects from the viewpoint of contract theory, and identify factors that affect the efficiency of such contracting as well as the distribution of its outcome among the contracting partners. The traditional dual-structure hypothesis that has made the monopsonic power of the prime contracting firm a focal point is criticized for being at best one-sided.

In Section 2, I turn to the corporate groups consisting of major manufacturing companies, trading companies, insurance companies, and banks formed either along the lines of former *zaibatsu* networks (Mitsubishi, Mitsui, and Sumitomo) or with major banks as nuclei (Fuji, Daiichi-Kangin Bank [DKB], and Sanwa). The relatively loose reunification of former *zaibatsu* member firms began in the early 1950s, when the government exercised discretionary foreign exchange control and the industry was yet to be restructured in order to catch up with the Western economies. Consequently, the revival of a former *zaibatsu* connection, or a closer tie with a major bank and a major trading company, may have been considered advantageous for rent-seeking purposes. Most manufacturing companies were engaged in a limited line of business and their earnings were very much subject to the business conditions of a single market. Also during that period, the rationing of foreign exchange for the acquisition of raw materials, as well as the payment of a patent royalty for the importation of advanced technology, was controlled by the government, which used market shares of

[1] The Agency for Small- and Medium-Sized Enterprises, *A Survey of Division of Labor Structure (Automobile)*, 1977.
[2] See Kazuichi Sakamoto, *Gijitsu Kakushin to Kigyo Kozo* (Technological innovation and the structure of the firm), Minerva, 1985, chap. 3.

firms in relevant markets as a criterion for determining their eligibility for foreign exchange. Group affiliation guaranteed the companies involved certain market shares through reciprocal customer relations within the group. Securing supplies of raw materials and developing overseas markets had to be entrusted to trading companies because transaction costs were high due to the inexperience of manufacturing companies in international transactions and the cumbersome foreign exchange controls. Since manufacturing companies had not been able to accumulate much equity capital, they also had to depend on external financing for investment, and thus a close association with major banks appeared to be beneficial.

A recent statistical study by Thomas Roehl has shown that in the 1950s companies in major corporate groups in fact enjoyed a higher rate of profit, on average, than nonaffiliated companies.[3] But for the period between 1961 and 1975, Richard Caves and Masu Uekusa, Iwao Nakatani, and Thomas Roehl report that group-affiliated nonfinancial companies did not realize as high a rate of profit on average as comparable independent competitors.[4] I discuss their results in more detail later, but suffice it to say here that the plausible joint profit-maximizing hypothesis has not been verified as the reason for the existence of corporate grouping, at least for that period. Had corporate groups become outmoded by then?

There are many possible motives for forming and maintaining a corporate group. Insulation from unfriendly takeover was one of the possible motives cited in Chapters 4 and 5. In Section 2 of this chapter, I discuss the function of protecting affiliated companies from business adversity, as dramatized by the rescue operations for affiliated companies that have fallen into difficulty. I also attempt to put the role of the bank, as discussed in Chapter 4, in a broader perspective and to explain how this insurance aspect of corporate grouping is linked to another important feature of the J-firm, namely that a great proportion of the wealth of the firm's quasi-permanent employees is fixed in the form of potential claims for their future seniority premiums and separation payments, and therefore is exposed to firm-specific risk. In other words, I argue that the phenomenon of corporate grouping and the emergence of ranking hierarchy within the J-firm are closely linked and complementary.

[3] T. Roehl, *Corporate Grouping in Japan*, Ph.D. dissertation submitted to University of Washington, 1985.
[4] R. Caves and M. Uekusa, *Industrial Organization in Japan*, Brookings Institution, 1976; I. Nakatani, "The economic role of financial corporate grouping," in M. Aoki (ed.), *The Economic Analysis of the Japanese Firm*, North-Holland, 1984, pp. 227–58; Roehl, *Corporate Grouping in Japan*.

As some firms have grown into large multinationals, diversifying their business risks through hedging operations in the international financial market, ever-increasing product diversification, and so on, while strengthening their financial foundation through the accumulation of equity capital, it has become increasingly clear that those firms do not necessarily need group affiliation to remain viable. For them, it is becoming more important to develop new innovative products to remain competitive in the international market.

The conventional view is that the J-firm has been particularly proficient at adopting, assimilating, and improving technologies that have originated elsewhere, particularly in the United States and Western Europe, but weak in developing breakthrough innovations. A significant change is under way in Japan, however, in the area of science and technology. Recent evidence, which I present in this chapter, suggests that Japan has been increasing its human and financial inputs to basic research and development at a remarkable speed since 1978. Accordingly, the output of research and development has started to grow. It is generally believed that Japan is now ahead in such products as fiber optics for telecommunications, certain new materials such as industrial ceramics, and numerically controlled machine tools and robots. If this is the case, then Japan must rely on its own resources to retain leadership in those areas. Is there any uniquely Japanese way of organizing innovative effort?

In Section 3, I examine whether the difference in the micro-micro structures that the J-firm and the A-firm have developed to process, use, and accumulate information has any bearing on the direction and organization of the production of knowledge, that is, innovation. In Chapter 2, I argued that the J-firm places greater emphasis on the efficient use of on-site information and the benefits of knowledge sharing among employees than the A-firm, which relies more on the efficient utilization of specialized a priori knowledge. An isomorphic contrast may be found in the production of knowledge as well. The J-firm has been oriented more toward the development of knowledge within the firm, through production experience, and has emphasized closer interaction between the firm's R&D laboratory and manufacturing division. On the other hand, the A-firm seems to be more inclined to seek innovative opportunities through a more scientific approach. This difference may partly explain why innovation in Japan is less likely to be commercialized by small independent firms founded by the scientist cum entrepreneur and financed by venture capital, or through the acquisition of a smaller entrepreneurial firm by a large firm, but instead in the form of product diversification by the established firm.

Yet the increasing need for a multidisciplinary approach to innovation and the development of communications technology may make the existing line of business of the established firm too narrow. As a result of this concern, new corporate linkages across traditional industrial boundaries and groups have started to emerge in the form of joint research and development efforts, information processing networking, and other such ventures. Section 3 touches on this new trend in industrial organization.

Following a discussion of the function of corporate grouping and the entrepreneurial activity of the J-firm, Section 4 turns to the issue of management monitoring. The monetary incentives for Japanese managers are severely curbed by the stringent personal income tax system and the relatively egalitarian pay structure extended to top management in the ranking hierarchy. I discuss an alternative social mechanism operating in Japanese society at large through which the capability and leadership of top managers in arbitrative management is evaluated and ranked. This discussion relates the industrial system of Japan to its political-economic system, which is the subject of Chapter 7.

1.   The subcontracting group

A.   *Efficient contract design: incentive versus risk sharing*

Let us begin by considering a stylized model of the prime manufacturer–supplier relation in the automobile industry and analyzing its generic element.[5] Setting aside large supplier firms, such as those supplying steel plate and tires, which are autonomous and unaffiliated with the association of supplier firms subcontracting to a prime manufacturer, we will find it useful to distinguish, as Banri Asanuma did, between the two types of suppliers who maintain somewhat subordinate relations with the prime manufacturer, directly or indirectly.[6] One type of supplier has a relatively unique stock of production knowledge and directly supplies essential components to the prime manufacturer. These components are based on the supplier's own design as approved by the prime manufacturer. This type of supplier may provide such

---

[5] For similarities as well as differences in subcontracting relations between the automobile industry and the electric machinery and electronics industry, see Banri Asanuma, "Manufacturer-supplier relationships in Japan and the concept of relation specific skill," *Journal of the Japanese and International Economies,* 2 (1988), in press.

[6] B. Asanuma, "The Organization of parts purchases in the Japanese automotive industry," *Japanese Economic Studies,* 13 (1985), pp. 32–53.

components as advanced electronic equipment or brakes, which may be patented products or products in which the prime manufacturer does not have comparable technological expertise. Or some of the suppliers may be contracted to assemble particular models of final products, while producing specific body frames. Although such suppliers are relatively autonomous technologically, their capital is often partly owned by the prime manufacturer. Therefore, these suppliers are considered in the capital *keiretsu*.

Another type of supplier is one that has less specialized technological expertise and supplies less crucial components (such as lamps or plastic parts) to the primary manufacturer, according to the contracting firm's specification. These firms are normally referred to as subcontractors *(shitauke)*. They are considered to have relatively weaker bargaining power vis-à-vis the contracting firm because they lack special technological expertise. As a result, the subcontractor has long been regarded as an entity that social policy needs to protect from the possible exploitation of monopsonic power by the contracting firm. In fact, the *shitauke* firm is a legal concept defined in the Basic Law for Medium and Small Enterprises and the Law for Preventing the Delay of Payment of Subcontracting Fees as a firm with 300 or fewer employees, or with ¥100 million or less paid-in capital, which has a contractual relation with a larger firm for supplying a part, processed product, or material.

Notwithstanding this legal and conventionally accepted distinction, let us call the group of all suppliers directly or indirectly associated with the prime manufacturer on a relational contracting basis the *subcontracting group* and its members *subcontractors*. Subcontractors are stratified in the group according to the range and level of technological knowledge possessed by each. As we shall see shortly, the essential factors to consider in an analysis of the contracts between the contracting firm and the supplier are the relative bargaining power and the difference in their attitudes toward risk as determined by, among other things, the latter's technological expertise. The more indispensable, and the less easily replaceable the technological know-how possessed by a supplier, the stronger the supplier's bargaining power is likely to be in the determination of the terms of transaction vis-à-vis the prime contracting firm. Also, the wider the product range of a supplier, the less prone to product-specific risk the supplier is likely to be. In this sense, Asanuma's classification of suppliers, which focuses on the mode of product design, may provide more insight than the legal distinction; the classification is based on whether the supplied component is designed by the supplier itself under the approval of the prime contracting firm (because the latter has only incomplete know-how regarding relevant technology) or is produced according to the specifications provided by the prime manufacturer.

The nature of the contract between the prime manufacturer and the first-tier subcontractor in the subcontracting group has been clarified in a recent case study by Asanuma.[7] The contract between the prime contracting firm and its subcontractor is normally written for the duration of a particular model, say, a four-year period. The prime contracting firm guarantees not to switch suppliers or to start producing the item itself within this period. The prime contracting firm thus does not vary its dependence on the first-tier supplier for the supply of particular components in response to the business cycle. The contract is renewable for a new model unless the subcontractor has not met the quality and cost standards set by the prime contracting firm consistently in the preceding contract period.

A contract agreed upon at the start of a new model does not specify definite quantities of supply. The contracting manufacturer specifies only target quantities at the outset. The actual delivery of supply is to be specified every month and fine-tuned daily through the medium of *kanban*, as demand for the model evolves. The contract, however, specifies the rules by which the price is to be determined. An initial price is determined on the basis of detailed cost estimates submitted by the subcontracting supplier and is carefully examined by the prime contracting firm. The unit profit margin for the subcontractor is added to this cost estimate. The prime manufacturer may rely on a single subcontractor for the supply of a component for a particular model, but, whenever possible, maintains a long-term relation with other suppliers for the supply of similar components for other models (the so-called two-vendor policy) so that one subcontractor's estimate of the cost of the supply can be checked by comparing it with estimates by others. The threat of a potential switch to another supplier at the time of contract renewal for a new model may also strengthen the bargaining power of the prime contractor over the determination of the profit margin allowed the subcontractor.

The price can be adjusted between the prime manufacturer and each member of the first-tier group regularly, normally twice a year, just like the collective bargaining with the union regarding biannual bonuses. The prime manufacturer guarantees the amortization charges for the transaction-specific equipment and tools, like jigs and dies, committed by the supplier over the life cycle of the model. If actual demand turns

[7] Ibid.

out to fall short of predicted demand, the supply price will be readjusted by the prime manufacturer to cover the full capital cost of the supplier. The prime manufacturer also allows an increase in the cost of materials to be passed on as a supply price increase, but it is less ready to agree to passing on increases in labor and energy costs. In addition, there are provisions in the contract for changing the price in response either to cost changes resulting from design changes by the prime manufacturer or to cost reductions due to the subcontractor's process innovation (the so-called rationalization). Normally the cost reduction by the subcontractor is allowed to be absorbed by the subcontractor during the period of the current contract so that the latter has proper incentives for cost-reducing effort.

Ignoring the fact that the above rules for price adjustment are based on a vector of cost components and assuming simply that the price is adjusted on a single overall cost observation, one may envision that the contract formula of price revision at a regular interval is given by

$$(1) \qquad p = b + \alpha(c - b),$$

where p is the unit price for a component, b the target price including negotiated profit margin based on the estimate of normal cost, and c the realized average cost during the interval preceding the price revision. If the sharing parameter α is zero, the contract is set at a fixed price; all of the risk of cost fluctuations is borne by the subcontractor. If α is 1, the contract is cost-plus, so the contracting prime manufacturer bears the entire risk. If $0 < \alpha < 1$, the risk is shared.

Suppose that the realized unit cost can be decomposed into three components:

$$c = c^* + w - e,$$

where c^* represents the ex ante expected cost including profit margin and w a random variable representing unpredictable cost fluctuations observed only by the subcontractor in the course of doing the work. The third term, e, represents the reduction in cost achieved as a result of the subcontractor's innovation effort. The level of c^* is known to the contracting prime manufacturer at the time of contracting through the cost analysis and price negotiation. Although the contracting firm does know the distribution of w, which is assumed to be normal with mean zero and variance σ^2, it does not observe the realization of w so that it cannot distinguish the effects of cost fluctuation due to factors beyond the control of the subcontractor from the one realized by the innovation effort of the subcontractor. The innovation is not costless, and the cost $H(e)$ is financed from the gross profit of the subcontractor, with $H(.)$ exhibiting increasing marginal cost (diminishing returns to scale with respect to effort). Then the profit to the subcontractor net of rationalization cost is

(2) $p = (1 - \alpha)(b - c^* - w + e) - H(e)$.

Let us denote the variance of net profit by s^2. Then from the relation (2) we have

(3) $s^2 = (1 - \alpha)^2 \sigma^2$.

As the standard deviation of net profit and that of cost are observable, the value of α may be estimated from relation (3). Seiichi Kawasaki and John McMillan have attempted such an estimation using aggregate company data. Their estimated value of the sharing parameters vary depending on industry and firm size, but on the average are greater than one-half, tilting toward the cost-plus end (risk-sharing end) rather than the fixed price end.[8]

Suppose that the subcontractor is more risk averse than the contracting firm (the assumption is to be examined shortly). In the framework of a principal-agency problem, Bengt Holmstrom and Paul Milgrom have shown that under certain regularity conditions, the efficient method of periodical price revision agreeable between the risk-averse prime manufacturer (principal) and the risk-averse subcontractor (agency), while the stochastic element of cost follows a certain stochastic law, may be found in the class of linear contract described in (1).[9] If the subcontracting contract is in fact efficient (in the sense of Pareto), the chosen value of α will reflect the following conditions (I discuss the factors determining the level of profit margin, which in turn affect the value of b, in Section B):

[C.1] *Risk sharing (1):* The value of the share parameter, α, is larger if the subcontractor is relatively more risk averse than the prime manufacturer.

---

[8] S. Kawasaki and J. McMillan, "The design of contracts: evidence from Japanese subcontracting", *Journal of the Japanese and International Economies*, 1 (1987), pp. 327–49.

[9] B. Holmstrom and P. Milgrom, "Aggregation and Linearity in the Provision of Intertemporal Incentives," mimeographed, Yale University, 1985. Suppose that the subcontractor's activities take place in continuous time, but that the payment is made by the contracting firm only at discreet points in time. Suppose that production costs follow a Brownian motion, of which the subcontractor controls the drift. The Brownian motion results in the accumulated production cost at the time of payment being normally distributed. Assuming that the utility functions of both parties are of the constant-absolute-risk-aversion type, they have shown that the optimal contract is linear in the end-of-period accumulated production cost as represented in (1).

[C.2] *Risk sharing (2):* The value of the share parameter, α, is larger as the uncertainty involved in the unit cost fluctuation becomes greater (as the variance σ^2 is greater).

[C.3] *Incentive for innovation:* The value of the share parameter, α, is smaller as the effect of the innovation effort relative to cost becomes greater (as the effort elasticity of innovation is greater).

Conditions [C.1] and [C.2] reflect the risk-sharing aspect of the long-term subcontracting contract. Condition [C.3] reflects the incentive aspect. If the value of the sharing parameter α is high, then a large proportion of the effect of possible cost overruns beyond the control of the subcontractor would be shifted to the prime contracting firm, although a large proportion of windfall gains from the cost underrun has to be yielded to the prime contracting firm as well. Thus the subcontractor would be more protected from the risk of uncontrollable cost fluctuation. However, in this case, the cost-reduction effect due to the innovation effort of the subcontracting firm must be shared with the prime contracting firm to a greater extent. Then the subcontracting firm may be less motivated to make the innovation effort (moral hazard). There is thus a trade-off between the provision of insurance to the risk-averse subcontracting firm (insurance) and the provision of incentives for its innovative effort (monitoring). The empirical result by Kawasaki and McMillan mentioned above may indicate that the price adjustment in the subcontracting group is characterized more by the sharing of risk than is the monitoring device.

But is it really the case that the subcontractor is significantly more risk averse than the contracting firm? Is it not contrary to the presumption of the traditional business cycle buffer theory in which the subcontractor is assumed to bear the brunt of business cycle risk? If the subcontracting contract is characterized more as the insurance device, then how is the moral hazard problem dealt with (i.e., how are proper incentives for cost-reducing innovation by the subcontractor given)? If there is a trade-off between insurance and incentives in the subcontracting relation, why has the trade-off not been resolved by the integration of subcontracted activities under the umbrella of the prime manufacturer, and why has the subcontracting group persisted instead? I now turn to these questions.

B. The relational quasi rent and its stratified division

A reason often cited for the extensive use of subcontractors by the J-firm is that, since it grew so fast, it could not generate enough internal resources to integrate these activities to the extent that the A-firm did over its longer course of growth. This may partly explain the genesis of the extensive subcontracting relations observed in the Japanese manufacturing industry. But if this were the only reason, and there was no intrinsic advantage in subcontracting relations over more complete integration, the former would have been gradually replaced by the latter as the growth rate of the economy slowed down and the internal resources of the J-firm accumulated in the 1970s and the early 1980s. On the contrary, the degree to which the J-firm relies on subcontracting relationships has increased over this period.[10] This also contradicts Alfred Chandler's thesis that the trend in modern economies is toward increasingly vertically integrated production.[11]

Because of the long-term relational contract, the subcontractor may be thought of as being related to the prime contracting firm in a somewhat similar way as the in-house division of the integrated firms. On the other hand, even though the contracting firm has minority holdings (capital *keiretsu*) in the stock of the subcontractor, the latter retains considerable autonomy over its operations. Many upper-tier subcontractors are very active in pursuing their own research and development, as the development of new technology endows them with considerable bargaining power vis-à-vis the contracting firm in the future negotiation of profit margins. In fact, it is not rare for technologically advanced suppliers to have simultaneous relational contracting with multiple prime manufacturers, even if a significant share of capital stock is owned by one prime manufacturer, a sure sign of bargaining power.[12] Because the subcontracting group has this dual nature, integrational and autonomous, its organizational characteristics may be referred to as *quasi integration,* meaning that the prime manufacturer is not as integrated as the A-firm, but that its relation with suppliers is much more specific and enduring than in the case of spot contracting.

[10] The index of vertical integration constructed by Michael A. Cusmano and defined as in-house manufacturing and other operating costs divided by sales minus operating profits was 0.41 for Toyota in 1965 and 0.49 at Nissan in 1955, but lowered to 0.26 at both companies in 1983. See M. A. Cusmano, *The Japanese Automobile Industry,* Harvard University Press, 1985. The percentage of small firms (defined to be firms with less than 300 employees) doing subcontracting also increased from 58.7 in 1971 to 60.7 in 1976 and 65.5 in 1981. See MITI, *Survey of Industrial Situation,* 1981.

[11] A. Chandler, *The Visible Hand: the Managerial Revolution in American Business,* Harvard University Press, 1977.

[12] For example, the Toyota corporate group owns about 28 percent of the stock of Nihon Denso, which supplies advanced car electronic equipment, but the latter is also a member of the associations of first-tier suppliers for Mitsubishi Auto Industry, Ltd., Fuji Heavy Industry Co., and Isuzu Motor Co.

Relative economies of quasi integration in the form of the subcontracting group vis-à-vis a higher degree of integration may be found partly in the informational efficiency of the operational coordination between the prime manufacturer and the supplier, which is very similar in its functioning to the horizontal operational coordination among in-house shops of the prime manufacturer. In Chapter 2, I mentioned that a certain type of nontree technological structure among production units may be transformed into a simple tree structure by subgrouping intricately connected component units (see Section 2.3) and placing each subgroup under the control of a separate firm. This possibility suggests that even if the entire technological process may be complicated, a simple treelike relation may be defined among firms. Then horizontal coordination of the *kanban* type may become viable for the group of those firms.

In fact, the *kanban* system is applied to communications between first-tier suppliers and the prime manufacturer in the Japanese subcontracting group in the auto industry to realize just-in-time delivery of supplies. It often extends even to transactions between first-tier suppliers and second-tier suppliers. Market information regarding fluctuating demands for a variety of final outputs of the prime manufacturer is fed directly into the final assembly line of the prime manufacturer, and from there communications necessary for associated upstream adjustment are dissipated beyond the corporate boundary of the prime manufacturer by the medium of *kanban* without the intervention of a single controlling tower, while pressure to respond to local shocks such as quality defects and machine malfunction, is placed firmly on each supplier. Successful autonomous quality control at the level of the subcontractor enables the prime manufacturer to abolish specialized inspector jobs and to reduce the costly discarding of finished or in-process products at the downstream end of the production process.

The savings on information and transaction costs resulting from the horizontal coordination of operations in the subcontracting group and autonomous problem solving by its member firms dramatically manifests itself in the functional hierarchy of the prime manufacturer in Japan, which is much simpler and smaller in comparison with that of the large American integrated firm. This is made possible because fewer personnel are needed for planning and monitoring (such as accounting and supervising). In American auto firms, the chief executive officers are normally six or seven management layers away from a typical plant manager, whereas in Japanese auto plants managers are often appointed to the board of directors (which consists almost entirely of "insiders") and at most two levels below the chief executive officer.[13]

The horizontal operational coordination beyond corporate boundaries and autonomous problem solving by subcontractors are made possible only by the quasi-permanent association of particular suppliers with the prime manufacturer. The situation is isomorphic in that the quasi-permanent association of employees with the firm and the concomitant development of their contextual skills make possible the efficient operation of the intrafirm nonhierarchical, integrative coordinating mechanism. Just as the workings of the ranking hierarchy depend on the employer and the employee's desire to maintain their reputation, so the workings of the stratified subcontracting group depend on the desire of the prime manufacturer and its suppliers to do the same.

The prime manufacturer must maintain its reputation of commitment to the subcontractor in order to elicit the subcontractor's commitment regarding relation-specific investments in expertise, equipment, and research and development. Such mutual commitment is also thought to help shorten the lead time from design to development to commercialization. According to a study of the U.S. and Japanese automobile industry by Robert Cole and Taizo Yakushiji, the lead time is a few years shorter for Japan precisely because the effort put into developing a new model can be initiated concurrently by the prime manufacturer and the subcontractors. If there is no relational contracting, the development effort at the supplier level cannot be initiated until the prime manufacturer has completed the design.[14]

On the other hand, the subcontractor must maintain its reputation for quality, timely delivery of supplies, continual innovative effort, and so on, if it is to secure a stable and profitable position in the subcontracting group. If a lower-tier subcontractor scores well by these measures over a long period, then it may be selected to a higher-tier position. On the other hand, if a subcontractor loses a contract with a major prime manufacturer, it may have difficulty in finding another good business partner. This situation is analogous to that of the ranking hierarchy, wherein the quasi-permanent employee is motivated not

---

[13] R. E. Cole and T. Yakushiji, *The American and Japanese Auto Industries in Transition,* Center for Japanese Studies, University of Michigan, 1984. Another illustration is that GM employed 161,000 salaried employees (and 380,000 hourly workers) in 1986 in the United States, whereas Toyota, which is about one-third the size of GM in terms of sales, employed only 62,000 blue- and white-collar employees in 1984. The total figure of GM includes 127,000 employees of its Electric Data Systems and Hughes Aircraft subsidiaries.

[14] Cole and Yakushiji, *American and Japanese Auto Industries in Transition.*

to shirk and to develop contextual skill, because losing one's ranking in the hierarchy would spoil one's job history.

Transactional economists – such as O. E. Williamson and Bent Klein, Robert A. Crawford, and Almer A. Alchian – have argued that needs for investment in transaction-specific assets tend to develop integration rather than relational contracting.[15] In such situations, once the investment is made, the supplier is locked in with a particular buyer, who may try to exploit this monopsonic position to appropriate rents. The supplier who foresees this opportunity may become reluctant to make any transaction-specific investments. Symmetrically, if a transaction-specific investment is made only by a particular supplier, the buyer may be locked in and the supplier may try to exploit its monopolistic position to appropriate rents. In order to avoid such opportunistic haggling, these authors have argued, the manufacturer would be induced to integrate the supplier as an in-house division up to the point where inefficiency from overbureaucratization would set in. In my opinion, the Japanese experience indicates that the case for integration due to such opportunistic behavior is overdrawn.

Ronald Coase, who was a leading light in the development of the transaction cost approach,[16] has noted:

A defrauding firm may gain immediately but if it can be identified, future business is lost and this, I claimed, would normally make fraud unprofitable. A similar argument suggests that opportunistic behavior of the type we are discussing would also normally be unprofitable and it has added force since a firm acting in this way will certainly be identified. That the implementation of long-term contracts is commonly accompanied by informal arrangements not governed by contract . . . and that this seems to work suggests to me that the propensity for opportunistic behavior is usually effectively checked by the need to take account of the effect of the firm's actions on future business.[17]

Coase described the content of long-term contracting between General Motors and its supplier of automobile frames, A. O. Smith, at some length to support his argument, which is very similar to that presented in Subsection A for the Japanese case. He argued that "it is difficult to believe that this business relationship could have continued for over 50 years if either General Motors or A. O. Smith had acted opportunistically." The ranking hierarchy of suppliers in the Japanese

---

[15] O. E. Williamson, *The Economic Institutions of Capitalism,* Free Press, 1985. B. Klein, R. A. Crawford, and A. A. Alchian, "Vertical integration, appropriable rents, and the competitive contracting process," *Journal of Law and Economics,* 21 (1978), pp. 297–326.

[16] See R. Coase, "The nature of the firm," *Economica,* n.s. 4 (1937), pp. 386–405.

[17] R. Coase, "The third lecture on 'the nature of the firm,'" the conference celebrating the fiftieth anniversary of the "Nature of the Firm," Yale University, 1987.

subcontracting group may be considered nothing but an elaborate systematization of similar relationships.

Then, just as the mutual commitment of the employer and the employee is the source of the organizational quasi rent at the J-firm, one may say that there arise group-specific economic returns attributable to the relational cooperation between the prime manufacturer and its subcontractors. One may call such returns *relational quasi rent* in the sense that it is generated by the unique informational efficiency of relational contracting in the subcontracting grouping. How is this relational quasi rent distributed among the prime contracting firm and supplier firms within the subcontracting group? What factors determine the distribution?

These questions, formally speaking, boil down to the question of how the equilibrium value of parameter b in formula (6.1) is determined. Given an estimated ex ante unit cost, it is determined by the relative bargaining power of the subcontractor vis-à-vis the prime contracting firm. One may suppose that the bargaining equilibrium is characterized as the perfect equilibrium of a Rubinstein-type model, as described in Section 5.1 for union–management bargaining. However one important characteristic of the subcontractor–parent relationship is distinct from the union–management relationship: There may be alternative suppliers, with equal or inferior technological expertise, to which the prime contracting firm may be able to switch if an agreement with the incumbent supplier cannot be reached.

A bargaining model with such a switching possibility was analyzed by A. Shaked and J. Sutton in the context of employment bargaining with involuntary unemployment.[18] The equilibrium outcome tends to favor the prime contracting firm more than the Nash bargaining solution does, as switching to another equally qualified partner becomes easier in terms of time (in the limit in which the switching time approaches zero, the spot market result obtains; i.e., the whole rent, if any, can be appropriated by the prime contracting firm). As already noted, the prime contracting firm in fact tries to strengthen its bargaining position by adopting the so-called two-vendor policy, but the effectiveness of such strategic behavior by the prime contracting firm would be limited if the supplier has transaction-specific technological and communicational expertise. Suppose that the length of switching time in the Sutton-Shaked model is a proxy for the difficulty of switching in terms of technological expertise and/or informational processing

---

[18] A. Shaked and J. Sutton, "Involuntary unemployment as a perfect equilibrium in a bargaining model," *Econometrica*, 52 (1984), pp. 1351–64.

capacity of the incumbent supplier. Also assume that the efficiency of the communicational channel between the prime manufacturing firm and the subcontractor in the use of the *kanban* system, cooperative developmental effort, and the like, increases with the duration of relational contracting. Then we can claim:

> [C.4] *Stratification of the subcontracting group:* Given an estimated ex ante unit cost, the value of target price *b* is higher (lower), the more (less) unique the technological knowledge that the subcontractor possesses and that the prime contracting firm cannot easily replace by its own production or another potential supplier, and the longer (shorter) the tenure of the subcontractor in its relation with the prime contracting firm. Consequently subcontractors are stratified within the subcontracting group in the sharing of the quasi rent according to their technological expertise and tenure.

The relational quasi rent acquired by each firm in the subcontracting group according to its unique technological expertise, if any, is likely to be shared, in turn, by the body of its stockholders and the body of its quasi-permanent employees, because its technological efficiency is partly due to employees' contextual skills. The quasi-permanent employees of first-tier subcontractors are normally found to enjoy a considerable level of earnings, although it may not be precisely comparable to the levels possible at the prime manufacturer. This suggests that, although the pressure on first-tier subcontractors and their employees for efficient operational coordination and quality control, as well as technological development, is strong, they also enjoy a reasonable share of the relational quasi rent made possible by avoiding a high degree of integration. But it also seems true that quasi integration is a way to secure the benefit of quasi-permanent employees at the prime manufacturer and at stronger first-tier supplier firms by restraining the expansion of the bodies of quasi-permanent employees at those levels. As one goes down hierarchical tiers in the subcontracting group, the technological expertise of lower-tier subcontractors becomes less and less specialized. The fact that their supplies may be easily replaced by other competitors makes their bargaining power over participation in the relational quasi rent extremely weak.

Table 6.1 reveals that scale differential in the rate of increase in value-added productivity began to widen after 1975 in favor of larger establishments, which suggests that the bargaining power of lower-tier subcontractors had become weaker. If we look only at contractual wages, it appears that workers at small establishments are less severely

Table 6.1. *Rate of increase in wages and value-added productivity by establishment size, 1960–83*

No. of employees	500 or more	100–499	30–99	5–29
Wages				
1960–5	8.1	11.0	12.2	15.0
1965–70	14.7	14.9	14.4	14.2
1970–5	18.1	18.2	17.3	17.3
1975–83	7.5	6.9	6.7	6.7
Value-added productivity				
1960–5	6.9	10.0	11.9	14.5
1965–70	17.2	16.8	16.5	16.3
1970–5	10.8	13.8	13.1	13.8
1975–83	11.6	9.2	8.6	8.2

Source: Ministry of Labor, *Monthly Labor Survey;* Ministry of International Trade and Industry, *Industrial Statistics.*

Table 6.2. *Ratios of welfare-related labor costs at establishments with 30–99 employees to those at establishments with more than 1,000 employees, 1973–82*

	Welfare costs legally required	Welfare costs legally not required	Costs for retirement compensation
1973–5	76.1	44.8	32.2
1976–9	70.1	34.8	33.9
1980–2	72.0	29.4	29.2

Source: Ministry of Labor, *Analysis of Labor Economy,* 1983.

hit. In fact, if one compares wages paid to workers in the same age and the same job tenure category, the differentials according to establishment size are not so great. For example, regularly paid wages to male workers of establishments with 10 to 99 employees in the manufacturing industry in the age categories 20–24 and 25–29 were 98.6 percent and 94.5 percent, respectively, of those paid to workers of establishments with 1,000 or more in 1983.[19]

[19] Ministry of Labor, *Basic Survey of Wage Structure,* 1983.

But, if one compares benefits paid in the form of nonstandard wages, such as bonuses, pensions, and separation payment, there is evidence of a greater differential between larger and smaller firms, as Table 6.2 indicates. It is also at these smaller firms that one can find a larger proportion of employment of "part-timers" who are underpaid and deprived of various benefits such as job security, bonuses, and pensions.

One may then conjecture, depending on further empirical verification/falsification, that larger firms in the subcontracting group have gained an increasingly larger proportion of the relational quasi rent, delivering to their quasi-permanent employees sizable shares of this rent in the form of nonstandard wage benefits, while the bargaining power of smaller firms within the group has been declining, with employees there gaining only near-competitive wages. This may seem reminiscent of the old dual-market hypothesis, but the current structure is characterized more by fine gradational stratification, starting with the coalitional structure of the prime contracting manufacturer at the apex of the subcontracting group and going down to that of upper-tier subcontracting firms of relatively stronger bargaining power to the near-competitive system at the lowest tier. In the early 1960s, there was substantial differential in regularly paid wages by firm size, but this differential narrowed and almost disappeared in the period of high growth, and does not seem to have reemerged since. Scale differential appears more conspicuously in the form of nonstandard wage benefits.

Another way in which our model may depart from the traditional theory of subcontracting may be found in its risk-sharing aspect. As represented by (6.1), the efficient relational contract is characterized by two parameters, α (share parameter) and b (power parameter); the value of each is affected by the relative risk attitude of the supplier. The more risk averse the supplier is vis-à-vis the prime contracting firm, the higher the efficient value of α and the lower the equilibrium value of b, other things being constant. Kawasaki and McMillan, in the empirical study referred to earlier, concluded that the level of the risk-sharing parameter, α, in fact increases with the degree of estimated risk aversion of the subcontractor, which in turn decreases with the size of the firm. They also showed that the level of profit is negatively correlated to the degree of estimated risk aversion.[20]

This implies that, contrary to the traditional view, which sees the prime manufacturer as using monopsonic power to force the subcon-

[20] Kawasaki and McMillan, "The design of contracts."

tractor to bear the brunt of cost and demand fluctuations for the purpose of insulating itself from business cycle risk,[21] the following holds:

[C.5] *The insurance function of subcontracting group:* The prime manufacturer absorbs a proportion of contract-specific risk, acting as a partial insurer for lower-tier, risk-averse subcontractors, extracting a larger portion of the relational quasi rent as a sort of insurance premium.

Since the prime manufacturer and major first-tier suppliers are likely to be diversified in their production, at least in a variety of outputs, they are relatively free from product-specific market risk. Their greater financial resources endow them with the capacity to resist the cost of business cycle risk. On the other hand, subcontractors, particularly at a lower tier, are likely to be specialized in a narrower line of business and more limited variety of output. Therefore they are more likely to be prone to product-specific risk, while lacking adequate financial resources to bear the risks of product demand and business cycle. Therefore it is in the mutual interest of the prime contracting firm and the subcontracting supplier to share the burden of risk, and to assign an increasing portion of it to the former as the level of the contract is lowered. But this is not in conflict with the fact that the greater monopsonic power of the prime contracting firm and the risk aversion of the subcontractor reduce the "level" of the target price of the latter's output, whence reduce its sharing in the relational quasi rent.

The gradational stratification of the subcontracting group in Japan does seem to be facing a turning point, however. Since the realignment of the exchange ratio, which began with the intervention of G-5 in the fall of 1985 and was accelerated by declining energy and other material costs, the advantages of the low-cost production of lower-tier subcontractors are being overriden by the potential lower-cost supply from abroad. The prime manufacturers have begun to consider the relative merit of obtaining supplies from sources abroad, either through foreign suppliers and/or their own subsidiaries. Inasmuch as most strong first-tier subcontractors are looking for foreign bases of operation themselves, the substitution of foreign suppliers (or Japanese subsidiaries in foreign countries) may not reach the first-tier supplier immediately, but it may well have an adverse effect on employment opportunities at the lower end of the subcontracting group. It is yet to be seen, how-

[21] For example, see Takafusa Nakamura, *The Postwar Japanese Economy,* translated by Jacqueline Kaminski, University of Tokyo Press, 1981 (originally published in 1980 by the University of Tokyo Press under the title *Nihon Keizai: sono Seicho to Kozo*), chap. 5. See also Caves and Uekusa, *Industrial Organization in Japan,* chap. 6.

ever, whether the phenomenon of the dilemma of industrial democracy will come to manifest itself in the form of rising macro unemployment.

2.   The insurance function of corporate grouping and its waning

In this section, I deal with the corporate groups of *zaibatsu* origin, or financial *keiretsu* type, which are formed by companies from different industries and are relatively autonomous but connected through mutual minority stockholding. Hereafter I refer to these simply as corporate groups. One who is not familiar with the workings of a group of firms that are not product market rivals but enjoy respective monopolistic positions in separate markets may suspect that the primary function is to maximize the joint profits of the group. A parable along these lines was presented by Caves and Uekusa:[22] Imagine a general equilibrium situation in which many oligopolistic firms produce and exchange multiple commodities. Markets are not free from monopoly power, so that equilibrium price ratios are not in general equal to marginal opportunity costs of production. Suppose now that a subgroup of firms linked by a complex network of input–output relations band together and strike a trade arrangement among themselves in order to maximize their joint profits. They can do so by trading among themselves at internal "optimal" price ratios equal to the marginal rates of opportunity costs among themselves. They would jointly trade with outsiders at prices that would make profit-maximizing use of their joint monopoly–monopsony power.

As Caves and Uekusa have rightly pointed out, such joint profit maximizing would require a high degree of centralized coordination to enforce discriminate pricing between insiders and outsiders as well as to override incentives for individual profit maximization for the sake of collective profit maximization. The joint profit-maximizing arrangement would increase the joint profit (and profits of some member firms), but may decrease profits of some member firms. The pre–World War II *zaibatsu* may be regarded as groups that implement such centralized coordination. The general trading company acted as a sole trading agent for member firms and was in a position to manipulate the terms of transaction with outsiders. The holding company pooled the profits of the operating firms.

However, the post–World War groups of companies – those of *zaibatsu* origin or those clustered around the principal banks – do not

[22] Ibid., chap. 4.

operate under such centralized coordination. The President Club, lacking a formal governance structure and a special staff to coordinate member actions, normally functions only as a forum for the exchange of information. It may sometimes mediate possible disputes among affiliated companies, coordinate a rescue operation for a troubled affiliated company, or explore the possibility of mutual cooperation in new ventures that may be beyond a reach of a single company (e.g., atomic energy development, ocean and space development, setting up of value-added communications networks, or large-scale integrated plant exports such as the Mitsui-Iranian Petroleum Development Project). The decision whether or not to participate in such a joint project is up to individual companies. There is no mechanism apart from moral obligation, by which to enforce any consensus reached at the meeting. The initiative for joint projects has been shifting from the bank and the trading company to individual companies in relevant fields that tend to be willing to expand their cooperating partners beyond the group boundary.

Transactions among affiliated companies are never exclusive, and affiliated companies are freely engaged in transactions with outsiders. For example, as Table 4.3 shows, bank financing from member banks to an affiliated company is on average only between 13.2 percent and 27.8 percent of all financing, and the rest comes from outsiders. Outside opportunities are presumably important if affiliated companies are not to weaken their relative bargaining power over the terms of transaction by relying on a single supplier/buyer too heavily. From the viewpoint of banks, it is desirable to spread risk, as well as to pool it, by mutually participating in loan consortia organized by other banks affiliated with different groups.

Yet, one may argue that repeated transactions, or relational contracting, with affiliated companies may save on the costs of transaction. They may save on the cost of negotiating and drawing separate contracts with different partners and they may save on the cost of monitoring everything from the quality of supplies to the soundness of an investment project. Self-binding discipline may be imposed to maintain the company's reputation as a good business partner, and consequently benefits will arise from repeated transactions. Although the business relationship in the corporate group is relatively more horizontal and reciprocal than that in the subcontracting group, the above-mentioned aspect of repeated transactions may be considered similar to the functioning of the subcontracting group, as discussed in the previous section. Further, interlocking directorate holding is often observed between close business partners within the corporate group and provides another mechanism for mutual monitoring.

Caves and Uekusa have compared profitability in affiliated companies of major corporate groups before and after interest payments to banks with that in independent competitors using data for 243 large companies over the period 1961–70. After controlling for other possible determinants of profitability, they found that profits before interest on total assets were weakly negatively related to group affiliation. Further, they found a weak tendency for group affiliation to reduce the variability of profit, as well as a significant positive relation between group affiliation and the level of interest payments on borrowed capital. From these observations, they concluded that "rents due to group affiliation are captured by the banks, the central organs of the present-day groups."[23]

They do not seem to deny that appropriable rent arises in corporate grouping. However, their finding seems to be inconsistent with the prediction of the transaction cost approach. If, as mentioned above, transaction cost savings are the only motive behind group formation, why are there more profitable independent companies than group-affiliated companies? Is it not possible for any reputable company to obtain those transaction cost savings without being a member of the President Club or relying on a particular bank, but by developing relational contracting with selected business partners? Further, is it not the case that a company that is free from monitoring by the bank and other business partners through the board will have more room to switch partners, if necessary, as well as enter into a new line of business? If so, why have nonbank-affiliated companies not broken away from corporate groups when the bank's stockholding was, at most, the legally set 10 percent (5 percent at present)?

Some of the results reported by Caves and Uekusa have been reaffirmed by Nakatani in a study of 317 nonfinancial companies covering the period 1966–74.[24] He found that the rate of profit before interest payments to total assets is 1.1 to 2.7 percent lower for group-affiliated companies than for comparable nonaffiliated companies after controlling for other possible determinants of profitability. He also found that the variability of profitability measured by the variance of the profit rate was significantly lower for group-affiliated companies than for the selected independent companies. However, in examining corporate

---

[23] Ibid., p. 87.
[24] I. Nakatani, "The economic role of Financial corporate grouping," in M. Aoki (ed.), *The Economic Analysis of the Japanese Firm.* North-Holland, 1984.

performance, Nakatani went beyond the framework used by Caves and Uekusa and found that group-affiliated companies pay higher and more stable average compensation to their employees after controlling for firm size as well as the age and gender composition of employees. In the light of our notion of the J-firm, this suggests that the bargaining power of employees at group-affiliated companies is stronger than at other companies and that these employees are relatively better insulated from income risks.

How should we interpret these results? One possibility would be to suppose that *one* of the major functions of the corporate group is to ensure that incomes will be evened out for the constituent bodies of affiliated companies, the stockholders and the employees. The principal bank acts as the nexus of this mutual arrangement, extracting higher interest payments from affiliated companies as a sort of insurance premium. Let us see whether this hypothesis can endure a test of economic logic.

First, this hypothesis requires that we answer the following questions: Why is it reasonable to assume that the affiliated companies of corporate groups are risk averse? Since the individual investor can diversify his/her wealth among many investments belonging to different risk classes, isn't individual risk cost associated with any single investment negligible, and consequently isn't the aggregate of negligible individual risk costs in one company over the entire body of stockholders also negligible? If so, it is appropriate for management of the company to behave risk neutrally. The existing financial literature provides affirmative answers to the last two questions.[25] Why, then, does the group of companies have to develop a risk-sharing (insurance) contrivance? This question cannot be answered unless we take into account the position of quasi-permanent employees in the J-firm and the nature of games there, a point that is not dealt with in the financial literature.

Let us begin with the following purely theoretical observation. If the capital market is complete and perfectly competitive, and if there is no transaction cost or tax, the efficient allocation of risk bearing among financial investors in the economy can be achieved through the market. Neither intercorporate stockholding nor other risk-sharing mechanisms can expand the opportunity already available to wealth holders through the capital market, and they become redundant.

In order to illustrate the point, let us assume that there exist only

---

[25] For example, see K. J. Arrow and Robert Lind, "Uncertainty and the evaluation of public investment decisions," *American Economic Review*, 59 (1970), pp. 364–78.

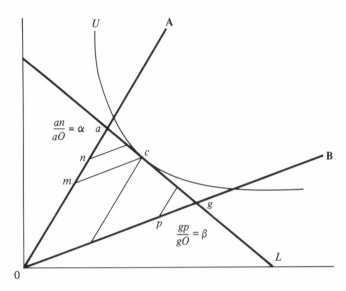

Figure 6.1. Optimal risk bearing in the competive capital market.

two firms, denoted by A and B. The profitabilities of investment projects undertaken by the two firms are assumed to be uncertain and
dependent upon two disjoint events, 1 and 2, the occurrence of which
cannot be controlled by the firms. The horizontal axis in Figure 6.1
represents profit when event 1 occurs, and the vertical axis represents
profit when event 2 occurs. Let vectors **A** and **B** represent profit prospects
of firm A and firm B, respectively. Suppose that an individual
owns a certain share a in firm A's stock and that the tradability of
shares in A for shares in B is represented by the straight line L. If the
risk attitude and risk assessment of the individual are represented by
the indifference map U, as depicted in Figure 6.1, his/her subjectively
optimal portfolio selection would be point c. In other words, the individual
can insure against uncertain events in the best possible way by
exchanging a proportion am/aO of his/her shares in A for shares in B
at the market rate.

If the market tradability as represented by L is determined in such
a way as to equate the demands for, and the supply of, shares in A and
B and every individual investor chooses an optimal portfolio as
described, then this general equilibrium situation achieves the efficient
allocation of risk in the economy. Suppose now that α (= an/aO) percent
of A's stock is owned by firm B and β (= gp/gO) percent of firm

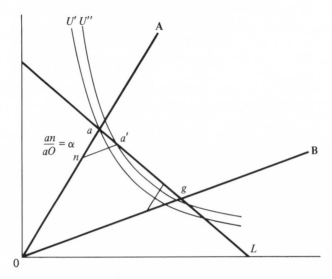

Figure 6.2. Risk sharing through cross-stockholding under nonsalability conditions.

B's stock is owned by firm A. If the market values of cross-stockholdings are equal, the opportunities open to the investor do not change, as can be seen from Figure 6.1.[26] Therefore cross-stockholding or any other type of risk sharing arrangement among firms cannot do more than what the market can do with an appropriate initial allocation of stocks among individuals.

That much is obvious, as we have assumed the unlimited tradability of stock in the perfectly competitive market. Now instead of tradable stock, let us consider a claim for the sharing of uncertain revenues of firm A that is not freely transferable in the capital market. Let us call this claim a "nonsalable share." If such an asset existed, the role of the cross-stockholding would be changed. Let us employ a similar example to Figure 6.1 and imagine a situation in which the individual cannot sell his or her share a in firm A's revenue. If the indifference maps for this individual are as depicted in Figure 6.2, the utility level under the

[26] Strictly speaking this is so provided that short sales are possible. More generally, for any combination of cross-stockholding among two firms, there exists a corresponding initial allocation of stocks among individual stockholders for which the equilibrium relative price ratio will equate the valuations of the cross-stockholding so that individual opportunities will not change from the initial position by the introduction of cross-stockholding.

nonsalability constraint without cross-stockholding is represented by the curve U' going through a. But if there is cross-stockholding (or another risk-sharing arrangement) so that the position of the revenue claimant of firm A's can be shifted to the point a', he/she is clearly better off than at point a, enjoying a higher utility level U''. Cross-stockholding (or other risk-sharing arrangement) between firms can remedy, albeit incompletely, the inefficiency caused by the absence of salability of individual shares in the revenue of firm A.

In the above example, the nonsalability constraint was just an imaginary hypothesis, but recall that the potential wealth of the quasi-permanent employee of the J-firm is related to the performance of the employing firm, and its salability is limited. Under the seniority compensation scheme, the quasi-permanent employee bears a portion of the cost of investment in firm-specific human capital when he/she is a junior employee, but can reap returns on the investment only when he/she becomes a senior employee. Further, there is the posting of bonds repaid only at the time of retirement in the form of a separation payment. The important point is that not only is the potential wealth of the quasi-permanent employee in the form of a seniority premium and separation payment unportable, but the risk involved in acquiring it is firm-specific and not diversifiable.

If employees of the A-firm quit in midcareer, they too may be penalized by a reduction in the pension benefits provided by the firm. But as long as they continue to work for the firm, their own, as well as their employer's, contributions to the pension plan are funded outside the employing firm and are diversified in the capital market by professional financial managers. By the Employees' Retirement Income Security Act, not more than 10 percent of the funds can be invested in the stock of the parent company. Further, the so-called prudent-man rule is imposed on the pension manager in his/her portfolio selection, and the pension funds are insured by the Federal Pension Benefits Insurance Corporation. Thus the pension wealth of the employee of the A-firm is virtually free from firm-specific risk. There is a clear line dividing the risk-bearing functions of investors and employees.

In contrast, a substantial amount of wealth owned by the quasi-permanent employee of the J-firm is at stake in the employing firm, as already mentioned. In other words, risk bearing is shared by investors and employees and, the latter's risk is not salable as the former's in the financial market. In this situation, cross-stockholding within the corporate group may mitigate the variability of revenues to affiliated firms as well as that of their quasi-permanent employees. It is true that mutual dividend receipts by affiliated companies may not be significant relative to their own operating revenues, but when they incur current losses they can make them up through the realization of capital gains on stockholdings. In fact, it is common for Japanese companies to make up operating losses by selling off a portion of holding stock, as needed, primarily to other affiliated companies and often on the condition that they repurchase the stock once they have recovered from the business adversity. Thus the phenomenon of corporate grouping in Japan may be linked to the other important characteristics of the J-firm, that is, to its ranking hierarchy and coalitional structure.

As shown earlier, cross-stockholding itself functions as an incomplete risk-sharing scheme. However, the direct risk-sharing arrangement between transacting partners may also be able to mitigate the variability of operating revenue. In this case, cross-holding functions as a mutual monitoring device forcing each partner to comply with the requirements of an arrangement that may not necessarily be in its short-term interest. This can be seen as follows.

Imagine that there are two vertically related firms, the upstream firm U and the downstream firm D. Suppose that the supply price p_u of the primary resource to U as well as the demand price p_d of the final output of D are stochastic variables, reflecting the market uncertainty uncontrollable by these firms. Let p_i be the price of the intermediate good transacted between U and D. If there is no transactional arrangement between the two firms, then p_i is given by the external market, which is assumed to be perfectly competitive. If the two firms are revenue maximizers, the amount of the primary input by U would be such that its marginal value product evaluated by p_i is equal to p_u at any given moment, while the amount of the final output by D would be such that its marginal cost evaluated by p_i is equal to p_d at any given moment. The resulting variability of each firm's revenue may be high.

Suppose that both firms are interested in reducing the variability of revenue as well as increasing the level of expected revenue. If so, they can enter into a mutual agreement for reducing the variability of the revenue of each. In order to be group efficient, both firms must jointly adjust the level of operations in exactly the same manner as they would under the perfectly competitive intermediate market so that joint revenue is maximized. The question is what type of nonmarket arrangement is appropriate for distributing the maximized revenue between the two firms so as to minimize their risk costs?

Suppose that the two firms agree on an arrangement to share the maximized revenue I^* at each moment according to the rule

$$I_u = \alpha I^* + \beta \text{ and } I_d = (1 - \alpha)I^* - \beta,$$

where I_u and I_d are revenues of the upstream firm and the downstream firm, respectively, α is a share parameter, and β is a transfer parameter. Under a certain regularity condition, it is optimal for risk-averse firms to set α in such a way that

$$\alpha = \frac{A_u}{[A_u + A_d]},$$

where A_u and A_d are the measures of absolute risk aversion for each firm, as defined by Arrow and Pratt. In other words, there is no other arrangement to make both risk-averse firms better off ex ante. According to this rule, the fluctuating joint revenue should be shared (before transfer) in inverse proportion to the relative intensity of risk aversion. If both firms are equally risk averse, then they ought to share the fluctuation of joint revenue equally, which would be possible under the competitive arrangement only by chance.

This rule is equivalent to minimizing the aggregate risk costs defined by

$$[A_u \alpha^2 + A_d(1 - \alpha)^2]\sigma_{I^*} = A_u \sigma_{I_u} + A_d \sigma_{I_d},$$

where σ_x denotes the variance of the variable x; that is, to minimize the sum of the variability of revenue (measured by its variances), weighted by the respective intensity of risk aversion. The difference between the minimized value of the aggregate risk cost under the prescribed rule and the expected value under the competitive market arrangement measures the savings on risk cost made possible under this arrangement. This saving may be divided between the two firms according to their respective bargaining powers. This division is captured by the parameter β.

Saving risk cost among firms as modeled above is only possible through a long-term transactional relation. Under this risk-sharing arrangement, at any given moment the instantaneous revenue maximization possible under the competitive intermediate market is not likely to be realized for each firm. However, if either firm defaults on the risk-sharing relational contracting and tries to realize the short-run maximized revenue by switching to the competitive market, the Walrasian market mechanism would be reactivated and long-run risk costs would consequently arise. In order to save the risk cost (the variability of revenue) on average in the long run, each firm must bind itself to nonrevenue-maximizing relational contracting. Cross-stockholding among member firms may serve as a mechanism by which each party can monitor whether the other is abiding by the relational contract.

The above model may be applied to more specific bank–borrower relations in corporate groups. In such a scenario the bank may be identified with the upstream firm U, and the affiliated borrowing company may be identified with the downstream firm D. In a depressed state of business, the affiliated company may be granted additional loans and/ or have the repayment of existing loans rescheduled by the bank to help it overcome its difficulty. On the other hand, the former may incur redundant loans when its business is in relatively good shape. It has been often observed that the risk-averse, group-affiliated company does not pay back all debts to the bank, even when it can do so, for fear that it may not be able to obtain financing in bad times. Instead, the company that maintains such long-run relations with the main bank may be able to receive an extraordinary "rescue operation" from the latter and other affiliated companies when it falls into real difficulty. The rescue operation may range from an extension on emergency loans, an interest moratorium, dispatches of management teams from the bank and technological assistance from other affiliated companies, reemployment of redundant employees by affiliated companies, to a buy-product campaign within the group. In Chapter 4 the rescue operation by the main bank was interpreted as the bank's effort to maintain its reputation as a responsible monitor, but here we see that it may also function as a business insurance payment from the viewpoint of the troubled borrower.

Since the bank sustains long-run relations with multiple companies, it can diversify risk so that the risk cost involved in any single loan may be relatively smaller. In the light of the above model, it is then collectively more rational for the bank to absorb a portion of the fluctuations of affiliated companies' revenues. In return, this insurance function may enable the bank to absorb a portion of the total cost savings in the form of relatively higher effective loan rates made possible through the manipulation of compensating balances of affiliated companies. The apparent abnormal statistical finding of Caves and Uekusa as well as Nakatani that group-affiliated companies pay a higher rate of interest to the bank is thus consistent with the prediction of our insurance model.[27]

---

[27] Recently, the risk-sharing hypothesis in the context of major bank–borrower relationship was challenged by Akiyoshi Horiuchi and associates (A. Horiuchi, Shinichi Fukuda, and Frank Packard, "What role has the 'main bank' played in Japan?" *Journal of the Japanese and International Economies*, 2 (1988), in press. But in my judgment, the empirical results that they presented for that purpose did not conclusively reject the risk-sharing hypothesis. If the major bank functions as an insurer, there is a danger of moral hazard on the side of the borrower, owing to negligence of management efficiency. In such a situation, there is an incentive on the side of the bank to

However, even if the above theoretical explanation is consistent, we have not yet explained why profitable independent companies exist side by side with group-affiliated companies. Is it because the group-affiliated companies are more risk averse than successful independent companies? If so, why? One or more of the following may be cited as possible answers:

(A) Most group-affiliated companies, particularly of *zaibatsu* origin, were established earlier than independent companies, and accordingly the average tenure of their employees is longer. Therefore there is more need for a nonfinancial market arrangement to insure their quasi-permanent employees. This hypothesis is consistent with the aforementioned Nakatani finding that on average affiliated companies pay higher compensation to employees.

(B) Many successful independent companies listed on stock exchanges are led by founders cum managers who exhibited extraordinary entreprenurial talents in the post–World War II period, whereas the affiliated companies, particularly of *zaibatsu* origin, are managed by career-salaried managers who tend to play safe and not jeopardize their career opportunities.

(C) When groups were reformed between 1955 and 1965, many nonfinancial-affiliated companies were engaged in a limited line of business, with the notable exception of trad-

---

terminate its relational contract with badly run companies. (Incidentally, this possibility also suggests that the risk-sharing hypothesis and the monitoring hypothesis may not be mutually exclusive as Horiuchi et al. seem to imply.) Therefore their finding of negative correlation between the borrower's profitability and the probability of its changing its main bank is not necessarily contradictory with the risk-sharing hypothesis, although a risk-sharing arrangement requires a long-run relational contract between the major bank and the borrower, as explained in the text. Second, since the payment of the insurance premium by the borrower may take the form of the maintenance of a high compensating balance at good times, there may not be a clear negative correlation between the borrower's profitability and the amount of its debt under the risk-sharing scheme insurance. Therefore their empirical finding of the absence of negative correlation does not necessarily reject the risk-sharing hypothesis. I agree with their claim, however, that risk sharing between the main bank and the borrower does not explain the "rigidity" of the loan rate.

In view of the criticism by Horiuchi et al., it may be worth repeating here that the insurance function of corporate grouping is not limited to the main bank–borrower relationship. Cross-stockholding and the consequential accumulation of capital gains realizable in bad times may constitute a very important source of insurance in corporate grouping. Also it may be emphasized again that risk sharing is but one possible function of corporate grouping. Insulation from takeover as discussed in Chapter 5 is another important function of corporate grouping.

ing companies. Also during that period, foreign exchange for the acquisition of raw materials and patents was rationed on the basis of market shares of companies. As stated at the beginning of this chapter, group affiliation guaranteed affiliated companies certain market shares through reciprocal relational contracting within groups. After the foreign exchange control was lifted in the mid-1960s some group-affiliated companies may have been slow to adapt to this new competitive environment because of the conservative inertia of the insurance function of corporate grouping.

As the J-firm grows in size, however, its need for the insurance provided by affiliation in a corporate group decisively declines. The firm may bear more risk by diversifying into different lines of business, hedging foreign exchange risk, and so on, while protecting employee risk through its accumulated corporate assets. The insurance function of corporate grouping may have been on the wane since the mid-1970s, although it still seems to serve as the insurance of last resort for many affiliated companies. Instead, the horizontal linkage of firms in different lines of business seems to be growing among high technology–oriented, multidisciplinary research and development efforts. This linkage is present even beyond the traditional boundaries of corporate groups. Why does this linkage occur in the form of cooperation among independent firms, rather than merger and acquisition? Is there any economic explanation for this phenomenon? I now turn to these questions.

3.   The direction and organization of R&D

The main concern of Japanese firms in the mid-1970s was how to overcome the first negative growth experienced since the end of the war, which was brought on by the first oil shock. One step they took in this direction was to "slim down" their operations *(genryo keiei)* by reducing the amount of external debt and the number of employees. Although this was a painful experience, it allowed the major Japanese firms to regain their confidence and then, toward the end of the 1970s, to shift all their attention to the critically important research and development (R&D) effort. They gradually became aware that they had achieved their postwar objective of catching up with Western technology. They reasoned that, for competitive reasons, Western firms would now be more cautious about transferring advanced technology, and innovation would be required if firms were to remain competitive in global markets. At the same time, there was great anticipation of the coming of the microelectronic revolution and other high-tech advances.

Accordingly, there was a quantum leap in the ratio of research expenditure to gross national product from the steady 1.70 percent level in 1975–8 to the 1.80 percent level in 1979. Since then the ratio has continued to increase. In 1985 it reached the 2.77 percent level and surpassed the U.S. level for the first time. This increase was largely due to private initiative. About two-thirds of the ¥8,890 billion spent on research in 1985 came from private companies.[28] Contrary to the widely held view, the government played a relatively small role in this area. Its share of research funding in 1983 was only 22.2 percent, which included grants-in-aid to national and private universities.[29] Human resource inputs to research have been increasing as well since the late 1970s. The number of researchers rose from 255,000 in 1975 to 370,000 by 1984, which is approximately equal to the American figure on a per capita basis. About 6 out of 10 were employed by private companies, 3 by universities, and 1 by public research institutions.

Research output has also begun to increase. According to a survey by the Management and Coordination Agency, technology exports by all industries in 1986 reached ¥293 billion and thus narrowed the gap with the technology imports to 79 percent.[30] Until 1978, the value of technological exports was less than half the value of technological imports.

Statistics on patents also indicate that research output has increased considerably. Among noncommunist, highly industrialized countries,

[28] Management and Coordination Agency, *Report on the Survey of Research and Development, 1986.*
[29] In the United States, as much as 46.0 percent of research expenditures in 1983 were financed by the government, of which 28.6 percent was directed to defense-related research. The defense-related research financed by the Agency for Self Defense was only 0.5 percent of Japanese research expenditures in 1983.
[30] According to Bank of Japan statistics, the technological trade deficit is substantially larger (exports are only about 30 percent of imports). The discrepancy between the MCA and BOJ statistics may be attributed to the following factors: (1) the BOJ statistics count only royalty payments, but the MCA statistics include payments for all technology-related services such as the provision of know-how, engineering guidance associated with plant exports, etc.; and (2) the MCA statistics cover only private companies engaged in research and development, whereas the BOJ survey covers all institutions engaged in foreign exchange transactions, including public research corporations active in technological imports, such as the Space Development Corporation and department stores. In the MCA statistics, industries for which technological exports exceeded technological imports were textiles, chemicals, iron and steel, and construction.

236 Information, incentives, and bargaining

Table 6.3. *Research intensity by firm size (manufacturing), 1986*

Size of the firm by capital (yen)	Number of researchers per 10,000 employees (March 1986)	Ratio of research expenditure to sales (1986)	Annual growth rate of research expenditures (1985–8)
5–10 m	332	1.98%	29.1%
10–100 m	299	1.62	18.7
100 m–1 b	336	1.58	0.8
1–10 b	440	2.15	17.4
10 b	619	3.44	17.4
Average	468	2.69	16.1

Source: Management and Coordination Agency, *Report on the Survey of Research and Development,* 1986.

Japan is the only country that has exhibited a steady increase in the number of domestic patent applications since the beginning of 1970s.[31] Although patents in general are considered a less important gauge of inventiveness today than they were in the past, it may still be worth noting that the Japanese are becoming markedly more inventive by this scale. The share of foreigners in Japanese patent applications peaked at 25.9 percent in 1971, but has steadily declined since then, and dropped to 10.0 percent in 1984. In contrast, Japanese-invented patent applications in the United States have increased from 5.1 percent in 1975 to 15.4 percent of total U.S. patent applications in 1983. According to recently completed research commissioned by the National Science Foundation, the share of Japanese-invented patents granted in the United States has also increased, from 8.8 percent in 1975 to 16.5 percent in 1984.[32]

These figures suggest an increasingly active research and development effort by the private corporate sector since the late 1970s. Table 6.3 provides some information on the distribution of those activities among firms of various sizes. It is apparent that large firms with capital

---

[31] Between 1975 and 1978, the number of patent applications remained roughly at the level of 160,000, but since 1979 it has increased at the annual rate of approximately 10 percent and rose to 285,000 in 1984. The number of patents granted has also increased from 44,000 in 1978 to 61,000 in 1984.

[32] Francis Narin and Dominic Olivastro, "First interim report: identifying areas of leading edge Japanese science and technology," submitted to NSF by CHI Research/Computer Horizon, Inc., May 1986.

in excess of ¥10 billion are engaged in the most intensive research activities, in terms of both human and financial resources. Research expenditures at firms of this size have also increased the fastest in recent years, if small firms with capital in excess of ¥5 million but no greater than ¥10 million are excluded. Although this class of small firms may include subsidiaries of large firms specializing in research and development, these data are still striking, in view of the fact that this class also includes conventional small-sized firms that are not particularly active in research and development. Contrary to the often-heard view that innovative small firms are not viable in Japan because of the shortage of risk-bearing capital and immobility of researchers, these figures indicate that Japan does have research-intensive small firms, particularly in high technology–oriented fields such as microelectronics, software, new materials, and machinery.

Keeping in mind the increasing intensity of research and development by large and small firms in Japan, I now turn to the following questions: Is there anything unique about the nature and direction of research and development carried out by Japanese firms, small and large, in comparison with Western firms? If so, do these charcteristics support the claim that the Japanese firm is strong in application-oriented, downstream technology, but weak in truly innovative scientific research, despite the sharp increase in basic research in Japan? Let us begin with the first question.

A.   *Stylized characteristics of R&D: isomorphic structure of manufacturing and R&D*

The research-intensive electric machinery and electronics industry provides a good picture of the typical R&D process in Japan. Many of the major firms in this industry have diversified their products, which range from electronic home entertainment products (videocorders, TVs, etc.) and home appliances (rice cookers, microwave ovens, refrigerators, etc.) to industrial turbines, generators, semiconductors, and both laptop and main frame computers. Accordingly, they are multidivisional and command a large subcontracting group, although they are not systematically organized, as is the automobile industry. Although there are some variations, most firms in the industry have two types of research and development (R&D) facilities: corporate and divisional. Let us refer to the former as the central research laboratory and the latter as the engineering department of the manufacturing division.

Although the central research laboratory has become more important recently, the engineering department of the manufacturing division has traditionally played the central role in the development process within the J-firm. The engineering department is located on the site of the manufacturing base, and engineers assigned there normally have good practical knowledge of the manufacturing process through value engineering and participation in value analysis groups: Value engineering is the effort to reduce the manufacturing cost by design before actual manufacturing starts, and the value analysis group is the group, often including workers from the shopfloor, that meets to discuss how to reduce the manufacturing cost by improving the design after the actual manufacturing process has started. Engineers in mid-career may be transferred to the production department after a new product has been designed to supervise the setting up of production lines for the product.

The principal task of the divisional engineer is to develop and apply engineering know-how of the manufacturing division to related uses. The close linkage between the engineering department and manufacturing may help move new products from the design stage through production to the market quickly and reliably without sacrificing quality. While the production process is being set up, many engineering problems arise and may persist until the normal rate of production is achieved; these problems are often more readily solved with the expertise of the engineer who has developed the product. The engineer, if specialized only in design, may not know how to handle all the engineering problems that may arise in later stages of development. If there is a prospect that members of the design team may be transferred to supervise the setting up of a production line after the completion of the design stage, they become more aware of the importance of interacting with, and obtaining feedback from, *genba* (the spot, meaning the production site) in the developmental stage.

If a potentially promising development project proposed by the engineering department requires more basic scientific knowledge than the department possesses, the project may be commissioned to the central research laboratory. When this happens, one or more young engineers from the engineering department are dispatched to the central research laboratory to participate in the project team. After the team has solved the basic problems, the project is handed back at a relatively early stage to the engineering department of the commissioning manufacturing division for detailed design and testing. In the process, the dispatched engineers are transferred back to the original department. They are responsible not only for completing the project, but also for implementing research results, by converting them into a manufacturing process through value engineering and other methods.

The central research laboratory has been increasing in importance since the mid-1970s, both in terms of budget allocation and of the personnel department's effort to recruit and assign promising engineering and science graduates to it. More basic research projects have become legitimized now that basic research is being emphasized at the firm level as well as the societal level. Yet, in comparison with the A-firm, the functional demarcation between the central research laboratory and the engineering department of the manufacturing division seems to remain relatively fluid, rather than clear-cut because of the centrally administered personnel transfers between them. The main concern at the central research laboratory is to enhance the in-house stock of engineering knowledge with the addition of more basic scientific knowledge, although the end output may not fit into the firm's traditional line of business. (For example, the traditional brewing techniques of food processing companies or the amino acid fermentation techniques of chemical companies may be used in the screening and breeding of microorganisms genetically modified by the method of recombinant DNA. Some research-intensive companies in the declining textile industry are trying hard to enter carbon fiber, optic fiber markets, and others.)

To explore the potential of in-house knowledge, the central research laboratory, as well as the divisional engineering department, systematically scans relevant scientific and engineering information in scientific and technical journals and has its researchers actively participate in scientific conferences, maintain school ties with professors and classmates, attend graduate schools abroad, and so on. The engineering knowledge accumulated in-house provides the basis for research and development, but outside information gives clues to the direction in which research should go and to the feasibility of possible research agendas. If the initial design and development stage of a project initiated at the central research laboratory successfully progresses, the project may be handed to the engineering department, just like commissioned projects, at a relatively early stage in order to speed up the lead time to manufacturing.[33] In the hands-off process, normally one or two researchers from the central research laboratory engaged in the project are transferred to the engineering department for permanent assignment.

Stephen Marglin has pointed out that the distinction the Greeks drew between *techne* and *episteme* has an interesting implication for

---

[33] See D. Eleanor Westney and Kiyonori Sakakibara, "Comparative study of the training, careers, and organization of engineers in the computer industry in Japan and the U.S.," mimeographed, MIT, 1985.

the organization of production. Quoting the French philosopher Jean Pierre Vernant, Marglin writes: "The Greeks looked down their noses at the craftman because craftmanship, the *techne* of production, was derived from tradition and dealt with approximation, to which 'neither exact measure nor precise calculation applies' [Vernant]. Thus *techne* belonged to an entirely different realm from *episteme,* or science, which was based on logical deduction from self-evident first principles."[34] The Western tradition of subordinating *techne* to *episteme,* Marglin argues, has legitimized the control of production according to a priori knowledge, with the result that workers have become subordinate to engineers and management.

In contrast, at the J-firm practical problem solving is delegated to the lowest possible level of the functional hierarchy where knowledge of circumstances exists. This, together with horizontal communications among operating units, provides the characteristic less rigid hierarchical control over the manufacturing operation in the J-firm. It is interesting to note that this parallels the practice of research and development at the J-firm, which has been inclined to expand in-house engineering knowledge – *techne* – with the aid of *episteme,* not vice versa. In other words, there is a striking isomorphism between the way research and development is directed and organized, on one hand, and the way in which operating tasks are performed and coordinated, on the other. Emphasis on *techne* as opposed to *episteme* in the former may be considered isomorphic to emphasis on the efficient use of onsite knowledge (the knowledge of circumstance) in the latter. The isomorphism between nonhierarchical, horizontal communications in the operation coordination, on one hand, and knowledge sharing between the central research laboratory and the engineering department and between the production site and the engineering department, on the other, ought to be quite obvious.

Just as the accumulation of human resources (contextual skills) needed for the efficient working of a decentralized horizontal information structure is promoted by the incentives of the ranking hierarchy, so is the isomorphic organization of R&D.[35] Engineering students at Japanese universities are said to be firmly grounded in general theory and well trained in problem solving in mathematics and statistics, but are offered fewer specialized courses in subfields of engineering. Therefore after they enter the J-firm out of school, they spend consid-

---

[34] "What do bosses do, again? An essay on the moral economy of work," mimeographed, World Institute of Development Economic Research, June 1986, p. 12. The quotation from Vernant is from his *Mythe, et pensée chez les grecs,* Paris, 1965.

erable time becoming familiar with specific design processes during on-the-job training. Some selected researchers and engineers may be sent to graduate school abroad for more specialized training. Researchers and engineers in their 20s are rotated among various projects, but they are not given administrative tasks such as drafting research proposals, which are assigned to more senior researchers. Although they normally progress through a special promotional hierarchy that is distinct from those for blue-collar and white-collar job categories, salaries differ very little at the lower ranks of all these promotional hierarchies. By the time they reach 30, researchers and engineers are promoted at virtually the same speed, and outstanding contributors are not immediately rewarded, except that their reputation is enhanced (and some may be sent to a foreign graduate school). However, contributions at a young age may still have important implications for one's long-term career within the firm.

By building a good reputation, divisional engineers may be promoted in their mid- or late 30s to line managers in the manufacturing division and may be screened for further advancements in the managerial ranking hierarchy within the division. Many of the members of top management in leading Japanese manufacturing firms have been selected from divisional engineers promoted in this way and, depending on the divisional background of the selected president, strategic orientation of the firm may be discerned.

As for a researcher who is first assigned to the central research laboratory, he/she may move to a divisional engineering department after the age of about 35, and may act as a "carrier" of a development project in which he has been actively involved. This means that he will be responsible for moving a new design to a more detailed stage of design and testing. In view of the strategic position of the engineering department with respect to career advancement, this transfer is normally considered a major promotion. Further promotion at about the age of 35–40 leads to entry into the managerial ranking hierarchy. Although entry to the managerial ranking hierarchy may entail better prospects for lifetime income and prestige, some researchers want to stay in the central research laboratory, where they can pursue careers as project leaders and managers of corporate research and development.

As just mentioned, under the ranking hierarchy of the J-firm, researchers and engineers are not rewarded for their performance by salary increases and rapid promotion at an early stage of their career.

[35] For an excellent case study on this subject, see Westney and Sakakibara, "Comparative study." I owe the description of the following paragraph to their study.

As a result, their income differs substantially from that of their American counterparts. Although the costs of formal training at graduate school abroad after job entry are financed by the employing firm, the uniformly lower salary of young researchers and engineers may mean that a substantial portion of the costs of research and engineering training is borne by the researchers and engineers themselves, as Carmichael's model suggests (see Section 3.2). Only after they are promoted to higher ranks (possibly managerial ranks), do they see any significant returns to their investment. Therefore, a midcareer departure often amounts to a financial penalty. Because they are promoted internally according to their track records on various development projects and their managerial leadership in moving from the development stage to manufacturing, they are motivated to contribute to firm-specific development projects rather than to develop individually marketable research capabilities or to contribute to purely scientific discovery that is relatively remote from the possibility of quick commercialization. Thus the ranking hierarchy tends to promote *techne* rather than *episteme*.

Inasmuch as the midcareer departure of the researcher or engineer is discouraged, the firm is less fearful that the results of ongoing research and development projects will be leaked prematurely. This allows it to promote free intrafirm communication between those working on research projects as well as between those in the laboratory, engineering department, and manufacturing division. On the other hand, the interfirm immobility of researchers and engineers not only restricts the stock of knowledge within the firm to the area connected with the company's line of business, but also makes it time-consuming to acquire new knowledge in other disciplines that may be useful. This is problematical, as the multidisciplinary approach toward innovation is becoming more important. Later I discuss a new phenomenon of Japanese industrial organization that is currently evolving to handle this problem.

B.   The chain-link model

From stylized observations in Subsection A, we may derive the following general principle for the direction and organization of R&D at the J-firm:

> [R.1] *The pull by techne:* At the J-firm, the motivation to make the best economic use of accumulated stock of in-house engineering knowledge (what the Greeks called *techne*)

exercises a "pull" upon the R&D agendas rather than new scientific knowledge (what the Greeks called *episteme*) "pushing" the development of new products or processes.

In other words, the production of new manufacturing knowledge (i.e., innovation) within the J-firm does not develop in a hierarchical order, stemming from the discovery of a new scientific principle and proceeding through sequential applications to downstream engineering problems, ending with the production and marketing of new products. Rather, it is stimulated by the search for new economic uses for the accumulated in-house stock of engineering knowledge with the help of, and possibly the development of, scientific knowledge.

However, according to the generally accepted model of innovation, innovation proceeds linearly from scientific research to development, from development to production, and from production to marketing. This model – what a few authors have called "the linear model" – has recently been criticized by Stephen J. Kline and Nathan Rosenberg for distorting the reality of innovation.[36] They have proposed an alternative model that places importance on feedback from downstream phases in the linear model to upstream phases as well as interactions between science and innovative process at every phase of the innovation process, from invention to marketing. By relying on a slightly modified version of their model, I can now elaborate on the above characteristic of the direction of R&D at the J-firm and examine its implication.

Kline and Rosenberg call their alternative model the "chain-link model" (see Figure 6.3). Instead of having one major path of activity – starting with invention and ending with marketing, as in the linear model – this model has five:

(C) *The central chain of innovation*: The path begins with an invention or an analytic design and continues through development (detailed design, test, redesign, etc.), production, and marketing. According to Kline and Rosenberg, two types of designs may initiate innovations: invention and analytic design. "An invention is a new means for

[36] S. J. Kline, "Research, invention, innovation, and production: models and reality," mimeographed, Stanford University, 1985; S. J. Kline and N. Rosenberg, "An overview of innovation," in R. Landau and N. Rosenberg (eds.), *The Positive Sum Strategy*, Academy of Engineering Press, 1986, pp. 275–305. See also M. Aoki and N. Rosenberg, "The Japanese firm as an innovative institution," International Economic Association roundtable conference, Tokyo, 1987.

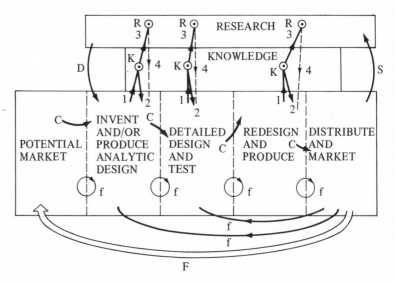

Figure 6.3. Elements of the "chain-link" model. Key: C = central chain of innovation, f = short feedback loops, F = long feedback loop, K-R = links through knowledge to research and return paths [If problem is solved at node K, link 3 to R is not activated. Return from research (link 4) is problematic – therefore dashed line.], D = direct link between research and problems in invention and design, S = support of scientific research. *Source:* Stephen J. Kline and Nathan Rosenberg, "An overview of innovation," in Ralph Landau and Nathan Rosenberg (eds.), *The Positive Sum Strategy,* National Academy Press, 1986, p. 290. An earlier presentation and discussion appears in Stephen J. Klein, "Research, invention, innovation and production: models and reality," mimeographed, 1985.

achieving some function not obvious beforehand to someone skilled in the prior art. It therefore marks a significant departure from past experience. Analytic design . . . consists of various arrangements of existing components or of modifications of designs already within the state of the art to accomplish new tasks or to accomplish old tasks more effectively or at lower cost. It is thus not invention in the usual sense. However, analytic design is currently a more common initiator of the central-chain-of-innovation than invention."[37] This central-chain path is the only flow path

---

[37] Kline and Rosenberg, "An overview of innovation," p. 292.

of information considered in the traditional linear model, but the chain-link model departs from the linear model even in this respect as it takes noninventive analytic design to be the starting point of the process of innovation.

(f,F) *A series of feedback links*: There are two types of feedback mechanisms. One, which I call the *short feedback loop* and denote by lowercase f, connects each downstream phase in the central-chain path to its previous phase (for example, from distribution and marketing to production, from production to design, from design to invention or analytic design). The other, which I call the *long market feedback loop* and denote by uppercase F, feeds perceived market needs and users to various upstream phases of invention, especially to particular possibilities for new invention or analytic design.

(K-R) *The chain-link of science and innovation*: The linkage between science and innovation is not solely a unilateral one from the former to the latter at the beginning of the innovation process, as the linear model envisions. When a problem is confronted in technical innovation, stored knowledge is called upon at all the developmental phases, and developmental activities may in turn contribute to the accumulation of the stock of knowledge all along the central-chain path. This linkage alongside the central chain of innovation is the basis for naming this the chain-link model. It is only when the accumulated knowledge from all known sources fails to solve the problems of a specific development task that the much more costly process of mission-oriented research is invoked to do so.

(D) *From science to invention*: New science *(episteme)* makes possible, albeit very rarely, radical innovations (recent examples include semiconductors, lasers, atomic bombs, and genetic engineering).

(S) *From market to science*: The products of innovation, such as new instruments, machine tools, and technological procedures, are used to support scientific research (current examples include the CAT scanner, experiments in the space laboratory, and the use of digital computers in the laboratory). There is another qualitatively different path from markets to research. Many government agencies and large corporations in developed countries seek areas of potential innovation and support long-range research in

246 Information, incentives, and bargaining

order to solve social and military problems (e.g., research in AIDS and the Star War program) or to suggest advances in the quality or performance of old products (e.g., research in superconductors and new materials).

In terms of these five paths of information and cooperation, the characteristics of the Japanese R&D process may be elaborated as follows:

(C) In the central-chain-of-innovation path, the J-firm has been more active in the downstream phase of the innovative process, such as the redesigning of existing products, rather than new invention, although there have been some notable cases of and an increasing emphasis on analytic design.

(f,F) The J-firm has been making effective use of short feedback loops, for example, from marketing to production (feedback of consumers' complaints, opinions and suggestions for product improvements), from production to redesign (through value engineering and value analysis), from product design to analytic design, and so on. Such short feedback loops are activated by horizontal communications between adjacent functional units, often facilitated by the rotation of personnel between them. The J-firm has been weaker in utilizing the long feedback loops and perceiving the potential of a radically new product (although there have been some exceptions, of course). A major reason for this is probably that such long-loop feedback requires the entrepreneurial leadership of management, but at the J-firm management is usually more concerned with the efficient use of in-house human resources than with exploring market potential and organizing the R&D process according to the perceived market potential.

(K-R) The J-firm is most concerned with using the science-innovation interactive path at the developmental stage (redesign, testing, etc.). As indicated earlier, engineers of the manufacturing division of the J-firm are very active in scanning outside scientific information and using it to develop their own stock of knowledge *(techne)* for new products and process innovation.

(D,S) The Japanese have made rather weak contributions to scientific invention. Currently, there is growing public interest in allocating more resources to scientific research. Also, Japan is developing the capability of allocating various expensive products of recent innovation to supporting pure science. Since the beginning of the 1980s, Japan's contributions in some fields of pure science have been increasing. Whether Japan can make true breakthroughs remains to be seen, however.

Thus the chain-link model by Kline and Rosenberg provides a good framework for characterizing the Japanese R&D process. According to the traditional linear model of innovation, the J-firm (the Japanese in general) may be characterized as uninventive and uninnovative. Such a characterization may, however, miss an important aspect of Japanese competitiveness.[38] According to the chain-link model, the J-firm may be considered innovative in one sense. In terms of this model, the proposition [R.1] may now be rephrased as follows:

[R.1*] The strength of the J-firm lies in the design and production phase of the innovation process, since it makes effective use of short feedback loops (horizontal communications) from marketing to production and production to redesign and effectively exploits stored knowledge, in-house and at an outside source, with design and production phases of the innovation process.

Here I interpret *stored knowledge* in as broad a sense as possible to include engineering knowledge and other forms. I have already noted that the J-firm puts more emphasis on *techne* than on *episteme*. However, the line between the two is not sharply drawn, and one should remember that the spectrum of knowledge covered ranges from pure scientific knowledge that is remote from any particular engineering application at one end to the highly specialized knowledge of a particular individual that may be impossible to analyze or express in formal language but is still useful in a specific context at the other. One may say that this aspect of the J-firm's innovative process lies in its ability to recognize the ambiguity of the distinction between *techne* and *episteme,* rather than ranking them in a hierarchical order as the Greeks did.

In the next section, I discuss how the J-firm tries to develop or modify these characteristics to meet emergent challenges from global markets and high technologies, what kinds of problem it encounters in this respect, and how it tries to solve them.

---

[38] See N. Rosenberg, "Problems in the economist's conceptualization of technological innovation," in *Perspectives on Technology,* Cambridge University Press, 1976, pp. 61–84.

C.   Emerging intercorporate R&D linkage

I have argued that the J-firm emphasizes the later phases of the development process (the central chain of innovation), such as the redesign of existing products and improvement of production processes, rather than radically new invention or analytical design. This orientation is made possible by the effective use of the short-loop feedback mechanism (horizontal communications) between neighboring functional departments. The development of the in-house stock of engineering knowledge with the aid of scientific knowledge at outside sources is another mechanism supporting the said orientation. Thus, in one sense, the direction of R&D at the J-firm may be said to be *constituent based.*

Toward the late 1970s, however, some firms consciously began to move up the development process, or the central-chain-of-innovation, toward an earlier phase, such as the analytical design phase. It is generally agreed that the Japanese have now reached the technological frontier in semiconductors, robotics and programmable machine tools, optic fibers, and new materials such as ceramics and composites, and are just catching up in some fields of biotechnology. The J-firm now recognizes that to simply stay on the frontier it must become more active in the initial phase of the development process.

If the J-firm is to become more involved in analytical design and invention, it may have to make two types of adjustment in its R&D process and organization. One is to amplify even further the characteristic Japanese approach to R&D processes in upward directions alongside the central chain of innovation. Another is to activate long market feedback loops that perceive potential market needs and make them clear objectives of analytic design of radically new products. So far only a few Japanese companies have effectively mobilized such long loops.

As already noted, visible efforts have been taken in the first direction. The position of the central research laboratory has been enhanced and more funds have been allocated to basic research. Also, as Kline and Rosenberg have pointed out, given current computer capabilities and current trends in computer-aided design plus increasing capabilities to model physical processes accurately, analytic design is becoming a more important initiator of the central chain of innovation than invention.[39] The J-firm is accumulating such capabilities at a noticeable rate in hardware and software terms.

---

[39] Kline and Rosenberg, "An overview of innovation," p. 293.

The second type of adjustment may be more difficult for the J-firm to make, however. To activate the long market feedback loop is to conceive of potential new markets and organize the first phase of the development process according to perceived, though not yet actualized market needs. Such a task requires more *entrepreneurial* leadership from management than merely constituent-based management. Once the potential for a new market is conceived, a research team must be organized according to the needs of the set goal. There is no assurance, however, that in-house human resources are adequate for the research task. For example, in order to explore the technological possibility of developing bioelectronic integrated circuits, do integrated electric firms in Japan have the needed stock of trained specialists in biochemistry? Not likely. Can they then recruit the specialist they need from biochemical or pharmaceutical firms by attractive offers? It is difficult to recruit midcareer specialists from established firms other than from Western firms without causing some conflict with the imperative of the firm-specific ranking hierarchy (see the discussion on the reputational effect in Section 4.2). How, then, can the J-firm meet the challenge of organizing an increasingly important multidisciplinary development project that may be vital for its future survival but beyond the capability of its in-house staff?[40] One way to overcome the limits of a J-firm's accumulated stock of knowledge is to acquire, as the A-firm often does, or to merge with, another firm that possesses the needed stock of knowledge. The J-firm has begun to do this abroad, but domestically there has been only scattered evidence of acquisition or merger. This is basically due to the potential difficulty of meshing two independent ranking hierarchies into one without spoiling the incentives of employees brought up in each of them (see Section 5.3).

One new approach to R&D in recent times has been to involve two or more firms having different types of knowledge bases. According to the Agency for Science and Technology, 20.0 percent of the firms it surveyed in 1985 were linked with other firms or institutions (such as

[40] For example, in recent years, medical science has benefited immensely, not only from such related disciplines as biology, genetics, and chemistry, but also from nuclear physics, electronics, and material science and engineering. In pharmaceuticals, there have been explosive advances in the related fields of biochemistry, molecular and cell biology, immunology, neurology, and scientific instrumentation. In other fields, more productive seed varieties, such as the high-yielding rice varieties developed at the International Rice Research Institute in the Philippines, were the work of geneticists, botanists, biochemists, entomologists, and soil agronomists. The trend toward smaller and smaller electronic devices has created a situation in which further technological progress no longer requires knowledge of the kind in which electronics engineers have been trained, but knowledge based in theoretical chemistry (and perhaps even biology).

universities and public research institutions) through the exchange of information, commissioned research, and joint research projects.[41] In 1980 the figure was only 12.8 percent, and by 1990, 25.5 percent of the firms expect to have such a collaborative linkage. The main reason for collaboration, according to a majority of the respondents (67.2 percent), was "to complement and exploit what is lacking and/or heterogeneous to its own technology, human resources, know-how, research facility and equipment, etc." Naturally, then, linkage with other firms in the same industry (discipline) is less common and is in fact declining, except for the much publicized research cooperatives organized by the Ministry of International Trade and Industry (52 cooperatives in 1985) and Ministry of Agriculture (5 cooperatives), or the joint research projects with foreign firms. Instead, joint research projects among firms in different industries (disciplines) are on the rise. The survey identified 89 firms engaged in joint research and development projects of some importance with capitally unrelated firms in different industries.

This intercorporate linkage through the R&D effort differs from relational contracting in the subcontracting group in that the linkage runs across the traditional boundaries of industries. It also differs from the mutual insurance scheme in corporate groups in that the partners may not necessarily be bound by an equity relation and it may be more entrepreneurial by nature. The linkage is fluid, flexible, and ad hoc. Whether the intercorporate linkage that fuses different stocks of knowledge for the purpose of generating new technology is a transitory phenomenon in a movement toward eventual integration, or whether a new type of industrial organization is replacing the old corporate group remains to be seen. On the other hand, one should not preclude the possibility that innovative technological fusion may be achieved by an entrepreneurial effort of diversification by established firms. Thus one may envision that Japanese industrial organization will become more diverse and fluid as the age of technological innovation advances.

Finally, I should touch on the role of small firms in the R&D organization. As noted earlier, some small firms are quite active in R&D in such fields as software, computer peripherals and parts, and operating and precision machinery. Some of them are subsidiaries of large firms specialized in research and development. There are also rela-

---

[41] Agency for Science and Technology, "Survey on international R&D activities involving R&D investment bewteen Japan and advanced countries," *Science and Technology White Paper, 1985.* Also see Economic Planning Agency, *Economic White Paper, 1986.*

tively new startups by ambitious researchers and engineers who have spun off from large established firms. Or they may be older firms that want to fuse traditional, indigenous technologies *(techne)* with emerging high technology to generate new products. Such firms often try to attract midcareer researchers and engineers from large firms by offering generous salaries. They can do so more freely than established large firms, as their ranking hierarchies are less structured and are not bound by the implicit agreement not to raid each other's ranking hierarchies (Section 3.2). By and large, researchers and engineers at small research-intensive firms in Japan originally acquired their expertise at large firms or are pursuing their development efforts in the context of the infrastructure provided by large firms. Therefore, it seems unlikely that those research-intensive small firms will pursue a radically different direction in R&D from that of large firms, although the former may sometimes realize an ingenious fusion of traditional technology with high technology that large firms may not have entertained.[42]

What is conspicuously lacking in Japan in comparison with the Western experience, and what is not likely to emerge in the near future, is the small firm set up by university scientists to commercialize new scientific inventions, specifically in the biomedical, biochemical, and artificial intelligence fields, such as the firms that have emerged in Silicon Valley. As already emphasized, however, there has been increasing emphasis on basic research in Japan, and according to a recently completed study commissioned by the National Science Foundation, fields related to potential biomedical and biochemical products – such as pharmacy, agricultural and food sciences, microscopy, and organic chemistry – are among those in which Japan has made substantial scientific progress in recent times, as measured by the science citation index.[43] Therefore the conspicuous absence of science-based firms organized by scientists may be partly attributable to the regulation that prohibits national university professors from engaging in private business. What may not be ignored, however, is that innovation in biomedical and biochemical products, as well as artificial intelligence, requires a highly multidisciplinary approach, so that the compartmentalization of academic research at Japanese universities may be partly

---

[42] For example, there is a firm that applied the indigenous *nishijin* weaving technique to solve some difficult problems associated with manufacturing optic fibers. A firm that has achieved about 70 percent share in the world market for dicing saws used in the final process of integrated circuit manufacturing was a small firm that manufactured conventional industrial sawing machinery about 15 years ago.

[43] Narin and Olivastro, "First interim report."

responsible for the lack of entrepreneurial leadership needed for setting up science-based firms.[44]

4.   Business organizations and social ranking of top management

In Section 5.2, I cited three functions of management at the J-firm – collective bargaining, personnel administration, and arbitrative strategic decision making – and we have just finished looking at an increasingly important activity of the J-firm: R&D. Corresponding to this activity, there has emerged yet another important function of management: *entrepreneurial* direction.

When R&D activity leans toward the development of *techne*, – that is, toward the improvement of existing (often borrowed) productive technology – managerial leadership in R&D may remain a modest one, and may basically rely on its internal body of engineers for knowledge as the basis of R&D and on the established line of its own business for the commercialization of R&D outputs. However, as the R&D activity becomes more involved with the development of new *techne*, thus necessitating closer interactions between *episteme* and *techne* as well as the feedback of market potential to the conception of new analytic design, managerial leadership may have to become more entrepreneurial. As already noted, in its search for new technological knowledge the J-firm tends to rely on the internal knowledge base, and thus managerial leadership of R&D does not lose its fundamental constituent-based characteristic. Yet if multidisciplinary research is to be car-

---

[44] Japanese universities have been downgraded by foreign observers as less dynamic and less innovative in comparison with the advanced industrial laboratories. I recognize that Japanese national universities lag behind first-rate American research universities both in research and graduate-level education except in a few fields. There are many reasons for this that cannot be elaborated within the perspective of this book. Having admitted this, however, I would like to note the following two points: First, the Japanese have made substantial progress in some scientific fields in recent times, and the role of the university in it is not entirely negligible. Particularly in such advanced fields as material science (e.g., superlattice), computer architecture and pattern recognition, and organic chemistry, a much larger proportion of Japanese contributions to major scientific journals came from the university sector in 1981–84.

Second, under the condition of low mobility of researchers and engineers between firms, laboratories of university professors have been playing nonnegligible roles as information clearinghouses. Professors of major faculties of engineering have decisive roles in allocating new graduates among leading firms. Those students maintain personal ties with professors after graduation, and through these ties scientific and engineering information flows remarkably freely between industry and academia, except for top trade secrets. It seems to me that the widespread view that the low mobility of engineers and researchers in Japan is detrimental to rapid technological diffusion and that Japanese universities do not play a significant role in technological progress is somewhat simplifistic.

ried out effectively, management may have to take a unique leadership role, precisely because of its limited constituent basis, in establishing a new relation with another firm that has the complementary knowledge base needed for the cooperative research effort. In investing a large amount of funds in R&D that has a highly uncertain outcome and in assessing the commercial potential of possible outcomes in new markets, management needs to exercise far-sighted judgment that cannot be based simply on existing constituent interests. Although it is basically constituent based, entrepreneurial management may have to break away from some old constituents and establish new constituent bases (customers, engineering knowledge, employees' operating skills, etc.) if the managing firm is to be competitive.

Thus, in order to exercise efficient and effective leadership, Japanese management needs to assume increasingly complex and intertwined bargaining, administrative, arbitrative, and entrepreneurial roles. How are such multidimensional roles of management to be assessed and monitored? How is the efficient and effective manager rewarded? What incentives drive the manager of the J-firm to perform those multidimensional roles?

The incentive structure of management of the J-firm appears to be somewhat unique. The monetary incentive may of course be an important component of managerial motivation, but managerial positions in the J-firm have rather limited monetary rewards. Rather, the top management of the J-firm is usually selected from the internal managerial organization, so that a top manager's status is more like the pinnacle of internal career advancement, rather than a position that is essentially distinct from the status of salaried employees in the promotional hierarchy. As a result, the gap in salary and bonus incomes between the top-ranking manager and lower-ranking managers, or even between the top-ranking manager and blue-collar employees, is comparatively narrower in the J-firm. A Japanese president's pre-tax salary, including bonus, is generally not more than 6 to 8 times greater than the income of the highest paid blue-collar employee, whereas in the United States, even if bonuses and stock options are excluded, the salary of the chief executive officer is usually 12 to 18 times greater than that of the highest-paid blue-collar worker. Note, too, that bonus and stock options create still greater differentials.[45]

---

[45] Loopholes for salaried income tax are virtually impossible to find in Japan. Instead, the expense account of the company is treated rather generously by the tax authority, and on-the-job consumption by management is phenomenal, to the degree that the amount of expense accounts of Japanese companies exceeds that of dividend payout to stockholders, which is about 10 percent of corporate earnings.

For American executives, a stock option is a particularly attractive reward scheme, as capital gains are more advantageous from the viewpoint of tax obligation. In Japan, stock option plans are not common, especially not in large companies. This is partly because the treasury stock (stocks owned by the issuing company) is not legalized, except in special cases, and therefore the supply of stocks available for the plan would be limited to newly issued stocks. But the discretionary allotment of newly issued stocks at a discount is also strictly regulated by the Ministry of Finance and subject to heavy gift tax.

If the monetary reward cannot be the primary incentive for the manager to excel, what is the basic prize for achieving the pinnacle of internal promotional hierarchy? If it is only the highest rank itself, then once the highest rank is achieved, what motivates the top manager to perform the multidimensional task skillfully?

Before considering these questions, let us recall the mechanism by which management is screened and selected for promotion in the internal hierarchy of the J-firm and then see how this monitoring mechanism is succeeded by the one applied to top management. Needless to say, managers are evaluated and screened according to their own contribution to the company's rent-producing objective. But what is particularly conspicuous in the J-firm is that managers at every level are subject to strict monitoring by both peers and subordinates.[46] If managers of any rank fail to build a good reputation and elicit emotional support form his/her subordinates, his/her effectiveness in the formal organization would be curtailed over time. Therefore, managers of any rank take pains to build up their reputations not only among their superordinates but also their subordinates. A good part of reputation building comes from their own capabilities in specialized management roles and their contributions to the organization, but it also comes from their ability to delegate decision making to the satisfaction of subordinates and to strike a proper balance of interests among them. In other words, one may say that an important consideration in evaluating managers in the promotional hierarchy of the J-firm is their arbitrative performance, as monitored by their subordinates. The successful managers are normally highly skilled in this respect.

Managers admitted to the top rank in the promotional hierarchy carry this cultivated trait to the new position and can enhance their

---

[46] It has been observed that many Japanese *sarariman* (salaried men) spend a considerable amount of after-work time with colleagues from the same work group at bars and the like, discussing their work, but also gossiping, criticizing, backbiting, or praising their superordinates and peers. It is a sort of review session of management in a quasi-social setting.

reputation by performing their mediating job with a new dimension of skill and efficiency. Their mediating role now extends beyond the internal organization and they must be engaged in a mediating function of a higher order, between the qualitatively different constituent bodies of the J-firm, the stockholders of diverse background, the body of quasi-permanent employees, suppliers and dealers in relational contracting, and others. They are expected to deliver a reasonable rate of return to stockholders (see Section 4.3), dealers, and suppliers (see Section 5.3), as well as reasonable earnings and promotabilities to quasi-permanent employees (Section 5.2) and research opportunities for researchers and engineers (Section 6.2). At this stage, not only their arbitrative skill, but also entrepreneurial leadership will count as an increasingly important qualification for the top job, since the economic success of the firm, gauged by the market performance of the product, is the ultimate requisite for satisfying the economic needs of the diverse constituent bodies of the firm.

Despite the increasing importance of entrepreneurial ability, however, the arbitrative skills of chief executives of large firms are subject to scrutiny in a broader context beyond the internal organization of the firm. They are normally elected to executive positions of relevant industrial association ex officio. The industrial associations play a significant role in settling any disputes among member firms, absorbing the common interests of member firms, and relaying them to relevant bureaus of economic ministries with a view to promoting industrial policy making to their interests. As the "voluntary investment adjustment" in the steel industry in the 1960s and the "voluntary auto export restraint" to the United States in the 1980s exemplify, quota allocations, as needed, are normally administered by the industrial association. In intra-industrial negotiation for quota allocation, relevant economic ministries, such as the Ministry of International Trade and Industry, may mediate settlements, but the working out of the final plans depends greatly on the arbitrative ability of the executive committee of an industrial association.

Some business leaders, whose ability to promote industrial interests and to arbitrate the interests of member firms in the industrial association is recognized, may be further selected to an executive position of a broader-based business organization, such as Federation of Business Organizations *(Keidanren),* Committee for Economic Development *(Keizai Doyukai),* Chamber of Commerce and Industry, Nihon Managers Association *(Nikkeiren),* or *Kansai* Business Organization *(Kankeiren),* as well as various governmental councils, such as the Economic Council, which reports to the prime minister with regard to national economic planning. By that time they may have retired from the position of chief executive to the chairman of the board of directors or the honorary position of councilor of their company, and may be able to devote all their energy and time to the so-called *zaikai* (business community) activity. Here they play the important social and political functions of arbitrating possible disputes among industries, raising funds for various social and political contributions, and absorbing the general interests of the business community and promoting them through the political-economic process to be dealt with in Chapter 7.

As we are about to see, the structure of the Japanese government's bureaucracy is isomorphic to the structure of industry with respect to diffuse decision making, horizontal coordination and bargaining, and constituent-based leadership; bureaucrats are also evaluated according to their policy-making leadership and arbitrative skill in their own administrative ranking hierarchy. In fact, Japanese society in general has high regard for the skillful mediator, who is respected for his "impartial" and "unselfish" dedication to public welfare. Social recognition of this order, symbolized by a decoration from the emperor, and promotion to the rank of the First Order are something to which the top management of large companies seems to aspire. Although one cannot deny that personal ambition and aspiration to excel are strong drives in successful businessmen, the point here is that social recognition is an effective institutionalized mechanism in Japan, distinct from the monetary incentive, that drives top managers to perform the unique function of arbitration, as well as to exercise leadership, at the J-firm and beyond.

However, the economic environment that has made the social ranking system workable seems to be changing. Now that multidisciplinary R&D is becoming more important for innovative activity and that competition among firms for global markets is becoming even keener, the practical utility of industrial associations of growing industries may be declining and large member firms may no longer depend on the intervention and protection of the government through the industrial association. The position of the once-powerful iron and steel industry, which used to boast of its strategic position in the economy with the slogan "iron is the state" and the successive elections of its men to the prestigious presidency of *Keidanren*, is declining, while commerce, which used to be ranked after manufacturing, is gaining substantial recognition in the business community. As a result, the *zaikai* is no longer a tightly knit entity. The smokestack industry, for example, pushed for wage restraint as well as a reduction in corporate tax rates in exchange for the introduction of the sales tax in the ill-fated 1987 tax reform bill, but the consumer industries and the commerce sector were critical of the organized attempt of *Nikkeiren* at wage restraint and strongly opposed the introduction of the sales tax.

It is my opinion that the cohesiveness of the *zaikai* is bound to grow weaker and that, as a result, the hierarchical ranking of companies and industries and their top managers recognized by their positions in economic organizations, will be less neatly defined in the years to come. Nonetheless, I believe that ranking by reputation, as symbolized by the imperial decoration, will remain an important part of the reward system for top management.

CHAPTER 7

Bureaupluralism

A treatise on the Japanese economy can never be complete without a discussion on the role of the government, as many in the West believe that a large share of credit for the economic development of Japan goes to the government. The bureaucracy is viewed as a coherent, farsighted planner, which, in close cooperation with the ruling Liberal Democratic Party (LDP), gives a clear growth-oriented boost to the market economy by means of its promotional and protective industrial policy, indicative economic planning, fiscal incentives, stabilizing monetary policy, and so on. An eloquent exposition of this view may be found in the developmental state theory of Chalmer Johnson,[1] but its variations, sophisticated and vulgarized, are not difficult to find among academics, journalists, politicians, and the general public in the West.

There is, however, an equally powerful opposing view, often held by economists, which may be referred to as the market-supremacy theory. It sees the role of the government as being complementary and subordinate to the workings of the market mechanism. According to this view, although the government has certainly provided a favorable environment, the main impetus to growth has come from the private sector – from active business investment demand, high private saving, and industrious and skilled labor operating in a market-oriented environment. Government intervention has merely accelerated trends already put in motion by private market forces. For example, it is argued that economic planning administered by the government may have helped generate a consensus concerning midterm as well as long-term expectations for firms to make macro-consistent investments. However, the government has never been able to promote growth where there was no private initiative.

This market-supremacy view regards the polity as *pluralistic,* and sees intense competition in the private sector among various interest

[1] C. Johnson, *The MITI and the Japanese Miracle: the Growth of Industrial Policy,* Stanford University Press, 1982.

258

groups, among firms, between city dwellers and rural farmers, and so on. Philip Trezes has summarized this view as follows:

The bureaucracy has indeed had an extensive and active part in economic life, but it has been constantly subject to conflicting pressures, ranging from narrow royalty to individual ministries to the demand of competing special interest groups. And politics in Japan has hardly been more orderly a process of bargain and compromise than in any other democracy.[2]

In the developmental state theory, the government is a benevolent guardian of the national interest, whereas in the market supremacy–pluralist theory the overarching notion of national interest is eschewed, each bureaucratic agency is regarded as an agent of the jurisdictional constituent that is its principal, and public policy is regarded as an outcome of bargaining among bureaucratic agencies.

Somewhere between the two is the notion offered by corporatist theorists, which was originally developed for the analysis of political processes in some European countries, particularly Austria and Nordic countries such as Sweden, Norway, and Finland. In those countries powerful industrial unions, business associations, and other peak interest associations penetrate into the state and jointly participate in important economic and other public policy making. In this theory, the state is neither an autonomous agent, as in the developmental theory, nor the simple black-box processor of pluralist demands, as in the pluralist theory. The state mediates, filters, and sometimes shunts aside, demands put forth by peak interest associations according to its own preference. Some authors, represented by John Pempel and Kei-ichi Tsunekawa, believe that this theory applies to the Japanese polity as well, with one important qualification. In Japan, they argue, because of the lack of industrial unionism and the "weakness" of enterprise unionism, "Japanese labor has been dealt with piecemeal at the level of the individual enterprise while economic growth in the 'national interests' has been able to proceed without central regard to the specific demands of collective labor."[3]

Reserving my assessment of the corporatist theory in the context of Japanese polity for a later discussion, I submit here that both the developmental theory and the pluralist theory are one-sided and only partly valid. Indeed, as the developmental theorists argue, the Ministry

---

[2] P. Trezes, "Politics, government, and economic growth in Japan," in Henry Rosovsky and Hugh Pattrick (eds.), *Asia's New Giant,* Brookings Institution, 1976, pp. 753–812.
[3] T. J. Pempel and K. Tsunekawa, "Corporatism without Labor? The Japanese anomaly," in Phillippe Schmitter and Gerhard Lehmbruch (eds.), *Trends toward Corporatist Intermediation,* Sage Publishing Co., 1979, pp. 231–70. The quotation is from p. 264.

of International Trade and Industry (MITI) has an impressive track record of policy making and implementation, which has helped infant industries become internationally competitive industries. But there have also been more than accidental cases in which the "mighty MITI" has miscalculated the potential of private industries. In the 1950s it unsuccessfully tried to coerce some steel companies into curtailing their investment plans and some automobile companies into merger for fear of "excessive competition" in the private sector.[4] The ministry's ambition to strengthen its regulatory power on the eve of liberalization of foreign capital investments by the enactment of the Law of Special Measures for Strengthening the International Competitive Ability of Designated Industries (1964) was buried by the fierce lobbying of industrialists and bankers who opposed stronger state intervention. A recent jurisdictional dispute between the MITI and the Ministry of Post and Telecommunications (MPT) over the communications industry seems to indicate that proposed policies of both ministries were very much shaped by their desires to secure regulatory power in the promising high technology domain rather than to pursue consistent national policy.[5] Thus it seems oversimplistic to picture the MITI, as the developmental theory does, as a consistently farsighted, mighty, and rational entity; and it seems important to examine the information and incentive structures of the bureaucracy if we are to understand the nature of bureaucratic behavior in Japan and its implications for economic efficiency.

The market supremacy-pluralist theory also seems to overlook an important aspect of bureaucratic behavior. It may seem obvious to foreign observers that the price support system for rice administered by the Ministry of Agriculture, Forestry and Fishery (MAFF) and the stringent zoning regulation over farmland delegated to prefectural governments are attuned only to the interests of farmers. But, by leaving partisan actions promoting and sustaining farmer protection to LDP politicians (and often opposition party politicians as well) elected from rural areas, the ministry maintains a posture of neutrality and claims that it is acting in the national interest with regard to food security. Considering the potential vulnerability of the resource-meager Japa-

---

[4] See, for example, Eugene Kaplan, *Japan: The Government–Business Relationship*, U.S. Government Printing Office, 1972.

[5] See, for example, C. Johnson, "MITI, MPT, and telecom wars: how Japan makes policy for high technology," in Berkeley Roundtable on the International Economy (BRIE), *Creating Advantage: American and Japanese Strategies for Adjusting to Change in a New World Economy*, in press.

nese economy to major shocks, this argument has been rather hard to challenge in a politically effective manner until recently and is in fact even supported by consumerist organizations, such as the powerful Japan Housewives Association, and the mass media. It finds its way even into textbooks for fifth graders approved by the Ministry of Education. Ministries and their constituent interest groups do not appear to be in a simple principal–agent relationship and the former sometimes appear to assert their autonomy as the delineator of public interests.

In this chapter, I develop a hybrid view of the Japanese polity. Specifically, I argue that the dualistic role of mediating private interests and promoting public interest is intrinsic to the Japanese bureaucracy. That is, bureaucrats of each agency act partly as agents of its jurisdictional interests out of their own incentives, shaped by the unique tenure structure and the prospect of a postretirement prize (the ranking hierarchy). On the other hand, in order to replenish and accumulate the political resources necessary for effective interest representation, the bureaucratic agency needs to legitimize its cause by asserting and proving that its action is beneficial to the public interest, which lies beyond specific interests.

In Section 1, I clarify this dualistic nature of the bureaucracy by breaking open the black box of the bureaucratic structure and process, as we did for the J-firm in Chapters 2–5. The analysis of the intrabureaucratic structure and process will clarify some important characteristics of the bureaucracy that are identical – isomorphic – to those of the J-firm, such as decentralized responses to emerging problems at the place where the most relevant on-site knowledge is located, coordination through bargaining rather than hierarchical direction, the ranking hierarchy as an incentive scheme, and constituent-based leadership. But there is one subtle, yet significant difference between the two. That is, the centralization of personnel administration stops at the individual ministerial level in the bureaucracy. In other words, parallel ranking hierarchies coexist for individual ministries. The lack of the "duality principle" (Chapter 3) – the principle that the decentralization of the information structure is associated with and complemented by the centralization of incentive ranking hierarchy for its efficient operation – may prevent the bureaucracy from being innovative in its policies under some circumstances.

In Section 2, I show that political developments since the 1960s have been marked by an increasingly inclusive pluralistic tendency mediated by the LDP-bureaucratic alliance, which I call *bureauplur-*

alism.[6] A parallel trend occurred in the J-firm in the private sector, which evolved as a coalition of the body of stockholders and the body of quasi-permanent employees. In the sense that the J-firm is an important constituent under bureaupluralism, I disagree with the theory of "corporatism without labor" as a characterization of the Japanese political economy. In my judgment, the interests of labor are duly reflected in the Japanese political economy. As I argued in the first part of this book, labor is a viable member of the J-firm since its interests are represented by the enterprise union. Management of the J-firm arbitrates between the interests of labor and those of various types of investors such as banks, other corporate partners, and individual stockholders. The situation is analogous to one in which the state acts as a machinery for mediating business and labor interests represented by peak private associations in the corporate state. Elsewhere I have characterized the governance structure of the Japanese firm as an instance of *managerial corporatism.*[7] It is a micro version of corporatism.

In Japan, arbitration between business and labor interests takes place at the firm level, before they are further mediated at the industrial and national levels and presented to the state at the macro level. This process is just the reverse of what goes on in the corporatist process in Nordic countries and Austria, where mediation between labor and business interests is initiated at the macro state level and then disaggregated and modified down through the industrial and firm levels. The latter process is known as "wage drift" when referring specifically to the wage-determination process. In the case of Japan, wage determination (and other strategic business decisions such as investment) is decentralized at the firm level and only those matters encompassing interests across individual firms are amalgamated and presented at the macro level. If the term *corporatism* can be applied to Japan at all, one may say that the corporatist process in Japan works from the "bottom up," whereas in European countries it works from the "top down."

[6] This same development is coined by other authors as "bureaucratic-led, mass-inclusionary pluralism" (T. Inoguchi), "channeled pluralism" (S. Sato and T. Matsuzaki), "patterned pluralism" (M. Muramatsu and E. S. Krauss), etc. See Takashi Inoguchi, *Gendai Nihon Seiji Keizai no Kozu: Seifu to Shijyo* (The framework of contemporary Japanese political economy: government and markets), Toyo Keizai Shinpo-sha, 1983. Seizaburo Sato and T. Matsuzaki, *Jiminto Seiken* (LDP governmental power), Chuo Koron-sha, 1985. Michio Muramatsu and Ellis S. Krauss, "The conservative policy line and the development of patterned pluralism," in Y. Yasuba and K. Yamamura (eds.), *The Political Economy of Japan,* vol. 1, *The Domestic Transformation,* Stanford University Press, 1987, pp. 516–54.

[7] M. Aoki, *The Cooperative Game Theory of the Firm,* Oxford University Press, 1984, chap. 11.

The concept of the J-firm as a coalition of labor and investors arbitrated by management appears to match Muramatsu et al.'s concept of "labor–business coalition at big business" *(daikigyo roshi rengotai)*[8] as a dominating actor in pluralist politics in Japan. Because of its increasing economic strength, this coalition has recently begun to move away from state intervention and to rely more upon markets for the arbitration of interests. On the other hand, as Muramatsu et al. pointed out, interest groups receiving benefits such as farmers, traditional small businesses, pension recipients, and so on, tend to depend more on the state and are particularly threatened by and vulnerable to situations created by the increasing international pressure for a more open economy. In Section 3, I discuss a current dilemma and the possible transformation of the Japanese polity in reaction to this situation.

1. Two faces of the bureaucracy

The Japanese bureaucracy is neither a monolithic, rational social engineer nor a passive black-box processor of pluralist interests. It is a multitude of entities (ministries, agencies, and their bureaus, divisions, etc.), each of which has its own jurisdiction,[9] acquires its political resources through interactions with other bureaucratic and private entities, and is staffed with career civil servants whose motivations are conditioned by a unique structure of rewards and tenure. Each bureaucratic entity seems to have two faces in its operation: one is that of a delineator of public interests in its jurisdiction, and the other is that of an agent representing the interests of its constituents vis-á-vis the other interests in the bureaucratic coordinating processes: budgetary, administrative, and planning.[10]

The first face of the bureaucrat as a delineator of public interests is the focal point of the developmental state theory. The bureaucrats formulate and implement policy in their jurisdictions by drafting and enforcing laws, providing informal administrative guidance, allocating fiscal resources, and so on. As time evolves, a policy once established in the national interest may eventually become obsolete. Once insti-

---

[8] M. Muramatsu, Mitsutoshi Ito, and Yutaka Tsujinaka, *Sengo Nihon no Atsuryoklu Dantai* (Pressure groups in post-war Japan), Toyo Keizai Shinpo-sha, 1987.

[9] Strictly speaking, there are bureaucratic entities that do not have any jurisdiction in the private sector and whose functions consist of intrabureaucratic coordination. I discuss this division of functions within the bureaucracy later.

[10] For example, the computer industry is a jurisdictional constituent of the Machinery and Information Industries Bureau of the Ministry of International Trade and Industry (MITI), and the banking industry is a jurisdictional constituent of the Banking Bureau of the Ministry of Finance (MOF).

tuted, however, a law, and even informal administrative guidance, has its own institutional inertia. Unless innovative policy is introduced at a point when institutionalized intervention becomes obsolete, it may become adversarial to jurisdictional interests as well as detrimental to public welfare.[11]

The first face of the bureaucracy is closely intertwined with the second representative face. In acting as a representative, each bureaucratic entity provides its constituents with access to policy making. In contrast to high-level political appointees in the American executive branch, Japanese career bureaucrats are insulated to a great extent from changes in the cabinet and from electoral results. How, then, are they able to respond to the needs of their constituents? What incentives drive them to act as quasi agents of their constituents? How is the representation face related to the first one?

A.   Stylized facts

Each ministry is structured as a ranking hierarchy, just as the J-firm is. Most elite bureaucrats start their careers by passing the upper-class A *(ko-shu)* civil service examination while they are enrolled in one of the country's prestigious universities. Upon graduation they are recruited by particular ministries and placed at a lower rank of the administrative job cluster. There is a tacit pecking order among ministries regarding which ministry will get the best and brightest. The Ministry of Finance (MOF) normally gets the first pick, followed by the Ministry of Home Affairs and the Ministry of International Trade and Industry (MITI). Those elite bureaucrats referred to as the "qualified" persons on the "career" *gumi* (team) – who number a little more than 10,000 – normally remain in one ministry until they retire from the bureaucracy, except for an occasional temporary transfer *(shukko)* to related ministries in midcareer. However, throughout their bureaucratic careers they are regularly rotated among various sections and bureaus within a ministry. This practice doubtlessly prevents career bureaucrats from being confined to narrow jurisdictional interests and gives them a better and broader understanding of public interests.

Every type of job – administrative, legal, technical, and so on – has its own hierarchy, composed of seven ranks. Promotion within each hierarchy from the seventh rank to the first rank is based on seniority

[11] Such a cyclic aspect of government intervention has been studied by T. Yakushiji, "The government in a spiral dilemma: dynamic policy intervention vis-à-vis auto firms, c. 1900–1960," in M. Aoki (ed.), *The Economic Analysis of the Japanese Firm,* North-Holland, 1984, pp. 265–310.

and merit. Parallel to the system of ranking hierarchies there is a functional hierarchy of administrative positions (i.e., administrative hierarchy), just as in private companies. As the bureaucrat moves to a higher rank in the ranking hierarchy, he/she also moves from a lower to a higher administrative position. The bureaucrats who pass the class A examination progress through the administrative hierarchy quite rapidly during the first years of their career, in comparison with employees of the J-firm. Many become heads of sections *(kakaricho)* at the average age of 29.1 (most of them are in the fifth rank). Progression beyond that rank, however, becomes increasingly competitive. The average age of a director of a division *(kacho)* is 42.1 (most of them have achieved either the second or the first rank by the time of such appointments). Beyond the first rank, some may be selected to "specific job rank" *(shiteishoku)* and may be named director-in-general of a bureau *(kyokucho)* or given another comparable job. The average age of a director-in-general is 50.2[12] At the pinnacle of bureaucratic jobs is the permanent vice-ministership *(jimujikan)* of a ministry, which is attained at the average age of 55. The term of office of a permanent vice-minister is normally only one to two years.

Since the administrative hierarchy is pyramidal, a bureaucrat is pressured to depart from a bureaucratic career after he/she becomes the section director, if he/she does not continue to rise in the administrative hierarchy. By the time that a member of the bureaucrat's entering class becomes a permanent vice-minister, all except the most successful would have retired. Those bureaucrats who quit the bureaucracy after attaining positions higher than that of section director in the administrative hierarchy "descend from the heaven" *(amakudari)* of the elite bureaucracy and become available as human resources for national and local politics, business management in private and public corporations, and other consulting activities.[13] The bureaucrats in this group are assigned to available *amakudari* and other less prestigious positions by the ministerial secretary bureau of the ministry, particu-

---

[12] M. Muramatsu, *Sengo Nihon no Kanryosei* (The bureaucracy in postwar Japan), Toyo Keizai Shinpo-sha, 1981, chap. 2.

[13] The history of the *amakudari* phenomenon is not old. It began in earnest in the 1950s, possibly caused by the need and pressure not to block the opportunities for career advancement for younger bureaucrats. Since the so-called career team in the bureaucracy more than doubled in size between the Manchurian Incident in 1931 and the end of World War II, these pressures became very intense during the 1950s. This coincided with the beginning of the era of high growth, and relatively high-paid positions in the private sector and in expanding public corporations were available to retiring bureaucrats. Demand and supply happily matched. See C. Johnson, "The reemployment of retired government bureaucrats in Japanese big business," *Asian Survey*, November 1974, pp. 953–65.

larly the personnel section or secretarial division. Each ministry operates on the principle of a centralized personnel administration, just as the private companies do. Obviously, the longer a bureaucrat survives in the ranking hierarchy of the ministry, the better are his/her prospects for post-bureaucrat *amakudari* positions. Thus *amakudari* positions are provided as the final prize in the competition among bureaucrats in the ranking hierarchy.

Amakudari positions are diverse and there is a strong "push" from the ministry to expand *amakudari* and other job opportunities for retiring bureaucrats in its jurisdiction and possibly to find such positions in new areas as well. Some of the most successful retired bureaucrats obtain executive positions in various public corporations, foundations, and so on, that are under the supervision of their ministries. Even less successful ones can obtain administrative positions in diverse organizations supervised directly by the ministry or financed through public corporations in the ministerial jurisdiction. For example, it is said that the MOF controls 19,000 such positions. Some top-ranking retiring bureaucrats even become high-ranking managers, such as directors or presidents of private companies, industrial associations, foundations, research institutes, and the like. Some retiring bureaucrats move into politics and run for the Diet or for governor. Recently there has also been a growing tendency among relatively young ambitious bureaucrats to retire in midcareer and to run for political office before climbing up to the top of the bureaucratic administrative hierarchy.

By expanding and maintaining its own network of *amakudari* (and other less prestigious) positions in the interface between the polity and the economy as well as in the private sector, the ministry can reward its bureaucrats for their devotion to the ministry and at the same time extend its visible and invisible influence throughout its jurisdiction. But its influence is not unidirectional. There is "pull" from the jurisdiction as well. Although the midcareer recruitment of a retiring bureaucrat to a managerial position in a private organization may hamper the potential progress of a firm's own employees in the managerial hierarchy, it may also benefit the organization despite that cost. By putting to use the expertise and the personal communication network (*jinmyaku* or human context) that was cultivated during their tenure, *amakudari* bureaucrats can gain access to important policy information, which may very well be relevant to the interests of the constituency to which they have been recruited. They may even be able to promote the interests of the constituency that recruited them.

Thus the *amakudari* practice seems to provide a subtle, yet important mechanism for giving attention to constituent interests in the bureaucratic process. Kent Caldor, who has done interesting work on this subject, has provided evidence that the relatively "disadvantaged" segment of the private sector is quite active in the recruitment of *amakudari* bureaucrats. For example, companies located in the Kansai area rather than in metropolitan Tokyo, or companies that are either unaffiliated with major corporate groups, foreign-owned, or less dominated by Tokyo University graduates on the boards of directors, have relatively larger numbers of *amakudari* bureaucrats on their boards. Caldor thus characterizes the practice of *amakudari* as an "equalizing process."[14]

Another important mechanism that gives the private sector access to the policy-making process is the increasingly active and influential LDP *"zoku"* ("tribes"). The *zoku* of a ministry is an informal group of influential LDP Diet members clustered around the ministerial jurisdictions. A Diet member is recognized as a *zoku* member of a particular ministry by acquiring influential power related to the affairs of that ministry. This influence can arise after one has served successively as parliamentary vice-minister *(Gyosei Jikan)*, chairman of a subsection of the Policy Research Council *(Seichokai)* of the LDP corresponding to the appropriate ministerial jurisdiction, and in other important roles such as minister. From their experiences, *zoku* members gain considerable expertise and access to information regarding the activities and affairs of the relevant ministry. They sometimes exercise tacit or overt influence over the appointments of bureaucrats retiring to important positions in public corporations and other institutions.

Until the late 1960s, bureaucrats were considered to be much better informed and to have more expertise than LDP politicians. Although bureaucrats are rotated among various sections and bureaus in order to prevent them from becoming too closely tied to specific interests, *zoku* politicians are continuously involved in certain strategic issues in related ministries. Given such a steady involvement, *zoku* politicians have come close to, and in some cases have even surpassed, the bureaucrats in their policy-making capabilities.[15] The commitment of the *zoku* is, needless to say, indispensable for the ministry in ensuring the passage of desired legislation in the Diet. Thus, the bureaucrat must treat the *zoku* carefully and cordially.

[14] See K. Caldor, "Elites in an equalizing role: ex-bureaucrats as coordinators and intermediaries in the Japanese government-business relationship," mimeographed, 1985.
[15] See Nihon Keizai Shinbun-sha, *Jiminto Seichokai* (The Policy Research Council of LDP), 1983 for a detailed account of *zoku*.

The *zoku,* together with *amakudari* bureaucrats, have become important vehicles in recognizing and channeling emerging constituent demands to the relevant ministries. Notwithstanding the growing receptiveness of bureaucratic entities to constituent interests, however, the relationship between the bureaucracy and its constituents is not a simple principal–agent relation, as bureaucratic congressional relations are viewed in the United States.[16] Strictly speaking, in principal–agent relations, an agent must follow the principal's instructions, and the authority of an agent can be terminated by the principal at any time. But Japanese ministries are authorized to draft and propose laws on their own initiative, as they deem necessary, to the Diet through the Prime Minister. Furthermore, Japanese ministries are perpetual bodies established by statute and staffed with career bureaucrats whose terms of employment do not normally terminate with either a change in the cabinet or an electoral result. Thus Japanese ministries have relatively more autonomy than a typical agent in the ordinary principal–agent relation. Through incentives provided by the ranking hierarchy, bureaucrats are only remotely related to the interest of specific jurisdictional constituents. What, then, is the objective of a ministry? The following simple conceptual framework may shed some light on these questions.

B.   Why two faces?

Although career-long competition among individual bureaucrats within the ranking hierarchy is keen, a primary concern for them all is to maintain and increase the political influence of their ministry. Their ambitions, idealistic and personal, cannot be fulfilled unless the ministry is politically viable. In addition, the more politically powerful the ministry and the more instrumental the role of the bureaucrat in it, the better are his/her chances for a postretirement position in the private sector and in the influential network of communications connecting the bureaucracy and the private sector. However, to remain politically viable a ministry must bring in and accumulate the political resources needed for policy making and implementation, just as the economic viability of the J-firm depends on the efficient accumulation of firm-specific resources, both financial and human.

---

[16] See, for instance, B. R. Weingast, "A principal–agent perspective on congressional-bureaucratic relations," unpublished; and T. M. Moe, "The new economics of organization," *American Journal of Political Science,* 28, 1984, pp. 739–77.

The resources that a ministry can mobilize to implement its policy include

1. Budgetary funds allocated to the ministry and available for public expenditures in the interests of its jurisdictional consitutents; fiscal financial funds made available as loans to, or investments in, the interests of its jurisdictional constituents through public financial corporations under its control[17]

2. Its incumbent officials recruited through the highly competitive civil servant examination and trained on the job; the network of its *amakudari* bureaucrats through which ministerial policy may be effectively propagated to the private sector and its constituent interests may be effectively absorbed

3. The authority to propose laws to the Diet through the Prime Minister, and good working relations with *zoku* politicians who can be relied upon to enhance the possibility of enaction in the Diet

4. The legitimized capacity to carry out regulatory power either according to statutes, or by moral suasion referred to as administrative guidance *(gyosei shido).*

The reproducibility of these resources appears to depend mainly on two factors: the "utility" of ministerial policy to its jurisdictional constituents and the reputation of the ministry among the general public as a delineator of national interests. These two factors are inseparable determinants of the political stock of a ministry.

The utility of ministerial policy to its jurisdictional constituents is basically determined by the effectiveness of its representation of the constituents' interests in the bureaucratic process. The MITI is interested in the efficient development of internationally competitive industries; the MOF is interested in securing the profitable operation of banks, securities companies, and insurance companies; the MAFF is interested in keeping the farmer's standard of living at par with that of urban working households, and so on. However, it is not enough to merely represent interests in order to accumulate political stock. Unless a ministry has a good reputation among the general public as a delineator of national interest, it will have difficulty legitimizing and sustaining its command of political resources. The MITI, for example, has to legitimize its policy of protecting infant industry from the view-

---

[17] A large proportion of funds allocated to public finance corporations originate in postal savings, and its allocation is determined by the annual Public Investment and Financing Plan drafted by the MOF and legislated by the Diet.

point of national interest in maintaining industrial competitiveness and national prosperity; the MOF has to legitimize its regulatory power over the financial industry in terms of financial stability, accountability, and responsibility; and the MAFF has to warn against excessive dependence on foreign food supplies from the viewpoint of national security in order to legitimize the sustained protection of farmers through the rice price support program.

As can be easily imagined, however, the utility of a ministry to its constituents and reputation among the general public may not necessarily be harmonious. Even among the constituents of a ministry, there may be partly harmonious, partly conflicting interests. For instance, the exercise of certain regulatory power may be of protective value to incumbents in a particular market, but may deter new outsiders from entering. Depending upon the life-cycle stage of the targeted industry, the same regulatory power may increase or decrease the political stock of a ministry, as what Yakushiji calls the "dilemma of policy intervention" illustrates:[18] Once the policy of fostering the stable structure of a particular industry becomes successful, the industry inevitably starts to drift away from intervention. At this stage, the bureaucracy tends to become coercive and, unless a new relation is created, the intervention is no longer effective. If a ministry (or a bureau or a section) commits itself to a specific interest and in so doing sacrifices others, the legitimacy of the budgetary demands required to sustain that policy may be questioned. If a ministry fails to enhance public welfare because its policy is not innovative, its overall reputation will slide and it will have more difficulty recruiting competent and promising college graduates.

How can a policy be legitimized as being in the public or national interest? How is the balance between jurisdictional interests and the national interest struck within the bureaucracy? The answer is that each ministry has to build its political resources through competitive and cooperative interaction with other ministries. The bureaucratic process by which this takes place is discussed next.

2.   The bureaucratic process

A.   Stylized facts

In Section 1, I spoke as though each bureaucratic entity (ministries, bureaus, divisions, and sections) controls and represents its own juris-

---

[18] Yakushiji, "The government in a spiral dilemma."

dictional constituency. Strictly speaking, however, there are two types of bureaucratic entity, only one of which has a clearly delineated jurisdiction. Bureaus (and sections), which are often referred to as *genkyoku* (the "original bureaus"), are of this type. The Banking Bureau of the MOF, the Automobile Industry Division in the Machinery and Information Industry Bureau of the MITI, the Senior Citizen Welfare Section of the Ministry of Welfare and Health, the Postal Savings Bureau of the MPT, the Economic Bureau of the MAFF, and the Local Bond Division of the Ministry of Home Affairs are obvious examples. The other type consists of bureaus whose primary function is to coordinate, budget, plan, and monitor ministry affairs and to manage personnel. Let us call them coordinating offices. The Budget Bureau of the MOF, the Coordination Bureau of the Economic Planning Agency (EPA), the Administrative Inspection Bureau of the Management and Coordination Agency, and the Minister's Office of each ministry are examples.

Genkyoku bureaus maintain close contact with the various organizations that represent their jurisdictional constituents. With these organizations as intermediaries, each *genkyoku* bureau looks after its constituents' interests and implements the regulations covering its jurisdiction. Following Muramatsu et al., it is convenient for the purpose of later discussion to distinguish two types of organization in this relationship: sector groups and benefit-recipient groups.[19] The first type comprises those organizations that represent market-based economic and professional interests. Examples corresponding to the above *genkyoku* include, the National Federation of Banking Associations and the Automobile Industrial Association. The second type comprises those organizations that are "existent relying on, or at least symbiotic with government activities."[20] An example is the National Association of Senior Citizen Clubs. The Specific Postmasters Association and the National Center of Agricultural Cooperatives may be thought of as sector groups by definition, but they have come to behave like benefit-recipient groups, because the incomes of their members are now determined by government activities to a substantial extent.

One of the most important bureaucratic processes that directly deals with the distribution of political resources, the budgetary process, may be stylized as follows: Each *genkyoku* is responsible for drafting annual budgetary demands *(gaisan yokyu)* related to its jurisdictional inter-

---

[19] Muramatsu, et al. *Sengo Nihon.* They consider the third type of pressure groups, cause-promotional groups, such as environmental groups. But I exclude this type from consideration as they are peripheral to the discussion here.
[20] Ibid., p. 3.

ests. In this process, "requests" *(chinjyo)* for the allocation of budgetary funds and preferential tax treatments are made by constituent members to the working officials concerned. These requests are often backed up by politicians. The first draft of budgetary demands at the bureau level is coordinated and adjusted at the Minister's Office of each ministry. At this point, the *zoku* politicians and the minister exercise their political influence. By representing the interests of constituents successfully, politicians can obviously increase their own political stock, that is, vote-getting power. On the other hand, the bureaucrats of each ministry cannot ignore the pressures of *zoku* politicians at this stage, because their political influence on behalf of the ministry is valuable at a later stage of the interministerial budgetary process. This reciprocal dependency of the ministry and its *zoku* politicians has recently been strengthened.

Primary budget demands at the ministerial level are then submitted to, and scrutinized by, the Budget Bureau of the MOF, and at this stage hard bargaining between MOF bureaucrats and other ministries takes place. Toward the end of each calendar year the Budget Bureau normally acts as a referee of the budget distribution game and, in consultation with and after obtaining approval from LDP leaders, drafts a final budgetary plan. This plan is still subject to the "second budget revival demand" by each ministry, but at this stage only powerful *zoku* politicians are able to exercise their influence and effect rather marginal changes. The final plan must still be discussed and approved by the Diet. At this stage, the budget for additional minor expenditures may be appropriated after negotiation between the ruling LDP and opposition parties representing the interests of small shopkeepers, government employees' unions, and others.

This brief description of the budgetary process reveals one fundamental feature of the administrative process – *quasi-social bargaining.* Each *genkyoku* ministry represents constituent interests and is engaged in quasi-social bargaining. This bargaining is not directly multilateral, however, and it is subject to the multilayered arbitration of coordinating offices (first by the Minister's Office of each ministry and then the Budget Bureau). The arbitration activity of coordinating offices is directed less by a well-defined policy objective than by ad hoc rules of thumb such as "incrementalism" (Y. Noguchi) or "minus x percent ceiling on budgetary demands." The essential feature of these rules may be stated as follows: The budget allocations to (or the budget demands by) ministries increase (or decrease) equiproportionally every year.[21] Therefore, once a budgetary allocation pattern is set, the

---

[21] See Y. Noguchi, "Decision making rule in the Japanese budgetary process," *Japanese Economic Studies,* 7, 1979.

discretionary power of the coordinating office becomes rather limited from then on.

The limited power of the coordinating office is more apparent in the case of economic planning. Economic planning is officially discussed and formulated by the Economic Council upon the request of the prime minister and is then reported to the cabinet for its official sanction.[22] The council is dominated by representatives of business leaders, but also includes academics, representatives of the mass media, consumers, labor unions, and *amakudari* bureaucrats in various capacities. The prime minister sets the general tone of the plan at the outset in his official letter of request for planning. Economic planning then becomes a sort of interest arbitration process within that framework. The Planning Bureau of the EPA functions as the secretariat for the council. It prepares the agenda and statistics and draws up a draft of the plan, which is then subjected to minor revisions at the final meeting of the council. During the deliberation of the plan at the Economic Council, bureaucrats of other ministries are dispatched to this bureau or sit as observers at council meetings to make sure that the plan will not be drafted counter to their ministries' interests. Economic planning does not produce a "plan" as such, but rather creates a consensus on, or an atmosphere for, very general economic targets by giving pluralistic interests their due share and a place in the future perspectives.

The economic plan does not have binding power over any party. However, it may legitimize, in a very broad sense, the budgetary demands of ministries consistent with the plan in the first few years of its "implementation." Therefore the MOF carefully intervenes in the planning process, behind council meetings and through its *amakudari* bureaucrats in the council, to ensure that no commitment will be made to limit its discretionary power in the budgetary process. Thus, the coordinating role of the EPA in the actual allocation of fiscal and other political resources is at best modest, although its role of interest mediating in setting national economic targets and promoting macroeconomic stabilization through the consensual formation of expectation should not be overlooked.[23]

Finally, note that, parallel to this official coordination among ministries, "shadow bargaining" takes place among corresponding *zoku*. *Zoku* politicians are normally influential members of the LDP, and it sometimes happens that an important jurisdictional dispute between ministries is settled among them, and/or the budgetary arbitration by

---

[22] See R. Komiya, "Planning in Japan" in M. Bornstein (ed.), *Economic Planning: West and East,* Balinger, 1975, for a detailed description of economic planning process.

[23] For the stabilizing effect of economic planning, see M. Aoki, "Aspects of the Japanese firm," in Aoki (ed.) *The Economic Analysis of the Japanese Firm.*

the MOF is revised. As an example of the latter, note that the administrative decision regarding the level of the support price of rice has often been undermined by the partisan pressure of the so-called *komegiin* (parliamentary member for rice). In view of the growing power of LDP, some ministries are making a greater effort to get their bureaucrats, both retired and midcareer, elected to the Diet.

B.   Quasi-pluralistic bargaining nested within the bureaucracy

This subsection considers a simple model of interministerial bargaining. The model is intended to provide a conceptual framework for the analysis of the nature of quasi-pluralistic bargaining nested within the bureaucracy, but not to be a realistic descriptive model of the Japanese bureaucratic process. Let us imagine that there are only two *genkyoku* ministries, I and A (say, the MITI and the MAFF), and one coordinating office (say, the Budgetary Bureau of the MOF). Imagine a representative constituent of each Ministry (say, the J-firm or the agricultural cooperative) and let its cardinal utility indicator, defined on a reasonable domain of the set of feasible policy instruments of both ministries, be u^I or u^A.[24] We can complicate the model by introducing more than two *genkyoku* ministries and more than one constituent for each ministry, but the simple model suffices for a while. Issues unique to n-person bargaining ($n > 2$) will be referred to later, when the need arises. I also ignore the problem of preference aggregation of different members within a ministerial constituent. I have treated such a problem for the case of the J-firm in Chapter 5.[25]

Let $\hat{u}^I$ and $\hat{u}^A$ be the level of utility of I and A in the status quo.[26] Suppose that by policy changes in the provision of public goods, promotional industrial policy, protective farm policy, and so on, the utility opportunities for I and A may be expanded from the status quo point as drawn in Figure 7.1. Each point of the utility opportunity set enclosed by the frontier, lying to the northeast of the status quo, represents the distribution of social surplus net of tax burden between I and A, for which a particular mix of political resource allocation between ministries is associated. It is conceivable, however, that an

---

[24] The set of policy instruments corresponds to the set of bargainable subjects in intra-firm bargaining.

[25] The utility indicator of each ministerial constitutent may be considered the Nash utility product of its members.

[26] At the more fundamental theoretical level, one may conceive of the $\hat{u}^I$ and $\hat{u}^A$ as referring to the utility levels achievable at the Hobbs-Roussauvian "original state" where there is no state action.

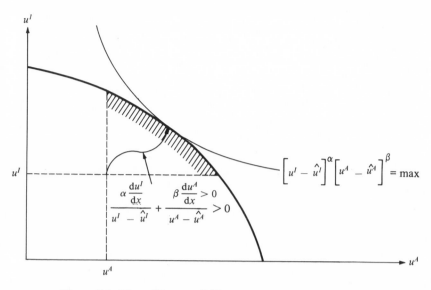

Figure 7.1. The utility possibility set.

allocation of political resources under the jurisdiction of I (alternatively A) has an external effect on the utility level of A (resp. I). For example, the industrial policy for promoting the machinery industry by ministry I may have beneficial effects on the productivity of agriculture by an improvement in rice-planting machinery, while the rice price support policy by ministry A may secure the domestic rice supply, albeit at a comparatively higher price, to members of the J-firm.

Suppose that the coordinating office, as a mediator of the bargaining game between the *genkyoku* ministries, tries to allocate political resources in order to maximize the weighted Nash utility product:

$$[u^I - \hat{u}^I]^\alpha [u^A - \hat{u}^A]^\beta,$$

where α and β denote the weights attached to I and A by the coordinating office such that $\alpha + \beta = 1$. The weights may reflect the relative size of the population, or the relative voting power of each constituent, or some a priori political belief. For example, the farmer's interest may be given more weight by the coordinating office because the farmer is overrepresented in the Diet or because the coordinating office is committed to the traditional agrarian philosophy. If the weighting is "neutral" in the sense that weights reflect only the relative population sizes of the corresponding constituencies, then the coordinating outcome may be said to be *democratic* in the Nash sense (see Chapter 5). At that outcome, the political resource is allocated in such a way that its last marginal unit yields the same percentage utility gain from the status quo for each member of the population. If the weighting is determined by the coordinating office on an a priori value basis, one may characterize the resulting Nash solution (i.e., the maximand of the weighted Nash product) as "imposed."

Suppose, alternatively, that ministries I and A are engaged in direct competitive (strategic) bargaining, which may involve some risk of disagreement (stalemate at status quo). Imagine that under this risky situation, both ministries are trying to maximize their expected utilities:

$$\frac{[u^I - \hat{u}^I]^{1-a}}{1 - a} \quad \text{and} \quad \frac{[u^A - \hat{u}^A]^{1-b}}{1 - b},$$

where a and b (>0) represent the degree of risk aversion of the corresponding ministries toward the risk of breakdown on interministerial bargaining (the degree of risk aversion is measured by half of the risk premium per unit variance of u^I or u^A). Both ministries may want to avert the risk because the failure to reach an agreement may spoil their reputation by defaulting on the expected delivery of utility to their constituents, as well as hamper the public welfare (in the sense of failing to realize a potentially possible bargain outcome that is Pareto-superior to the status quo). The more risk-averse the ministry is (the greater the value of a or b), the less bold it is throughout the competitive bargaining.

When the bargain process is at equilibrium in Zeuthen's sense (see Section 5.1), one may say it is power-equilibrating. When it is at perfect equilibrium in the sense of Rubinstein (Section 5.1), one may say it is politically stable (with regard to strategic disturbance). As stated in Section 5.1, under certain conditions both equilibrium bargaining outcomes in the sense of Zeuthen and Rubinstein maximize the Nash product of the ministerial utility functions given above. Therefore if

$$\frac{1 - a}{1 - b} = \frac{\alpha}{\beta},$$

the Nash solution dictated by the coordinating office and the competitive bargaining equilibria in the Zeuthen and Rubinstein senses are identical.

The above assumption concerning the proportional equality of ministerial risk (taking) attitude with the population size of its constituent body may not be that farfetched. If the constituency of a ministry is relatively small, then its blocking of the Nash bargain outcome may be criticized by the majority for being sectarian, selfish, and the like, and may not be sustainable for a long time. Therefore, the relatively unimportant ministry in terms of constituency size may be less bold in competitive bargaining. On the other hand, the reputation of the ministry whose constituency is large may be more vulnerable if it fails to deliver the benefit to its constituency, so that it may behave more aggressively in bargaining. Therefore one may assert that

> [P.1] *The equivalence of a politically stable bargain outcome and democratic coordination:* The democratic arbitration by the coordinating office concerning the allocation of political resources is power-equilibrating and politically stable if the bargaining power (risk-taking attitude) of each ministry is proportional to the size of population it represents. Conversely, the power-equilibrating and politically stable allocation of political resources can be achieved through the democratic arbitration of the coordinating office.

This proposition may be considered obvious. Note, however, that the democratic coordination defined here refers to the allocation of resources that equalize the marginal percentage utility gain from the status quo by a marginal unit of political resources for every citizen, but not the allocation that would be supported by the majority vote of citizens (or by the preference of the median voter). Such an allocation may be democratic in a particular sense of the word, but neither power-equilibrating nor politically stable when the allocation of political resources is subject to bargaining. On the other hand, if each individual has an identical utility indicator and every unit of public expenditure is directed to a ministry without causing any external effect, then the administrative rule of thumb called incrementalism, which would increase the distribution of fiscal funds to each ministry equiproportionally every year, may be democratic, power-equilibrating, and politically stable at the same time (provided that the initial distribution is the Nash bargaining outcome).

The above proposition suggests that *genkyoku* ministries need not be engaged in direct competitive bargaining with each other, but through the intermediary of the coordination office in order to achieve the politically stable allocation of political resources. That is to say, each *genkyoku* ministry may negotiate vis-à-vis the coordinating office concerning the interministerial allocation of political resources. Suppose that the coordinating office assesses the relative political power of each *genkyoku* ministry and uses it as the weight to be attached to the ministry in the allocation of political resources (possibly after suitable adjustments according to its own value judgement or institutional constraint, if necessary). Let us call this institutional arrangement *quasi-pluralistic bargaining nested within the bureaucracy.*

Suppose that the weights used by the coordinating office are α and β and that these values are known to each *genkyoku* ministry. In order for ministry I to be able to put forth the case for an allocational change dx successfully to the coordinating office, it is not sufficient to prove that the change is beneficial to its constituent; that is,

$$\frac{du^I}{dx} > 0,$$

but it must also prove that the change is in the "public interest" in the following "Nash-improving" sense:

$$\alpha \frac{du^I/dx}{[u^I - \hat{u}^I]} + \beta \frac{du^A/dx}{[u^A - \hat{u}^A]} > 0 \tag{N.I}$$

where du^I/dx and du^A/dx are the utility changes from the allocational change, dx. The symmetric condition also applies to the ministry A. The last condition says the weighted sum over every citizen of the percentage changes in utility relative to the status quo must be positive. That is, even though a proposal for political resource reallocation by ministry I is in the interest of its constituency (the first term is positive), if it would hurt the other constituency to a larger extent (the second term is negative and larger in its absolute value than the first term) so that the left-hand side becomes negative, such a proposal would not be accepted by the coordinating office as being against the public interest. Only when the left-hand side becomes equal to zero does the allocation reach an equilibrium and maximize the Nash utility product.

When the weighting used by the coordination office reflects the democratic value, the quasi-pluralistic bargaining nested within the bureaucracy may be able to locate a stable political resource allocation more efficiently (in terms of allocation and time) than the "pressure group pluralism" in which bargaining is entrusted to agents of concerned pressure groups (such as elected representatives, the labor union, the farmers' association, and the business association). There are three reasons for this.

First, the centralized arbitration by the coordinating office may be more informationally efficient than direct multilateral bargaining in an

n-person context such as one involving more than two ministries. The coordinating office can centrally propose an allocation of political resources among multiple ministries, elicit its effects on percentage utility gain (loss) for each constituent via a corresponding ministry, and then revise the proposal according to the aggregated rule analogous to formula (N.I). N-person bargaining can be transformed into n bilateral communications, with the coordinating office functioning as an information clearinghouse, just like an auctioneer in the *tâtonnement* process.

Second, the asserted approximate equivalence of the Nash bargaining solution with the politically stable equilibrium à la Rubinstein can be attained on the assumption that each ministry rotates in a proposal (an offer) concerning a division of political resources in a preordered sequence. Even if the players do not rotate, this extra freedom does not affect the perfect equilibrium outcome in the two-person context. But it does seriously change the situation when several players are bargaining over which coalition is to form.[27] If, on the other hand, n-persons simultaneously announce demands, any Pareto-efficient allocation can be a (Nash) equilibrium of the noncooperative game. In facing such an indeterminancy intrinsic to the n-person game, the arbitration by the democratic coordinating office can make the single power-equilibrating outcome à la Zeuthen a focal point. The political power of a coordinating office in the bureaucracy, such as the Budgetary Bureau of the MOF, in enforcing a chosen outcome is more likely to be stronger than an arbitrative agent in social bargaining. In addition, the bureaucratic imperative of reaching a decision within a certain institutionally set time frame (say, the budgetary period) may help the quasi-pluralist bargaining nested within the bureaucracy reach an equilibrium under the leadership of the coordinating office in a time-efficient manner. In particular, when the condition stated after proposition [P. 1] holds, the coordinating office may use the simple principle of incrementalism as a rule of thumb for allocating political resources and still get the democratic and politically stable outcome.

Third, the permanent processing and accumulation of information by the career bureaucrats of ministries, together with repeated interactions between the ministries and the coordinating office, may help clarify the objective and efficient bargaining frontier more precisely

---

[27] "In these . . . cases, a player may well wish to avoid making a proposal at a time when he has the opportunity to do so because he anticipates having a more favourable proposal accepted in the future." K. Binmore, "Perfect equilibria in bargaining model," in K. Binmore and P. Dasgupta, *The Economics of Bargaining,* Basil Blackwell, 1987, p. 78.

than in the case of direct bargaining between agents whose contracts with the principals (pressure groups) may be terminable at the discretion of the latter. It is true that even ministries are sometimes observed to distort and misrepresent information to their own advantage in interministerial bargaining, but such seems to be more frequent under situations in which bargaining issues are to be settled once and for all. In repeated bargaining such as budgetary negotiations, the coordinating office and ministries may come to mutually share, albeit to a limited degree, knowledge relevant to bargaining. The ex post disclosure of misrepresentation may spoil the credibility of subsequent cases made by the ministry and may trigger the coordinating office's effective sanction in the form of the withdrawal of fiscal resources over succeeding periods. On the other hand, the agent in direct social bargaining may resort to overrepresenting the demands and needs of clients to secure its position as a bargaining agent (or to secure reelection).

However, in the quasi-pluralistic bargaining nested within the bureaucracy, weighting by the coordinating office may not reflect democratic values. One possibility is that the coordinating office may have to follow a weighting dictated by the law, even if the law becomes obsolete. If this situation persists, the coordinating outcome may become less efficient and politically unstable. Unless the law is revised, bureaucratic action may become coercive. Alternatively, some social pressure group may inherit an unproportionally stronger influence over the determination of weighting (policy making) through the inertia of old policy and/or its unproportional representation in the legislative body that has ultimate sanction over the allocation of political resources.

The imposed outcome of the quasi-pluralistic bargaining nested within the bureaucracy may involve not only an undemocratic distributional bias, but also allocational inefficiency, if the imposed value blocks the introduction of new policy instruments (accordingly some allocations of political resources). For example, suppose that UU in Figure 7.2 is the utility frontier possible under the currently available set of policy instruments and the point A is the chosen point under the imposed value. The dotted curve NN going through point A is the indifference curve of the imposed Nash utility product. Imagine that the democratic Nash utility product generates indifference map, $N'N'$, $N''N''$, . . . and that the introduction of new policy instruments (e.g., the reduction of farmer's protection policy, or the dezoning of farm land for alternative uses) shifts the utility possibility frontier to $U'U'$. Point C represents the democratic, power-equilibrating, and politically stable outcome under the policy innovation. The imposition of undemocratic values would block the movement from A to C, how-

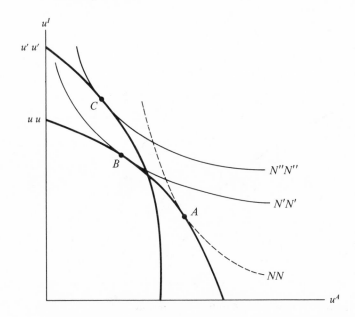

Figure 7.2. Blocking of policy innovation by conservative inertial policy orientation.

ever, as C would yield a smaller value of the imposed Nash utility product. Such blocking involves the undemocratic bias, represented by AB, and the efficiency loss, BC, due to the failure of the policy innovation to be instituted. The imposed value orientation which would lead to an outcome such as A rather than C may be referred to as *conservative inertia*.

Another possibility is that the coordinating office may deviate from democratic weighting in the anticipation of long-run democratic effects from the introduction of a new policy instrument. For example, suppose that the weighting reflecting the current population composition dictates the democratic Nash solution at point A on the current utility frontier UU in Figure 7.3, where the indifference curve NN corresponds to the democratic Nash utility product. Suppose that the adoption of a new policy instrument (say, a policy to promote an infant industry) would currently lead to the Nash-inferior solution B, but would enhance the utility frontier to $U'U'$ in the long run as well as shift the demographic composition (e.g., by the immigration of rural population to the urban area) in such a way that the eventual democratic Nash solution would be at C. Point C is Pareto-superior and

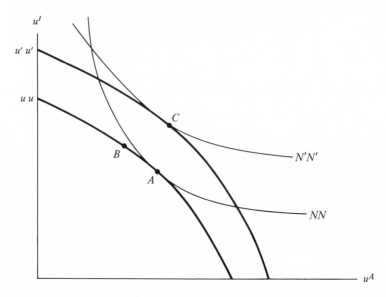

Figure 7.3. Promotional policy orientation.

would be in the public interest in the long run. But such policy may not be preferred by the shortsighted current population. In this situation, the adoption of policy innovation is imposed in the sense that the weighting leading to C does not reflect the current democratic value, but it may be referred to as *promotional* in the sense that it would promote the public welfare of future population.

The job of foreseeing and advocating a promotional possibility may not be limited to the coordinating office, but rather may be decentralized to *genkyoku* ministries. It may be imagined that each ministry advocates and competes in presenting its own case for a promotional possibility, which may eventually improve the public welfare, although the result may be contrary to the current interests of some segments of the population. In this case, the coordinating office may play the role of judging the merits and demerits of competing demands and adjudicating among them. Through this process, there may emerge a ranking of *genkyoku* ministries in the long run according to the track records of policy innovation.

In actuality, the policy orientation of the bureaucracy may not consistently be democratic, conservative-inertial, or promotional. It is possible that each of them alternately dominates the others at various phases of the political cycle. For example, the conservative-inertial policy orientation will not last without spoiling the efficiency of the economy and the political stability of the polity. To repeat, by stability of the polity, I mean the strategic-disturbance-free (perfect) equilibrium in the Rubinstein sense. That is the equilibrium that will not be disturbed by rational bargaining agents who try to exploit all possible opportunities to their own advantage. (Under the conditions stated in [P. 1] above and in Chapter 5, it is identical with the democratic Nash solution.) In order for the polity to restore economic efficiency and political stability, it would have to introduce policy innovation, democratic or promotional.

The promotional orientation, on the other hand, has to prove itself to be in fact promotional by realizing a Pareto-superior improvement (the improved public welfare). Otherwise, the policy innovation would be conceived of as simply coercive and detrimental to general public welfare, and as destabilizing the polity. The policy outcome under a successful promotional orientation tends to gravitate toward the democratic Nash solution, realizing pluralistic value and political stability. However, once the democratic Nash solution becomes formalized into written statute or conventionalized, then the subsequent policy derived from that statute/convention may eventually become conservative-inertial as economic conditions change. Such would be the case when the distribution of population over various ministerial jurisdictions changes, or a new technological possibility makes jurisdictional demarcation among ministries obscure and obsolete. Then the polity may be destabilized and forced to start a new cycle.

C.   Semi-isomorphism: the J-firm and the bureaucracy

In Chapter 6, we saw that there is an isomorphic structure between the operating division of the J-firm and its R&D organization. In this subsection, I briefly review a similar isomorphic structure that exists between the organizational patterns of the J-firm and those of the bureaucracy. Such an isomorphism at various societal levels suggests that it is a deep-seated structure of the Japanese social organization and must be made clear if one hopes to understand the Japanese social system. Although I emphasize isomorphism at the operating level, however, I also note that there is one important difference between the two in the way that control is exercised over its employee/bureaucrats through the incentive ranking hierarchy, which may have a potentially different implication for leadership behavior at the "strategic" level of each system. Therefore, we may call the structural semisimilarity and semidifference existing between the bureaucracy and the J-firm semi-

Table 7.1. *Semi-isomorphic structure: bureaupluralism and the J-firm*

	The bureaucracy	The J-firm
At component unit	Diffused reception to emergent demands of constituent interests; rigid jurisdictional demarcation	Autonomous problem solving to emergent events
Between component units:	Hierarchically layered quasi-pluralistic bargaining	Horizontal coordination
Incentives and control	Parallel ranking hierarchies	Centralized ranking hierarchy
Leadership type	Constituent-based	Constituent-based
	$\left\{\begin{array}{l}\text{Democratic}\\\text{Promotional}\\\text{Conservative-inertial}\end{array}\right.$	$\left\{\begin{array}{l}\text{Arbitrative}\\\text{Entrepreneurial}\\\text{Conservative-inertial}\end{array}\right.$

isomorphism. The following discussion on this semi-isomorphic structure is summarized in Table 7.1.

We have observed that the bureaucrat is rotated among various sections and bureaus within the administrative hierarchy of a ministry in much the same way that the quasi-permanent employee of the J-firm is rotated among various jobs. This practice trains the bureaucrat to be a quasi-agent who is able to recognize and screen the interests of jurisdictional constituents in a broader public perspective. He/she is delegated a substantial degree of authority to formulate a policy relevant to his/her jurisdictional assignment, although the policy must be within the framework of the strategic orientation of the ministry and sanctioned by the MOF for budget backing.

The situation is analogous to that in the J-firm where the quasi-permanent employee is trained to develop a wider range of skills and related knowledge useful for coping with emergent events autonomously at the assigned operating level. In both cases, the emphasis is on delegating operational/administrative problem-solving tasks to those who have the relevant on-site knowledge and on making this decentralized decision making effective and consistent with the broader objective of the firm/bureaucracy. This is done by nurturing versatile/public perspectives of the quasi-permanent employee/bureaucrat within the competitive framework of the ranking hierarchy of the J-firm/ministry. This is a positive aspect of decentralized decision making. A negative aspect is that, because bureaucrats are so concerned with their own territory, it has become a sacred rule not to interfere with the affairs of other departments and ministries wherever jurisdictional lines are clearly drawn; this reinforces the tendency toward diffuse decision making. Even the central coordinating ministry, the MOF, can approve/disapprove budgetary demands of *genkyoku* ministries, but can never dictate any concrete policy to them.

Second, the Japanese organization, both the J-firm and the bureaucratic entity, has tended to coordinate interrelated operating activities and resolve conflicts of interest through bargaining by relevant functional units rather than "centralized control." In the bureaucracy, when bargaining involves many ministries – as in the budgeting process – it is mediated by a specialized coordinating office such as the Budgetary Bureau of the MOF. But as we saw in Section 2.B, this does not change the essential character of bargaining as far as the coordinating office follows the democratic value. Under this condition, "centralized coordination" would only reduce the cost of multilateral bargaining. The cost saving will be particularly high under stable conditions in which centralized coordination can be routinized by an automatic rule such as budgetary incrementalism.

At the interministerial level, the mutual interests binding coordinating and bargaining partners in a cooperative framework may become rather thin and, as I shall discuss shortly, efficient bargaining (coordination) on a "once-and-for-all issue" may sometimes be hampered by jurisdictional disputes and misrepresentation of information. However, as already pointed out, the potential disclosure of misrepresentation in repeated bargaining, such as budgeting, is very costly to a ministry. Also note that the accumulation of political stocks of each ministry partly depends on its contribution to the public welfare. The mutual concern with public welfare may deter ministries from consistently engaging in uncooperative, inefficient haggling with each other in repeated bargaining, which may deplete their own political stocks.

Third, the Japanese organization, industrial and bureaucratic, has tended to be constituent-based in its managerial/political leadership. In Chapter 6, we saw that R&D activity of the J-firm is primarily directed toward the development of engineering knowledge accumulated within itself through the manufacturing process. Thus even entrepreneurial leadership in the J-firm is characterized as constituent-based in terms of knowledge relied on and human resources carrying out innovative activities. Isomorphically, the policy innovation of the polity also seems to rely on emerging phenomena in the society in order to be effective. For example, in Section 5.3 we noted that elements of drastic policy innovation in the post–World War II reform that have survived to the present day (e.g., the removal of *zaibatsu* control and enterprise-based unionism) appear to be accelerating evolutionary trends that were already underway before the end of the war, and that otherwise the reform was quickly reversed (e.g., the regulation on the stockholding by banks). As another example, the promotional policy of the MITI during the 1950s would not have been effective if there had not already been entrepreneurial energy and ambition on the side of the private industrial sector.

A policy innovation may not only promote economic interests of some groups, but may also hurt other groups. The LDP-bureaucratic alliance since the beginning of the 1960s seems to have carefully avoided potential political conflicts of policy innovations by compensating interest groups adversely affected by them through income assurance schemes and other means (e.g., income assurance to farmers through support of the price of rice during the promotion of the industrial development). In the sense that only those policy innovations that have yielded Pareto-improving outcomes have been formed and most effectively implemented, the political leadership in the quasi-pluralist bureaucracy may be reckoned as having been constituent based.

One important difference between the overall structure of the bureaucracy, with its various ministries and agencies, and that of the J-firm is the lack of centralized personnel administration. It is true that the Agency for Personnel Administration is responsible for recommending annually to the cabinet a revision of the pay schedule for various ranking hierarchies within the central government bureaucracy, which is based on its annual survey of wages in the private sector. But important personnel decisions such as individual hirings, promotions, transfers, and *amakudari* assignments are administered by each ministry. In order to promote interministerial communications, the temporary *shukko* (dispatch) of bureaucrats to other ministries is increasingly practiced,[28] but the lifetime careers of those bureaucrats hinge on the personnel decisions of parent ministries. Accordingly, their ultimate loyalty remains with parent ministries.

As discussed in Chapter 3, the centralization of personnel administration is an important mechanism through which the J-firm ensures that individual employess will comply with the organizational objective despite the wide-ranging delegation of decision making to the lower level of the functional hierarchy and nonhierarchical coordination. In short, the centralized administration of the ranking hierarchy complements and substitutes for decentralization in the functional hierarchy in the J-firm (the duality principle). The training of employees in a wide range of skills and the practice of rotating personnel between functional units may thus discourage personnel from asserting inefficient sectarian interests in the organization. There is no such

---

[28] The number of *shukko* bureaucrats increased from 2,106 in 1975 to 3,345 in 1983.

safeguard in the government bureaucracy as a whole, only in the individual ministry. As noted already, this may not be a serious problem as far as the political environment is fairly stable and thus interministerial coordination can be routinized. However, when jurisdictional demarcation becomes an issue because of a drastic environmental change, for example, the lack of centralized control in personnel administration, together with the decentralized delegation of decision making to each *genkyoku,* may result in a fierce jurisdictional dispute and haggling among concerned ministries, each of which may endeavor to expand its own jurisdiction.

, The tendency for the bureaucracy to represent diffuse interests in a rapidly changing environment may make it increasingly difficult to formulate and implement an innovative promotional policy. As discussed in Chapter 6, an increasingly innovative orientation of the J-firm under entrepreneurial leadership may also undermine the interest of some constituent within the firm, such as a particular type of skilled worker. But the centralized administration of personnel and emphasis on training for versatile skills within the J-firm may ease, at least to some extent, the burden of the drastic internal reorganization by internal transfers and the retraining of affected workers.[29] In contrast, in the case of the government bureaucracy, each ministry administers its own incentive hierarchy and relies on specific interest groups for *amakudari* arrangements. In the absence of the duality principle, ministries may be motivated to fiercely resist a policy change that may deprive them of vested political stocks, such as regulatory power and discretionary grants to their constituents.

In view of its quasi-pluralistic character and the absence of the duality principle, the bureaucracy may be led to develop an intrinsic conservatism toward radical, promotional innovation. This may also explain why, more often than not, the Japanese polity appears to need

---

[29] Too much concern with potential damage to a particular constituent group may also hamper entrepreneurial leadership in the J-firm and result in conservative-inertial management. For example, the prolonged, inefficient practice of work sharing in the steel and shipbuilding industries in the late 1970s to early 1980s, which I referred to in Section 5.2.B, may have largely stemmed from the mistake of management in its forecast of future demands, but may also have been attributable to the unduly high weighting given to the welfare of employees, particularly those who worked at plants located in company castle towns. The situation may be analyzed in terms of Figure 7.2, with constituent A being interpreted as the quasi-permanent employee and constituent I being interpreted as the stockholder. Too much concern with the welfare of employees might have prevented management from making the more drastic innovative strategic business decision to close down old and inefficient plants and move decisively into high-tech-oriented diversification at an earlier time. This caused not only a profit squeeze (distribution bias measured by the difference between A and B), but also a loss of efficiency (measured by the distance between B and C). Such a mistake is severely penalized by the market in the case of industry.

extraordinary external shocks *(gaiatsu)* of a degree that might threaten national integrity and viability, in order to implement radical social changes that decisively deprive vested interests of certain social groups. In the next section I argue that the conservative tendency has indeed begun to manifest itself in the Japanese polity in changing technological and international environments, but that the polity is also experiencing mounting international pressure for a structural change that would make it conform more with the Western norm.

3.   Bureaupluralism

A.   The evolution of bureaupluralism

It is generally believed that the model of a ruling "triad" applies to the Japanese polity of the 1950s.[30] According to this model, the orientation of national policy was determined by elitist bureaucrats in central economic ministries such as the MITI and the MOF, conservative LDP political leaders, and big business leaders. The strategic policy agenda was to make Japan's industries viable in the international market. The bureaucracy channeled relatively scarce fiscal resources and foreign exchange to big business. To "rationalize" (make efficient) the industry and establish management's prerogative, the management of big business frequently confronted the union with the backing of the conservative political leadership. Allied with the union were populist socialists and Marxist intellectuals. To achieve industrial development in the face of their anticapitalistic rhetoric, and often at the real sacrifice of unionists as well as small businesses, the triad remained exclusive.

In retrospect, however, the policy orientation of the triad, albeit exclusive, was promotional rather than conservative-inertial in paving the way for the subsequent phenomenal economic growth.[31] When

---

[30] See, for example, Haruhiro Fukui, *Party in Power: the Japanese Liberal Democrats and Policy-Making,* University of California Press, 1970.

[31] The two historical events in 1960 – the anti-Anpo (U.S.–Japan Mutual Security Treaty) movement, culminating in the cancelation of Eisenhower's visit to Japan and the resignation of Prime Minister Kishi, and the aforementioned Miike labor dispute – marked the end of confrontational politics of the 1950s. The surge and decline of the New Left in the Anpo movement gave the coup de grace to the dogmatic Marxian doctrine of class conflict, which had been influential among intellectuals since before World War II. The Ikeda cabinet, which succeeded Kishi, reoriented the conservative LDP toward the "politics of tolerance and patience." The first item on the cabinet's agenda was to facilitate the early settlement of the Miike dispute in a conciliatory manner. The "Income Doubling Plan," which had been actually formulated by the Kishi cabinet, did not come to be recognized as a truly national objective until the decline of confrontational politics. The potential energy of the nation, which had been building up latently during the economic development of the 1950s and flared up politically in 1960, began to be funneled into the economic arena.

industrial development started to generate more social surplus in the 1960s, the polity became increasingly attentive to the demands of various social groups in addition to big business: Farmers, for example, were assured that their incomes would be at least par with those of working-class families in cities through a price support scheme for rice, and that they would be provided with various public goods such as irrigation and snow disaster prevention; small shopkeepers and business owners were given access to low-cost capital financing by public finance corporations, lenient tax treatment, and protection from competition in the form of regulations limiting the entry of large businesses to traditional areas of commerce;[32] veteran families were provided with a steady flow of pension benefits; and so on. The LDP functioned as a network for absorbing pluralistic interests, old and new, and channeled them into the bureaucratic process. The bureaucracy provided an administrative framework through which pluralistic interests could be screened and duly recognized. Fiscal resources increased every year because of the high growth of national income, and annual increments were distributed almost equiproportionally among ministries (the so-called budgetary incrementalism). Ministries struck a balance between the interests of their own constituent groups within this budgetary framework. The political stock of ministries and LDP politicians was enhanced substantially in this period through the absorption of pluralistic interests, and unprecedented stability of LDP rule followed. The 1960s was the heyday of pluralistic politics mediated by the bureaucracy–LDP alliance, which we may call *bureaupluralism* for the sake of convenience.[33]

Pempel and Tsunekawa, among others, are of the opinion that labor was excluded from this broadly based interest absorption and mediation process.[34] But I suggest that the bureaupluralism of this period did not entirely ignore the interests of labor either. During these years, labor in big business, stylized as the quasi-permanent employee of the J-firm in the earlier chapters, became an integral element of the J-firm, while the J-firm's interest as a whole was effectively absorbed by the MITI and other economic *genkyoku* ministries through the intermediary of various business associations. The quasi-permanent employee of the J-firm also benefited from periodic income tax reductions made possible by the continuous growth of the tax base. The Ministry of Labor, albeit weaker in its ranking in the bureaucracy, served as the quasi agent protecting specific interests of labor in the workplace as

[32] See H. Patrick and T. Rohlen, "Small-scale family enterprises," in Y. Yasuba and K. Yamamura (eds.), *The Political Economy of Japan*, pp. 381–4.
[33] See Muramatsu and Krauss, "The conservative policy line."
[34] Pempel and Tsunekawa, "Corporatism without labor?"

well as in the nonunionized sector by the enforcement of labor law and protective regulations. Even opposition parties, such as the Socialist Party (SP), functioned as mediators of working class interests in the political process. For example, the SP often engaged in deals with the LDP in the budgetary legislative process in order to deliver higher levels of pay to government employees, and the LDP increasingly accommodated such deals.

The election of Tanaka, a primary school graduate with no background as an elite bureaucrat, to the prime ministership in 1972 symbolized the broadened pluralistic nature of the Japanese polity.[35] His power stemmed from the fact that, through several ministerial experiences at various important ministries and with exceptionally gifted social skill, he cultivated awesome power over the assignments of top-ranking bureaucrats to various positions in and outside the bureaucracy. He more or less built and administered a de facto centralized ranking hierarchy that the bureaucracy formally lacked. With the rise of Tanaka, the balance of power within the LDP-bureaucratic alliance was decisively tilted toward the LDP politicians, although no single politician has ever acquired comparable influence over the careers of elite bureaucrats since he left office. In spite of Tanaka's enormous popularity at the time of his inauguration, a series of subsequent events, such as the collapse of the Bretton-Woods system and the first oil shock, triggered the shakeup of the financial foundation of expansive pluralism. The concomitant disclosure of the Lockheed scandal ended his prime ministership.[36]

In a shift to the non-accommodating monetarist stance by the mone-

---

[35] The high speed of economic development in the 1960s caused various spillover effects such as environmental pollution, congestion, and a lack of decent housing stock. The political failure to absorb the discontent of city dwellers regarding these social costs of growth culminated in successive defeats of LDP candidates in the late 1960s and early 1970s in important gubernatorial and mayoral elections in major metropolitan areas such as Tokyo, Osaka, Kyoto, and Yokohama. The LDP and central bureaucracy led by Tanaka quickly responded to the crisis of conservative politics by accommodating welfare- and environmental-oriented policies of local "democratic" governments. The new system of social security introduced in 1973 by the Tanaka cabinet provided social security benefits as generous as those in the United States. Pollution control was set at the level stipulated in the original Muskie Act, which was considered unrealistic in the United States.

[36] Tanaka tried to make his primary policy objective solving the deficiencies of the social infrastructure and private housing by the Plan for Remodeling the Japanese Archipelago. However, at the time the plan was announced the Japanese government was concomitantly supplying an excessive amount of liquidity by converting mounting export proceeds at the out-of-dated fixed rate of ¥360 = $1 in a vain effort to rescue the fixed exchange system that had insulated the Japanese financial market in the post–World War II period. Feverish land speculation was ignited and the first oil shock aggravated the impact of great inflation.

tarist authority in the aftermath of the great 1973–4 inflation,[37] the central government began resorting more and more to national bond issues for financing expanded social securities and other expenditures. The ratio of bond issues to total revenue of the general account of the central government exceeded 30 percent in 1977, an upper limit that the MOF insisted be kept. A tax reform that included a general consumption tax seemed to be inevitable, and the MOF began to maneuver for its early introduction. However, Prime Minister Ohira committed a tactical mistake in making the introduction of a new value-added tax a campaign issue in 1979, and the near defeat of the LDP made tax reform politically infeasible for some time to come. Instead of ushering in a tax reform, the MOF put a zero-percent ceiling on annual increases in budgetary demands, except for defense expenditures and foreign aid, in the early 1980s as a means of keeping the fiscal deficit at a manageable level. Later the ceiling was further lowered to minus 10 percent. The availability of fiscal resources in the 1980s for administering bureaupluralism was thus severely curtailed in comparison with the preceding decades.[38]

Meanwhile, in the second half of the 1970s, as noted earlier, big business trimmed its reliance on external debt considerably, as well as its organizational size relative to sales, through the so-called *genryo keiei* (trimming management), with the cooperation of enterprise-based unions. Regaining the confidence that had been shaken by the anticorporate public sentiment in the aftermath of high inflation and land speculation in the mid-1970s, business leaders became increasingly frustrated by and critical of the mounting fiscal deficit and the size of the bureaucracy. They called upon the government to make a similar organizational change. The demand for government services began to decline among private enterprises that had gained a substantial competitive edge in the global market, particularly when the supply of services involved the exercise of discretionary regulatory power of the bureaucracy. What Muramatsu et al. have called an "employee-employer coalition in big business," which corresponds to our notion of the J-firm, became more autonomous and started to drift away from government intervention.[39] In addition, in the face of mounting trade disputes, it became increasingly difficult for the bureaucrat to maneuver away from the pressure of foreign governments and businesses to

---

[37] See Section 4.2.
[38] This measure of restraining budgetary demands had a side effect: It reduced the MOF's discretionary power in budget allocation, as a near-final budgetary plan of each ministry is formulated at the ministerial level, before it is presented to the MOF.
[39] Muramatsu et al., *Sengo Nihon*, p. 277.

remove protective regulations. In the early 1980s the inefficiency and ineffectiveness of the existing pattern of fiscal budgeting and regulatory power became the public issue.

Under pressure from the business community (the J-firm), the government, upon the Diet's approval in 1981, appointed the second Ad Hoc Council on Administrative Reform *(Rincho)* headed by a widely respected business leader, Toshio Doko, and authorized it to report on a broad administrative reform plan *(gyokaku)* for solving the fiscal imbalance in the long-term and for realizing a small efficient government. The scope and range of *Rincho* recommendations were considerable, if not perfect, and they were implemented fairly effectively by the Nakasone cabinet.[40] Bureaupluralism, which had continued to expand its constituents since the 1950s on the basis of growing fiscal and other political resources, came to be checked but pluralism has not lost too much ground.

A revived attempt at major tax reform that focused on the introduction of indirect taxes was defeated in 1987 through the strong opposition of small and medium businesses, but the plan also failed to mobilize the support of the employee–employer coalition because the proposed corporate and individual income tax cuts did not promise them any clear-cut benefits. Many think that an overhauling of farming protection policy is long overdue on the political agenda. The price support policy, which helps maintain the domestic price of rice at five times the international price, is becoming an extremely costly welfare policy in disguise. There is also increasing pressure on Japan to expand domestic demand in order to absorb domestic savings, yet such a policy may be extremely difficult to implement unless property zoned as farmland in the vicinity of urban areas is released for residential, industrial, and commercial uses. Farmers and their families, who constituted more than 50 percent of the population until 30 years ago, have dwindled to less than 10 percent of the population and are rapidly aging, yet they enjoy much more than proportionate representation in the Diet and solid bureaucratic support. (The number of *kome giin* is

[40] Through the recommendation of *Rincho* and its implementation, a stringent budget ceiling was imposed on every ministry, and some administrative regulations by *genkyoku* were curtailed, whereas some coordinating offices, such as the Management and Coordination Agency, were given greater power; the profitable and innovative National Telephone and Telegram Public Corporation was smoothly privatized and the debt-striken Japan National Railways (JNR) was privatized and dissolved, against the fierce opposition of the then-management and the union; a pension reform was introduced to curtail the extra benefits that had been awarded to government employees.

said to exceed one-third of LDP members. In addition, opposition parties, particularly the Socialist Party, are normally strong supporters of the farmer protection policy.)

Japan seems to need a truly promotional policy to curtail the cost of administering pluralism and to make the domestic economic structure more open to and compatible with emerging world economic environments. Is it necessary to significantly modify the structure of the polity in order to effect such a change? Or will the conservative inertia of bureaupluralism make it virtually impossible to find an immediate solution to this problem?

B.   *Bureaupluralism at bay and its dilemma*

The fundamental dilemma that bureaupluralism is facing may be described as follows: If the tendency toward diffuse decision making is a deep-seated characteristic of the Japanese social system, as suggested by the semi-isomorphism between the J-firm and the bureaucracy, why shouldn't it make the polity absorbed more into the economy? Is it not effective and efficient for the bureaucracy to impart regulatory power exercised through various interfaces between the polity and the economy to relevant segments of the private sector? As a series of measures taken in the *gyokaku* shows, this "privatization" tendency is in fact being advocated and is beginning to take place in some advanced and developing segments of the private sector.[41] A significant degree of privatization may require the bureaucracy to adopt a more modest role of general policy maker, particularly in the field of the economy. Such a change would not be a smooth one because of conservative resistance in the bureaucracy, but the advanced sector, as represented by the J-firm, is exhibiting a growing reluctance to bear the increasing costs of administering bureaupluralism. On the other hand, various benefit-recipient groups (such as veterans) as well as backward and declining economic sector groups (such as farmers and small shopkeepers) are being threatened by the prospect of increasing deregulation and competitive pressures from abroad and therefore tend to rely more on the protection of bureaupluralism.

How will this dilemma of bureaupluralism – the dilemma between the drift of the advanced segment of the economy on one hand and the

---

[41] This tendency of delegating decision making beyond the organizational boundary is occurring in the industrial organization as well. The so-called spinning-off tendency of the J-firm corresponds exactly to that. See Section 5.3.

increasing dependence of the declining segment on the other – be resolved? Three potentially important forces that may alter the nature of Japanese policy away from bureaupluralism are

1. the further strengthening of the LDP role in the arbitration of pluralist interests;
2. the centralization of administrative coordination or personnel administration in the bureaucracy; or
3. the shift to rule-bound neo-neoclassical administration.

Can any of these resolve the dilemma?

The first of these is already at work to some extent. LDP leaders are gradually taking over the arbitrative role, and the bureaucracy is concentrating more and more on its administrative function. One of the reasons for this change is the growing number of jurisdictional disputes among ministries. The jurisdictional dispute is a common feature of all bureaucracies, but its significance in Japan has recently increased because of (1) the growing competition among ministries for scarce fiscal resources and (2) the increasing importance of cross-jurisdictional policy issues and demarcational ambiguities caused by rapidly changing technological and international conditions.[42]

LDP politicians not only intervene in jurisdictional disputes but also resist any attempt to minimize the importance of the concerns of their respective constituent groups. Disputes and opposition to bureaucracy-led policy plans (such as tax reform) in the LDP are becoming more overt and their settlement is now entrusted more to intra-LDP bargaining and adjudiction by its leaders. I have argued that, in the heyday of bureaupluralism, LDP politicians engaged in shadow bargaining parallel to the primary bargaining conducted by the bureaucracy. Their role seems to have been reversed recently, so that the LDP now takes an initiative in arbitrating pluralistic interests.

If LDP arbitration is to avoid falling into the trap of conservative inertia stemming from ad hoc problem solving and is to resolve the dilemma of bureaupluralism, stronger political leadership – which is capable of envisioning and implementing a consistent and efficient policy – will be required. However it will be difficult to generate such leadership in the environment of consensus building that exists under

---

[42] Among such changes are the breakdown of traditional industrial boundaries caused by the development of multidisciplinary high-technology industries (such as biotechnology), the increasing integration of national economies into the global markets, and the resulting necessity of coordinating international and domestic economic policies as well as overhauling regulatory systems in ways consistent with international norms and demands.

the said dilemma. As the preliminary attempt by Nakasone suggests, one political choice that might lead to the needed policy orientation might be to rely on the increasingly self-reliant "labor–employer coalition" at the J-firm. Policy would then be directed more toward deregulation, consistent with the Western norm, in order to resolve the dilemma in favor of the internationally viable J-firm, which is predominantly urban based. But given that the constituents of the majority of incumbent LDP parliamentary members are benefit recipient groups that rely on bureaucratic protection, such political reorientation may not yet be politically feasible.

Theoretically, another way to resolve the dilemma of bureaupluralism is to introduce consistent, promotional leadership through centralization of the functional hierarchy or ranking hierarchy in the administration, to restore the duality principle. There have in fact been some attempts to centralize interministerial coordination within the administration, as reflected in the September 1985 cabinet decision to reorganize the prime minister's secretariat and in the role given to the newly created Management and Coordination Agency. Both of these changes were based on recommendations in the report of the *Rincho*.[43] But newly created coordinating offices in the prime minister's secretariat are predominantly staffed by officials temporarily dispatched from the ministries concerned, and it appears doubtful that those offices can exercise autonomous coordinating functions free from interministerial haggling. Even such a modest attempt at functional centralization seems to be difficult to reconcile with incentives created by the administration of the diverse ranking hierarchies in the separate ministries.

As an alternative to a centralized form of administrative coordination, I. Nakatani recently suggested that personnel administration in the bureaucracy be centralized.[44] He argued that through a unified per-

[43] According to that decision, "in order to strengthen the Cabinet function of systematic coordination," the Prime Minister's secretariat is to be reorganized to include a Domestic Policy Coordination Office, a Foreign Policy Coordination Office and a National Security Office. Two of the explicit functions of the Management and Coordinating Agency are to "coordinate and integrate administrative structure" and to "review the restructuring of administrative organs and fix the number of personnel for them." When this agency was created, it was generally expected that its impact would be rather limited. As it turned out, it started to play a certain active role in implementing and monitoring administrative reform, as seen in its role in the privatization of the JNR. One reason for the rather unexpected strength of this agency is that the Administrative Inspection Bureau is empowered to monitor administrative activities of governmental agencies and public corporations and to make necessary recommendations.

[44] I. Nakatani, "Sekinin kokka – Nihon-eno sentaku" (Choices open to the responsible state – Japan), *Asteion* (Fall 1987), pp. 38–40.

sonnel administration by "personnel headquarters," and through the regular rotation of bureaucrats among ministries, the sectarian fusion of *zoku* politicians and bureaucrats would be curbed and the conservative inertia of bureaupluralism could be overcome. One problem with this proposal, however, is that in centralizing the bureaucratic ranking hierarchy one may concentrate an enormous amount of power at the proposed headquarters. As episodes in the Tanaka era and the experience of many organizations indicate, a person or a group that effectively controls the allocation of persons usually acquires tremendous power in the Japanese organizational context. This seems to be an inevitable consequence of using ranking as a major incentive scheme. Further, it is not clear if the centralization of administrations would be compatible with, and even desirable in the face of the growing privatization in viable segments of the economy. The dilemma of bureaupluralism may be the price for pluralism.

A third alternative would be to have the bureaucracy operate under more explicit, neutral, and codified rules rather than rely on pragmatic, case-by-case administration. The overall policy orientation may be ideally provided by the democratically mature legislative body. Such a move would tend to change the basic nature of bureaupluralism and, in some circumstances, might place the bureaucracy in the role of an adversarial regulatory agency, rather than pluralistic agent, with respect to its constituency. In view of its emphasis on rationality, we could refer to this approach as neo-neoclassical administration.

Of course, there have always been rules for the bureaucrat to follow, but they have been applied flexibly and, whenever necessary, have been reinterpreted to fit the given situation. The flexible interpretation of laws and rules might have saved bureaupluralism from conservative inertia in its heyday. However, the favorable conditions that made discretionary and pragmatic adaptation workable are disappearing. Discretionary maneuvering on a case-by-case basis with limited resources may not be neutral toward various groups in its welfare effects (undemocratic bias). Further, international pressure to make regulatory rules more transparent, neutral, and consistent with international trade practices is mounting. Finally, the increasing uncertainty of economic environments may sometimes make a pragmatic and adaptive approach potentially more destabilizing. This in fact occurred in the 1970s; the sudden accumulation of fiscal deficits caused by the move to meet pluralistic demands for social security was followed by sudden reversion to fiscal stringency.

Furthermore, the inertia of bureaupluralism may make it difficult to effect a complete and smooth transition to the neo-neoclassical administration. I presume that in the neo-neoclassical bureaucracy each *genkyoku* bureau has its own special jurisdiction based on the principle of functionalism. However, the shift to functionalism will require a significant shaping of the incentive structure of the bureaucracy. As I have said, the bureaucracy developed and extended its influence on the basis of intricate networks with pluralistic interests of the economy. Restructuring the relation between the polity and the economy according to the neoclassical functionalist principle may mean severing this network of mutual interests. Any radical attempt to this effect may be resisted by the bureaucracy as well as the affected segments, particularly those segments of the economy in decline. For example, within the MOF the regulation of banking, securities, and international finance is compartmentalized in separate *genkyoku* bureaus, and financial deregulation is often hampered by interbureau jurisdictional disputes. However, *Rincho*'s informal inquiry about the possibility of spinning off those *genkyoku* bureaus from the MOF into the consolidated Agency for Monetary Finance and making the MOF a purely coordinating office was said to be flatly rejected by the MOF. It is crucial for the MOF to integrate those *genkyoku* bureaus if it is to maintain the attractive *amakudari* network under their jurisdiction.

Thus it is likely that the dilemma of bureaupluralism will persist for some time to come. It might be that the LDP-bureaucracy alliance will retain its role as quasi agent of benefit recipients, backward groups, and those in a declining economic sector, while limiting itself gradually to a laissez-faire policy-making role in the jurisdiction where private entrepreneurial initiatives are active. Ultimately, however, such a move would not resolve the dilemma. Whether the tension created by the dilemma will give rise to stagnant, inactive conservatism that could pose a threat to efficiency, fairness, political stability, and international harmony, or whether the Japanese polity will continue maneuvering to meet political exigencies with its renowned flexibility and eventually arrive at some kind of solution that is consistent and harmonious with pluralism and the future international environment remains to be seen. Whatever the case, the new international order will be influenced by the course Japan is now taking, and vice versa, although at present its direction is still unclear.

CHAPTER 8

Culture and economic rationality

The preceding chapters have shown that an isomorphic structural pattern occurs at various levels of Japanese organizations: the workshop, as composed of the J-firm, the production department, and R&D department, and the government bureaucracy. In contrast to the hierarchical coordination prevalent in Western organizations, this structural pattern features relatively autonomous operating units connected horizontally without hierarchical control. In the normal course of affairs, the role of leadership here is to facilitate horizontal communication among operating units and to make strategic decisions in a constituent-based manner. We have seen that such a structural pattern is very effective in allowing an organization to adapt its operations to a continually changing environment in a time-efficient manner.

One problem with this structure is that radical organizational innovation and strategic reorientation requiring some constituent groups to make a sacrifice are not likely to occur endogenously unless they are brought on by a significant external shock such as would affect organizational viability. The Japanese organization may thus exhibit a tendency toward "progressive conservatism." It is progressive in that it is capable of adapting itself to continually changing environments in a Nash-improving (consensual-building) manner, and it is conservative in that it is resistant to radical reorientation involving non-Pareto-improving change. Radical organizational innovation and strategic reorientation that forces some constituent groups to make a sacrifice would in general occur as a matter of organizational survival in response to drastic environmental shocks. There may be cases in which initiatives for radical organizational innovation and strategic reorientation come from entrepreneurial/promotional leadership, but even then the leadership seems to need to rely on those constituent groups that are most viable in changing environments.

This general theorizing about the Japanese organization suggests that small groups are the robust core of the organization. In the small group, tasks, information, and outcomes are shared by the members

298

(although not necessarily in completely egalitarian ways), and each group interacts with other groups both inside and outside the organization in a manner designed to preserve its own integrity as much as possible. Unless the integrity of the small group is maintained, the Japanese organization may not operate effectively. However, this small-group orientation is generally considered unique to Japanese culture, in contrast to the emphasis on the individual in the West. Does it imply that the Japanese way of organizing work and rewarding those participants is also culturally unique and not easily emulated elsewhere, even though it is comparatively more efficient in certain industries? Or, even if Japanese-type organizational practices are feasible in the Western context, should they be emulated at all, if it would inevitably curtail individuality and the organizational capacity to innovate radically? Or can the Western individualistic-innovative orientation be reconciled with some aspects of Japanese industrial organization to generate a superior hybrid organization?

There are two opposing views about the cultural uniqueness of Japanese organizational practices. In one view, Japanese practices are culturally unique and therefore not exportable. In the other view, Japanese practices have a rational, universalistic aspect. A discussion of this controversy is far beyond the scope of this book, the primary objective of which has been to present an economic analysis of the workings of the Japanese industrial organization and the economy. However, it may be worthwhile to summarize some of my arguments in terms of the cultural issue, particularly because few economists have given it direct attention.

In the following, I first summarize some representative views on the cultural issue. I suggest that, although the small-group values inherited from the cultural tradition have played a significant role in shaping Japanese organizational practices, in order to be efficient the J-firm had to consciously design and develop efficient *intergroup* coordination mechanisms and an accompanying incentive structure. Groupism is not a sufficient condition for the competitive performance of the J-firm. I argue further that it is not a necessary condition either. Therefore some aspects of Japanese-type organizational practices may be adopted in the West, where desirable, in a manner consistent with enhanced interaction among integratively developed individuals. On the other hand, the Japanese organization may gradually accommodate an increasingly individualistic value orientation of a new generation without losing its essential characteristics, with the aid of developing communications technology.

1.   Culturalists versus rationalists

The view that Japanese organizational practices are culturally unique is prevalent in both the academic and public world. Among those practices usually quoted are consensual decision making, the mutual exchange of "paternalistic" personnel practices on the side of the employer and "loyalty" on the side of the employees, and the penetration of the workplace (the J-firm) into what seem to Western eyes to be the personal and private affairs of the employee (through an emphasis on enterprise welfare, the careful nurturing of enterprise consciousness, etc.). An early statement of this view, which I call the culturalist view, is found in an influential sociological study by James Abegglen that dates back to 1958. He concluded his pioneering study about personnel practices of the Japanese factory with the following remarks:

If a single conclusion were to be drawn from this study it would be that the development of industrial Japan has taken place with much less change from the kinds of social organization and social relations of preindustrial or nonindustrial Japan than would be expected from the Western model of the growth of an industrial society.[1]

However, he did not regard Japan at that time as being at a midpoint in its development toward the Western model of an industrial society: "The Japanese system is on the whole self-consistent."[2] The system was capable of assimilating modern technology in a manner consistent with the historical customs and attitudes of the Japanese. Therefore, one might argue that there are two distinct systems here, a Western and a Japanese one.

Abegglen argued that there are two broad differences between the two. First, industrial organization (the factory, or the company) is not much different from that found in other types of social groups in Japan. The factory recruits obtain and maintain their membership in much the same way that domestic and social groups do. Closely related to this characteristic is "the lack of individualization that most sets off the day-to-day functioning of the Japanese production unit from its American counterpart."[3] It may be remembered from the discussion in Chapter 2 that in the Japanese workplace job specialization is an ambiguous concept (highlighted by the institutionalized job rotation), responsibility is shared by the members of the small work group, and reward is separated from job description.

[1] J. Abegglen, *The Japanese Factory*, Free Press, 1958, p. 129.
[2] Ibid., p. 130.
[3] Ibid., p. 140.

Abeggan's theory had an immediate impact on the West as well as Japan no doubt because he regarded the Japanese system as a "consistent" system parallel to the Western system, rather than as a transitional phase to the more modernized system idealized in the West. The latter interpretation had been espoused in Japan by modernists as well as anti-establishment Marxists.

The dichotomy of the "individuated" Western system and the group-oriented Japanese system was subsequently elaborated upon in an anthropological study by Chie Nakane. She formulated the dichotomy in terms of *tate* (vertical) versus *yoko* (horizontal) principles.[4] Since her characterization of the Japanese social system based on this dichotomy became so widely accepted and the position of the present book is somewhat at odds with it, a brief summary of it seems in order.

By the vertical principle, she meant the superior–inferior relationship among members of the group (p. 24), and by the horizontal principle the cooperative or colleague relationship developed across homogeneous attributes of members of the group. In every society, the horizontal and vertical categories coexist, but, depending on the society, one of these principles may dominate the other. In particular, if the division of labor develops sufficiently so that each occupational group cuts across various institutions (industrial organizations), the group becomes more homogeneous within, while clearly differentiated and autonomous vis-à-vis outsiders, so that the horizontal (market?) principle dominates. However, if the division of labor does not develop sufficiently, the autonomy of the occupational group is swallowed by an institutional group comprising many members of different attributes. The dominant order in this case will be the vertical one, in which members having different attributes are related through the superior–inferior relationship.

As one might expect, Nakane claimed that the vertical principle was prevalent in Japan, and the horizontal principle in the West. The degree of function of vertical relationships might differ depending upon the groups, but "the stronger the functioning of the group, the more likely it is that its human relations have been built along these lines. This structural principle is latent in all social groups in Japan" (p. 66). Further, the principle of hierarchical ranking permeates social values so that those hierarchically ordered institutional groups themselves come to be ranked vertically, culminating in the consolidating authoritative power of the central administration. What is the source

---

[4] Chie Nakane, *Japanese Society*. Quotations below are from the Tutle paperback edition, 1984.

of the strength of this structure? It lies in "its effectiveness for centralized communication and its capability of efficient and swift mobilization of the collective power of its members" (p. 66). From this statement, it may appear that the *tate* principle may be equated with the centralized information structure (which we also called vertical hierarchy in Chapter 3).

Although Nakane's theory as summarized above has been widely accepted, she is careful to qualify the argument in a subtle way. In the Japanese group, she argues, the vertical relation is actually nothing more than ranking based on seniority in its actual working; and the functional distinction between the leader and the subordinates is often ambiguous. The entire group becomes one functional body in which all individuals are amalgamated into a single entity (p. 72) and the subordinate often de facto performs the work of his leader. The ranking of the group members does not always reflect the real internal working procedure, and its has only symbolic importance in external activities of the group (p. 71).

Nakane has argued that the strength of the undifferentiated roles in the Japanese group lie in the adjustability of the group's activity to changing situations. Individual jobs in the group may be redefined flexibly as emergent events call upon the group to maximize its output. To facilitate this flexibility, work is assigned to "a group"; gains from individual contributions are shared by the "whole group." This system entails a somewhat unfair distribution of work and outcome, since an able man tends to carry a greater burden without receiving a corresponding share in the outcome. Therefore, in the absence of individual monetary incentives, it becomes crucial for management to preserve and promote a sense of personal and emotional connection among the members of the group. Successful mobilization of group dynamism along this line is, Nakane claims, the driving force of Japan's industrial development.

Although Nakane states that the second parable "qualifies" the first, it seems to me that the two parables presented above are not quite happily integrated yet. In the first parable, the vertical relation means the centralized information structure, whereas in the second it means the ranking hierarchy devoid of functional connotation and entirely based on seniority rule. In the second, the structure of the group may even be said to have a "horizontal" character in the sense that information is shared by its members, the decision-making authority is diffused, and its outcome is shared.

In Chapters 2 and 3, I pointed out that there can be two notions of hierarchies: vertical hierarchies and horizontal ones. Note that my usage of the words *vertical* and *horizontal* differs from Nakane's use of *tate* and *yoko*. The former refers to the centralized information system and the latter to the ranking hierarchy as an incentive device. When Nakane refers to the Japanese social system as being dominated by the *tate* principle, she seems to suggest that the Japanese system is hierarchical both in a vertical and horizontal sense. The view I have presented in this book, however, is that the Japanese organization has developed a nonhierarchical information structure (in the vertical sense), but that the nonhierarchical nature of this information sructure makes it necessary to centralize the administration of the ranking hierarchy (horizontal in our sense) in order to ensure that employees will comply with, and cooperate for the purpose of achieving, organizational goals. From this perspective, we can be more sympathetic with the second qualifying parable told by Nakane, but critical of the first one.

On the other hand, the market-oriented (*yoko* in the Nakane's sense) nature of incentive schemes in the West seems to necessitate the centralization of communications and decision making within the organization in order to strengthen the weak foundation of authority in the egalitarian social context. Either a vertical or horizontal hierarchy may be necessary to sustain an organization (the "duality principle"), but both need not coexist except in the truly authoritarian society. To characterize the Japanese social system in terms of an overarching notion of the *tate* principle may unduly exaggerate its authoritarian nature. In any case, for the purposes of this discussion, I assume that Nakane's central point is that the successful mobilization of group dynamism is the key to understanding Japan's industrial development.

Although culturalists like Abegglen and Nakane have argued that the core of the Japanese organization is the small group whose values are consistent with the historical customs and attitudes of the Japanese and are thus unique to Japan, there is a new view which appeared on the scene in the 1970s and is represented by Ronald Dore and Kazuo Koike, emphasizing the rationalistic and universalistic aspect of Japanese organizational practices. According to this view, some aspects of Japanese organizational practices, hitherto considered unique to Japan, may be regarded as rational responses to imperatives of advanced industrial development. Therefore they may be emulated in the Western context, or close analogues may even be found in the West.

Through an in-depth field study comparing organizational practices at English Electric and Hitachi, Ronald Dore found a "sufficient consistency" (p. 264) in differences between the Japanese and British employment systems, based on individualistic (market-oriented) and organization-oriented principles, respectively.[5] But he went on to propose that it is possible to distinguish between the differences due to the cultural tradition of the two countries and those related to employment-systematic characteristics. Upon examining the historical development of the "Japanese employment system," he discovered that some, but on the whole very few, of its features were the result of unconscious habits or of a certain pattern of traditional behavior or conscious adaptations of earlier employment patterns; some features were consciously borrowed from abroad or wholly indigenously invented. For example, the system of seniority pay was devised and developed as a management response to the excessive mobility of skilled workers in the early years of this century.[6]

This observation may naturally lead one to consider the feasibility and desirability of transferring institutions from one country to another. Dore has observed:

The Japanese employment system is (apart from certain features stemming directly from Japanese cultural traditions) simply one national manifestation of a phenomenon characteristic of all advanced societies – namely the adaptation of employment systems to:
1. The emergence of the giant corporation.
2. The extension of democratic ideals of a basic equality of condition for all adults at the expense of earlier conceptions of society as naturally divided into a ruling class and an underclass.
The Japanese have got there ahead. They made that adaptation earlier than Britain did, first because – a characteristic of late development – the larger corporation set the pace in industry from the *beginning of industrialization,* and second because the great post-1945 flood of egalitaraian ideas hit Japan (backed with the full authority of an occupying army) *before* union–management relations had acquired any institutional rigidity.[7]

---

[5] Ronald Dore, *British Factory – Japanese Factory: The Origins of National Diversity in Industrial Relations,* University of California Press, 1973, p. 264.

[6] Recently Dore's view that the manager's rational personnel policy was largely responsible for the emergence of the Japanese employment system has been challenged by Andrew Gordon, who interpreted its evolution in terms of the interplay between management (which sought efficient personnel administration), the bureaucracy (which sought stable industrial relations for national purposes), and labor (which sought status and membership in the J-firm). See Andrew Gordon, *The Evolution of Labor Relations in Japan: Heavy Industry 1653–1955,* Harvard University Press, 1985. But Dore has also noted that "it should not be forgotten that many of the modern features of the 'system' were established as a result of union pressure in the period of intense hardship and insecurity after the [Pacific] war" (p. 337). Gordon has extended the role of labor well back into the 1920s.

[7] Dore, *British Factory – Japanese Factory,* pp. 338–9.

Although the institutional inertia characteristic of Britain, the pioneer of industrialization, may have slowed down the adaptations of institutions to the said conditions, changes are nevertheless occurring there as well. These changes – in the structures of bargaining and union organizations, pay and promotion systems, enterprise welfare, and the corporate ideology – "might be characterized, however loosely, as in a Japanese direction," (p. 340) although he did not suggest that *all* the features of the Japanese system are likely to appear in Britain or elsewhere. More neutrally, one may say that there is a tendency for countries to move toward the organization-oriented employment system, although national diversity stemming from differences in cultural tradition, the historical development of industrialization, and the exigencies of other imperatives would continue to exist.

The sharpest attack on the culturalist view has come from Kazuo Koike, who has argued emphatically that most work practices at large Japanese firms are the natural outcome of rational behavior.[8] His argument revolves around the formation of workers' skills. Long-time employment, a wide range of job experiences, and the scheme of internal promotion within a single firm are conducive to the development of a wide range of workers' skills. The enterprise-based union provides an appropriate institutional framework through which the workers' interest in developing skills and deriving economic gains therefrom can be most effectively voiced. Although Japanese firms may have developed institutions conducive to in-house skill formation in more visible ways, the internal labor markets of Western firms and the enterprise-level bargaining prevalent in American manufacturing industries function in essentially the same way.

Throughout the present book, I have tried to make clear the rationality of Japanese practices, as Koike has. The "undifferentiated" ambiguity of job demarcation and the institutionalized practice of job rotation has been understood as contributing to the formation of the contextual skills of workers. In contrast to the culturalists, I have emphasized competition throughout "quasi-lifetime" employment and the principle of "pay according to rank" as an incentive device. Even the gift exchange of "job security" for "diligence," as well as

---

[8] His main work on this subject is *Shokuba no Rodo-kumiai to Sanka* (The labor union and participation on the shopfloor), Toyo-Keizai Shinpo-sha, 1975. Major points of this book are succinctly summarized for English readers in "Skill formation systems in the U.S. and Japan: A comparative study," in M. Aoki (ed.), *The Economic Analysis of the Japanese Firm,* North-Holland, 1984. See also "Skill formation in mass production: Japan and Thai," *Journal of the Japanese and International Economies,* (1987), pp. 408–40.

work sharing as opposed to layoffs in response to (moderate) business downturns, has been interpreted as a rational equilibrium outcome of the (strategic or cooperative) game between the employer and the employee.

However, there are some slight differences between Koike and myself in the degree of emphasis we place on the commonality of Japanese and Western practices. Koike seems to be more concerned with commonality, whereas I have been concerned with the contrasting ways in which the duality principle is satisfied in Japan and the West. To repeat, Japanese organizations tend to cluster toward the end of an organizational spectrum characterized by the combination of decentralization in information structure and centralization in personnel administration (incentive structure), whereas Western organizations tend to cluster toward the end of an organizational spectrum characterized by the combination of centralization in information structure and decentralization in personnel administration.

In Chapter 2.3, I pointed out that the information-processing mode of the Japanese type may be more efficient in continually stable environments, whereas centralized information processing may be more efficient in drastically changing environments or highly stable environments. The fact that the above-mentioned contrast in the organizational modes of Japan and the West persists despite the difference in performance characteristics of the two indicates that there is a cultural trait in the dominant organizational pattern in each economy. Otherwise, decentralized and centralized information-processing modes coexist in each economy, depending upon the environments of each organization, such as markets and technology. Then, an interesting issue is whether two economies can emulate superior aspects of the other in spite of a probable cultural difference, without losing its own superior aspects. The full treatment of this topic is far beyond the scope of this book so that I restrict myself in the rest of this book to an examination of the role of small groupism, on which cultural and business anthropologists put so much emphasis. In particular, I ask whether the Japanese organizational mode would collapse if the group orientation of the Japanese changed (or whether the group orientation has to be as strong as it has been in Japan for a Japanese-type organizational mode to be viable elsewhere).

2.   Is group orientation sufficient and necessary?

I begin with the assumption that group orientation, exemplified by such practices as the ambiguous demarcation of jobs and the sharing of responsibility and outcome within the small group, is indeed a distinctive characteristic of the Japanese factory and that this group orientation may be culturally conditioned by the collective memory of agrarian village life. Economic development during the proto-industrial period in Japan depended primarily on increases in the scale and productivity of rice production. But most Japanese land was not actually suited to rice paddy cultivation in its original form. To make the soil suitable for rice planting, collective control over the water supply had to be developed, initially in the form of *tameike* (reservoir) in plain fields and at a later stage in the form of large-scale irrigation along river systems. At the right moment, seedlings raised in nursery beds had to be transplanted to rice paddies with a sufficient supply of water and concentrated labor inputs. This task required collective coordination among villagers with respect to water allocation from collective sources of water supply and mutual help. At an early stage, the convention, called *ageta* (paddy drainage), developed in the village in plain fields such as *Kinai,* to ensure that the water supply would be reduced equiproportionally across families in the event of a water shortage and unirrigable land would be converted to alternative uses such as cotton planting. As large-scale irrigation systems developed, flood control in the typhoon season before harvest time required collective, ad hoc responses to unpredictable climatic changes. In addition, because of Japan's climate, weeding, insect control, and timing of the water supply demanded the constant attention of farmers.[9]

There is no doubt that through centuries of agrarian experience up to as recently as a generation ago, the Japanese developed the customs of mutual help, collective coordination, risk sharing, ad hoc and flexible adaptation to continual and incremental environmental changes, diligent work habits, and penetration of communal life into the private sphere, which are now viewed as characteristics of modern Japanese factory life. But the important point is this: The group approach to work would not automatically ensure an efficient work system in the context of large organizations. If the task of a work unit is carried out by a relatively egalitarian and cohesive work team, the work team may tend to become autonomous and assert its own localized interests by taking advantage of its monopolistic position within the organization. Coordination between work units then becomes problematical.

This problem was not unknown even in the proto-industrial period.

---

[9] For the work system of rice production and the importance of the irrigation system, English readers may refer to Thomas Smith, *The Agrarian Origin of Modern Japan,* Stanford University Press, 1959.

When the water supply was managed by the village in a self-sufficient, closed manner, a risk-sharing convention such as the *ageta* could be used to solve the coordination problem fairly automatically. But a great leap forward in civil engineering in the Warrior Period (fifteenth and sixteenth centuries) made the development of large-scale irrigation systems across villages possible. Villages in the Edo period, which were organized as coherent, *relatively* homogeneous user units of the irrigation system and were not under the control of castle-towns except for tax obligations in kind often engaged in fierce disputes among themselves over the distribution of water resources. Those disputes, known as *mizu-arasoi* (water-disputes), sometimes led to bloody clashes among neighboring villages in times of water shortages. Elaborate arbitration schemes, conceived as fair and equitable solutions, had to be developed along the irrigation system to cope with social conflict. The great agrarian leaders of the Edo period, like Sontoku Ninomiya and Chiyozaburo Mutsugawa, were associated with the organization and effective management of such arbitration schemes, which emerged largely outside *samurai* control.

The need to coordinate groups and resolve conflicts among them is no less important in the context of modern industrial organizations. In order to prevent individual work groups from having full control over their own interests in the context of decentralized information processing, the J-firm has consciously designed and developed two important institutions: the semiautomatic coordination mechanism among work units, as exemplified by the *kanban* system, and the centrally administered rotation of personnel among work units. As noted already, the *kanban* system was developed through the ingenious effort of industrial engineers at the Toyota factory who borrowed the idea of replenishing on-shelf stock from the American supermarket system and adapted it to the requirements of manufacturing coordination and inventory control. When the *kanban* system was introduced, it met with the resistance of workers on the shopfloor, who held a strike. This incident suggests that the change was not entirely consistent with the interests of small work groups. The institutionalization of the *kanban* system is, when successful, able to avoid the cost of ad hoc, case-by-case bargaining/arbitration because of its automatic rule-oriented settlements.

The practice of rotation of personnel *beyond* work units is also used to facilitate communication between units and to prevent the development of unit-specific interests. Such rotation is found, for example, among engineers in the manufacturing division, who may be transferred to the central research laboratory to help develop the analytic design of a new product, or to the production site to lead the value engineering group or supervise the setting up of a new manufacturing process. As I mentioned in Section 6.3, such transfers may facilitate the formation of feedback loops between the downstream and upstream phases of design as well as between the manufacturing process and the design process, and thus help reduce the time spent on these activities, from the conception of the analytic design of a new product to its commercialization.

Interwork unit rotation may be considered a magnified version of job rotation within the small group. Although job rotation on the shopfloor began somewhat autonomously on the initiative of the foreman and subforeman,[10] the practice of interunit rotation has been cultivated by management and has been centrally administered by the personnel department of the J-firm. Although the J-firm has come to rely less on hierarchical control over operating tasks – in order to make sure that work units, and the members of each work group therein, comply with the organizational goal and do not develop group-specific interests – the personnel administration of the Japanese firm has become much more centralized in comparison with that of Western firms.

Thus one may conclude that small-group orientation has certainly contributed to the organizational practices of the J-firm and that a trace of cultural tradition may be detected in them. But small-group orientation alone is *not sufficient* for their formation. Institutional devices such as horizontal coordination and a centrally administered ranking hierarchy for restraining the development of small-group interests are necessary to form a consistent, viable, and efficient system. If that is indeed the case, we should now reverse the path of inquiry and ask: Even if small group dynamics has played a role in the formation of the J-firm, is the small-groupism still *necessary* for the efficient operation of the J-firm? Further, is a Japanese-like system – which relies on less hierarchical coordination as an alternative mechanism and recognizes the body of employees as a constituent – viable and able to remain efficient without small groupism?

As pointed out in Chapter 2, before horizontal coordination can operate efficiently the constituent units must have autonomous problem-solving capability; that is, the workers on the shopfloor must have a wide range of skills (see proposition [I.2] in Section 2.3). Such skills have certainly been nurtured by the group-oriented teamwork in the Japanese context. But what is essential here, as Koike has emphatically

[10] See Kazuo Koike, "Skill formation systems: Japan and U.S.," in M. Aoki (ed.), *The Economic analysis of the Japanese firm,* North-Holland, 1984, p. 63.

argued, is the development of "intelectual skills" in workers, which will let them cope flexibly with unusual local emergencies, frequent shifts in their tasks, and a new technology, but not groupism per se. Intelectual skills may be nurtured by a carefully designed intrafirm career development program combined with a more flexible job rotation scheme, even at Western firms, although such a program may call for enhanced cross-jurisdictional interaction and cooperation among workers compared with the segmented job classification scheme. If such a career development program is feasible, and desirable from the perspective of individual development, the incorporation of elements of Japanese-like information processing at the shopfloor level may become a viable alternative to the traditional job control unionism even in the Western context, in industries that are required to adapt to market pressures and continual technological innovation quickly and flexibly. Indeed, various experiments in this direction have been attempted worldwide within the framework of management–labor cooperation.[11] Whether or not such attempts will eventually generate

[11] There are many recent anecdotal experiments on more flexible job classification schemes in the United States that would enhance the integrative skills of workers. A true hybrid of the two Japanese and American giant firms, New United Motor Manufacturing Incorporated (NUMMI) founded in 1983 at Fremont, California, provides a particularly interesting example in that it shows that the Japanese rotation scheme may be a viable alternative even in the U.S. union setting. Before actual production started at the beginning of 1984, the management of NUMMI and the UAW Local 2244 exchanged a letter of intent, and in June 1985 completed their first collective bargaining agreement in which the job categories for hourly workers were reduced to three: general maintenance, tool and die, and assembly line, from the traditional 200 or more categories at a comparable unionized factory of the same size. All blue-collar workers are now organized into egalitarian teams, each composed of seven members who are rotated among jobs under the direction of a team leader. There are two pay levels, skilled and unskilled, with annual bonuses. Team leaders made 50 cents more per hour in 1986, but there are no "pay-for-knowledge" differentials, as in GM's operating work team system mentioned earlier.

Through this team system, together with the application of a *kanban* system adapted for the geographical distances of supply sources in Japan and the Midwest, NUMMI was able to eliminate such specialized jobs as reliefmen (normally 500 workers at a comparable unionized plant), quality inspectors (250), material handlers (250), repairmen (250), and nonworking union representatives on payroll (40). Combined with an on-site stamping plant, which not only allows for just-in-time deliveries but also increases time efficiency through the Toyota "quick-die" process, the work-team approach has been able to reduce the work force at NUMMI by about one-third relative to comparable North American factories. The labor accord at the Fremont plant is expected to have an impact on the shaping of future industrial relations in the American auto industry, particularly in newly built plants. According to an interview with a NUMMI manager, 1,500 GM managers from 50 plants and 40 local unions had visited the NUMMI plant by the end of 1985. The design of a new GM assembly plant now being built in Kansas has adopted many ideas from NUMMI. At GM's plant in Van Nuys, California, a new collective agreement closely resembling the NUMMI agreement was ratified in 1986.

The emphasis on the integrative approach is also exactly the point that Swedish

a new paradigm of organizational practices will only be answered after painstaking effort on the side of management and of labor, rather than through the theorizing of scholars. Once the efficient and humanistic nature of the integrative approach is understood, however, such an effort would be worth the pain.

The ongoing development of information and electromechanical technologies as well as artificial intelligence will be used to develop intelectual skills and to enhance the capacity of individuals rather than to replace them, as discussed at the end of Chapter 2. This possibility also suggests that more opportunities will be available for the J-firm too. The practice of rotating jobs so that workers will have a wide range of job experiences, the sharing of knowledge among workers, and inter-disciplinary communication at the operating level – all of which con-tribute to the development of a localized problem-solving capacity in the Japanese factory – have traditionally been maintained through face-to-face communication or a tacit mutual understanding among workers and their leaders. If it is possible to fuse these human inputs and developing technologies, Japanese group dynamism may move in a new direction and release individuals from some of the conformist pressures of the small group. Such a change is desirable not only to make the established in-house career development program more con-sistent with the needs of increasingly individualistic employees, but also to enhance the organizational capacity to innovate (see discussion in Section 6.3). This does not mean, however, that the essential aspect of the Japanese system that lies at the heart of its competitive strength

management and labor unions have agreed to aim for as a key to productivity growth and the enhancement of the quality of work. In Sweden, in the 1970s, a movement was under way to give employees more voice in the affairs of the employing firm through employee participation in the corporate governance structure, as in other European countries (under the so-called codetermination or comanagement system). In the 1980s, however, the focus of participation has clearly shifted to the shopfloor level. The need for decentralized and autonomous problem solving with the workers' participation was formally agreed to in the historical Development Contract signed between SAF (Swedish Employers' Confederation), LO (Labor Union Association), and TCO (White-Collar Central Union) and subsequent Development Contracts at the enterprise level. One of those enterprise-level contracts at Volvo states that the "development of work organization . . . creates opportunities for making better use of the employees' experience and knowledge. Jobs, management practices, and control systems which stimulate and involve the employees shall be the goal in this respect." Also for that purpose, "responsibility and decision-making can be delegated, within an organizational unit and within well defined sections, to groups of employees who organize their work together themselves." This contract is noteworthy in that the pow-erful Swedish unions have come to recognize that participation in horizontal, auton-omous coordination is more effective than participation in vertical control over man-agement (i.e., comanagement) for enhancing the quality of work in the factory. For a discussion of codetermination see M. Aoki *The Cooperative Game Theory of the Firm,* Oxford University Press, 1984, chap. 10.

will have to be changed – that is, its reliance on the contextual skills of workers and enhanced communication among them.

Even if small-group dynamism, supposedly culturally unique to Japan, is thus not essential to the incorporation of elements of decentralized information structure into Western firms, and even if such incorporation is practically desirable for the revitalization of manufacturing industries in the West, the issue of incentive compatibility remains: Can Western firms emulate some elements of the workings of a decentralized information structure without modifying the traditional market-oriented, decentralized incentive scheme? Or can Western firms adopt some elements of centralized personnel administration in spite of alleged cultural differences? In view of the duality principle, this is a vital question.

We have stressed that Japanese organizations have solved the possible malfunction of the decentralized information structure due to small groupism through the development of the centralized personnel administration, which relies on the centralized authority of the personnel department and the administration of the ranking hierarchy. As explained in Section 3.1, ranking hierarchies in Japanese business organizations are different from managerial ranking hierarchies and blue-collar job ladders in the internal labor market at the Western firm in that positions therein are not specifically associated with well-defined job descriptions. Employees of different ranking may perform the same job. One of the important criteria for promotion is seniority, although competition in the same age group is keen. Japanese ranking hierarchies thus operate as a scheme to screen employees on the long-run basis and multidimensional criteria. One may argue however that such farsightedness and relative ambiguity of ranking criteria are only harmonious with the high symbolic value attached to ranking by the Japanese.

Yasusuke Murakami and his collaborators, Shunpei Kumon and Seizaburo Sato, indeed noted that there is a marked parallel between aspects of the Japanese management (such as the seniority wage and advancement system, high interjob mobility within each firm, and intrafirm welfare system) and the autonomous ranking hierarchy ("homo functional hierarchy" in their words) characterizing the traditional *ie* (house) principle of the *samurai* organization. They argue that "the Japanese management system is clearly a variant of *ie*-type organization."[12] They further maintain that the evolutionary devel-

---

[12] Y. Murakami, "*Ie* society as a pattern of civilization" *Journal of Japanese Studies*, 10 (1984), p. 356.

opment of the *ie* principle can account for the "unique" historical cycle of Japan since the eleventh century. If so, doubt may be cast on the workability of the "straightforward" trasplantation of the ranking hierarchy as a principal incentive scheme into an individualistic and market-oriented context.[13]

Although a non-market-oriented, job-description-free ranking hierarchy may be uniquely effective in the Japanese cultural context, the essential issue at hand, however, is to provide incentives for a long-term, if not lifetime, association of employees with the firm, as well as for the provision of an in-house training program, to promote and use employees' contextual skills to operate efficiently and effectively in a firm-specific information structure. Although the paternalistic and automatized aspects of the seniority wage and advancement system have been unduly emphasized in the "Japanese management" literature, it may be well to recall that the essence of ranking hierarchy is a competitive screening device to motivate and sort out employees according to their learning achievements. This aspect of the ranking hierarchy may be emulated even in a competitive environment. For example, the sharing of information rents – economic surplus made available from the efficient operation of the decentralized information structure – with employees according to their achieved skills based on more formal criteria may deter their interfirm mobility, while promoting intraorganizational competition. The sharing of information rents, different from that of the oligopolistic rents, will not necessarily distort allocative efficiency. For a systematic and consistent introduction of such a firm-specific incentive scheme, however, strengthening of the function and authority of the personnel department is essential. As an interesting study by Fred Foulkes suggests, there is indeed growing evidence that the personnel department is gaining its importance in the management structure of well-run, nonunionized companies in the United States.[14]

Western and Japanese firms can thus learn much from each other that will help make their industrial organizations more efficient and more humanitarian in spite of the cultural barrier. The hope is that the symbiotic development of human capacity and technology may help to fuse cultural differences into a new hybrid in the future.

---

[13] In this sense, it is interesting to note that NUMMI is experimenting on the Japanese-type work team, but implementing a much simpler structure of ranking as remarked in note 11.

[14] F. Foulkes, *Personnel Policies in Large Nonunion Companies,* Prentice Hall, 1980.

Author index

Subject index